W. Dirk Raat is professor of history at State University College in Fredonia, New York. He is also the author of *El Positivisimo durante el Porfiriato* (1975) as well as *Mexico: From Independence to Revolution, 1810–1910* and *The Mexican Revolution, 1910–1940: Historiography and Bibliography*, both forthcoming.

REVOLTOSOS

Mexico's Rebels in the United States, 1903–1923

REVOLTOSOS

Mexico's Rebels in the
United States, 1903–1923

by W. DIRK RAAT

 Texas A&M University Press COLLEGE STATION

Library of Congress Cataloging in Publication Data

Raat, W   Dirk, 1939–
　　Revoltosos : Mexico's rebels in the United States,
1903–1923.

　　　　Bibliography: p.
　　　　Includes index.
　　　　1. Mexicans in the United States—History—20th
century.   2. United States—Foreign relations—Mexico.
3. Mexico—Foreign relations—United States.   4. Mexico
—History—1867–1910.   5. Mexico—History—1910–1946.
6. Refugees, Political—United States—History—20th century.   I. Title.
E184.M5R3　　　973′.046872　　　80–6109
ISBN 0–89096–114–X　　　　　　AACR1

Manufactured in the United States of America
FIRST EDITION

To my parents,
Elmer W. Raat
and
Iris Calkins Raat

Contents

List of Illustrations

Preface

THIS is a book about rebels and authority; revolution and the suppression of revolution. *Revoltosos* is a study of Mexico's rebels in the United States between the Immigration Act of 1903 and the end of the Red Scare era in the early 1920s. The *revoltosos* were insurgents and political refugees, on the Right and the Left, who used the United States as a base for revolution (and counter-revolution) in Mexico. As exiles in revolt, the *revoltosos* were the object of suppression by American and Mexican authorities in both the domestic and foreign branches of government. The machinery for containing their revolutionary nationalism involved a binational police and espionage system, from American private detectives in the pay of Mexico to U.S. immigration officers and secret service agents (the counterpart of today's FBI, CIA, and the Mexican *Servicio Secreto*). The general governmental reaction, coming in an era of nativism, anti-radicalism, and wartime hysteria, was extreme—in spite of the fact that most *revoltoso* activity was not in violation of U.S. laws. These actions affected not only the *revoltosos* but the Mexican and Mexican American community in general, and seriously threatened the nineteenth-century traditions of humanitarianism and civil liberties.

One cannot honestly say that there has been scholarly neglect of the topic at hand, only that the work to date has been extremely narrow in range. U.S. historians have ignored the topic, and most "Mexicanists" have limited themselves to narratives about specific groups or individuals (e.g., the *magonistas* or *maderistas;* Ricardo Flores Magón or Francisco Madero) and have dealt with the subject only in the context of Mexican revolutionary history. To remedy this, the present study attempts to treat of a variety of

revoltoso groups, to integrate the domestic themes of Mexican
with those of U.S. history, and to relate the domestic histories of
both countries to that of Mexican and American foreign relations.

Mexico's *revoltosos*, as her exiles in revolt were called by the
authorities, were a varied group, often appearing to be an inco-
herent conglomeration of rival elements. Ideologically they ranged
from the socialist and anarchist followers of Flores Magón (called
Liberals and *magonistas*, or "floresmagonistas," and known as
members of the *Partido Liberal Mexicano*, the PLM) to the
reactionary, pro-clerical proponents of Porfirio Díaz's nephew,
Félix Díaz (*felicistas*). Along the spectrum one could also find
Pizaña "Seditionists," *orozquistas, zapatistas, obregonistas, reyistas,
maderistas, maytorenistas, vazquistas, villistas, carrancistas, huertistas, científicos*, and other assorted groups of the Right and Left.
The *magonistas* and the "Seditionists" of south Texas were the most
consistently radical. As for tactics, all of these groups, including
the radicals, made alliances with their rivals from time to time.
The one characteristic they shared was a hostility to the established
Mexican government and a desire to use the United States as a
revolutionary (or counterrevolutionary) base.

It was the policy of the Department of Justice and the Bureau
of Immigration to favor moderate *revoltosos* while opposing radicals and revolutionists. For example, the anarchistic and socialistic
leaders of the PLM were consistently pursued and suppressed by
governmental authorities, as were the *magonista* "Seditionists" who
advocated secession from the United States. Similarly, the followers
of Bernardo Reyes and Pascual Orozco were quickly and efficiently
suppressed, due in part to a public image that unfairly pictured
them as revolutionary nationalists and anti-imperialists who en-
dangered American lives and property in Mexico. On the other
hand, after May 1911 Francisco Madero's supporters were often
tolerated as the desirable "reformist" alternative to advocates of
class warfare and revolution.

Of the various *revoltoso* groups surveyed in this study, radicals
and moderates, especially the *magonistas* and *maderistas*, receive
more attention than do reactionaries. So too is this the case concerning the activities of their North American counterparts. For
example, the counterrevolutionary plot and reactionary coalition of

1915 led by Victoriano Huerta's Mexico City Chief of Police, Eduardo Iturbide, and the State Department's Mexican desk officer, Leon Canova, have been omitted from the narrative. Several explanations can be offered for slighting these more conservative *revoltosos*, among which are limitations of space, editorial considerations, treatment by other historians, and the central focus of this work, which has been to narrate the politics and diplomacy of suppression and of those *revoltoso* groups, like the *magonistas*, that were the object of such suppression.

Two words that normally appear in studies of this sort are used most sparingly in this book. They are "precursors" and "Chicanos." As for the first, I must agree with Professor John Womack—who first spoke of the "mistake of precursorism" at the Oaxtepec Conference in 1969—that "precursorism" is a form of "presentism" in which one moment in a country's or individual's past is treated as little more than preparation for another (usually more important and greater) moment in the country's or individual's past. For the Revolutionary School of official Mexican historians, that later moment is, of course, the Constitution of 1917. Concerning "Chicano," I find the word perfectly appropriate when describing the contemporary psychological, political, educational, and ideological concerns of Mexican Americans, but for these same reasons I am reluctant to employ the concept of "Chicanoism" when speaking of the historical phenomena of the early *revoltosos*. By so doing I am not making any pretensions about my own objectivity, or ignoring the essentially subjective nature of the historical task, only recording for the reader my preference in this matter.

To produce this book I have depended on a large number of institutions and people. For three summers between 1973 and 1975 the Research Foundation of the State University of New York provided me with grants and fellowships that facilitated my travel and research in Mexico and the United States. During the fall and winter of 1976–1977 I was the recipient of a generous fellowship from the American Council of Learned Societies and a sabbatical leave from the State University of New York. This enabled me to complete my research in Mexico and to initiate the writing phase of this project. Needless to say, without this kind of financial aid the present book would not have become a reality.

For their courtesy and efficiency I wish to thank the staffs of the following libraries and archives. In the United States: The Nettie Lee Benson Latin American Collection and the Eugene C. Barker Texas History Center, University of Texas at Austin; the Western Historical Collection, University of Colorado at Boulder; the El Paso Public Library; the Arizona Historical Society, Tucson; the Nebraska State Historical Society, Lincoln; the Sherman Foundation Library at Corona-del-Mar, California; the Bancroft Library, University of California at Berkeley; the Missouri Historical Society and the Western Historical Manuscript Collection at the University of Missouri, Columbia; in New Jersey, the Stevens Institute of Technology Library; the National Archives; the Library of Congress; the Federal Records Center at Laguna Niguel (formerly Bell), California; the Federal Record Center at Fort Worth, Texas; and the Daniel A. Reed Library of the State University College at Fredonia (especially Gary D. Barber, Margaret Pabst, Jon Weekly, and John Saulitis). In Mexico: the Archivo de la Secretaría de Relaciones Exteriores and the Biblioteca José María Lafragua; the Archivo General de la Nación; the Fundación Cultural de Condumex; the Colección Porfirio Díaz in Cholula; the Biblioteca Manuel Orozco y Berra; the Biblioteca Daniel Cosío Villegas at the Colegio de México; and the Hemeroteca Nacional.

I am deeply indebted to several individuals who aided me in my research. Stanley R. Ross and Michael C. Meyer were especially helpful in providing me with Mexican archival information. To my Mexican colleagues I state my thanks, especially Berta Ulloa, Lucila Flamand, Salvador Victoria, and Andrés Lira. For either bibliographical advice or interpretations I owe much to Marvin D. Bernstein, Paul J. Vanderwood, William H. Beezley, Juan Gómez-Quiñones, Nettie Lee Benson, James D. Cockcroft, John M. Hart, Charles B. Mosher, Frederick Stirton Weaver, Morgan D. Dowd, Roger Daniels, William T. Hagan, Susan Cobb, and João Cabral. At the National Archives, archivist Donald Mosholder was most enterprising on my behalf, as were William O. Hendricks at the Federal Records Center in southern California; Stephen R. Niblo, formerly at the University of the Americas; and Norman A. Carlson at the Bureau of Prisons in Washington, D.C. Several people unselfishly shared their own research notes with me, including C. L. Sonnichsen, Cornelius C. Smith, Jr., Joseph Fichandler, Robert Jordan, and Pietro Ferrua. Rudolph de Jong, director of the International Institute of Social History in Amsterdam, aided me in locating several *magonista* materials, especially the unpublished manuscript of Max Nettlau, parts of which were translated from the German by Susanne Behr.

Ron Warren, Jay Boylan, Michael Anton, and Lotte Morse of the Fredonia Instructional Resources Center helped in photographic work and graphics. I am grateful to Mary Notaro for her care in typing the entire manuscript at various stages.

Three men in particular were of special importance to me as I worked through this study: John Womack, Jr., who read major portions of the manuscript and provided me with necessary criticism and encouragement; Douglas H. Shepard, who read the entire manuscript and made recommendations on style; and my mentor and teacher, now retired from the University of Utah, C. Gregory Crampton, who taught me Mexican history and showed me how to love Mexico and the Southwest.

I owe a special debt of gratitude to my many friends for their care and to my family for their companionship, support, and interest.

While offering thanks to those who assisted me, I reserve to myself full responsibility for any errors of fact or interpretation.

Permission has been granted by Duke University Press to reprint excerpts from my article "The Diplomacy of Suppression: *Los Revoltosos*, Mexico, and the United States, 1906–1911," *Hispanic American Historical Review* 56 (November 1976): 529–550. Copyright 1976 by Duke University Press.

Abbreviations in Archival Citations

AGN/RRM
Archivo General de la Nación, Ramo Revolución. Política Interior. Correspondencia de Francisco I. Madero, 1910–1912. Mexico City.

AGN/RRV
Archivo General de la Nación, Ramo Revolución. Política Interior. Correspondencia varios, 1910–1919. Mexico City.

AREM
Archivo General de la Secretaría de Relaciones Exteriores de México, Mexico City.

Bureau of Prisons
McNeil Island Registers, Federal Records Center, Seattle, Washington; Leavenworth files, Federal Records Center, Kansas City, Missouri; United States Bureau of Prisons, Department of Justice, Washington, D.C.

CM Files
Compañía Minera de Cananea, S.A. de C.V. Company files of Greene Consolidated Copper Company, Cananea Cattle Company, and related companies. Tucson, Arizona.

CPD
Colleción Porfirio Díaz, University of the Americas, Cholula, Puebla.

Dip. Des
Records of the Department of State, Record Group 59, Diplomatic Despatch-

es from U.S. Ministers in Mexico, 1823–
1906, Microfilm Publication, Microcopy
No. 97. National Archives, Washington,
D.C.

Dom. Letters   Records of the Department of State,
Record Group 59, Domestic Letters, Mi-
crofilm Publication, Microcopy No. 40.
National Archives, Washington, D.C.

Fall Papers   Correspondence and miscellaneous materials from the files of Albert B. Fall,
Henry E. Huntington Library, San Marino, California. Copies provided to the
author by C. L. Sonnichsen, Arizona
Historical Society, Tucson.

FRC Fort Worth   Records of the Bureau of Customs, Record Group 36, Letterpress Volume, Eagle
Pass, Texas 1909–1913. Federal Archives
and Records Center, Fort Worth, Texas.

FRC Laguna Niguel   U.S. v. Magon, et al., Judicial Records
for the Southern District of California
and Arizona, 1906–1920. Federal Archives and Records Center, Laguna Niguel, California.

FSAR   Records of the Department of State,
Record Group 59, Foreign Service Applications and Recommendations, 1906–
1924. National Archives, Washington,
D.C.

Knox Papers   Philander Chase Knox Papers, Library
of Congress Manuscript Division, Washington, D.C.

NF   Records of the Department of State,
Numerical File, 1906–1910. National
Archives, Washington, D.C.

RDS   Records of the Department of State
                            Relating to the Internal Affairs of Mexi-
                            co, Microfilm Publication, Record Group
                            59, file 812.60, Microcopy No. 274. Na-
                            tional Archives, Washington, D.C.

RG 38   Records of the Office of the Chief of
                            Naval Operations (ONI, Office of Naval
                            Intelligence), Record Group 38. Nation-
                            al Archives, Washington, D.C.

RG 60   Records of the Department of Justice,
                            Record Group 60. National Archives,
                            Washington, D.C.

RG 85   Records of the Immigration and Natural-
                            ization Service, Record Group 85. Na-
                            tional Archives, Washington, D.C.

RG 94   Records of the Adjutant General's Of-
                            fice, 1780s–1917, Record Group 94. Na-
                            tional Archives, Washington, D.C.

RG 165   Records of the War Department Gen-
                            eral and Special Staffs (WCD, War
                            College Division; MID, Military Intel-
                            ligence Division), Record Group 165.
                            National Archives, Washington, D.C.

RG 267   Records of the U.S. Supreme Court,
                            Record Group 267. National Archives,
                            Washington, D.C.

STC   Silvestre Terrazas Collection, Correspon-
                            dence, Papers, and Photos, Bancroft Li-
                            brary, University of California, Berkeley.

Taft Papers   William Howard Taft Papers, Library of
                            Congress Manuscript Division, Washing-
                            ton, D.C.

REVOLTOSOS
Mexico's Rebels in the United States, 1903–1923

> The anarchist is the enemy of humanity, the enemy of all mankind.
>
> Theodore Roosevelt, 1908

Prologue: Aliens, Radicals, and Suppression, 1903–1923

IT was a glorious day, warm and clear. It was, as the local newspaper declared, "President's Weather." It was a bright Friday in September in Buffalo, New York. The nineteenth century and the "gay nineties" refused to leave town, even though it was the year 1901, and the Pan-American Exposition was celebrating an era and crowning it with the arrival of the president of the United States. It was to be a splendid occasion, a sight made more appealing by the presence of the fashionable people-in-waiting who had left their exclusive Delaware Avenue mansions to join in the festivities. It was 6 September 1901, and two men from Ohio were about to meet for the first time.

One of the Ohioans needed no introduction to the crowd. He had been governor of Ohio and was now Mr. President—William McKinley. The other man was a blacksmith who would soon need no introduction to the crowd. Although born in Detroit, he now claimed Cleveland as his home. He was a young man of twenty-three who had been waiting since Thursday evening for the arrival of Mr. McKinley. His few friends and the Reverend Benedict Rosinski called him Leon.

McKinley had been in Buffalo on Thursday, touring the Exposition grounds. Leon had seen McKinley riding around in his carriage but had not been able to get close enough to greet him. But Friday was different. There was a public reception in front of the Temple of Music. A crowd had gathered. All were swarming to get near the president. Leon pressed forward, his left hand bandaged, his right hand extended to greet his leader. And the two men met.

While shaking hands with the president, Leon triggered the gun, which sent two bullets into McKinley, the first shot knocking the president backward. Immediately reacting to the pistol's crack, secret service agent Foster attacked the assailant and, shoving him in the face, knocked him to the ground. Leon would have been killed had not the local police restrained the agent.

The president was suffering from severe abdominal wounds, but the first reports were cautiously optimistic. After a few days it appeared that Mr. McKinley would survive this ignoble attack. Then, a week later, on a Saturday morning at 2:15, McKinley's heart stopped. The president was dead. He had been killed by an alleged Polish "anarchist" named Leon Czolgosz. As the Buffalo newspapers so carefully noted, the last syllable of the last name is pronounced with a "t" before the "z," as in "Tzar," a most un-American-sounding name.[1]

It was not a glorious day, that sad, gloomy Saturday in Buffalo, New York. The nineteenth century refused to leave town as the memory and specter of anarchist terror filled the air. Earlier, in the 1880s, there had been the violent anarchism advocated by the German agitator Johann Most. Under his direction the revolutionary wing of the Socialist Labor Party had embraced Bakunin's "Black International" in an attempt to destroy existing class rule. Then there had been the eight-hour-day strikes in 1886, terminating with the so-called Haymarket affair of that year: a strike, workers killed by police, the protest meeting at Haymarket Square in Chicago, the bomb, public hysteria, convictions, and the executions of four anarchists. Again, in 1892, there had been the assault by Russian-born anarchist Alexander Berkman on Henry Clay Frick, the reactionary manager of the Carnegie Steel Company. Finally, and almost worst of all to the Puritans in Babylon, there were the free-love doctrines so recently and openly espoused by that female anarchist Emma Goldman, the lover and mistress of Most and Berkman. And now, the president was dead.

It was especially not a glorious day for the upper-class families, of Anglo-Saxon origin and Protestant religion, who had left their three- and four-story palaces along Delaware Avenue to attend

[1]Dunkirk (N.Y.) *Evening Observer*, 6 and 7 September 1901.

memorial services in honor of their fallen Republican president. It was not even a glorious day for the Polish-American, Catholic, weak and tormented Czolgosz. Nor would it be for the alien community in general.

The nativist impulse was still very strong in America, especially during times of economic depression and political troubles. Its roots were economic, religious, and racial. In the 1880s the trade union movement saw the seemingly inexhaustible supply of immigrant workers as a form of cheap labor that would undermine the American worker's standard of living. Protestant leaders were alarmed over the religion of the newly arrived immigrants, most of whom, being from southern and eastern Europe, were Jewish, Roman Catholic, or Greek Orthodox. The "best minds" of America were convinced that of all the world's "races," only the Anglo-Saxon, Aryan, Teutonic, or Nordic had superior innate characteristics. It was further believed that democratic institutions were Germanic in origin and could thrive only among Anglo-Saxon peoples. Spokesmen for nativism argued that the only protection for "democracy" was to exclude foreigners from American soil through restrictive immigration acts and policies. Throughout the late nineteenth century these arguments were made to the Congress and the public by such organized groups as the American Federation of Labor (1886), the American Protective Association (1887), and Henry Cabot Lodge's Immigration Restriction League (1894).[2]

The death of McKinley saw the resurgence and merging of these anti-radical and nativist traditions of nineteenth-century American life. With Czolgosz's assault the authorities were quick to assume an alien, anarchist conspiracy. Although Czolgosz's stepmother asserted that her stepson was too weak mentally and physically to be interested in anarchism, Buffalo police had somehow extracted from Czolgosz a confession in which he allegedly affirmed his admiration for the doctrines of Emma Goldman. With rumors circulating of an anarchist plot to kill Vice-President Roosevelt, a general investigation of the Polish quarter of Buffalo was immediately ordered.[3]

In Chicago, one day after the attack on McKinley, warrants

[2]Roger Daniels, *Racism and Immigration Restriction*, p. 5.
[3]*Evening Observer*, 6 and 7 September 1901.

were issued for the arrest of nine well-known anarchists. The chief of police, acting on his belief that "Chicago anarchists will never again become so active as they were just prior to the Haymarket riot," placed a dragnet around the city as a prelude to a general roundup of subversives. Several anarchists were quickly arrested, including Abraham Isaak and Emma Goldman. By 9 September Scotland Yard was publicizing reports alleging that a steady stream of anarchists had been flowing into the United States from Europe during the previous six to eight months. With the death of Mc-Kinley on 14 September, public sentiment was aroused against "anarchy" and its devotees.[4]

Politicians were urged to pass legislation and support constitutional amendments that would suppress anarchism and anarchistic societies. In his annual message to Congress of 3 December 1901, Theodore Roosevelt proposed the exclusion of "all persons who are known to be believers in anarchistic principles or members of anarchistic societies."[5] In March of 1903, these cries were answered when Congress, for the first time, passed an act requiring an inspection of the political opinions of immigrants. The Immigration Act of 1903, fusing nativist with anti-radical sentiments, added "anarchists" to the restriction list.

Sections 2, 38, and 39 of the act excluded from admission to the United States and from naturalization to U.S. citizenship "anarchists, or persons who believe in or advocate the overthrow by force or violence of the Government of the United States or of all government." Illegal aliens could be deported within a three-year period beginning with the date of entry. As an amalgam of previous legislation, the 1903 act detailed the duties and responsibilities of the commissioners, inspectors, and other officers, and went on to outline administrative and jurisdictional procedures.[6]

Over the next twenty years, immigration legislation tended toward more inclusive definitions of radicalism and additional numerical restrictions. The nationalistic and anti-foreign sentiments of World War I were apparent in the acts of 1917, 1918, and 1920.

[4]Ibid., 7 and 9 September 1901.
[5]As quoted in William Preston, Jr., *Aliens and Dissenters*, p. 31.
[6]U.S., *Statutes at Large*, vol. XXXII, 1213–1222.

By 1917, the literacy test, advocated by Roosevelt as early as his 1901 speech, became law. By 1919 the country had abandoned all time limits on deportation in radical cases, had accepted the principle of guilt by association, and had penalized belief as well as teaching and advocacy. The 1920 act went further, excluding aliens who wrote, published, or even possessed radical literature. Later post-war legislation would continue the exclusion of Asiatics and eventually develop a quota system based on a blatantly racist criterion.[7]

Throughout this period the procedures for processing aliens became more summary. In 1893 the Supreme Court held in *Fong Yue Ting* v. *U.S.* that deportation was an administrative and not a criminal proceeding. Thus, unlike the general body of law, immigration laws were enforced, not through the courts (except as a last resort), but by an administrative body, the Department of Labor (or, between 1906 and 1913, the Department of Commerce and Labor).[8]

Local commissioners and inspectors were delegated broad authority that allowed them wide discretion in interpreting and enforcing the immigration laws. Several techniques and practices came to predominate: arrests without warrants; detentions for long periods, often incommunicado; private preliminary hearings and interrogations (in which evidence in support of a warrant was often obtained—a form of self-incrimination); excessive or, at times, no bail; denial of counsel until a relatively late stage. This system also afforded the alien no protection from dishonest and incompetent lawyers. Adopted informally, these practices became a normal part of deportation.[9]

Any alien who was considered by the examining inspector to be unqualified for entry was detained for an examination by a board of special inquiry. These boards were usually composed of immigration officials, with the examining inspector—without any special legal training—often acting as detective, prosecuting attor-

[7]Preston, *Aliens and Dissenters*, p. 227; Daniels, *Racism and Immigration Restriction*, pp. 8–10; Roy L. Garis, *Immigration Restriction*, pp. 109–141.

[8]See Milton R. Konvitz, *Civil Rights in Immigration*, pp. 44–49, 103–109, and Kate Holliday Claghorn, *The Immigrant's Day in Court*, p. 305.

[9]Preston, *Aliens and Dissenters*, p. 13.

ney, interpreter, and judge. The inspector's summary and the board's recommendation would then be forwarded to the office of the secretary of labor, where rubber-stamping was routine.[10]

A lack of judicial safeguards or due process enabled the Bureau of Immigration and Naturalization to act quickly and efficiently against alleged revolutionaries and to apply to the removal of radicals the same abusive tactics that applied to all aliens. Immigration and Justice Department officials were quick to seize on these summary methods in the mass arrests and deportations of the Red raids of 1919–1920. Caught in the police dragnets of those years were Alexander Berkman and Emma Goldman, and later, in 1923, the Mexican anarchist Enrique Flores Magón.

Deportation was not the only repressive weapon to be used in the war against aliens and radicals during these years. Between 1912 and the early 1920s, socialists, Wobblies (members of the Industrial Workers of the World, the I.W.W.), and a number of naturalized citizens of German birth were deprived of citizenship. In some of those cases citizens were "denaturalized" by judges equating radical beliefs with a lack of good character.[11] In other instances the provisions of extradition treaties and neutrality statutes were invoked in order to deport and imprison radicals. Equally questionable were the practices of closing foreign-language newspaper offices, harassing the editors, and seizing their properties.

Between 1917 and 1921, federal troops were used to put down labor strikes and domestic disorders. The military sent intelligence operatives into I.W.W. circles and placed many suspected radicals under surveillance. Troops occupied labor and lumber camps. The Post Office engaged in mail interceptions, denied second-class mailing privileges to radicals, and practiced outright censorship during the wartime years. For those few individuals who escaped these measures, there was always the post-war enforcement of the draft, sabotage, sedition, and espionage acts of World War I. The enforcement of these acts brought about the death of the I.W.W. in particular and radicalism in general.[12] As Warren G. Harding ushered in his days of "normalcy," the federal penitentiaries were

[10]Claghorn, *The Immigrant's Day in Court*, pp. 319–322.
[11]Ibid., pp. 16–17.
[12]Preston, *Aliens and Dissenters*, pp. 88–151.

filled with political prisoners, including the Mexican rebels Ricardo Flores Magón and Librado Rivera. The death of Flores Magón at Leavenworth in 1922, along with the forced deportation of Librado Rivera to Mexico at the end of 1923, marked the end of an era for Mexican *revoltosos* in the United States.

ONE
The Early *Revoltosos* and Their
American Allies, 1903–1911

... los gobiernos no saben hacer otra cosa que
sostener al fuente y tener aplastado al debil.
Ricardo Flores Magón, 1911

1. *Magonistas* and *Magonismo*

DURING the last decade of the nineteenth century, U.S. economic interests, in the form of capital and industrial surpluses, extended into
Mexico and continued to expand during the administrations of
Roosevelt, Taft, and Wilson. In 1890, the total U.S. investment was
around $130 million. At the turn of the century, American capital
invested in Mexican enterprises amounted to a little over $200 mil-
lion. By 1910, according to figures published by the Mexican government, total foreign capital amounted to over 2 billion pesos, of
which 1.2 billion pesos (or over $500 million U.S.) was American.
By 1914 the figure had grown to $580 million.[1]

Of the largest businesses in Mexico in 1910–1911, seven were
owned by American interests either outright or as joint enterprises
with the Mexican government and other foreign nationals. Anglo-
American interests dominated the express, petroleum, mining, and
utilities industries, and the American Smelting and Refining Company and the Greene Cananea Copper Company were the second-
and third-largest concerns in all of Mexico (only the multinational
Ferrocarriles Nacionales de México was larger).[2] American-con-
trolled enterprises brought in alien technicians, managers, and railway workers while making little effort to train Mexicans for the
better jobs.

[1]See Marvin D. Bernstein, *Foreign Investment in Latin America*, pp. 7–8.
For Mexican government statistics see Montgomery Schuyler (Mexico) to the
Secretary of State, 9 December 1912, Records of the Department of State
Relating to the Internal Affairs of Mexico, Microfilm Publication, Record Group
59, file 812.60, microcopy 274 (hereafter cited as RDS). For a general analysis
of the late-nineteenth-century events see Federick Stirton Weaver, "Capitalist
Development, Empire, and Latin American Underdevelopment: An Interpre-
tive Essay on Historical Change," *Latin American Perspectives* 3 (Fall 1976):
33–42.
[2]José Luis Ceceña, *México en la órbita imperial*, p. 86.

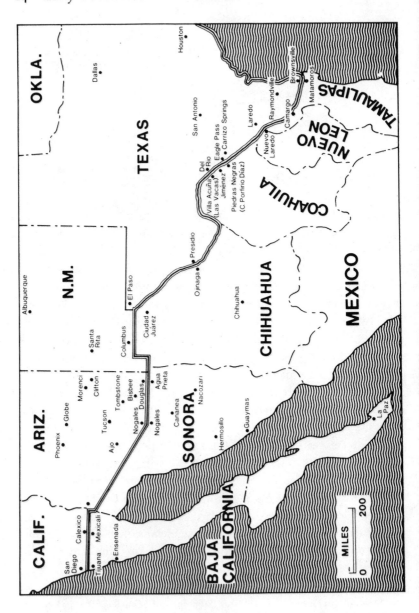

Revoltoso Country

Most of America's magnates of commerce and industry were attracted to Mexico because of the liberal concessions granted to foreigners. The names of Doheny, Morgan, Harriman, Guggenheim, Rockefeller, and Hearst were as well known in Mexican business circles as they were in the United States. With the exceptions of the plantation and oil interests of the coastal regions and the financial community in Mexico City, American investments tended to congregate around the northern Mexican states of Baja California, Sonora, Chihuahua, Coahuila, and Tamaulipas. This is where U.S. investors controlled substantial mining, timber, ranching, and agricultural enterprises.

Some of these capitalists, like Southern California publisher Harrison Gray Otis or Arizona rancher and copper king William C. Greene, held extensive properties on both sides of the American-Mexican border. These individuals cooperated with the U.S. government in a common struggle with the *revoltosos*. After all, Otis and Greene were involved at home in class warfare with radical labor. Otis confronted the I.W.W. in southern California, Greene fought the W.F.M. (Western Federation of Miners) in Arizona. Thus, owning concerns in Mexico, these men were as interested in the Mexican government's fight against the revolutionaries in Mexico as they were in the U.S. government's war against the radicals at home. And, more than that, they were active in promoting an intergovernmental campaign against *revoltosos* in both countries.[3]

When speaking of these American private and public interests in Mexico and other "underdeveloped" areas, Roosevelt often used the rhetoric of expansionism. Writing to Andrew Carnegie in 1907, he spoke about the great advances in the standard of international conduct, both among "civilized and strong" nations and "weaker and more backward" peoples.[4] It was the "white man's burden" to civilize, modernize, and capitalize these "backward" peoples. The United States had a moral duty to act as the policemen of the hemisphere. The enforcement of international law meant not only the

[3]For Greene's concern about the W.F.M. and the PLM, see C. L. Sonnichsen, *Colonel Greene and the Copper Skyrocket*, pp. 184–187. For Otis, who was owner of the California-Mexico Land and Cattle Company, see Lowell L. Blaisdell, *The Desert Revolution, Baja California, 1911*, pp. 26–28 and 174.

[4]Roosevelt to Carnegie, 5 April 1907, reproduced in Elting E. Morison, ed., *The Letters of Theodore Roosevelt*, V, 638–642.

prevention of violence in underdeveloped countries but also the enactment of policies by the governments of such countries to protect and promote the rights and interests of American businessmen.[5] By acting "civilized," Mexico's dictator Porfirio Díaz won from Roosevelt the accolade of being "the greatest statesman now living."[6]

Although differing from Roosevelt in temperament and tactics, William Howard Taft and his secretary of state, Philander C. Knox, shared the former president's assumptions about the need to maintain existing markets while finding new outlets for U.S. capital and goods. Taft was aware that American exports were changing, that the sale of manufactured goods was beginning to exceed that of raw products. He agreed with the vice-president of the Chamber of Commerce for Latin America, who in 1910 said "in the main it may be stated categorically, that our manufacturers will find their best acceptance in non-manufacturing, but wealthy, lands, such as Latin America."[7] Having experienced the recessions of 1903 and 1907, Taft was aware of the need for direct governmental intervention in support of U.S. trade and enterprise abroad, if only to avoid the perils of overproduction, a glutted home market, and the disorders of depression.

Below the border, Roosevelt and Taft found a good friend and colleague in don Porfirio Díaz. Coming to power in 1876, Díaz did not relinquish his presidential authority until forced to do so by Francisco Madero early in 1911. Sharing with North Americans their faith in liberal capitalism, Díaz stubbornly held to the belief that government cooperation with private enterprise would lead to progress and modernization for Mexico. Private enterprise in many instances meant foreign, especially U.S., investments, and Díaz was determined to attract and hold U.S. capital in Mexico.

This he accomplished through a variety of policies designed to make foreign capital safe and profitable. Low taxes, liberal conces-

---

[5]Robert Freeman Smith, *The United States and Revolutionary Nationalism in Mexico, 1916–1932*, pp. 23–30.

[6]Roosevelt to James Creelman, 7 March 1908, *Letters*, VI, 963–964. For Roosevelt's "hemisphere diplomacy" see George E. Mowry, *The Era of Theodore Roosevelt and the Birth of Modern America, 1900–1912*, pp. 143–164.

[7]Hugh MacNair Kahler, "Current Misconceptions of Trade with Latin-America," *Annals of the American Academy of Political and Social Science* (May 1911): 630.

sions, friendly courts, cheap labor, police protection, and a legal framework adjusted to the international legal order of the developed countries succeeded all too well in making Mexico "the mother of foreigners and the stepmother of Mexicans." As historian Robert Freeman Smith noted, "foreign businessmen and government officials considered Porfirian Mexico to be one of the most well-behaved 'backward' nations in the world."[8]

The result of these policies was a society that was partially developed economically, but primarily in its extractive sector, and an aging president and government that could not or would not make room for social groups that had been politically mobilized by the limited modernization.[9] In particular these were agrarian workers, *peones*, industrial workers, railroad employees, miners, middle-class intellectuals, and, in a few instances, hacendados who had been excluded from the system.[10] The leaders of these *revoltosos* foreshadowed the revolutionary events of 1911.

Their activities, which included issuing manifestos, arming strikers, issuing revolutionary programs and propaganda, and using guerrilla or *foco* tactics, eventually contributed to the distintegration of don Porfirio's rule. Of all the *revoltoso* groups in the pre-1911 era, the PLM (*Partido Liberal Mexicano*), or *magonista* movement, was the best organized and most extensive. Its activity accelerated governmental terrorism, and this in turn fed the ever-developing forces of revolutionary nationalism. The rebels sought the end of U.S. economic domination and the overthrow of Díaz.

Between 1905 and 1911 the PLM central Junta was intermittently located in San Antonio, St. Louis, and Los Angeles. From these centers the Junta directed operations along the border and in Mexico. PLM partisans were involved in the June 1906 strike at the Cananea copper works in Sonora, an event that was a kind of catalyst of revolution and governmental suppression in the history of the Mexican Revolution. That same year they participated in uprisings in Coahuila, Tamaulipas, and Veracruz. In 1906–1907 the

[8]Smith, *The U.S. and Revolutionary Nationalism in Mexico*, p. 5.

[9]This interpretation follows the model developed by Samuel P. Huntington in *Political Order in Changing Societies*, pp. 264–343.

[10]William D. Raat, "Ideas and Society in Don Porfirio's Mexico," *The Americas* 30 (July 1973): 34–40.

PLM was indirectly involved in a series of strikes affecting the textile industries of Puebla, Veracruz, Tlaxcala, Querétaro, Jalisco, and the Federal District. The year 1908 witnessed many uprisings and abortive attempts at revolution, not the least of which were the PLM-inspired raids at Viesca (Coahuila), Las Vacas (today Villa Acuña, Coahuila), and Casas Grandes and Palomas (Chihuahua). In 1910 and 1911 PLM "armies" were operating in Puebla, Tlaxcala, Morelos, Oaxaca, Veracruz, Tabasco, Yucatán, Chihuahua, Durango, Coahuila, Sonora, and Baja California.[11]

In surveying all of these campaigns, it is obvious that the *magonistas* were something more than mere "precursors" in the history of Mexico's Revolution of 1910. They not only set the stage for Madero's successful revolt, they were responsible for weakening Díaz's army and for keeping the momentum of revolution alive during the critical months and weeks before Díaz's self-imposed exile in May 1911. They were not only a prelude to Madero and the Revolution—in conjunction with other *revoltoso* groups, they *were* the Revolution of 1910.

The PLM had its antecedents in the *Club Liberal "Ponciano Arriaga,"* which was founded in San Luis Potosí in 1899. The central Junta organized in 1905 in St. Louis, Missouri, was known formally as the *Junta Organizadora del Partido Liberal Mexicano.* By July 1906, the Junta had developed a party platform and a revolutionary manifesto that not only called for the creation of secret clubs throughout Mexico but included a comprehensive social reform program (aspects of which were eventually incorporated into the Constitution of 1917). For propaganda purposes the newspaper

---

[11]A variety of sources narrate PLM activities from 1906 to 1911. The most authoritative account of the Cananea strike is Manuel González Ramírez, *Fuentes para la historia de la Revolución Mexicana,* III, *La huelga de Cananea.* For a general history see Florencio Barrera Fuentes, *Historia de la revolución mexicana: La etapa precursora,* pp. 201–210; James D. Cockcroft, *Intellectual Precursors of the Mexican Revolution, 1900–1913;* and Charles C. Cumberland, "Precursors of the Mexican Revolution," *Hispanic American Historical Review* 22 (May 1942): 344–356. For strike activity see both Moisés González Navarro, *El Porfiriato: La vida social,* pp. 298–300, and González Navarro, *Las huelgas textiles en el Porfiriato,* pp. 13–17. For the Baja revolt see Blaisdell, *The Desert Revolution.* An analysis of PLM structure and tactics can be found in Armando Bartra, "Ricardo Flores Magón en el cincuentenario de su muerte," in *Suplemento de Siempre!,* no. 565 (6 December 1972): ii–viii.

Regeneración was renewed and sent through the U.S. and Mexican mails to subscribers along the border and in the Mexican interior. A communications network was also set up to increase dues, subscriptions, and memberships (that is, the creation of regional, Liberal clubs and guerrilla *focos*).[12]

The initial leadership of the Junta, a group that Díaz blamed for much of the political unrest in Mexico, consisted of Ricardo Flores Magón (president), Juan Sarabia (vice-president), Antonio I. Villarreal (secretary), and Enrique Flores Magón (treasurer), and had as voting board members (*vocales*) Librado Rivera, Manuel Sarabia, and Rosalío Bustamante. Between 1907 and 1910, with Ricardo Flores Magón, Juan Sarabia, Antonio Villarreal, and Librado Rivera in jail, the leadership fell to Enrique Flores Magón and Práxedis G. Guerrero. Enrique, always faithful to his older brother, was to be Ricardo's constant companion and fellow revolutionist. Guerrero, a man of remarkable military and journalistic abilities, engineered many of the guerrilla actions of 1908 and 1910.

Of all these individuals, Ricard Flores Magón is usually considered by historians to have been the most influential in politically

---

[12]There exists an extensive literature on the *magonista* movement. In addition to items previously cited, see the following. Two important sources for printed documents are Manuel González Ramírez, ed., *Epistolario y textos de Ricardo Flores Magón*, and Isidro Fabela, ed., *Documentos históricos de la Revolución Mexicana*, X, XI. For excerpts from *Regeneración* see both Ricardo Flores Magón, *¿Para qué sirve la autoridad? y otros cuentos*, and Armando Bartra, ed., *Regeneración 1900–1918*. For the PLM see Juan Gómez-Quiñones, *Sembradores, Ricardo Flores Magón, y el Partido Liberal Mexicano: A Eulogy and Critique*. For Flores Magón's prison correspondence between 1919 and 1922 see Ricardo Flores Magón, *Epistolario revolucionario e íntimo*. This last work also contains an excellent chronology. A pioneering effort is Lyle C. Brown, "The Mexican Liberals and Their Struggle against the Díaz Dictatorship," *Antología MCC*. See also José C. Valadés, "Los precursores de D. Francisco I. Madero," *La Opinión* (Los Angeles), 13 December 1929–24 January 1930. The classic study remains Ethel Duffy Turner, *Ricardo Flores Magón y el Partido Liberal Mexicano*. Two competent dissertations are Ward Albro, "Ricardo Flores Magón and the Liberal Party: An Inquiry into the Origins of the Mexican Revolution of 1910," and Ellen Howell Meyers, "The Mexican Liberal Party, 1903–1910." Also see William Weber Johnson, *Heroic Mexico*, pp 18–35; Manuel González Ramírez, *La revolución social de Mexico*, I, 39–114; the introduction by Sinclair Snow to John Kenneth Turner, *Barbarous Mexico*, pp. xi–xxix. Cockcroft, *Intellectual Precursors*, contains an excellent thirty-four page bibliography.

radicalizing the Mexican people between 1900 and 1911. Born in Oaxaca in 1873 and educated in Mexico City, he was forty-nine when he died in Leavenworth Penitentiary in the fall of 1922. Not only as a symbol of revolutionary anarcho-communism but as an object of intergovernmental suppression, Flores Magón's imprisonment nine separate times by the governments of Mexico and the United States in Mexico City, St. Louis, Los Angeles, Yuma and Florence (Arizona), McNeil Island, and Fort Leavenworth made him an incarnation of international class warfare.[13]

In 1900, at a time when Mexico's editors and publishers were feeling the brunt of Díaz's war on the press, Ricardo Flores Magón left his law career behind to become a militant journalist. With his older brother Jesús he founded the newspaper *Regeneración* as "an independent journal of combat" against centralism and autocracy. Later, at the Liberal Congress held in San Luis Potosí in February 1901, he publicly denounced the Díaz administration as "a den of bandits." By 1902, with the suppression of *Regeneración*, he became a writer for Daniel Cabrera's *El Hijo del Ahuizote* until its demise in February 1903. As a writer, spokesman, and organizer of anti-Díaz causes, Ricardo was fined and sentenced three times between 1901 and 1903, serving sentences in Mexico City's infamous Belem prison as well as the military compound of Santiago Tlatelolco. By June 1903 he had been prohibited to publish in Mexico. His alternatives were reduced either to living with rats, lice, spiders, mud, and excrement in prison or to living in what he thought would be the relative freedom of an alien exile radical in the United States. He chose the latter.[14]

In January 1904, Ricardo, accompanied by his brother Enrique and the revolutionary poet Santiago de la Hoz, crossed the border into Laredo, Texas. By February they had been joined by Camilo Arriaga, Juan Sarabia, Crescencio Villarreal Márquez, and Manuel Sarabia. The group immediately distributed a circular to their fellow *correligionarios* announcing their intent to reorganize the struggle against Díaz. Appeals were mailed to their former associates and subscribers to *El Hijo del Ahuizote* and *Regeneración*. With monies received from their friends, including Francisco Madero

---

[13]R. Flores Magón, *Epistolario*, chronology.
[14]Ibid.; also see Johnson, *Heroic Mexico*, pp. 18–25.

through his relatives in Texas, a few *revoltoso* publications were established. By the end of the year the Flores Magón brothers were publishing a new *Regeneración* from San Antonio, while Márquez and others had founded *1810* and *El Mensajaro* in Del Rio. After a local incident that resulted in the arrest of Enrique, the group decided to move the organization to St. Louis.[15]

The St. Louis experience of 1905–1906 brought about a significant shift in the orientation of the Liberals. What had begun as an anti-clerical, traditional liberal reform movement in 1901 was now transformed to a covert revolutionary operation that intended not only to overthrow Díaz but to change the entire political and social structure of Mexico. As was indicated before, a Junta was formed, secret clubs were invited to join, and a party platform and a manifesto were announced. Men of wealth and moderate views, like Camilo Arriaga and Francisco Madero, withdrew their support. As governmental authorities became aware of the increasing radicalism of the PLM, party leaders were once again harassed and imprisoned. To avoid these difficulties, the Flores Magón brothers and Juan Sarabia took refuge first in Toronto, Canada, and then in Montreal. By September 1906 the publication of *Regeneración* had been suspended when the St. Louis printing press was confiscated by local authorities.[16]

In the spring of 1907, a Liberal Party nucleus had reassembled in Los Angeles. Other supporters had joined Flores Magón, Villarreal, and Rivera, including Manuel Sarabia (Juan Sarabia's cousin), Práxedis Guerrero, and Lázaro Gutiérrez de Lara (the last of Cananea strike fame). With the aid of these individuals, Flores Magón was able to establish a new revolutionary organ called *Revolución*. The newspaper revived public awareness, and once again the PLM faced governmental hostility. That summer saw the attempted kid-

---

[15]L. Brown, "The Mexican Liberals," pp. 322–324; Bartra, *Regeneración*, pp. 43–49. Although many writers suggest that the Liberals went from Laredo to Chicago in 1904, there is no substantiating evidence. Most authors cite the authority of Cumberland, and he refers to correspondence between R. Flores Magón and Henry Weinberger on 9 May 1921. But González Ramírez's reproduction of the 9 May 1921 letter contains no reference to Chicago. See Cumberland, "Precursors," p. 345, and González Ramírez *Epistolario y textos*, pp. 239–240.

[16]Bernard Axelrod, "St. Louis and the Mexican Revolutionaries, 1905–1906", [Missouri Historical Society] *Bulletin*: 94–108.

napping by the Mexican government of Manuel Sarabia from Douglas, Arizona. More important, in August the Los Angeles police, aided by Furlong detectives, arrested Ricardo Flores Magón, Villarreal, and Rivera. They were held in the Los Angeles county jail for several months, eventually being transferred to Tombstone, Arizona. There they were found guilty of conspiracy to violate the neutrality laws and were sentenced to eighteen months in the territorial prison. After his release from the Florence penitentiary in August 1910, Flores Magón, never one to waste time, proceeded (with the aid of Anselmo L. Figueroa) to usher in *Regeneración's* third epoch with plans for a Baja California revolt and a new anarchist manifesto.[17]

The ideology of *magonismo* had undergone radical changes between the 1 July 1906 "Programa del Partido Liberal y Manifiesto a la Nación"[18] and the September 1911 "Manifiesto Programático" outlining the anarcho-communist position of the Partido Liberal. The Liberal Plan of 1906, a lengthy document that included an "exposition" and fifty-two provisions, was the product of many minds. As early as April a preliminary program had been drafted and was circulating among fifty or more of the leaders for their comments and revisions. The education section was written by Villarreal; Ricardo Flores Magón drafted the accompanying "exposition." The labor and peasant sections reflected the influence of Juan Sarabia in particular and American, Canadian, and Mexican labor leaders in general. When the final draft was completed, Juan Sarabia acted as the general editor. The manifesto and program were designed to appeal to many groups, including common soldiers, anticlerics, peasants, workers, schoolteachers, productive *latifundistas*, nationalistic businessmen (who disliked the competition of foreigners), and Yankeephobes of all classes. Published in Span-

---

[17]González Ramírez, *Epistolario y textos*, pp. 92–161. For Guerrero in particular, see Pietro Ferrua, *Gli anarchici nella rivoluzione messicana: Práxedis G. Guerrero*, and Práxedis G. Guerrero, *Artículos de combate*.

[18]The original "Program and Manifesto" appears in many published works. For example, see José D. Silva, *Plan de Ayala. Fuente de información de la Revolución Mexicana*, pp. 5–19, or Fabela, *Documentos históricos*, X, 41–68. An English version of the provisions section can be found in Cockcroft, *Intellectual Precursors*, pp. 239–245.

ish, it was soon circulating throughout Mexico and the American Southwest.[19]

The fifty-two provisions were specifically aimed at correcting the abuses of the Díaz regime. Díaz's conciliation policy with the Church was to go, with religious properties being taxed and nationalized. The presidential term was to be reduced to four years, with no reelection of either the president or state governors. Freedom of speech and press were to be guaranteed, and education was to be secular and obligatory. More public schools were to be built, and schoolteachers were to receive increased salaries. The conditions of rank-and-file soldiers were to be improved, and obligatory military service was to be suppressed. *Ejidos* (Indian commons) were to be restored, the Indian population was to be protected, and unproductive lands were to be taken from the hacendados and redistributed. Agrarian banks were to be instituted. Labor was granted several rights, including the eight-hour day, a minimum wage, and health and job security assurances. Progressive taxation was introduced, as well as penal and municipal government reforms. Finally, foreign workers were not to be paid more than Mexicans, and foreign capitalists were to hire native workers.

It is obvious that the intent of the Partido Liberal was to overthrow Díaz and usher in a democratic and popular system of government. Private property was to be preserved, but the excesses of capital were to be curbed. Class cooperation, rather than class warfare, was stressed. The middle-class aspirations of the working classes were to be realized, capital would be restrained but not abolished, and a democratic, progressive, popular welfarist state would replace the old order. Domestic and foreign capitalist elites were to be restrained in their exploitation of the human and natural resources of their country. In sum, the party was calling for revolution—a nationalist, middle-class, and "petit bourgeois" revolution.

After 1908 the thinking of the Junta leaders changed. Between 1908 and 1910 their position was one of a thinly veiled anarchism,

---

[19]Cockcroft, *Intellectual Precursors*, pp. 120–133; L. Brown, "The Mexican Liberals," pp. 325–328; Johnson, *Heroic Mexico*, pp. 27–30; González Ramírez, *Fuentes*, III, 111–112.

with the PLM manifesto of 1906 being used simply as a tactic to assure an ever-increasing membership. By September 1911 the Junta, now purified by the absence of the socialist wing, was privately and openly espousing an anarcho-communist position. The ideas of Marx, Engels, Bakunin, Saint-Simon, Kropotkin, and Malatesta formed the matrix of their communist anarchism.

Marxism, scientific socialism, and revolutionary unionism were some of the ingredients of the PLM philosophy. Anarcho-communism urged the abolition of government by "proletarians" in the name of the masses and of all mankind. Government and capital would be replaced by a community of workers, all engaged in useful pursuits, seeking, through a collective consciousness, the common good. To achieve this end, violence could be used but, when used, was to be educative and instrumental in bringing about the natural order of society. Since the state was the cause (and not the product) of private property, individual property would be replaced by communal ownership and use after the dissolution of the state.[20]

These ideas were translated into more concrete terms in September 1911 when Ricardo Flores Magón made an ideological appeal to Pascual Orozco, Jr., with the hope of wooing him away from the *maderistas* and over to the *magonistas*. Had the tactic worked, Orozco, who was a popular leader with a large following, would have been a significant addition to the *magonista* cause. After appealing to Orozco's ego, calling him an informed and honorable man, Flores Magón went on to denounce Madero and the forthcoming October elections. He argued that, of the several *revoltoso* groups seeking power, only the PLM was truly anti-government, non-personalistic, and aware of the lessons of history. Unlike Madero, he emphasized the point that economic freedom was prior to political liberty, and, since government was the guardian of capitalism, freedom could not emanate from government. It was necessary "to place the mines, factories, and machinery in the hands of the workers so that they could work without masters and distribute the product of their work among themselves." Government only

[20]Irving L. Horowitz, *The Anarchists*, pp. 44–47; Bartra, *Regeneración*, pp. 33–36; Arnaldo Córdova, *La ideología de la Revolución Mexicana*. pp. 173–187.

exists when there are two classes; Mexico's classless society of the future would need no government. He concluded with this exhortation: "Since the spilling of blood is inevitable, why do you not orient your guerrilla movement toward the conquest of true liberty, i.e., the emancipation of labor from the claws of capital?"[21]

Thus the ideology of *magonismo* had evolved from a traditional liberal, anti-clerical reform doctrine in 1901, through the ideas of bourgeois revolution in 1906, to the radicalism of anarcho-communism in 1911. In this it reflected the changing interests of the leadership and their socio-economic backgrounds (most of them were from petit bourgeois and semi-proletarian households). A small sample of key figures, either directly or indirectly involved in PLM fortunes, when looked at collectively provide us with a general profile of the leadership. For this purpose eight individuals have been selected: the Flores Magón brothers, Juan Sarabia, Antonio Villarreal, Librado Rivera, Práxedis Guerrero, Lázaro Gutiérrez de Lara, and Antonio Díaz Soto y Gama (an associate of Arriaga, co-founder of the Liberal Party in Mexico in 1899, and colleague of many *magonistas*).

The first observation that can be made about this group is that its members were relatively youthful. In 1910, the average age was 32.6, with Rivera the oldest at 46 and Enrique Flores Magón the youngest at 23. Ricardo Flores Magón was 37 (the same age as Madero); Sarabia and Guerrero were a youthful 28. In 1900, when the movement started, their ages averaged 22 years (quite in keeping with current thought about the average age of a politically mature generation).

Although age may not be as important a socializing factor as socio-economic forces, the group's youthfulness would account, in part, for the vigorous, activist, and idealistic quality of the movement. Age can also be a clue to familial behavior, which may be transmitted from one generation to the next. In this case, all had parents who participated in or were aware of the civil wars and Liberal Party movement of Benito Juárez between 1857 and 1872.

In surveying the socio-economic backgrounds of these individ-

[21]Flores Magón to Orozco, 18 September 1911, Archivo General de la Nación, Ramo Revolución, Política Interior, Correspondencia varios, 1910–1919, Mexico City (hereafter cited as AGN/RRV), doc. no. 43.

uals, all, with the exception of Guerrero and Gutiérrez de Lara, could be described as, to use the language of historian James Cock-croft, "low status intellectuals."[22] As such, they were either from petit bourgeois or semi-proletarian backgrounds. Peculiarly enough, Guerrero's family owned a hacienda in Guanajuato and could be described as aristocratic, religious, and conservative. Nevertheless, Guerrero abandoned his class to live as a common worker in the factories and mines of Colorado and Arizona. Gutiérrez de Lara was a lawyer, judge, and government employee with influential family and professional contacts in Mexico City. The others, how-ever, fit the "low status" description: Ricardo Flores Magón (jour-nalist), Enrique Flores Magón (carpenter and electrician), Villarreal (schoolteacher), Rivera (primary schoolteacher), Díaz Soto y Gama (provincial lawyer), J. Sarabia (poet, journalist, printer).[23]

This "low status" background explains, again in part, the petit bourgeois and proletarian objectives of the PLM. The Flores Ma-gón brothers, raised in the communal regions of Oaxaca, never lost their faith in the "liberalism" of their parents and the collective values of the Indian community. Both Rivera and Sarabia came from struggling households and knew the value of physical labor. Villarreal had spent four years in prison in Monterrey and learned first hand that in a tyranny there is very little difference between political and criminal acts. While the Flores Magón brothers and Rivera gravitated toward anarchism, the others formed the liberal and socialist wing of the PLM. Villarreal, the rough and burly schoolteacher, was less idealistic than the others and always to the right of Sarabia and Gutiérrez de Lara. The latter, along with Díaz Soto y Gama, eventually became active in the left wing of the anarcho-syndicalist *Casa del Obrero Mundial.*[24]

To summarize, then, as PLM binational leaders they were pri-marily but not exclusively "low status" intellectuals, with back-grounds or sentiments that identified them with petit bourgeois and proletarian groups. They were ideologically radical, as either so-

---

[22]Cockcroft, *Intellectual Precursors*, p. 88.

[23]Ibid., pp. 70–88. See also Bartra, *Regeneración*, p. 35, and Fortunato Lozano, *Antonio I. Villareal: Vida de un gran mexicano*, pp. 5–23.

[24]Cockcroft, *Intellectual Precursors*, p. 210. For Díaz Soto y Gama, see John Womack, Jr., *Zapata and the Mexican Revolution*, pp. 135–136, 186, 193–194.

cialists or anarcho-communists. Many of them (the Flores Magón brothers, Villarreal, Sarabia, Rivera) found it increasingly difficult to advance within the system. All were literate, indeed well educated (including the self-educated Sarabia); some were even bilingual. Familiar with the works of Tolstoy, Marx, Engels, Bakunin, and Kropotkin, many had been "politicized" by their prison experiences. They were a new generation of young, idealistic, and optimistic individuals (and, as will be seen, with female companions who made important contributions to the revolution). They were excellent propagandists of both the word and the deed. With the exception of Díaz Soto y Gama, all were Mexican exiles in revolt. They were the spokesmen, theoreticians, publicists, and policymakers of the PLM. And, equally important, apart from level and type of education, their make-up mirrored that of many of their followers.

The rank and file of the PLM were found in many Liberal clubs, which first started to develop in Mexico after 1900, especially after Camilo Arriaga issued a manifesto from San Luis Potosí. At least fifty clubs were formed that year as a result of the manifesto. After 1905, new groups came into existence, affiliated with the St. Louis Junta. Many of these started in the mining communities of Sonora and Arizona, like that formed by Gutiérrez de Lara in Cananea or Guerrero's *Obreros Libres* in Morenci. The July 1906 manifesto accelerated the creation of new clubs along the border and in Mexico. With over 750,000 copies of the manifesto in circulation,[25] the St. Louis post office box began to receive a steady stream of gifts, loans, and subscriptions. By the end of August 1906, *Regeneración* had a circulation of between 15,000 and 20,000. As clubs developed throughout Mexico and the American Southwest, new *revoltoso* newspapers were established.[26]

From membership lists compiled from subscriptions obtained through mail interceptions in 1906, Enrique Creel and the Chihuahua authorities knew of the existence of dozens of clubs in Mex-

---

[25]Bartra, "Ricardo Flores Magón," p. vi.

[26]Albro, "Ricardo Flores Magón," p. 76; Johnson, *Heroic Mexico*, p. 25. See also Richard Griswold del Castillo, "The Mexican Revolution and the Spanish Language Press in the Borderlands," *Journalism History* 4 (Summer 1977): 42–47.

ico and the United States (the state of Hidalgo alone had at least eleven clubs) and of hundreds of individuals who either subscribed to or corresponded with the Junta. On the American side, although a few members lived in Indiana, Illinois, New York, and Missouri, most active members lived and worked in Texas, Arizona, and California.[27] These people, Anglo, Mexican American, and Mexican, reflected the economic concerns of their regions, with railway and itinerant workers in the greater Los Angeles area (one Mexican government source estimated that there were over 12,000 Mexicans in Los Angeles in 1906, of whom 3,000 worked for the railroads),[28] miners and smelter workers in Arizona, and artisans and small merchants in Texas.

In Mexico, most clubs operated along the northern tier, with Sonora, Coahuila, and Chihuahua having the most *revoltoso* activity and PLM members. There was also limited but important political action in Durango, Baja California, and Sinaloa. Outside of the north, a second area of importance for the PLM was the east coast region, in particular the state of Veracruz and the adjoining east-central states of Hidalgo, Tlaxcala, San Luis Potosí, Puebla, and Mexico. Of lesser importance were Oaxaca, Tabasco, and the port city of Progreso (Yucatán). Although there were political clubs in all of the states of the Republic, there were few active members in the Yucatán peninsula, southern "Indian" Mexico, and the traditional and "Spanish," conservative, western states of Jalisco, Colima, and Nayarit.[29]

Membership was largest and most active in those northern areas of the Republic that underwent a mining boom, with a corresponding shift in population, during the last decade of the Porfiriato. For example, Sonora, Chihuahua, and Coahuila all advanced one

[27]See the lists of purported PLM members and clubs in the Silvestre Terrazas Collection, Bancroft Library, University of California, Berkeley (hereafter cited as STC), box 26, folder 4, and box 27, folders 9b, 11b, 13a.

[28]Operative's Report, Pacific Co-operative Detective Association, 23 October 1906, Archivo General de la Secretaría de Relaciones Exteriores de México, Mexico City (hereafter cited as AREM), L–E–1245. For a description of AREM legajos and expedientes see Berta Ulloa, *Revolución Mexicana, 1910–1920*, pp. 41–113.

[29]STC, box 26, folder 4; box 27, folders 9b, 11b, 13a. See also Bartra, "Ricardo Flores Magón," p. viii.

place in the rank order of populous states between 1900 and 1910.[30] Another significant correlation is that Sonora and Veracruz, the two states that witnessed the most PLM political and military activity, were also areas undergoing a type of modernization that led to the labor conflict and industrial strife of the mining fields of Cananea and the textile factories of Río Blanco.

The so-called Arizona-Sonora mining triangle was of great importance in the history of the *revoltosos*. Between 1870 and 1910, Sonora developed at a rapid pace. By the 1880s the Sonoran Railway linked Nogales, Arizona, to the Pacific port of Guaymas. The railway accelerated the wars against the Yaqui and opened the country to commercial, agriculture, and mining development. U.S. financial involvement came quickly, so that by 1902 Sonora ranked second in the list of states holding American investments. The development of large-scale mining led to an explosion in wage rates and to labor shortages on the traditional haciendas.[31]

The communities of Sonora, a product of the state's economic expansion, were true urban units populated with urban-centered middle groups of professional men, ranchers, merchants, artisans, miners, and other "prototype" petit bourgeoisie. The Sonoran middle class had many contacts with Arizona and the United States, sending their children to schools there and coming across the border to shop and trade. The Anglo influences and the ties of Sonora to the American Southwest led other Mexicans to call the Sonorans the "Yankees of Mexico." The Arizona-Sonora affinity was even greater for the *revoltosos*, who saw the country north of the Rio Grande in strategic terms as a source of arms, equipment, finances, and revolutionary exiles.[32]

The official governmental view of Flores Magón's followers was not very flattering. Del Rio informant Judge J. G. Griner said of the Jiménez rebels that they "are an undesirable element of people, most of whom have never done an honest day's work." Captain W. S. Scott of the U.S. Army called the *revoltosos* "idle vagabonds."

[30] For demographic data see Donald F. Roberts, "Mining and Modernization: The Mexican Border States during the Porfiriato, 1876–1911" (dissertation), pp. 69–114.

[31] Barry Carr, *The Peculiarities of the Mexican North, 1880–1928: An Essay on Interpretation*, pp. 4–6.

[32] Ibid., pp. 6–8.

And Mexico's consul in Laredo, A. V. Lomelí, referred to them as "a large mass of ignorant and poor people who are absolutely in the control of political agitators and socialists."[33] Although there were some drunks, tramps, desperadoes, outlaws, and other lumpenproletariat in the *revoltoso* ranks, they were a minority, with most followers being politically astute and aware of their own economic conditions.

From reports submitted to the Mexican government by private detectives and informants, a more precise picture of the composition of the *revoltosos* can be developed. The Mexican government, and especially Governor Creel's office, was very efficient in maintaining records on its enemies. In one month's time during 1906, Creel demonstrated his thoroughness by compiling a list of over six hundred PLM contributors, their home addresses, and the amount of their contributions.[34] Some reports were very detailed. For example, from a private investigator's report in 1909 it is possible to get a small sample of the skin color, clothing styles, and occupations of over forty *revoltosos* in the Clifton, Arizona, area.[35] From these and other accounts some generalizations can be made.

Most of the followers were male and under forty years of age (the average for the Clifton group was 34.5). Those in Arizona were either Mexican Americans of long standing, recent immigrants from Sonora and Chihuahua, or Anglo allies from the Western Federation of Miners. In Los Angeles and Laredo and in other railway centers, there were large numbers of railway shop and "gang" laborers. Occupationally they included artisans and craftsmen (e.g., carpenters, leathersmiths, blacksmiths), small merchants (e.g., restaurant owners), photographers, printers, journalists, schoolteachers, lawyers, miners, construction workers, factory workers, ranch man-

[33]J. G. Griner to the San Antonio District Attorney, 7 June 1907, Records of the Department of State, Record Group 59, Numerical File, 1906–1910, National Archives, Washington, D.C. (hereafter cited as NF), case 5028/7–8; Capt. W. S. Scott to the Adjutant General, 26 August 1907, Records of the Department of Justice, Record Group 60, National Archives, Washington, D.C. (hereafter cited as RG 60), file no. 43718; A. V. Lomelí to Sec. de Estado y del Despacho de Rel. Ext., 8 September 1906, AREM, L–E–1240, Segunda Parte.

[34]STC, box 27, folder 11b.

[35]Miguel López Torres to Sec. de Rel. Ext., 2 and 16 March 1909, AREM, L–E–954.

agers, and itinerant laborers. The majority were unskilled industrial workers, small-scale artisans and merchants, and middle-class professionals. These were the groups undergoing occupational changes in a modernizing society, the same petit bourgeois and working-class groups from which the leadership came.

In reviewing this list of occupations, one is immediately struck by the lack of *peones* and campesinos. Several factors can be suggested to account for this circumstance. Perhaps it was the traditional conservatism, regional orientation, and anti-intellectualism of the rural dweller that, except for the later guerrilla campaigns in Veracruz, accounted for his lack of direct involvement in the PLM. Because the PLM relied so extensively on journalistic devices for its propaganda, it is possible that the illiterate campesino and the migrant farm worker were mostly unaware of the PLM's ideas and activities.

Ideological factors should also be considered. With the emphasis that anarcho-communism placed on the abolition of government by "proletarians" in the name of mankind, no specific focus was placed on rural dwellers and laborers as such. In spite of the agrarian provisions of the PLM manifesto, socialists and revolutionary unionists replaced the ideologue and peasant alike with the proletariat as the central element in the struggle against the bourgeois state. In this respect one can see the influence on the PLM of the urban-based Los Angeles Socialist Party and the syndicalism of the Industrial Workers of the World. Finally, and this certainly explains one problem that the *zapatistas* had with the *Casa del Obrero Mundial* at a later date, the anti-clericalism of urban liberals was antithetic to the religious inhabitants of the country parish.[36]

Another group important to PLM fortunes was that of the female radicals. Between 1906 and 1911, the writers and contributors to *Regeneración* and *Revolución* advocated the emancipation of women, urging them to participate fully in the revolutionary process. In 1907, the first women's revolutionary organization in support of the PLM was organized by textile workers in Mexico City. It was called the *Hijas de Anáhuac*, and it grew to a membership of

[36]In any case the *Casa* directors rejected the *zapatistas* because of their religiosity and church support. See John M. Hart, *Anarchism and the Mexican Working Class, 1860–1931*, pp. 131–133.

over three hundred before being suppressed by the police. In spite of this, meetings of smaller groups were continued at the factories, and the *Hijas* survived to become an active *maderista* body after 1911.[37] Another women's organization, the Liberal Union of Mexican Women, provided funds and support for the PLM.

The *compañeras* of PLM Junta members also played more than supportive roles in helping the cause of the revolution. Ricardo Flores Magón's lifetime companion (and common-law wife) was María Talavera. In 1907, she was instrumental in developing socialist support for those *magonistas* in the Los Angeles county jail. While Flores Magón was in prison, she aided in shaping his thinking and the ideology of *magonismo*. During World War I she was tried by a federal court in Los Angeles in 1918 for violations of the Espionage Act. Enrique Flores Magón's wife, Teresa Arteaga, joined the PLM in 1905, worked to sustain *Regeneración* during this period, and has been credited with saving the life of don Ricardo in Los Angeles in 1907. She was later a friend and associate of Margarita Ortega, the famed *revoltosa* who was killed in the Baja California revolt.[38]

During 1907, Librado Rivera's wife, Evarista, was active in smuggling messages out of the Los Angeles county jail and keeping communications alive between *magonistas* in and out of the jails. Juan Sarabia's companion was Andrea Villarreal, the sister of Antonio. Andrea and her sister Teresa led a national campaign between 1907 and 1909 on behalf of the imprisoned *magonistas*. By 1910, they had established their own radical newspaper in San Antonio, *La Mujer Moderna*. Teresa also founded the socialist newspaper *El Obrero*. Finally, one should acknowledge the financial contributions of Elizabeth Trowbridge, wife of Manuel Sarabia.

One center of female radicalism was El Paso, Texas. In 1907,

[37]Virginia Ann Newton Mounce, "Mexican Women during the Porfiriato, 1877–1911" (thesis), p. 5; Ana María Hernández, *La mujer mexicana en la industria textil*, pp. 35–38; Margaret Towner, "Monopoly Capitalism and Women's Work during the Porfiriato," *Latin American Perspectives* 12 and 13 (Winter and Spring 1977): 98.

[38]María de los Angeles Mendieta Alatorre, *La mujer en la Revolución Mexicana*, pp. 38–40. For María Talavera's 1907 campaign see the *Los Angeles Daily Times*, 19 and 21 September 1907.

Isidra T. de Cárdenas established the weekly *Voz de la Mujer*. She too entered into the campaign to free Flores Magón from prison, sending public messages to Roosevelt and other national leaders. *La Voz de la Mujer* also carried excerpts from the Los Angeles *Revolución* in order to communicate the Junta's ideas to the readership of El Paso. One year earlier, the female radical señora Flores de Andrade fled from Chihuahua to El Paso. In Chihuahua she had organized the semi-secret "Daughters of Chauhtémoc," which worked with the Liberal Party. In El Paso she worked for both Flores Magón and Madero, collecting money, clothes, medicines, arms, and ammunition for the revolutionists.[39]

Finally, there was Teresa Urrea, the mystic, revolutionary Saint of Cabora. Between 1890 and 1906, she led an anti-Díaz movement in Chihuahua, Arizona, and Texas. In 1896, in the company of Lauro Aguirre, she stormed the customshouse at Nogales (to be pursued by the famous Emilio Kosterlitzky). In Texas and Arizona, they led the *teresista* movement against the dictator—even writing a book together called *Tomóchic*, an exposé of Díaz's Yaqui policy.[40]

After her death in February 1906, Aguirre kept the *teresista* cause alive by integrating it with *magonismo*. That year he responded to the PLM's call by writing *magonista* editorials for his El Paso newspaper, *La Reforma Social*. In 1906, at the time of his arrest with Villarreal, he had resided in El Paso for over ten years. In the years prior to the Revolution of 1911 the old *teresista* and *magonista*, now called a "revolutionary crank" by the locals, continued to be harassed by the agents of Díaz.

As has been suggested, by 1906 the PLM had not only established a central Junta, published a manifesto, established a newspaper, and called for members but had also developed a binational structure and set of tactics to implement their program. Fundamentally, the organization was structured on three levels: the clandestine clubs, the cellular and front groups, and the insurrectional

[39]See *Le Voz de la Mujer*, 28 July and 27 October 1907 (STC). For Flores de Andrade see Manuel Gamio, *The Mexican Immigrant: His Life-Story*, pp. 29–35.

[40]Carlos Larralde, *Mexican-American: Movements and Leaders*, pp. 58–64; Mario Gill, "Teresa Urrea La Santa de Cabora," *Historia Mexicana* 6 (April–June 1957): 626–644.

forces. The clandestine clubs (with their ties to the PLM to be kept secret) were to be small, highly disciplined underground political groups. They were to be modeled after the central Junta, and orient themselves politically by following the general ideology espoused in *Regeneración* and other Junta publications. Specific tactics would be defined by the central Junta and communicated to the clubs by means of special messenger or cryptograms. Their function was that of directing the other organizations and preparing the conditions for revolution.[41]

The cellular clubs operated openly as Liberal clubs. They privately acknowledged the PLM and sought to propagandize the masses and promote knowledge about the manifesto and program of 1906. Their major responsibility was to create broadly-based "front" organizations concerned with political and economic issues. To meet the needs of propaganda, the members of the Liberal clubs often established militant newspapers, again on the model of *Regeneración*. Once the "fronts" had been established, the cellular clubs were to become integrated with and indistinguishable from the popular movement. Labor unions and artisan's guilds were often the means through which the clubs operated, with the ultimate concern that of activating the masses on the national level.[42]

The operations of these clubs can be illustrated with the examples of Cananea and Río Blanco. In Cananea, in January 1906, Manuel M. Diéguez and Esteban B. Calderón created the *Unión Liberal Humanidad,* a secret organization that communicated with the St. Louis Junta. Since this type of clandestine group was incapable of inciting a mass movement, they went on to organize a *Unión Minera,* a local miner's syndicate that advocated popular labor reforms. The leadership's main hope was to transform the local *Unión* into a national movement to be known as the *Liga Minera de los Estados Unidos Mexicanos.* Similarly, in Veracruz in June 1906 a group of workers founded a secret club known as the *Mesa Directiva* and a popular front called the *Gran Círculo de Obreros Libres.* Although the directorate of the PLM did not actually plan the details of either the Cananea or Río Blanco strikes,

41Bartra, "Ricardo Flores Magón," p. vi.
42Ibid.

they did indirectly set the stage through their propaganda and agitation.[43]

The insurrectional forces were also known as guerrilla *focos*. The original concern was one of developing a fighting force that would be ready for combat on receiving the signal to revolt from the Liberal Junta. The object was to initiate simultaneous revolts that would ignite the fires of a general social revolution and mass movement. Once the insurrection had been sparked by this force, the guerrillas would transform themselves into a military and political cadre in order to assure a successful revolution. Although they called themselves *focos*, much of their strategy and logistics was conventional, not resembling at all in 1906 the modern insurgency forces of China and Cuba.[44]

With the military failures of 1906, the Junta became convinced that Mexico was not ready for a general mass insurrection. Thus the tactics and strategy from 1908 to 1911 changed to those of a prolonged undercover guerrilla war against the federal armies of Díaz. It was in this latter phase that Práxedis Guerrero, as *Delegado General*, and Jesús M. Rangel, as Third Guerrilla District Commander, were important. Rangel initiated a guerrilla movement in the Burro and Toro mountains of Coahuila that grew to include over five hundred guerrillas and lasted through the eve of the Revolution of 1910. Similarly, the revolutionists of Acayucán retreated to the Soteapan sierra and, with the aid of local campesinos, extended their fighting from Veracruz to Oaxaca and the Isthmus.[45]

In 1906, the country was divided into five military zones. The Northern Zone consisted of the states of Sinaloa, Baja California, Sonora, Chihuahua, Coahuila, Nuevo León, and Tamaulipas. There were approximately forty-four guerrilla groups throughout the country. The military coordinator for the entire country, who

[43]Bartra, *Regeneración*, pp. 18–20. Contrary to Rodney D. Anderson's interpretation, GCOL activity, in conducting a vigorous state and national campaign between June and December 1906, was in association with and not contrary to PLM directives and goals. Cf. Rodney D. Anderson, "Mexican Workers and the Politics of Revolution, 1906–1911," *Hispanic American Historical Review* 54 (February 1974): 101–102.

[44]Bartra, "Ricardo Flores Magón," pp. vi, vii.

[45]Ibid.

worked directly with the Junta, was known as the *Delegado General*. He was appointed by the Junta. Over each zone was a *delegado*, also appointed by the Junta, who had political and military authority. Under each zone and *delegado* were the guerrilla groups, each led by a *jefe de guerrillas* and a *subjefe*. At this level the local guerrilla leaders were elected democratically by the individual fighters. Thus a hierarchy of command was established that fused both democratic and authoritarian traditions. As time went on, this structure was altered to fit new conditions. By 1908, the number of groups had increased and the Northern Zone had been further sub-divided. At the zone level, however, military and political authority continued to be merged, with Santana Rodríguez in Veracruz being named both *Comandante Militar* and *Delegado Especial*.[46]

One major problem and weakness of the command structure was the confusion caused by overlapping functions of the clubs and the guerrillas. In addition, the guerrillas were not always in communication with the local clubs, and the two groups failed to coordinate their plans and actions. This explains, in part, the failure of the Viesca uprising in northern Coahuila on 25 June 1908. Crossing the Rio Grande in the evening, the rebels took the town with comparative ease, with no insurgents killed and only one wounded. The guerrillas controlled the town, molested no civilians, and allowed no disorders. Yet public opinion finally forced their retreat, for it was reported that they were not true revolutionists but simply bandits masquerading under the name of the Liberal Party. The populace did not rise to their cause, and the rebels had to return to Texas. Had the local Liberal club generated the appropriate propaganda, it is likely the citizens might have greeted them as an army of revolutionary liberation; instead they were thought to be a horde of "Tex-Mex" *bandidos*.[47] After 1910, the mass movement was not coordinated with the guerrilla effort, and the *magonista* movement eventually failed as a military effort.

As for other tactics, the PLM, contrary to Roosevelt's fears

---

[46]Ibid., pp. vii, viii. See also Ricardo Flores Magón and Práxedis Guerrero to C. Santana Rodríguez, 20 September 1910, in Fabela, *Documentos históricos* X, 99.

[47]Cumberland, "Precursors," p. 352.

about anarchists, did not engage in indiscriminate violence or acts of terrorism. Only after years of harassment did the Junta finally threaten to assassinate Díaz. The year was 1906, and Juan Sarabia, who was eventually sentenced to seven years in San Juan de Ulúa, was in the Chihuahua state prison. The early reports indicated that Governor Creel had threatened to kill Sarabia in jail. With the temporary suppression of *Regeneración*, the St. Louis Junta in flight, and arrests being made of PLM members in Arizona and Texas, Ricardo Flores Magón made his threat in a letter delivered to Díaz's door: "If Juan Sarabia dies in jail we will kill you." It was signed "The Scorpion." This threat was followed up by one from Andrea Villarreal, who said: "If Juan Sarabia perish [*sic*], the Liberal Party will kill Díaz." Needless to say the threats were never carried out, and Juan Sarabia did not die in the Chihuahua prison—instead, he suffered a heart attack at San Juan de Ulúa, nearly lost his eyesight, and died prematurely in 1920 from tuberculosis contracted while a prisoner.[48]

Kidnapping, although a tactic used by the officials against the *magonistas*, was usually only sanctioned by the PLM as part of a larger guerrilla action. For example, the Jiménez rebels of September 1906, after securing the town, kidnapped the mayor, the city treasurer, the collector of customs, and several leading citizens. This was done in order to undermine their authority in the eyes of the citizenry and to extort funds, arms, ammunition, horses, and saddles for the revolution.[49] In general, the PLM followed the anarcho-communist doctrine of engaging only in educative and purposive violence.

The one tactic in which the publicists of the PLM excelled was that of propaganda. The eighteen-year history of *Regeneración* reveals that *Regeneración* was *magonismo*, that there would have been no ideology without the newspaper. All PLM adherents were aware of this and imitated Ricardo Flores Magón in founding their own militant organs. From the late Porfiriato up to the early 1930s, over four hundred and fifty Spanish-language newspapers were

---

[48]For the assassination threats see the *St. Louis Post-Dispatch,* 10 February 1907.

[49]J. G. Griner Report, 7 June 1907, NF, case 5028/7–8.

published in the United States.[50] At the very least, thirty of them (and possibly as many as a hundred or more) were *magonista* publications. Most of them were suppressed by the authorities. Some of the labor-oriented newspapers were published in conjunction with the I.W.W., such as *La Unión Industrial* of Phoenix. Others were strictly socialist, such as Teresa Villarreal's *El Obrero* or Manuel Sarabia's *El Defenso del Pueblo*. And again, there was the anarchist weekly put out by Guerrero, *Punto Rojo*. As has been seen, the radical feminists published *La Mujer Moderna* and *La Voz de la Mujer*. Others worthy of mention are *Reforma* (put out by Tomás Sarabia, Manuel's brother), *Libertad y Justicia, El Clarín del Norte, La Bandera Roja, La Democracia, El Progreso, Renacimiento, Resurrección, Revolución, Los Bribones, El Liberal, Libertad y Trabajo*, and, last but not least, Aguirre's *La Reforma Social*.

As can be seen, then, the PLM was a fully mature revolutionary organization, consisting of a radical cadre of leaders, a large number of followers in Mexico and the United States, a developed ideology, program, and propaganda organ, a group of guerrilla *focos*, a variety of tactics, and a revolutionary base of operations from a "sanctuary" above the U.S. border. Although the PLM ultimately failed to achieve its revolutionary ends, it did provide a model and many precedents for other, more successful *revoltosos*, like the followers of Francisco Madero. Operating in the United States and along the frontier, the *revoltoso* insurgency made of the Mexican Revolution a northerner's revolution (Zapata notwithstanding). It is not surprising, then, that the Sonorans and the men from the north dominated Mexico's political destinies from 1917 to 1934.

To fairly evaluate the relative successes and failures of the PLM movement is not an easy matter, even with the hindsight of history. The reader today has the advantage of inheriting an entire tradition of writings on the theory of insurgency warfare. But in 1910 Flores Magón had read Marx, not Lenin, and could never experience the ideas of Mao Tse-Tung, Nguyen Giap, and Ernesto ("Che") Guevara. As an anarchist movement, and in the context of its day, the PLM did succeed in sustaining a revolutionary effort

---

[50]José C. Valadés, "Más de cuatrocientos periódicos en español se han editado en los Estados Unidos," *La Prensa* (San Antonio, Texas), 13 February 1938.

for several years. Outside of Spain very few anarchist societies can make that claim. The *magonistas*, articulating the hopes of the exploited, were most popular with the Mexican community along the border.

Yet the *magonistas* did fail, and with that failure, some would argue, Mexico aborted her radicalism before the Revolution was ever born. In many ways it may have been a self-induced abortion. As visionaries, the Junta's leaders were too simplistic in their planning. This led to the military defeats. Because these urban-oriented intellectuals did not speak the language of the countryside, they did not honestly seek or gain the aid of the campesino. Sometimes their anarchism was more an attitude than an ideology, and moral anger only led to factionalism and decline. Perhaps their greatest mistake, one they shared with their radical Anglo friends in the United States, was to underestimate the strength, power, determination, and resources of the opposition. By so doing, the American and Mexican radical community in the United States would lose the war before it began.

We Socialists, anarchists, hobos, chicken
thieves, outlaws and undesirable citizens of the
United States are with you heart and soul. . . .
                                    Jack London, 1911

2. An American Community of Radicals

WITH the suppression of the St. Louis Junta in the fall of 1906,
Manuel Sarabia (now using the alias "Sam Moret"), in order to
avoid arrest, decided to travel to Chicago. Arriving in November,
he stayed through the middle of May 1907 before leaving for Douglas, Arizona. In Chicago, Sarabia worked with the local Liberal
club, forming alliances with that city's radical community as well as
personal friendships with a variety of sympathizers (including, un-
knowingly, an agent for the Furlong Secret Service Company).[1]
    While at the Chicago office of Charles H. Kerr's *International
Socialist Review,* Sarabia met a young artist by the name of Ralph
Chaplin. Through Sarabia, Chaplin, during 1907 and 1908, made
contact with the local PLM club and was thereby introduced to the
horrors of Díaz's Mexico—e.g., the Yaquis' plight, slavery in the
Yucatán, political prisoners in the fortress of San Juan de Ulúa.
Chaplin learned about the liberal "muckraker" John Kenneth Turner and Turner's fact-finding mission to Mexico, and was shown
photographs that were to illustrate Turner's upcoming book *Barbarous Mexico.* Undergoing his own political conversion, Chaplin
(who in 1912 would become a "Wobbly," that is, a member of the
I.W.W.) then testified that "the struggle in Mexico, like that in Russia, India, and Ireland, was becoming my struggle; Enrique and
Ricardo Flores Magón were becoming my personal heroes, and
Porfirio Díaz my personal enemy."[2]
    Early in 1909, Chaplin, with letters of introduction and Tur-
ner's Mexican address in hand, went to Mexico City. Although he

[1]Thomas Furlong to Enrique C. Creel, 2 January 1908, AREM, L–E–
954Bls.
[2]Ralph Chaplin, *Wobbly,* pp. 104–106.

failed to contact Turner, he did work with the Liberal Party. Returning to Chicago in 1910, he remained loyal to the Flores Magón
brothers and Zapata in spite of the successes of Madero. In 1911, at
the request of the Los Angeles editors of *Regeneración*, he designed
small posters for use by the agrarian revolutionary forces in Mexico.
He was also active in translating Práxedis Guerrero's poetry into
English. Always faithful, "Wobbly" Chaplin eventually developed
a close friendship with his idol, Ricardo Flores Magón, when they
shared the same Leavenworth prison address after the hysteria of
World War I. Like many liberals, socialists, and I.W.W.'s in the
United States at this time, Chaplin made the *magonista* cause his
own.[3]

It was fitting that Chaplin's home town, the "drab wooden
metropolis" of Chicago, with its squalor and privations, would be
the site of the founding convention of the Industrial Workers of the
World in June and July of 1905. One could easily see in its formation the influences of America's foremost radical leaders of the day
—William D. ("Big Bill") Haywood, Eugene V. Debs, and Daniel
DeLeon. The I.W.W. was a confederation of several groups, especially the Western Federation of Miners, the Socialist Party, the
Socialist Labor Party, and the American Labor Union (the latter
consisted of railway employees, engineers, and musicians). In the
beginning the socialists were more influential than the anarchists,
but with the departure of many socialists after 1908, the ideology of
anarcho-syndicalism came to predominate. Although the founding
members were mostly of British and Western European stock (e.g.,
Irish, German, and English), the I.W.W. did publish propaganda
leaflets in French, Finnish, Swedish, Yiddish, Romanian, and Spanish. The first Spanish syndicalist newspaper published by the
I.W.W. in the United States was *La Huelga General* of Los Angeles. Eventually, *Regeneración* too would be considered by both the
authorities and the I.W.W. leadership to be, although not altogether
correctly, a Spanish I.W.W. weekly.[4]

[3]Ibid., pp. 107–117.
[4]*The Founding Convention of the IWW, Proceedings;* Paul F. Brissenden,
"The Launching of the Industrial Workers of the World," *University of California Publications in Economics* 4 (1966): 1–82.

Attending the I.W.W. convention in Chicago were delegates from the Socialist Party of St. Louis. This was to be expected, for St. Louis, by 1905, had become a kind of heartland haven for dissidents, rebels, and the disaffected of many countries. Among the nationalities represented there were Germans, Russians, Irish, Poles, Chinese, Turks, Italians, and Spaniards. Although not all were radicals, the local *Post-Dispatch* followed the practices of the day by equating exiles with radicals, especially those in the back yard.[5]

It was this city with its cosmopolitan population, its socialist and anarchist groups, and its inland location—centrally located with a railway link to Mexico, yet away from Díaz's minions and sympathizers along the border—that Ricardo Flores Magón chose as his North American sanctuary. In St. Louis he would become a close associate of the Spanish anarchist Florencio Bazora and the Russian immigrant Emma Goldman, both of whom conducted anarchist meetings there. And it would be the German and Russian residents of St. Louis—liberal, socialist, and anarchist—who first came to his aid in October 1905, when he was arrested on a libel charge initiated from Mexico. Their activities developed the public support that eventually led to the official release of Ricardo and Enrique Flores Magón and Juan Sarabia in January 1906.[6]

Another group in the United States that would lend support to the *magonistas* was the Western Federation of Miners, the organization that in terms of membership did the most to promote and develop the I.W.W. in 1905. Composed primarily of western metal miners, timbermen, engineers, smelter workers, and laborers, the W.F.M. was an industrial union based on the ideas of class solidarity and political action against capitalist employers. Through the *Miners' Magazine*, the union's official organ, articles about socialism and revolutionary unionism were sent to the members. The movement to establish the eight-hour day, which began in western mining camps, was promoted by the W.F.M. between the 1890s and 1910. In 1894, the W.F.M. was involved in the infamous Cripple

---

[5]*St. Louis Post-Dispatch*, 10 September, 1905.

[6]Barrera Fuentes, *Historia*, p. 159; Myers, "The Mexican Liberal Party," pp. 34, 35, 49. For the 1905 arrest see the *St. Louis Globe-Democrat*, 13 October and 17 December 1905.

Creek struggle and was in the center of the Colorado labor wars of 1903.[7]

It was also 1903 when the first significant labor trouble came to the Clifton-Morenci district in Arizona. Before that year the W.F.M. had hardly penetrated Arizona, with one local in Globe and no organization in Morenci. In June, some sixteen hundred strikers, mostly of Mexican extraction, led by a Rumanian known as "Three-fingered Jack" and a Mexican from Nacozari named Alvarez, attacked Morenci. They were quickly subdued by a joint force of Arizona Rangers and federal troops. The immediate cause of the strike was a territorial law, to become effective in June, prohibiting more than eight hours of work in the mines.[8]

The origins of the Morenci strike go back several years and reveal much about the conditions of Mexican labor in the Arizona-Sonora mining camps. At issue in Morenci was the decision of management to implement the eight-hour legislation in a fashion that discriminated against "cheap" Mexican labor. The Detroit Copper Company decided to offer nine hours' pay for eight hours' work to the underground miners, but provided no increases for allied and above-ground labor. In effect this meant that the skilled, Anglo-American underground miner would receive an average of four dollars for eight hours of work, whereas the unskilled, above-ground Mexican American and alien worker (mostly Mexicans and Italians) would get two dollars for ten hours of labor.[9]

This two-wage system was not simply the result of company caprice and avarice; it was the historical effect of two trends that had been accelerating since 1895. By 1903, a collision occurred in Morenci between the mounting tide of alien laborers from Mexico and the union movement then spreading southward from the Rocky Mountain zone into the intermountain areas of Arizona. Although there had always been a gap in wages between Mexican and Anglo workers in Arizona, the inequity increased significantly after 1885.

[7]Philip S. Foner, *History of the Labor Movement in the United States,* III, 393–412; Vernon H. Jensen, *Heritage of Conflict: Labor Relations in the Nonferrous Metals Industry up to 1930,* pp. 96–98, 170.

[8]A. Blake Brophy, *Foundlings on the Frontier: Racial and Religious Conflict in Arizona Territory, 1904–1905,* pp. 17–19; Jensen, *Heritage of Conflict,* pp. 356–357.

[9]Brophy, *Foundlings on the Frontier,* p. 18.

After 1895, the wage per diem for Mexican miners leveled off, a result of "cheap labor" competition from Mexico, while union efforts on behalf of Anglo miners resulted in continually increasing wages through 1910.[10] In this context, it is not so surprising that the Cananea strike of June 1906 in northern Sonora also focused directly on the two-wage grievance so common in the Arizona-Sonora area.

Needless to say, the first efforts of the W.F.M., in Globe in 1893 and in Cananea in 1902, had been to cultivate anti-Mexican sentiment in order to win Anglo support. Yet the W.F.M., unlike the craft unions, quickly learned that management too could exploit the race issue for its own benefits, especially when Mexican laborers from Arizona were used as "scabs" to break the 1903–1904 strikes in Colorado. Thus, as early as the 1903 W.F.M. convention, the delegates were being urged to change past practices and pay special attention to organizing immigrant workers. By 1905, when the Arizona State Union No. 3 could boast of nine chartered locals, the W.F.M. rank and file in Colorado and Arizona included Mexicans and Navajo Indians.[11] In addition, by early 1906, W.F.M. organizers were working with and among Mexican workers in Bisbee (southern Arizona) and Nacozari and Cananea (northern Sonora).

It was only natural that once the W.F.M. had decided to organize Bisbee, nearby Mexican mining towns would be affected. In the spring of 1906, funds originating with the local in Butte, Montana, were being redirected from the Denver headquarters to organizers in Bisbee. This practice lasted through the summer, with Bisbee organizer Joe Carter distributing literature and money to "agitators" in Nacozari and Cananea.[12] After the June strike at Cananea, the Denver convention of the W.F.M. not only urged the Mexican miners to join the union but passed a resolution in support of the Cananea miners' strike for higher wages.[13]

Several PLM district leaders in Arizona became members of the W.F.M. and distributed I.W.W. literature. When PLM leader

[10]Joseph F. Park, "The History of Mexican Labor in Arizona during the Territorial Period" (thesis), pp. 244–246.

[11]Brophy, *Foundlings on the Frontier*, p. 17; Foner, *History*, III, 402; Jensen, *Heritage of Conflict*, pp. 356–357.

[12]Rowen to William Greene, 20 and 23 July, 1906, files of Albert B. Fall, Henry E. Huntington Library, San Marino, Calif. (hereafter cited as Fall Papers).

[13]Foner, *History*, III, 402.

Lázaro Puente was arrested in Arizona in September, he had in his possession copies of *A Los Obreros Industriales* (an I.W.W. pamphlet), *The Industrial Worker*, and *Defensor del Unionismo Industrial de la Clase Trabajadora* (a Spanish version of the I.W.W. newspaper).[14] At the end of the year, the W.F.M. was fighting the hiring practices of the Cananea managers, who were excluding Cananea and Cripple Creek veterans as well as all W.F.M. members.[15]

The movement to organize Mexican workers increased significantly during 1907. The W.F.M. was active in Bisbee, Douglas, Clifton, Metcalf, and Morenci. By July, the W.F.M. was consciously organizing Mexicanos in order to remove any threat of cheap labor to the union worker's wage scale. Clifton was considered to be the "jumping-off place" for a W.F.M. thrust into the American Federation of Labor stronghold of "unspeakable Metcalf" and "Russianized Morenci."[16]

In challenging the A.F.L., the W.F.M. spokesmen alluded to the restrictive "racist" practices of the A.F.L. For example, in 1903, Samuel Gompers, president of the A.F.L., refused to grant a charter to the Sugar Beet and Farm Laborers' Union of Oxnard because it would have been inconsistent for the Federation to unionize Japanese workers while campaigning for their exclusion from the United States. Gompers was not moved by the appeals of Mexican farm workers on behalf of their "Japanese brothers," or even by the local A.F.L. argument that "forming the Orientals into unions . . . [would prevent them] from scabbing on white people."[17]

By way of contrast, the W.F.M. was proud of its I.W.W. credo with its "noble sentiments of democracy and disregard of race." As the editors of the *Miners' Magazine* noted:

> Let it be said here, without fear or favor, that, as a race, the Mexicans in the Clifton-Morenci district have shown more of a desire for economic independence than have the Americans. There is too much petty aristocratic, ten-cent millionaire ignorance and prejudice among many of the American wage-workers.[18]

[14]Arturo M. Elías to Sec. de Rel. Ext., 27 September 1906, AREM, L–E–1241, pt. 5.

[15]*Miner's Magazine* (Denver), 11 October 1906.

[16]Ibid., 21 February and 25 July 1907.

[17]Foner, *History*, III, 274–277.

[18]*Miner's Magazine*, 21 February 1907.

Thus the W.F.M. enthusiastically attempted the organization of the Mexican and Italian workers of the Clifton-Morenci district.

As government persecution mounted, the PLM and the W.F.M. increased their cooperation with each other. The forces of suppression made of them natural allies. For example, just as the Pinkertons tracked the I.W.W. and broke their strikes, so too did Furlong and other private detectives in the pay of the Mexican government harass the *magonistas* in the United States. With the arrest, federal "kidnapping" (the forced removal from Colorado to Idaho), and trial of W.F.M. leaders "Big Bill" Haywood and Charles Moyer in 1906–1907, a national campaign was initiated for their defense. The Haywood case set the pattern for subsequent I.W.W., syndicalist, socialist, and anarchist campaigns in support of the PLM.

When Manuel Sarabia was kidnapped from Douglas on 1 July 1907 by Mexican officials, his cause was immediately championed by W.F.M. organizers in Denver and Arizona, with the "kidnapping" of Haywood and Moyer being cited as the precedent that the American government established for Mexico to follow.[19] Likewise, Lauro Aguirre and other Liberals compared Haywood's persecution by the U.S. government to that received by the Flores Magón brothers and other PLM leaders by Díaz and Roosevelt.[20]

When Ricardo Flores Magón, Librado Rivera, Antonio Villarreal, and Manuel Sarabia were arrested and detained in Los Angeles in the fall of 1907 and the winter of 1908, the PLM cause became one with that of the American Left. With anguish the editors of the *Miners' Magazine* cried out that

> . . . they [Flores Magón, Villarreal, and Rivera] have heard the groans of agony and the moans of pain that have come from thousands of Mexican hovels and because they have lifted up their voices against Cossack barbarism in Mexico they are hounded by the vultures of capitalism and treated with no more consideration than wild beasts of the jungle.[21]

As for Manuel Sarabia, his cause received the special care and attention of the W.F.M.'s most prominent organizer, Mary Harris ("Mother") Jones.

[19]Ibid., 11 July 1907.
[20]*La Reforma Social* (El Paso), 3 September 1907.
[21]*Miners' Magazine*, 3 October 1907.

Mother Jones was at her radical best at the age of seventy-five, when she sat in an honored position on the platform of the opening session of the 1905 convention of the I.W.W. Always a maverick in the labor movement (never an ideologue, let alone an anarchist), she allied herself with whatever organizations and friends she thought could help her to aid the cause of labor. She was a personal friend of socialists—Antonio Villarreal, Lázaro Gutiérrez de Lara, John Murray, and Eugene V. Debs; of labor leader Samuel Gompers; and of the American president, William Howard Taft. At various times in her career she had organized for the United Mine Workers in West Virginia, the W.F.M. in Arizona, the Socialist Party in Minnesota, and the A.F.L. in Illinois. Always interested in the Mexican worker, she was a Pan-American delegate to Mexico City three times, in 1901, 1911, and 1921. As was understandable, she became more conservative in her old age (after eighty), opposing anarchism and, at times, being used by the A.F.L. and Gompers to persuade workers away from the radicalism of the I.W.W. An individualist and crusader to the end, on her hundreth birthday in 1930 (several months before her death) she sent a gift of $1,000 to an insurgent group of Illinois miners who were seeking to oust John L. Lewis from the presidency of the United Mine Workers.[22]

Her involvement with the Mexican rebels began in 1907, when she aided the W.F.M. in organizing a strike against the Phelps Dodge copper mine interests of Douglas, Arizona. When she returned to her hotel after a July street meeting, the editors of *El Industrio* burst into her room, yelling, "Oh, Mother, they have kidnapped Sarabia, our young revolutionist." On learning that the Mexican officials, in conjunction with the local Douglas authorities, had pirated Sarabia across the line, she immediately telegraphed the territorial governor, as well as President Roosevelt, and started a very loud publicity campaign through the local newspapers.[23]

Her libertarian ire aroused, Mother Jones patriotically declared:

That's got to stop. The idea of any bloodthirsty pirate on a throne reaching across these lines and stamping under his feet the constitution of our United States, which our forefathers fought and bled

[22]Edward T. Jones, ed., *Notable American Women, 1607–1950*, II, 286–288; Mary Jones, *The Autobiography of Mother Jones*, pp. ix, 142–143.

[23]Jones, *Autobiography*, pp. 136–140.

for! If this is allowed to go on, Mexican pirates can come over the border and kidnap any one who opposes tyranny.[24]

Her influence having been exercised, Manuel Sarabia was returned to Arizona from the Hermosillo penitentiary eight days later.

In 1908, when informed of the arrest and detention of Flores Magón, Rivera, and Villarreal, she immediately began a campaign on their behalf. "They were patriots," she said, "like Garibaldi and George Washington—these Mexican men in jail, fighting against a bloodier tyrant than King George against whom we revolted."[25] To meet the costs of their Tombstone trial, she raised $4,000, persuading the United Mine Workers to contribute $1,000 of the total, with the remainder coming from the A.F.L., the W.F.M., and other unions.[26] In addition, she wrote articles for the socialist review *Appeal to Reason* and circulated pamphlets like *Oh! Ye Lovers of Liberty!*, which called for the working people of the United States to respond to the needs of "our comrades and brave brothers" who are crying from the "bastille of capitalism in Los Angeles."[27]

Throughout 1909, she continued her fund-raising for other PLM members like Antonio de P. Araujo and Jesús M. Rangel, and aided in opposing the extradition of half a dozen others. She also visited *revoltosos* in Leavenworth and sent letters of moral support to the political prisoners in Yuma and Florence, Arizona. In November 1909, Flores Magón, Villarreal, and Rivera, writing from the Florence prison, saluted her as a "noble example . . . teaching a lesson humanity should not forget." They went on to say, "You, an old woman, are fighting with indomitable courage; you, an American, are devoting your life to free Mexican slaves. And they will be freed in the near future, and they will learn to call you Mother."[28] By 1910, in the company of John Murray and John Kenneth Turner, she testified about the horrors of Díaz's Mexico before the Committee on Rules of the House of Representatives.[29] The creation of

[24]Ibid., p. 138.

[25]Ibid., pp. 140–141.

[26]Ibid., pp. ix, 141. See also Jones to Flores Magón, 4 November 1911, in Fabela, *Documentos históricos*, X, 380–382.

[27]Jones, *Oh! Ye Lovers of Liberty!*, NF, case 1741/104.

[28]As quoted from the Jones Papers in Dale Fetherling, *Mother Jones: The Miners' Angel*, p. 81.

[29]"Statement of Mrs. Mary Jones," U.S., Congress, House Committee on

this special inquiry was the result of Samuel Gomper's interest in the *magonistas* and his influence with Congress.

When Mother Jones's defense committee succeeded in enlisting the powerful support of Gompers, the *magonista* cause was assured a national audience. He persuaded the 1908 convention in Denver to adopt the following resolution: "Resolved that the A. F. of L. extends its earnest sympathy to the aforesaid Magon, Villarreal, Rivera, et al., and commends to all affiliated organizations the consideration to proper means for their defense."[30] Sympathetic to the PLM goal of a liberal welfare state (as outlined in the 1906 manifesto), he fought their extradition to Mexico and, as indicated, pressured Congress into conducting an inquiry into the persecution of Mexican political refugees in the United States.

Others who shared Gompers's sympathies for the PLM included various American socialists. As individuals and groups, on the local and the national level, between 1907 and 1909 they were most active in raising funds, organizing defense committees, hiring lawyers, propagandizing and developing publicity, and making appeals to Congress and the president. In Los Angeles, at the request of Anselmo L. Figueroa, a leader of the Socialist Party of that city, two socialist attorneys were persuaded to take up the defense of Flores Magón and the others. Job Harriman (Social Democratic Party candidate for vice-president in 1900) and A. R. Holston provided an eloquent, if vain, legal defense of the men.[31]

Through Harriman, other local socialists were introduced to Flores Magón and the PLM. Harriman's friend, John Murray, a member of the trade-unionist wing of the Socialist Party, met the Liberals in jail. Harriman also arranged for John Kenneth Turner, then a correspondent for the Los Angeles *Express*, to interview the prisoners. Murray and Turner became the nucleus of the newly created Mexican Revolutionists Defense League, which soon included as participants other Los Angeles socialists like James

---

Rules, *Providing for a Joint Committee to Investigate Alleged Persecutions of Mexican Citizens by the Government of Mexico: Hearings on H.J.R. 201*, 61st Cong., 2d Sess., 8–14 June 1910, pp. 90–93.

[30] U.S., Congress, Senate, *Investigation of Mexican Affairs*, II, 2642.

[31] Myers, "The Mexican Liberal Party," p. 220.

("Jimmy") S. Roche, Ethel Duffy Turner, Primrose D. Noel, Lázaro Gutiérrez de Lara, and Elizabeth Trowbridge. Trowbridge, a wealthy Boston heiress, provided many of the monies that financed the group's undertakings. She personally provided for the families of Flores Magón and Librado Rivera in Los Angeles, backed the creation of the *The Border*, a Tucson publication dedicated to the protection of Mexican political refugees, and eventually financed Murray, Gutiérrez de Lara, and Turner in their fact-finding trips through Mexico. All of them wrote articles for *The Border*, *Revolución*, and the *Appeal to Reason*.[32]

The *Appeal to Reason* (sometimes referred to by foes as the *Squeal of Treason*) was easily the most influential socialist publication of the day. By 1911, its circulation exceeded that of all but a few standard magazines, and there were times when as many as a million copies were printed. Published in Girard, Kansas, with Fred Warren as managing editor, the *Appeal* featured several articles on the terrorism of Díaz's Mexico and the plight of Mexico's rebels in the United States.[33] In 1909, Warren, along with Socialist Party leaders John C. Chase and Eugene Debs, planned with Murray, Trowbridge, and Manuel Sarabia a Spanish page for the *Appeal*. Unfortunately, the project was interrupted in May 1909 with the arrest of Warren.[34]

Another important socialist voice was the *New York Call*, started in May 1908 with money that had been raised from Debs's lecture tour. The *Call* was particularly effective in late 1910 and early 1911 in reporting on *magonista* affairs, especially since the *Appeal* carried few articles on Flores Magón after July 1909. The *Call* was supported in its pro-*magonista* campaigns by socialist locals like the *St. Louis Labor* and *The Milwaukee Leader*. From 1908

[32]Ibid., p. 237. See also Turner, *Barbarous Mexico*, pp. xi–xiii; Harvey A. Levenstein, *Labor Organizations in the United States and Mexico: A History*, pp. 21–22; González Ramírez, *Epistolario y textos*, p. 221.

[33]See Ivie E. Cadenhead's articles; "The American Socialists and the Mexican Revolution of 1910," *Southwestern Social Science Quarterly* 43 (September 1962): 103–107, and "Flores Magón y el periodico The Appeal to Reason," *Historia Mexicana* 13 (1963): 88–93. Of more limited value is Robert E. Ireland, "The Radical Community, Mexican and American Radicalism, 1900–1910," *Journal of Mexican-American History* 2 (December 1973): 12–32.

[34]John Murray to Elizabeth Trowbridge, 16 March 1909, encl. in A. V. Lomelí to Sec. de Rel. Ext., 30 March 1909, AREM, L–E–954.

to 1922, through these publications and others, Debs periodically expressed his concern for the Flores Magón brothers and the PLM, concluding with an obituary in the 3 December 1922 issue of the *Call* entitled "The Assassination of Magón."[35]

Under the leadership of Debs, the Socialist Party, meeting in convention in Chicago in May 1908, unanimously passed a resolution in support of Flores Magón, Villarreal, Rivera, and Manuel Sarabia. During his presidential campaign in the same year, Debs, from the platform of the *Red Special* (the party's railway car), championed the cause of Flores Magón and the others.[36]

He also wrote an article for the *Appeal* that was later reprinted in pamphlet form in English and Spanish. In this pamphlet, entitled *"This Plot Must Be Foiled" (Complot que es necessario desbaratar)*, Debs commented that

> Ricardo Flores Magón, Antonio I. Villarreal, Librado Rivera, and Manuel Sarabia are our comrades in the social revolution! They have been doing in Mexico what we are doing in the United States and by practically the same means. If they ought to be shot so ought we. The truth is that they are four reformers in the highest sense of the term, highly educated, cultured, pure in mind, exalted in thought, noble of nature and lofty of aspiration. They are victims of a foul conspiracy between two capitalistic governments to put them to death.[37]

As Trowbridge had requested, publicity took precedence over everything else, and this the PLM received through the vivid words of Debs and his associates.

One of Debs's associates was John Murray. Born into an upper-class New York family in 1865, he was forced by bad health to move to the warmer climate of Los Angeles. There, in his twenties, he became active in the union movement. As a trade unionist, he, like Mother Jones, was able to move in and out of a variety of political circles. A proponent of cooperation between socialists and the

[35]Cadenhead, "The American Socialists," pp. 103–109. See also Ray Ginger, *The Bending Cross: A Biography of Eugene Victor Debs*, p. 268. The St. Louis group was active even earlier than 1907; see the *St. Louis Labor*, 11 and 18 August 1906. Finally, Debs's 1922 article has been reproduced in Flores Magón, *¿Para que sirve la autoridad?*, pp. 38–41.

[36]Debs to Trowbridge, 25 September 1908, NF, case 1741/100–104.

[37]*"This Plot Must Be Foiled,"* p. 4, NF, case 1741/100–104.

A.F.L., he was as much at home with Debs as with Gompers.[38]

On the encouragement of the Mexican Revolutionists Defense League, he left for Mexico on 8 May 1908, hoping to substantiate the charges made against Díaz by the Liberal Party leaders so that an exposé could be written and publicized. During his trip he visited Río Blanco, site of the 1907 textile mill strike; traveled to San Juan de Ulúa, where several Liberals, including Juan Sarabia, were imprisoned; and went as far south as the Valle Nacional in Oaxaca, where debt slavery was rampant. He also acted as a special messenger for Flores Magón, dispensing revolutionary instructions to Liberals in Mexico City and elsewhere concerning the imminent uprising scheduled for June 25.[39]

Murray arrived back in Los Angeles on 25 June, having first met with Lauro Aguirre in El Paso and Manuel Sarabia in Tucson. He had collected a substantial body of information on conditions in Mexico, but not enough for an effective exposé. His adventures did lead, however, to some articles that were published in *The Border*,[40] and were a valuable experience for Turner and others, who learned more of Mexico from him. Also, his services as an emissary were invaluable to the PLM.

After the Las Vacas and Palomas raids of 25 June–1 July, Murray traveled to Chicago. There he aided in the formation of the Political Refugee Defense League, founded originally to protect Russian refugees from the Czar. As secretary of the league, he was obligated to visit several local jails, document cases, and hire defense lawyers. At one time, the famous social reformer Jane Addams was treasurer of the league. In fact, between October 1908 and July 1909 several mass meetings of the league took place at Addams's Hull House in Chicago.[41] The league's most important case was, of course, that of Flores Magón in Arizona in early 1909.[42]

In his capacity as league secretary, Murray dealt with several

[38]Levenstein, *Labor Organizations*, pp. 21–22.

[39]Turner, *Barbarous Mexico*, pp. xii–xiv; Myers, "The Mexican Liberal Party," pp. 241–242.

[40]See, for example, Murray, "San Juan de Ulúa, the Private Prison of Díaz," *The Border* (February 1909).

[41]U.S., Congress, House, *Alleged Persecutions*, pp. 48–51.

[42]Tucson *Citizen*, 4 March 1909, AREM, L–E–954.

revoltosos from late 1908 through early 1910. Many of these cases grew out of the Mexican government's attempt to extradite those individuals who were allegedly involved in the Las Vacas raid of 1908. Grand juries in Del Rio and San Antonio indicted several in- dividuals who, it was believed, had participated in the Las Vacas uprising. In those cases (usually for murder and robbery) where extradition failed, the Mexican government sought their deportation or imprisonment on neutrality violation charges.[43]

In this connection, Murray's organization defended several *revoltosos*, including Calixto Guerra, Guillermo Adán, Inez Ruiz, Tomás Sarabia, Lauro Aguirre, Jesús M. Rangel, and Antonio de Pío Araujo. All were eventually released for lack of evidence with the exceptions of Rangel and Araujo, who were convicted and sen- tenced to two and one-half years at Leavenworth.[44]

With Araujo's conviction in January 1909, the league prepared an extensive appeal that was forwarded to the U.S. Circuit Court at New Orleans. To provide additional substance for Araujo's appeal, Mother Jones, Debs, Warren, Chase, and Murray collectively agreed to hire Clarence Darrow for the defense. It was hoped that Darrow, who had obtained national fame for his masterly defense of William Haywood, would eventually fight all of the league's political pris- oner cases.[45] But the Darrow defense of Araujo and the PLM did not materialize. Instead, with Fred Warren's arrest on a libel charge in May 1909, Darrow had to appear on behalf of the editor of the *Appeal to Reason*.[46]

As has already been indicated, Murray, with Mother Jones and Turner, appeared in June 1910 on behalf of the PLM and against Díaz in a congressional inquiry on persecutions of Mexican citizens by the government of Mexico. Murray's testimony included com- mentary and documents on the Manuel Sarabia kidnapping, the arrests and federal trials of Gutiérrez de Lara, and the general plight of the Las Vacas insurgents.

[43]U.S. Congress, House, *Alleged Persecutions*, pp. 53–62.

[44]Ibid. See also Turner, *Barbarous Mexico*, p. 255, and U.S., Congress, House, *Congressional Record*, 61st Cong., 2d Sess., 21 April 1910, 45, p. 5137.

[45]San Antonio *Daily Express*, 24 and 25 February 1909, AREM, L–E– 954. See also Murray to Trowbridge, 16 March 1909, AREM, L–E–954.

[46]Cadenhead, "The American Socialists," p. 107.

After 1911, he retained his interest in the Mexican Revolution. Between 1915 and 1918, he assisted Gompers in the formation of a Pan-American Federation of Labor. Like Mother Jones, he was an associate of Villarreal throughout his life. When Murray died in 1919, a close friend quietly observed that "the peons in the wastes of Mexico will mourn for John Murray."[47]

In 1908, Murray's associate, John Kenneth Turner, went to Mexico on his own fact-finding trip. Turner posed as a wealthy American businessman who wanted to invest in henequen and tobacco. Because of his limited understanding of Spanish, Gutiérrez de Lara accompanied him to act as an adviser and interpreter. Luckily, these "muckraking socialists" were never suspected of being Liberals by the planters and officials, even though they penetrated deep into the slave labor areas of the Valle Nacional and the Yucatán. What eventually was published in book form in early 1911 as *Barbarous Mexico* was first printed as separate articles in the *American Magazine*, the *Appeal to Reason*, the *International Socialist Review*, and the *Pacific Monthly*. An indictment of Díaz's repressive policies, *Barbarous Mexico* caused a sensation in the United States.[48]

In May 1911, after having served as a chief adviser to the *magonista* rebels in Baja California (eventually being replaced in that capacity by the recently released Antonio de P. Araujo), Turner retired to Carmel, California, to relax and write. At Carmel he became friends with many literary figures, including Sinclair Lewis, Upton Sinclair, and Jack London.[49]

London's association with Turner (and his own experiences as a fund-raiser during the Baja revolt) was reflected in his literary productions between 1911 and 1913. In the latter year he published a short story called "The Mexican," which was filled with allusions to Díaz's Mexico (Río Blanco, *rurales*, and so forth), the Los Angeles Junta, and the Baja Revolution of 1911. The main character is

[47]As quoted in Grace H. Stimpson, *Rise of the Labor Movement of Los Angeles*, p. 22.

[48]Turner, *Barbarous Mexico*, pp. xiv–xxiv. See also Alejandro Carrillo, "Una historia de amistad Yanqui-Mexicana," in Fortunato Lozano, *Antonio I. Villarreal*, pp. 167–172.

[49]Turner, *Barbarous Mexico*, pp. xxiv–xxv.

an amateur boxer named Felipe Rivera, a Mexican "rags to riches" Rocky.[50]

True to the naturalistic vogue of the day, London portrayed Rivera as "the primitive, the wild wolf, the striking rattlesnake, the stinging centipede," whose eyes did not simply burn, but "burned venomously." As the story proceeds, Rivera, an impoverished wanderer (not unlike London's early career as a hobo) joins a revolutionary junta located in the United States (evidently Los Angeles). When the junta needs $5,000 in order to purchase arms and munitions, Rivera agrees to attempt to obtain the money by fighting a professional boxer. At the arena all the ticket holders symbolize potential rifles. The audience, the other fighter, the seconds, the referee, all are gringos. He is the lowly outcast facing tremendous odds.

When Rivera defeats the other boxer, he becomes the destroying angel who is the Revolution incarnate—his victory is a victory for the Revolution, a defeat for Díaz and his gringo friends. "No Call of the Wild," the critics say. Granted, "The Mexican" is not great literature, and maybe even bad socialism—yet, for the historian, it is a testimony to the times: the romance, idealism, and violence of the magonista movement as seen through North American eyes. And those "eyes" belonged not only to London but to thousands of America's workers.

One measure of the success of the socialist and labor campaigns can be seen in the popular response of local groups to the national appeal. Between 1907 and 1909, a variety of organizations and individuals joined the magonista bandwagon. They included liberals, socialists, reformers, union workers, and syndicalists. For example, among these supporters were:

I.W.W., Local 84, St. Louis.
Socialist-Local, Wellington, Kansas.
Socialist-Local, Grand Rapids, Michigan.
United Mine Workers, McHenry, Kentucky.
Local 215, Womens' International Union Label League, Shreveport, Louisiana.
Socialist Party, Connellsville, Pennsylvania.
Womens' International Label League, Pasadena, California.

[50]See Jack London, The Bodley Head Jack London, pp. 296–322.

Rocky Mountain Miners Union, Local 247, W.F.M.

Socialist Party, St. Louis.

Citizens of Alvin, Texas (fifty-four signatories—farmers, merchants, druggists, jewelers, and real estate salesmen).

Citizens of New Haven, Connecticut.

Citizens of Wellington, Kansas.

Cigarmakers Local Union, Detroit, Michigan.

Socialist Party, Union City, Indiana.

Marshall Co. Local, Minnesota.

Socialist Party, Vineland, New Jersey.

Bonanza Miners Union, W.F.M., Rhyolite, Nevada.[51]

And ultimately it was financial contributions from these kinds of people that covered the legal expenses of 1909, and it was groups of this type that would be appealed to once again when the PLM leadership was arrested and jailed toward the end of the Baja Revolution in June 1911.

Of all the episodes involving the American and Mexican radical community at this time, certainly the Baja Revolution must rate as the most colorful and bizarre. In December 1910 the Flores Magón brothers, Librado Rivera, and Anselmo Figueroa, operating from their base in Los Angeles, instituted the first of their military plans, calling for PLM armies to develop anarchist strongholds in northern Mexico. These were to expand and embrace all of the Republic in a social revolution. Along with the Mexican Liberals, the Baja campaign attracted a host of Yankee misfits, including I.W.W.'s, socialists, anarchists, bandits, military deserters, soldiers of fortune, disgruntled union men, adventurers, roughnecks, and unemployed miners.[52]

While the Junta was planning the general strategy, John Kenneth Turner dedicated himself to buying second-hand munitions. He sent rifles, pistols, and cartridges to Holtville (near the border town of Calexico, across from Mexicali) packed in boxes that bore

---

[51]NF, case 1741/63, 74–75, 119, 126–130, 140.

[52]The best detailed study of the Baja revolt in English is Blaisdell, *The Desert Revolution*. See also Pablo L. Martínez, *A History of Lower California*, pp. 462–502, and Pablo L. Martínez, *El Magonismo en Baja California* (*Documentos*). A somewhat outdated study is Peter Gerhard, "The Socialist Invasion of Baja California, 1911," *Pacific Historical Review* 15 (September 1946): 295–304.

the label "Agricultural Implements." In Holtville, Turner's packages were merged with arms that the I.W.W. sent from Chicago via Goldfield and San Diego, California. From Holtville a certain Jim Edwards took them on a wagon drawn by mules into Mexican territory, where *revoltosos* immediately cached them.[53]

The first military success of the Baja revolt came with the taking of Mexicali on 28 January 1911 by Fabian socialist José María Leyva and a band of thirteen Mexicans, along with one Anglo Wobbly by the name of John Bond. One week after the Mexicali victory, a Canadian Indian by the name of Stanley Williams led thirty men in taking the small village of Algodones. By March, a split occurred when Leyva arrested Williams and threw him out of Mexico. Because of this, forty of Williams's followers left Leyva to fight for Madero in Sonora. That same month a socialist group of eighteen men under Luis Rodríguez, a fanatical I.W.W., took the village of Tecate. By April, with the death of Simón Berthold (truck driver, militant Wobbly, and subchief of the Lower California revolutionaries), Marine deserter and I.W.W. member Jack Mosby was elected by the non-Mexicans to take his place. In the meantime, Leyva had abandoned the Baja to fight for Madero in Chihuahua.[54]

On the propaganda front, on the eve of the "Battle of Tijuana," the celebrated anarchist Emma Goldman exercised her oratorical skills on behalf of the *magonistas* in Los Angeles and San Diego.[55] On 9 May, Rhys Pryce, a Welshman, disobeyed Flores Magón's orders and unexpectedly led his army of I.W.W.'s (mostly from San Diego), Irishmen, Italians, Germans, and—oh, yes—Mexicans, in capturing the border town of Tijuana. By June, Pryce had mysteriously departed the Baja scene, leaving Mosby in command of the Tijuana army. On 22 June 1911, Mosby's troops were pushed out of Tijuana by Mexican *federales* now serving under Madero (Díaz had fled Mexico in May).[56]

Mosby fled across the line and, on 26 June, was interned with his men by the U.S. military authorities at Fort Rosecrans in San Diego. Most of the one hundred individuals interned there were

[53]Martínez, *Lower California*, p. 468. For the I.W.W. shipments, see S. Platt to the Attorney General, 9 May 1911, RG 60, file no. 90755.

[54]Martínez, *Lower California*, pp. 468–473.

[55]Blaisdell, *The Desert Revolution*, p. 123.

[56]Martínez, *Lower California*, pp. 474–477, 483.

eventually released or, as the military commander at the Fort reported, "we just turned them loose on San Diego—which was a dirty trick." Many of these persons were later involved in the infamous I.W.W. "free speech" riots of San Diego in 1912.[57] As for Mosby, after having testified at the trial of Flores Magón he was sentenced to the penitentiary for desertion from the Marines, and was subsequently killed en route to jail when allegedly trying to escape (an American version of Díaz's *ley fuga*, the "law of flight").[58]

With Porfirio Díaz gone, Francisco Madero coming to power, and the PLM armies in northern Mexico in disarray, Flores Magón's "desert revolution" was almost over. When Dick Ferris, an actor, promoter, and clown, declared the separate Republic of Baja California with himself as self-appointed president, Flores Magón lost the support of patriotic Americans, Mexicans, and radicals who thought he was more of a "filibuster" than a revolutionist.[59]

Hoping to have a final rapprochement with the *magonistas*, Madero now sent Ricardo's brother Jesús, along with the recently released Juan Sarabia and the ex-*magonista* José María Leyva, on a peace mission to Los Angeles. Flores Magón, desperate and desolate, and not in a compromising mood, rebuked his older brother and former friends. The commission failed. Four days later, on 14 June, either by coincidence or plan, the Los Angeles Junta was arrested. Indicted and found guilty on a charge of violating the neutrality laws, the Flores Magón brothers, Rivera, and Figueroa were sentenced to twenty-three months in prison. PLM customs collector Araujo, also indicted, fled from his captors to the sanctuary of Canada.[60]

The Baja phase of the *magonista* movement proved to be tragic. Flores Magón was criticized for not taking the field personally, for not maintaining an efficient chain of command, and for allowing clowns and adventurers to take over the campaign. By mid-February, Gutiérrez de Lara's PLM army in Chihuahua went

[57]As quoted in Rosalie Shanks, "The I.W.W. Free Speech Movement, San Diego, 1912," *Journal of San Diego History* 19 (1973): 27.

[58]Blaisdell, *The Desert Revolution*, p. 195.

[59]Lowell L. Blaisdell, "Was it Revolution or Filibustering? The Mystery of the Flores Magón Revolt in Baja California," *Pacific Historical Review* 23 (May 1954): 147–164.

[60]Martínez, *Lower California*, pp. 481–484.

over to Madero. On 26 February, Villarreal exchanged harsh words with Flores Magón in Turner's home in Los Angeles, and he too then left to join Madero's armies in Mexico. It had been Gutiérrez de Lara and Villarreal who had originally won Gompers's support for the PLM by having written those editorials in *Regeneración* that were favorable to the A.F.L.[61] With these men gone, Gompers had second thoughts about Flores Magón's intentions in Baja California, and he too abandoned the *magonistas* for Madero, bringing Murray and Mother Jones with him.

In October, Mother Jones and Job Harriman visited the Flores Magón brothers in Los Angeles. This was one month after the PLM manifesto of 1911, in which the *magonistas* openly declared their anarcho-communism and called for "direct action" in lieu of "political action." It was also after Flores Magón had publicly insulted the A.F.L., called Juan Sarabia a "Judas," accused the socialists of swallowing propaganda, and asserted that Madero's money had bought off Debs and the socialist press.[62]

Mother Jones reported that they discussed politics for over an hour, "but they believed only in direct action" and "charged everyone with being a traitor, but themselves." After the meeting was over, Job Harriman, who was then a candidate for mayor of Los Angeles, told Mother Jones that he could not continue to be their lawyer "or have anything more to do with them." Mother Jones later went around to the various labor unions of the city and extracted a promise from them not to render any future aid to the PLM Junta.[63]

Flores Magón's disgust, anger, and despair had been mounting since 1908. Noting the struggles within the American socialist camp and the seeming inability of the radicals to aid him, he told his brother Enrique that "the American people, and even the organized

[61]This information about the editorial roles of Villarreal and Gutiérrez de Lara is based on the testimony of Librado Rivera as cited in Barry Carr, *El movimiento obrero y la política en México, 1910–1929*, I, 120, n. 169.

[62]Blaisdell, *The Desert Revolution*, p. 184.

[63]Mother Jones to Calero, 25 October 1911, and Mother Jones to Ricardo Flores Magón, 4 November 1911, AGN/RRV, docs. no. 71 and 84. See also Heriberto Barrón to Francisco Madero, 30 October 1911, Archivo General de la Nación, Ramo Revolución, Política Interior, Correspondencia de Francisco I. Madero, 1910–1912, Mexico City (hereafter cited as AGN/RRM), doc. no. 76.

workmen of this cold-blooded country are not susceptible to agitation. . . . With the exception of Pasadena [unions], there has been no real campaign in our favor." With indignation, he went on to assert that "this is really a public of pigs. Look at the Socialists; they have split in a most cowardly way in their campaign for the liberty of speech."[64]

After the failures of the June 1908 campaigns, Flores Magón ordered the PLM chapters to combine their efforts with those of the Anglo radicals. Instead of developing a broader front, the result was confusion, resentment, and the "capturing" of PLM members by the Americans. In a letter to his beloved María at the end of 1908, he complained about the racism and condescension encountered by Mexicans in the United States, even from Anglo radicals.[65] His unfavorable opinions of the American socialists were not changed by the 1909 experience, when the Darrow defense effort was redirected from the Liberals to Fred Warren. This only proved to Flores Magón that when times were tough and resources limited, the Anglo radicals would take care of their own first. With the schisms and failures of 1911, Flores Magón was a bitter man.

As tempting as it is to explain the break between the Junta and their American supporters in terms of personalities, that is, the misunderstandings generated by an irreconcilable Flores Magón in his dealings with the "politically naive" Mother Jones, this interpretation would be too simplistic. Of more importance than personalities were the ideological differences, as well as the conflicts and tensions within the American radical community.

It should not be forgotten that a handful of socialists, like Turner, did not abandon the *magonistas*; neither did the Italian anarchists in the United States, nor the I.W.W. After some initial grumblings about the Junta's treatment of Mosby and other Baja Wobblies, the I.W.W. continued its support of the Mexican anarchists. Ideologically, the PLM's anarcho-communism was compatible with the anarcho-sydicalism of the I.W.W.[66] Between 1915 and

[64]Ricardo Flores Magón to Enrique Flores Magón, 7 June 1908, encl. in Creel to Diebold, 19 August 1908, AREM, L–E–954Bls.

[65]Gómez-Quiñones, *Sembradores*, p. 34; González Ramírez, *Epistolario y textos*, pp. 169–170.

[66]Blaisdell, *The Desert Revolution*, pp. 184–186.

1926, for example, the I.W.W. (hardly a potent force itself after the repressions of World War I) supported a campaign on behalf of the imprisoned PLM leader Jesús M. Rangel until his pardon by Governor Miriam ("Ma") Ferguson of Texas.[67]

It should also be remembered that the I.W.W. ceased to function as a trade union after 1908. By that year the philosophy of anarcho-syndicalism dominated the thinking of the leadership, and the spring I.W.W. convention dropped the idea of "political action" from its preamble. The new policy was simply nonsense to Eugene V. Debs and many of the socialists. Thus, in 1908, Debs quietly permitted his dues to lapse and his membership in the I.W.W. to expire.[68] Similarly, Gompers, who began his career as a socialist, cooled very quickly to the competition coming from the I.W.W. and the W.F.M.

Between 1908 and 1912, as the I.W.W. became more uncompromisingly extreme, the Socialist Party became more conservative. The elections of 1910 confirmed the right-wing approach of practical politics, with reform-minded socialist ministers and lawyers being most successful. As the middle-class reformers joined the Socialist Party in large numbers, the radical working men left it. By 1912, the Socialist Party constitution was amended so as to expel any member who opposed political action or advocated sabotage as a weapon of the working class.[69]

As moderate socialists in the PLM (like Villarreal) split from the anarchists, so too did Murray, Jones, and Debs remove themselves from the I.W.W. With the Baja revolt, the I.W.W. and the PLM became closely intertwined in the minds of the American radical community. Among socialists, the presence of Emma Goldman in the California campaign did not help the PLM image. American labor, by and large, had responded to the liberal, reformist goals of the 1906 PLM but not to its anarchist objectives of 1911. Money had been raised to meet the cost of lawyers for the defense, not for arms and munitions for the revolution. Thus, realignment was a natural result, with Debs and the others fleeing from both the PLM

[67]Chaplin, *Wobbly,* pp. 178–179.
[68]Ginger, *The Bending Cross,* pp 255–256.
[69]Preston, *Aliens and Dissenters,* pp. 46–50.

and the I.W.W. The association of the I.W.W. with the PLM did not go unnoticed by U.S. authorities either: they continued their politics of suppression toward the *magonistas* and the Wobblies from the election of 1912 to the post–World War I era. That policy, as will be shown, started at Cananea after the June strike of 1906.

TWO
Don Porfirio and the Not-So-Loyal
Opposition, 1906–1911

Greene is a copper king and beneath the canopy of a Mexican sky he is licensed as an executioner.

The Miners' Magazine, 1907

3. A Specter Named "Cananea"

FORTY miles below the international boundary, in the northwestern state of Sonora, lies the copper mining town of Cananea. It is the town that Colonel William Cornell Greene built. Originally it was only a small Pima Indian village, but this Yankee *caudillo* had developed it into a city of 20,000 people by 1905. Although the origin of the term "Cananea" is uncertain, it is most likely a Spanish corruption of the original Andebe Indian usage. But to the contemporaries of Colonel "Bill," the name was biblical, referring to Canaan and the "Canaanitish Woman." "La Cananea," the Cananite woman, was described by Anglo pioneers as "a humble and beautiful Jewess with black eyes of fathomless depths, and with lone, silky tresses dark as the blackest night, with lips the color of ripe cherries, and with a form divine which would have caused Venus to turn green with envy."[1] "La Cananea," it was said, "flourished" in the area around the time of the establishment of the Cananea ranch.

The initial date of the ranch is unknown, but from its original name, *El Real de Cananea*, it is evident that it was a royal Spanish grant pre-dating 1817. The name was afterward changed by common usage to *Cananea Vieja*, to distinguish Old Cananea from a new grant in 1886. Meanwhile, the general meaning of "Cananea" was expanded by the Pima Indians of Arizona to include the mountain

[1]A. E. Zeh to George Young, 5 August 1921, in Young's unpublished history, "Greene Cananea Copper Company and Subsidiaries, A Historical Sketch" (Cananea, Sonora, August 1920), pp. 27–28, in the files of the Compañía Minera de Cananea, S.A. de C.V., Tucson, Arizona (hereafter cited as CM files).

ranges in northern Sonora on the western slope of the Sierra Madre Occidental.[2]

As such, the Cananea field embraced a wide region of mountains, mesas, and plateaus interspersed with arroyos and flat valleys. Unlike the country further west, it was definitely not desert land, either in climate or vegetation. Depending on the altitude (which ranged between 2,000 and 6,000 feet above sea level), the climate varied between the middle latitudes and the steppes, from hot rainy summers with mild winters in the higher areas to the drier steppe country, where the average annual temperature was around 65° F. Water flowed from the mountains through the arroyos, and small oak trees flourished on the hillsides. Surface ores were in abundance, and the plains were covered with mesquite and grama grass, which attracted herds of wild mustangs. It was a ranchman's heaven and a potential paradise for gold, silver, lead, and copper miners. Only the Yaqui and Apache spoiled the promoter's dream, at least until the strike of 1906.[3]

From Bisbee, in southern Arizona, one could see the Cananea mountains fifty miles away. By 1900, Arizona prospectors could reach Old Cananea by a wagon trail that went in a southwesterly direction for thirty-eight miles from the border community of Naco to the mines of Cananea. In colonial times the Spaniards knew Cananea as a potentially rich mining region. In the mid-eighteenth century, Jesuit padres operated the Cobre Grande mine for its silver. By the 1820s, a soldier, José Pérez de Arizpe, combined his operations with the Bacanunchi holdings of his relatives, the Arvallo family. Operating from their headquarters at the Hacienda de Beneficio (Old Cananea), José María Arvallo and José Pérez opened the silver and gold mines of Ojo de Agua (a few miles south of the present town of Cananea) and established a smelter near the old village of Cananea on San Pedro Creek (also called El Ritto). The hacienda was on the border of a vast plain, a mile and a half from the principal Cananea mines of El Ronquillo, Cobre Grande, and La Chivatera.[4]

[2]Ibid., pp. 11–12.

[3]Michael E. Bonine, et al., *Atlas of Mexico*, pp. 5–16. Cananea lies in the Sonoran basin and range complex.

[4]C. L. Sonnichsen, *Colonel Greene*, p. 40; Young, "Greene Cananea Copper Company," pp. 12, 24–25, CM files.

Most of the Pérez-Arvallo properties were eventually deeded to General Ignacio Pesqueira, the governor of Sonora between 1856 and 1876. Pesqueira worked the mines of Cananea and the veins of Ojo de Agua. From these mines copper and silver ores were extracted that were treated in the smelters at Old Cananea and Puertocitos (west of Cananea).[5]

In 1896, Greene obtained from Pesqueira's widow a ninety-nine-year lease on the Ronquillo, Chivatera, Cobre Grande, and San Ignacio mines. By late 1899, he had incorporated the Cananea Consolidated Copper Company, S. A., as a Mexican operating company. On 10 February 1900, in order to open stock to the U.S. market and attract American investors, Greene and his friends organized a holding company called the Greene Consolidated Copper Company, which controlled the capital stock of his Mexican corporation.[6]

As for the legendary Bill Greene, his spectacular career as a cattle baron and promoter extraordinaire between 1900 and 1906 has attracted more writers of fancy than of fact. His own friends created much of the legend, and since then Mexican and American historians have completed the mythologizing. Bisbee old-timer and newsman Joe Chisholm, Greene's contemporary, said that the "Colonel" (who was not an authentic colonel) "flamed on the horizon of the Southwest like a lurid meteor [and] . . . was a potential Croesus [who] killed men ruthlessly when they got in his way. . . . He was a superman." Arizona Ranger Thomas H. Rynning, another of Greene's friends, said that in the middle of a conversation during the Cananea strike Greene beat a Mexican to the draw, shot him dead, and continued without interruption. Not only did superman Greene capture Geronimo, according to writer Ralph Donham, he "once killed two Apaches single handed in a half-mile running gunfight on horseback." Through these feats, Big Bill, the "gun toting womanizer," certainly represented the "slap-dash energy of the Wild West."[7]

[5]Young, "Greene Cananea Copper Company," pp. 12–13, 20–25, CM files.

[6]Sonnichsen, Colonel Greene, pp. 44–46, 59.

[7]Joe Chisholm, Brewery Gulch, pp. 150–151; Thomas H. Rynning, Gun Notches: The Life Story of a Cowboy-Soldier, p. 302; Ralph A. Donham,

These portrayals continue today, even though Greene did not carry a weapon after he killed Jim Burnett in Tombstone in 1897 in a dispute involving land rivalry. As for the accounts of his private life, they are non-verifiable, more the product of frontier gossip and jealousy than of reality. Although a gambler, he was a legitimate businessman, not simply a confidence man. He was not always, as has been argued, careless, thoughtless, "hot tempered," and precipitous in his business affairs—his company accounts were orderly and his methods efficient enough to have made his Quaker ancestors proud. For contemporary Mexico and Mexicans, Greene was the American exploiter par excellence: a living embodiment of the Colossus of the North. As for the residents of the American Southwest, Greene had to be remodeled to fit their stereotype of a Wall Street Wyatt Earp, an image that epitomized the values of his friends and enemies.[8]

Between 1900 and 1906, Greene (originally from New York state) grew from a poor Arizona rancher with perhaps a few hundred dollars to a financial titan. It is estimated that he acquired property valued at almost $12,000,000 through his various schemes.[9] He had arrived in Sonora at a most propitious time, when Indian troubles were rapidly subsiding and the copper industry was on the verge of expansion to supply the new demand for electricity in Europe and the United States. In fact, until the recession of 1907, world copper prices would rise to new heights.[10]

Even after the recession, the industry remained optimistic, especially about the Arizona-Sonora copper fields. In 1908, the *Copper Handbook*, citing the authority of the famous early-nineteenth-century explorer and engineer Alexander von Humboldt, said that

---

"Buckaroo of Wall Street," *Arizona Days and Ways Magazine* (24 November 1957): 44; David M. Pletcher, *Rails, Mines, and Progress: Seven American Promoters in Mexico, 1867–1911*, p. 219.

[8]The best job of demythologizing Greene has been done by Sonnichsen in *Colonel Greene*, pp. 258–269.

[9]Marvin D. Bernstein, "Colonel William C. Greene and the Cananea Copper Bubble," *Bulletin of the Business Historical Society* 26 (December 1952): 189.

[10]Pletcher, *Rails, Mines, and Progress*, p. 223.

Humboldt predicted, nearly one hundred years ago, that the mineral wealth of the world would be developed in Sonora, which then consisted of the present states of Sonora and Sinaloa in the Republic of Mexico, and the territory of Arizona in the United States. This prediction is being borne out to the letter, as there is no richer mineral field, of equal area, upon the globe.[11]

Of the Mexican states referred to, Sonora, with its three mining districts of Arizpe (Cananea and Ajo mountains), Moctezuma (in the neighborhood of Nacozari), and Sahuaripa (east-central Sonora adjacent to Chihuahua), was easily the more important. In order to exploit the natural wealth of these regions, Greene formed, in time, a constellation of companies.

The Cananea Consolidated Copper Company (the "Four C's") held 37,000 acres of mineral lands and over 350,000 acres of timbered surface lands (a total of 630 square miles). The Greene Gold-Silver Company and the Greene Consolidated Gold Company exploited gold and silver mines in western Sonora and eastern Chihuahua. Greene also formed the Sierra Madre Land and Timber Company to cut the timber for the Cananea mines, and the Rio Grande, Sierra Madre, and Pacific Railroad to serve the timber company and to link Cananea with the west coast. Finally, the Casa Grande Irrigation Company was organized to dam the Gila River and irrigate the basin.[12]

For himself, Greene used his "dividends" to buy several ranches in Mexico and Arizona. The Cananea Cattle Company controlled over 600,000 acres of grassland, neatly sub-divided into several corporate divisions so as to evade the Mexican law that forbade any one concern or person to own over 10,000 hectares (24,700 acres). His Mexican interests included the famous Turkey Track Ranch, the best in Sonora—extensive, well irrigated, and stocked with fine Herefords. On the Arizona side, he ran the Greene Cattle Company, which included the San Pedro Valley Ranch and the San Rafael del Valle. All told, he managed over 40,000 head of purebred Herefords.[13]

At its height, Greene's Mexican fief comprised 646,545 acres,

[11]Horace J. Stevens, comp., *The Copper Handbook*, VIII, 219.
[12]Bernstein, "Colonel William C. Greene," p. 187.
[13]Sonnichsen, *Colonel Greene*, pp. 233–237.

extending from the towns of Bacoachi and Arizpe on the south to the Mexican-Arizona boundary on the north, with its western border at the Los Ajos mountains and its eastern at the La Mariquita range. When his heirs were finally forced to relinquish their empire to the Mexican government in 1958, they were compensated with 125 pesos per hectare, or over $2,586,000.[14]

The center of Greene's empire, and his pride and joy, was the company townsite of La Cananea, founded and owned by William C. Greene. La Cananea was declared a municipality on 13 October 1901 by the Sonora legislature. Located on a mesa overlooking the mines, the town was laid out in the familiar rectangular grid pattern, with a cemetery, plaza, park, school, church, and city offices. The Sonora Hotel serviced travelers and those looking for housing. It was here that, by 1906, the company managed and owned a few office buildings, eleven dwellings for foremen, over two hundred rental lots, a restaurant, a bakery, a meat market, a mercantile store, a two-story brick hospital, two sawmills, and a fine clubhouse. A nine-mile aqueduct brought water in from Ojo de Agua at the headquarters of the Sonora river.[15]

In most towns in Mexico, the most prominent architectural structure is the local Catholic church, but in Cananea it was Greene's two-story clapboard mansion—the House of Seven Chimneys. It was located on the western rim of the mesa, and Greene could look out from his wide veranda and see the smokestacks of the smelting plants below. With stables (he loved racing horses) outside and servants' quarters in the rear, the interior of the Big House was designed for comfort and elegance—sixteen-foot ceilings, fireplaces in every room, oak paneling, heavy wooden swinging doors with brass doorknobs, bathrooms in all of the five bedrooms (the downstairs bathtub was huge—large enough, as the legend-makers would say, "to hold a big-boned, fleshy-faced colonel, two maidens, and a bottle of champagne"), a kitchen and pantry, a stately reception hall, a library, massive furniture, and so on. Appropriately painted green with white trim, the Big House was and is the

---

[14]A. Frederick Mignone, "A Fief for Mexico: Colonel Greene's Empire Ends," *Southwest Review* 44 (Autumn 1959): 332, 337.

[15]*The Copper Handbook* (1906), VI, 544.

showplace of Cananea—a living symbol of Greene's wealth and power.[16]

Immediately west of the townsite was Ronquillo, the old town in the valley between the mesa and the reduction works. This area, adjacent to the power plant and the smelters, housed many Mexicans and grew without much supervision. To the west of Ronquillo were the concentrating plants, the administration buildings, the company-owned Banco de Cananea, and Greene's mineral holdings—divided into five zones, each including a number of mines. By 1906, the most important zone was the Veta Grande with its two enormous ore bodies, known as the Veta Grande No. 5 and the Oversight.[17] Here, too, was the community of Chivatera, where Greene had built a six-ward emergency hospital, and the company saddle town of Buenavista, wherein 346 lots were rented to the Mexican workers who lived in the 500 dwellings there.[18]

Porfirio Díaz, of course, had made all of this possible. Díaz, and his allies in the provincial governments, had granted and renewed liberal concessions to Greene, including exclusive exploitation rights and tax exemptions. Greene's operations, for example, benefited from a two-percent deduction on export duties, a concession that allowed Greene to increase his profits at the expense of competing mining concerns.[19]

In Sonora, the state government of Rafael Izábal contributed 15,000 pesos to the construction of a private company road that allowed Greene to transport his machinery to the Conchena mines. It was then "declared" a public road.[20] In Chihuahua, in 1904, Governor Enrique C. Creel gave the Sierra Madre company timber concessions amounting to about 3.5 million acres of forested land. In 1906, he facilitated Greene's exploitation of western Chihuahua by having the Chihuahua and Pacific Railroad build a branch line from Miñaca to Temosachic. In return for these favors, governors

[16]This description is based on observations made at Cananea by the author on 16 July 1975.

[17]The Copper Handbook, VI, 537–545; Sonnichsen, "Map: The Cananea Neighborhood," Colonel Greene, pp. 190–191.

[18]George Young to W. C. Greene, 8 June 1906, CM files.

[19]Bernstein, "Colonel William C. Greene," pp. 187–188; Jesús Luna, La carrera pública de don Ramón Corral, p. 112.

[20]Luna, Ramón Corral, p. 112.

Izábal and Creel were lavishly entertained, even being invited to the "Great Bear Hunt" of 1905 in the mountains west of Casas Grandes, along with such worthies as William G. Rockfeller, E. H. Harriman, James J. Hill, and Albert Bacon Fall.[21]

Fall was one of two attorneys and confidants who played essential roles in the success of Greene's enterprises (the other being Norton Chase, a Wall Street lawyer who represented Greene's interests in the financial and political circles of Mexico City, Washington, D.C., and New York City). During his early territorial days, Fall had been a judge and practicing lawyer involved in many extradition cases. In studying precedents for these cases, he eventually became a specialist in old Mexican and Spanish codes as well as Mexican law and procedures. Between 1903 and 1907, Fall occupied himself with building a private fortune in New Mexico and western Chihuahua through his services as Greene's top legal adviser for both the Greene Gold-Silver Company and the Sierra Madre Land and Timber Company. After making his money he became the sole possessor of the great Three Rivers Ranch north of Tularosa, New Mexico.[22]

Fall was not only Greene's lawyer, he was also his second in command for all the Mexican enterprises outside Cananea. He was vice-president of the Rio Grande, Sierra Madre, and Pacific Railroad. In 1907, he boasted to Roosevelt that Greene and he had, "within two years, invested in the state of Chihuahua alone something like ten million dollars in gold." Although he dropped his active partnership with Greene in July 1906, he continued to act as his legal adviser until Greene's death in 1911.[23]

Familiar with the terrain of northwestern Chihuahua, Fall was a personal friend of Enrique Creel and the Terrazas clan. After Madero's successful revolt in 1911, he rented his El Paso house to the elder Terrazas, then a political refugee from Mexico. In 1912, when New Mexico received statehood, he was made a U.S. senator. As such he tended to consider Americans in Mexico his special

[21]Sonnichsen, *Colonel Greene*, pp. 154, 157, 168–169.

[22]Ibid., pp. 54, 110, 221–222. See also David H. Stratton, ed., *The Memoirs of Albert B. Fall*, IV, 38–42, and Earl F. Woodward, "Hon. Albert B. Fall of New Mexico," *Montana* 23 (1973): 14–23.

[23]Fall to Theodore Roosevelt, 12 April 1907, Fall Papers.

constituency. Enamored with the Díaz-Creel system, which afforded foreigners special privileges and protection, he promoted the anti-Madero (later anti-Carranza) cause of many conservative *revoltosos* in the United States, often calling for military intervention in Mexico. In 1921, he was secretary of interior and Harding's special adviser on Mexico, at a time when Obregón's government was refused recognition by the United States because of the oil rights dispute. All in all, from 1903 to the Teapot Dome oil scandal of 1922, Fall had a long and consistent record of defending and promoting American property interests in Mexico.[24]

One Díaz concession that was critical for those interests, including Greene's, was the government's guarantee of an available supply of cheap, unorganized labor. In the mines at Cananea (which offered the highest wages in Mexico) the miner worked up to twelve hours in the shafts and pits for between 2.5 and 3 pesos. In the smeltery, *carreros*, who carted ore and coal, received between 3 and 4 pesos, and the *cargador*, who tended the furnace, might earn 6 to 8 pesos for ten hours labor. *Barreteros* (miners who worked with picks and crowbars) earned 3 to 4 pesos, and carpenters and other skilled craftsmen might make up to 6 pesos. Conditions were much worse in Greene's gold and silver operations in the Sahuaripa district, where laborers were paid as low as 1.5 pesos for an eleven-hour day.[25]

However, salary scales only reveal a small part of the worker's plight. Between 1900 and 1910, the peso (exchanged at a rate of 2 pesos to the dollar) lost half its purchasing power, while the cost of living jumped 200 percent.[26] In addition, there were the practices of the *tienda de raya*, the company store, in which management would give workers *boletas* or credit slips in lieu of real wages. This not only increased the indebtedness of the worker but

[24]Woodward, "Hon. Albert B. Fall," pp. 14–23; Michael C. Meyer, "Albert Bacon Fall's Mexican Papers: A Preliminary Investigation," *New Mexico Historical Review* 40 (April 1965): 165–166.

[25]Ramón Eduardo Ruiz, *Labor and the Ambivalent Revolutionaries: Mexico, 1911–1913*, p. 7; Esteban B. Calderón, *Juicio sobre la guerra del yaqui y génesis de la huelga de Cananea*, pp. 22–25; C. Nelson Nelson, "The Sahuaripa District, Sonora, Mexico," *The Engineering and Mining Journal* 82 (6 October 1906): 630.

[26]Ruiz, *Labor and the Ambivalent Revolutionaries*, p. 11.

frequently meant that he would have to buy inferior goods at higher prices. The practice not only saved the company the costs of handling large sums of cash, but also provided the store with 30- to 40-percent profits on the actual cost of goods.[27]

Another form of indebtedness for the Cananea workers was the cost of housing. In 1906, Greene rented a total of 570 lots to 746 householders. Lot rentals and water bills amounted to 3 pesos per unit each month. By 8 June 1906 the company's auditor reported that Mexican residents owed the Banco de Cananea over 47,700 pesos on secured notes and another 5,000 pesos for rentals on city lots.[28] Again, what was a cost for the Mexican worker was a profit for the foreign owners of the company.

A major grievance of the Mexican worker at Cananea was the unfair labor practice that favored Anglos over Mexicans, especially in housing and salaries. From the point of view of the Mexican, it appeared that the specter of unemployment, inferior housing, mine disasters, and disease haunted him more than his Anglo counterpart. At Cananea, out of a total population of 30,000, the Greene Consolidated Copper Company hired 3,251 Mexicans and 1,178 non-Mexicans (Mexicans 71 percent, foreigners 29 percent), paying the American worker more than the Mexican for the same amount and kind of work. Whereas the miner and mechanic might be paid 3 to 5 pesos per day, similar employment for American workers amounted to $3.50 to $8.00 gold per day. Again, a Mexican carpenter would be paid 5 pesos for the same work that an American earned $4.00 U.S. for doing. When one considers that the peso was worth less than half the American dollar, it would appear that the American often received two to four times the amount paid to his Mexican counterpart. Although the biwage system was common throughout Mexico and the American Southwest, it was naturally resented by Mexicans in both places, as was evidenced by the Morenci strike of 1903 and the Cananea revolt of 1906.[29]

Curiously enough, the Cananea company had a poor reputation with workers in the United States. Although salary scales were

[27]Nelson, "The Sahuaripa District," pp. 630–631.
[28]George Young to W. C. Greene, 8 June 1906, CM files.
[29]Ibid. See also Calderón, *Juicio sobre la guerra*, pp. 22–25.

similar to those in the mines in the United States, net earnings were actually less. Company officials assessed the American employees $2.50 gold for hospital fees and $2.50 gold for rent, and often discharged them from service after five to eight days, reducing the net earnings of the Americans by $1.00 to $2.00 gold per day. This meant that Greene attracted from the United States only the very poorest of skilled labor, the type likely to be persuaded more by the arguments of W.F.M. organizers than by those of Greene's managers.[30]

Another reason for the common resentment of foreigners was the Mexicans' conviction that Anglos looked on them as inferior. On this matter the Mexicans were unfortunately correct, as very few Anglos doubted their own natural superiority. Walter E. Weyl's statement that Mexican laborers were apathetic, inefficient, unproductive, passive, ambitionless, unintelligent, and untrustworthy, although extreme, probably epitomized the sentiments of most foreigners. As an intellectual and spokesman for industrial capitalism, Weyl mirrored the racism and class interests of capitalism when he argued that the improvidence of the lower classes was reflected in "their failure to be incited to more intense work by increased remuneration," or when he stated that there is no class consciousness in Mexico, no conflict between labor and capital. When these ideas are projected into the minds of American proprietors, managers, and foremen, it not difficult to conceptualize the attitudes of Mexican labor.[31]

It is not surprising that local Liberal Party leader Esteban B. Calderón proposed from Cananea, in May 1906, the formation of a national miners' union in order "to show the capitalists that we are not merely beasts of burden" and to oppose "white men with blue eyes."[32] Although the Cananea workers' plight was no worse than that of other industrial workers in Mexico, and although their material benefits were greater than those employed in agriculture or in the mines outside the copper industry, their grievances were

[30]John Dwyer, "The Greene Consolidated Copper Mines," *The Engineering and Mining Journal* 75 (14 March 1903): 416.
[31]Weyl, "The Labor Situation in Mexico," *Annals of the American Academy of Political and Social Science* 21 (January 1903): 77–93.
[32]Calderón, *Juicio sobre la guerra*, p. 48.

the product of frustrated expectations, and derived from a view that compared the quality of their lives, not with that of other Mexicans, but with that of Anglos in Sonora and the United States. Such are the costs of the belief in progress, a belief shared by socialists and capitalists alike.

Thus, with the exception of the presence of the PLM, the general labor situation in Cananea before the strike was not unlike that in other areas of Mexico where strikes and syndicalist agitation occurred between 1906 and 1910. The Cananea strike, like that at Río Blanco in 1907 and the railway disputes of 1908, was the offspring of industrial development. Occurring in a progressive sector of the economy in an industry tied to export markets, the Cananea strike was as much the result of modernization as of repression. Like the later strikers, the Cananea workers demanded from their foreign managers salaries and working conditions more akin to those provided foreign workers.[33]

And finally, since many of the specific grievances were aimed at the unfair labor practices of foreign managers, and since Porfirio Díaz obviously supported and protected these managers, the PLM knew in advance of the strike that if any protest were to succeed it would have to be political as well as economic. And if the PLM and the leaders of the local Liberal clubs did not actually plan the strike, this was due more to their own limited resources and to strategic and tactical considerations than to ideology or the workers' lack of consciousness. In other words, the grievances were real and had been articulated to the workers, but the time was wrong and the workers had neither sufficient arms nor sufficient finances to assure success.[34]

[33]Ruiz, *Labor and the Ambivalent Revolutionaries*, pp. 19–23; Carr, *El movimiento obrero*, I, 44–45. Surprisingly, John Dwyer, writing from Cananea in early 1903, asserted that the "labor difficulty is the principal one in the way of the Cananea Company," and prophetically declared, "that the company must inevitably substitute Mexican for American labor is certain" (Dwyer, "The Greene Consolidated Copper Mines," p. 416).

[34]Esteban Calderón, a Liberal leader and strike participant, swears that the local Cananea clubs did not have as their mission the organization of the strike. Calderón further argues that the Liberals gave reluctant leadership to the strike, knowing that without proper organization and finances the strike was doomed to fail. Since this testimony was given years after the Porfiriato, when there was no conscious reason to distort the truth, it should be given

Although the strike itself, and the accompanying violence, had neither been organized nor officially sanctioned by the Liberal clubs at Cananea, it is obvious that such developments were the indirect result of the organizational activities and incendiary propaganda carried on by the local Liberals and their PLM and W.F.M. supporters in Douglas, Bisbee, and St. Louis. They articulated the grievances of the workers and heightened both national and class consciousness, making the workers more aware of the "inevitable" class conflict on the horizon. In seeking to organize the miners into a union that was supposed to become a powerful auxiliary of the PLM, the Cananea leaders had simply prepared the way for a "spontaneous" and premature strike that would be met with repression.[35]

The first agitation came in 1905 and was carried on from Douglas, Arizona. Antonio de P. Araujo, an early supporter of the St. Louis Junta, began distributing copies of *Regeneración* to the workers at Cananea. Araujo had earlier aided Lázaro Puente (also known as Joaquín Fuentes) and Tomás Espinosa in the organization of the *Club Liberal Libertad* of Douglas. The Douglas campaign was also promoted by two journalists, José and Enrique Bermúdez. In May 1906, while José stayed in Douglas, Enrique established operations in Cananea, publishing a radical newspaper called *El Centenario*. This newspaper reflected the ideological concerns of the clubs and contained excerpts from *Regeneración*.[36]

Even after the June strike, Cananea Liberals like Plácido Ríos

---

credence. See Calderón, *Juicio sobre la guerra*, pp. 57, 81. The same testimony appears as "Testimonio de Esteban B. Calderón" in González Ramírez, *Fuentes*, III, 112, 117.

[35]As indicated previously, the best source for printed documents about the Cananea strike is González Ramírez, *Fuentes*, III, *La huelga de Cananea*. Lyle C. Brown's account remain the best narrative in English of the event. See his "The Mexican Liberals and Their Struggle against the Díaz Dictatorship," in *Antología MCC*. For a view derived from newspaper accounts in Bisbee, Douglas, and Tucson, see Herbert O. Brayer, "The Cananea Incident," *New Mexico Historical Review* 13 (October 1938): 387–415. Also see Pletcher, *Rails, Mines, and Progress*, pp. 236–259, and Sonnichsen, *Colonel Greene*, pp. 177–206. Finally, for a non-Mexican non-Anglo treatment see João Cabral, *O Partido Liberal Mexicano e a greve de Cananea*.

[36]Brown "The Mexican Liberals," pp. 327–328, 347–348; González Ramírez, *Fuentes*, III, 74.

would continue to run arms and act as emissaries between the radical communities of Douglas and Cananea. The Douglas Liberals were also aided at Cananea by W.F.M. organizers like Joe Carter, who, operating from Bisbee, distributed literature and money in Nacozari and Cananea. However, the most important leaders were at Cananea, especially Manuel M. Diéguez, Esteban B. Calderón, and Francisco M. Ibarra.[37]

Diéguez began work at the Cananea Consolidated in June 1904 at the rate of three pesos a day. By the time of the strike, however, he was earning seven pesos a day as the bilingual assistant to the paymaster at the Oversight mine. Calderón, a former schoolteacher, arrived in Cananea in March 1905 and immediately began work as a *carrero* in the smelter at three pesos a day. There he soon became ill with pleurisy, a result of constant exposure to the extreme variations in temperature between the hot furnaces inside and the cold air outside. In order to recover from his illness, he moved to the higher altitude of the Buenavista section of Cananea, living with his friend Francisco Ibarra, a grocer. While at Buenavista, Calderón noticed copies of *Regeneración* being circulated, and after Ibarra introduced him to Diéguez the three of them began to think in terms of organizing a political movement. After his recovery, Calderón took a new job at the Oversight mine as a miner, first as a blasting-powder distributor and later as an ore-car operator (at three pesos a day).[38]

In November 1905 the St. Louis Junta made an appeal to the Cananea workers to support the PLM in exile. Calderón and the others then contacted the Junta, and by 28 December 1905, they had been informed of their acceptance into the PLM. Thus, on 16 January 1906, a group of fifteen men secretly assembled and organized Cananea's first Liberal club, the *Unión Liberal Humanidad*. A written compact was agreed to by the members, including an article recognizing the leadership of the St. Louis Junta; the concluding section of the compact was later published

[37]See "Testimonio de Plácido Ríos" in either González Ramírez, *Fuentes*, III, 141–142, or Manuel Arellano Z., *Huelga de Cananea 1906*, pp. 27–29. For Joe Carter's activities see Rowen to Greene, 20 and 23 July 1906, Fall Papers.

[38]Calderón, *Juicio sobre la guerra*, pp. 23–28; Brown, "The Mexican Liberals," p. 329; González Ramírez, *Fuentes*, III, 106–109.

by the Junta in the March issue of *Regeneración*. During the five months of its existence, the club never consisted of any more than twenty-five members, and the leadership rotated in its offices, beginning with Diéguez as president, Ibarra as vice-president, and Calderón as secretary.[39]

Initially the *Unión* leaders contented themselves with propaganda campaigns in support of the St. Louis Junta, but, by April, Calderón and the others were no longer satisfied with such passive activity. On 6 April 1906, Calderón addressed a letter to Antonio I. Villarreal in St. Louis in which he outlined a proposal designed to arouse the Cananea workers from their ideological slumbers. First, he suggested a meeting of workers to be held on 5 May for the announced purpose of paying homage to General Ignacio Zaragoza, the liberal hero who had defeated the French at the battle of Puebla in 1862 (with, it should be noted, an army of ex-*guerrilleros*). During the course of the celebration the miners would be urged to form a local miner's union. When such a group was formed, the next step would be to extend the union movement to other parts of the country, with the aim of eventually joining all local unions into a national *Liga Minera de los Estados Unidos Mexicanos*. At the same time, the local unions would be expected to join the PLM movement, and thus merge local goals with political objectives.[40]

Peculiarly enough, the St. Louis Junta did not reply to Calderón, even though correspondence on other matters, such as the inquiry about measures for a new manifesto, continued throughout April. It is possible that the syndicalist ideas of Calderón were too radical for Villarreal. It should be noted that the more radical leaders of the Junta, like Ricardo and Enrique Flores Magón, had been forced to flee from St. Louis the month before, and by April were refugees in Toronto, Canada. Villarreal, by far the most conservative of the PLM leaders, was the only individual representing the Junta at the time. Thus, even though Calderón's tactics complemented the thinking of the PLM radicals, the Junta as a

---

[39]Calderón, *Juicio sobre la guerra*, pp. 32–40; González Ramírez, *Fuentes*, III, 3–9.

[40]Calderón, *Juicio sobre la guerra*, pp. 40–44; González Ramírez, *Fuentes*, III, 9–10. See also Brown, "The Mexican Liberals," pp. 330–331.

whole was disorganized and in a transitional stage (still formulating the ideology and tactics of the June "Revolutionary Instructions" and the July "Manifesto"), and therefore unable to make an authoritative response.[41]

Without waiting for approval, the *Unión* members obtained popular support for a *Cinco de Mayo* celebration and organized a *Junta Patriótica* to make the arrangements. Lic. Lázaro Gutiérrez de Lara agreed to serve as the principal speaker; Diéguez and Calderón also spoke. It was on this occasion that Calderón skillfully appealed to the nationalist sentiments of the workers in order to arouse their class consciousness. Racial and national pride could be used to unify workers against the American capitalists and imperialists; Díaz must be shown that sovereignty resides with the people. Calderón's speech came to the attention of the local authorities when it was published in the 12 May 1906 issue of *El Centenario*.[42]

As a result of the 5 May meeting, Gutiérrez de Lara created the *Club Liberal de Cananea* to appeal to the thousands of Cananea residents who were not employees of Greene's company. Again, although the evidence does not support the contention that the *Unión* and *Club Liberal* leaders actually planned and organized the strike, the secret meetings, propaganda activities, and incendiary speeches of 5 May and after set in motion forces that could not be controlled by the Liberals.[43]

The period between 5 May and 1 June was one of constant turmoil and agitation, with confrontations occurring between Americans and Mexicans, police and workers. By 9 May, the company police were arresting all persons who were out late at night in violation of an announced curfew. The last week of May was filled with rumors of violence and conspiracy. It was alleged that

[41]Article II of the "Instrucciones Generales a los Revolucionarios," 1 June 1906, called for all revolutionists to rise in arms if and when an uprising occurred at Cananea, without waiting for further instructions from the Junta. Evidently the Junta expected trouble at Cananea in the future but did not anticipate it for the immediate present. See "Instrucciones" in Fabela, *Documentos históricos*, X, 36.

[42]Calderón's speech is reproduced in both *Juicio sobre la guerra*, pp. 44–49, and González Ramírez, *Fuentes*, III, 10–13.

[43]Brown, "The Mexican Liberals," p. 332.

management had decided to raise the salaries of Americans and to cut those of the Mexicans. Then a Mexican policeman killed an American saloon keeper without apparent cause or provocation. On 30 May, company officials heard that several socialists and W.F.M. members were planning to dynamite the Banco de Cananea, take one million dollars from its coffers, seize arms and ammunition from the company store, and then start a bloody revolution against Greene and Díaz.[44]

Many officials, including company manager A. S. Dwight, were certain that Gutiérrez de Lara and Enrique Bermúdez were stirring up a race war against the Americans, allegations that, of course, they both later denied. On 31 May, several handbills appeared on the streets calling on the Mexican people to rise up in rebellion. One of these read: "CURSE the thought that a Mexican is worth less than a Yankee; that a negro or Chinaman is to be compared with a Mexican. . . . MEXICANS, AWAKEN! The Country and our dignity demand it!"[45]

Given this kind of emotional environment, it would not take much to ignite a major incident. This happened when foremen from the Oversight mine announced that, beginning on 1 June, all extraction of ores would be done on a contractual basis, with workers to be hired on a piecemeal basis. To the workers at the Oversight this meant more work for less pay and a reduction in the total work force. Although the announcement, if acted on, would directly affect only miners, most of the Oversight workers were angered by it, including white collar workers and union men from the United States.[46]

On the morning of 1 June, four hundred workers closed the Oversight mine. Summoned by the strikers, Díeguez and Calderón started the initial negotiations with the *presidente municipal,* Filiberto Barroso, and the local Ronquillo police chief, Pablo Rubio. It was soon decided that the workers' demands would have to be placed before Greene himself, and Calderón and fourteen others were selected by the strikers to act on their behalf. Calderón out-

[44]Brayer, "The Cananea Incident," pp. 391–392; Greene, Memorandum, 11 June 1906, "Brief resumé of the recent disorders in Cananea," CM files.
[45]Brayer, "The Cananea Incident," p. 393.
[46]Calderón, *Juicio sobre la guerra,* pp. 56–57.

lined a brief memorandum to serve as a basis for discussion, and subsequently a revised, more moderate statement was presented to the managers.[47]

Basically the workers stated that as a consequence of the new policy many of their "fellow-citizens" would be deprived of work, and for this reason they would no longer serve the company under the prevailing conditions. It was urgent and necessary "that foreigners should not alone act as arbiters of the welfare of the Mexican laborer." Thus, so that "the intelligence of the Mexicans be better appreciated," the company should increase all salaries by one peso, reduce the number of working hours to eight, and increase the number of Mexican foremen and chiefs. Greene, although apologetic and paternalistic, refused to meet any of the terms or even discuss the issue of discrimination in salaries.[48]

Persuaded of the company's intransigence, the strikers gathered their numbers and marched from Ronquillo, through the smelters and workshops, to the mesa, picking up recruits and closing the concentrator and the Veta Grande mine along the way. At the company lumber yard the demonstrators paused and called for the workers within to join them. When the strikers tried to force the gates, the manager, George Metcalf, and his brother directed water from high-pressure hoses at the crowd. Infuriated by this action, the strikers broke through the gates, only to be met by a hail of bullets. Although unarmed, they overpowered the Metcalf brothers, stabbing them to death with miners' candlesticks. When it was over, in addition to the two Metcalfs at least three Mexicans had been killed, and the lumber yard had been destroyed by fire (where the charred remains of two more bodies were later found). After firing the lumber yard, the mob then marched to the plaza, where they confronted Greene and his men. Another skirmish followed, resulting in more deaths, including that of an individual marching with a red banner.[49]

Alarmed by the violence, Greene, the American consul, and

[47]Ibid., pp. 61–76.

[48]The labor demands can be found in Calderón, et al., to the President, C. C. C. Co., 1 June 1906, CM files.

[49]Brown, "The Mexican Liberals," p. 335; Sonnichsen, *Colonel Greene*, pp. 182–183.

several company and town officials sent telegrams in all directions. Governor Izábal at Hermosillo was inundated with urgent messages from Greene, Barroso, and Rubio. Greene also telegraphed Díaz directly and communicated with Vice-President Ramón Corral through Izábal. The colonel also phoned Walter Douglas, the manager of the Copper Queen mine at Bisbee, and talked to Arizona Ranger Thomas H. Rynning, requesting troops and ammunition. Ignacio Macmanus, cashier of the Cananea bank, who had already been sent to Hermosillo to explain the situation to Izábal, sent pleas for help to Juan Fenochio, the *jefe* of the *Gendarmería Fiscal* for the Third Zone at Nogales, and to Colonel Emilio Kosterlitzky, Fenochio's subordinate at Magdalena.[50] (The *Gendarmería Fiscal* was a special military force, separate from the federal army, that reported directly to Díaz rather than the War Department, and was paid by the secretary of the treasury.)

General Luis E. Torres, the military governor and commander of federal troops for the First Military Zone of Sonora, was in Torin, away from both Hermosillo and Cananea. He kept sending requests for information to Izábal, who, about to have a nervous breakdown, initially failed to respond. Finally learning about the strike, Torres wired Díaz and headed for Nogales to catch up with Izábal. Meanwhile, Izábal contacted *Comandante* Luis Medina Barrón, the commander of a small group of *rurales* in Hermosillo, and made plans to go with Barrón to Cananea. As for consul W. J. Galbraith, he sent "I am the American Consul and must be protected" messages to President Roosevelt, the State Department, the War Department, and the military commander at Fort Huachuca in southern Arizona. From Huachuca a detachment of cavalry was sent to Naco, with unequivocal orders not to cross the border until further instructions were received. Before long, other Mexicans and Americans—soldiers, Rangers, cowboys, and miners—were marching from

[50]See González Ramírez, *Fuentes,* III, 26–29, for copies of many of the June 1 telegrams. Also see Greene to Díaz, 1 June 1906, Colección Porfirio Díaz, University of the Americas, Cholula, Puebla (hereafter cited as CPD), leg. 65, docs. 001073–001075; Fenochio to Díaz, 1 June 1906, CPD, leg. 65, doc. 001062; Kosterlitsky to Fenochio, 1 June 1906, CPD, leg. 31, doc. 006187.

all points in order to protect the fief of the man from the House of Seven Chimneys.[51]

The most ludicrous, and yet serious, events surrounded the activities of the somewhat bewildered and harassed Izábal. On hearing of the violence at Cananea, he issued orders instructing the *federales* at Arizpe, seventy miles south of Cananea, to march to Greene's mines. He then boarded a train at Hermosillo, accompanied by twenty *rurales* and a personal guard, and headed north for Nogales. Along the way he was instructed by Corral that the *rurales* could not enter the United States at Nogales to travel by train to Cananea via Naco, because this would create an unhealthy precedent for the Americans. His troops, therefore, were forced to march overland to Cananea from Imuris. Leaving the *rurales* there, Izábal continued by train to Naco.[52]

At around four o'clock on Saturday morning, 2 June, Izábal's special express, with Luis Torres aboard, arrived at Naco. Earlier, several ugly incidents had taken place there between some "gringos" and Mexican border troops, resulting in one American being seriously wounded after he had attempted to rush the line. At Naco, Captain Rynning of the Rangers, a former Rough Rider with Teddy Roosevelt during the Spanish-Cuban-American War of 1898, met with the Mexican officials. Rynning had brought with him to Naco a volunteer army of over 270 Bisbee cowboys, miners, and merchants, who were most anxious to get to Cananea to stop the race war, see some action, and protect the women and children —at least they thought that was why they wanted to go.[53]

At Naco the Mexican governor faced a dilemma. He hesitated to allow Rynning's volunteer army to cross the border on his own authority, yet the accounts of violence and disorder coming from Cananea seemed to require immediate action. When Rynning persuaded him that Kosterlitzky would not arrive in Cananea for several hours and that it would take two or three days for the infantry to arrive from Arizpe, he agreed to a legal fiction by

---

[51]González Ramírez, *Fuentes,* III, 26–27. See also the article "Consul Kept Wires Hot" in *St. Louis Post-Dispatch,* 3 June 1906.

[52]Pletcher, *Rails, Mines, and Progress,* p. 245.

[53]Rynning, *Gun Notches,* pp. 295–297.

which the Americans would cross as an unorganized mob and then be sworn into the Sonoran militia, agreeing to obey Izábal's orders. Rynning did some legal maneuvering himself: pretending not to know of Territorial Governor Joseph H. Kibbey's orders not to cross the border, he wired the governor to request a temporary leave of absence from the Rangers. Rynning and two other Rangers were then sworn in as high-ranking officers of the Mexican militia, and the troop train left for Cananea, arriving there at mid-morning. In the meantime, another telegram had been sent from Corral in Mexico City to Izábal, instructing him not to allow the entrance of any American auxiliary forces.[54]

On their arrival the volunteers made a show of force, marched past the smelters, and then retired to Ronquillo without firing a shot. In the afternoon the *rurales* from Imuris arrived. Izábal and Greene conferred, then talked to the crowd. At one point Izábal attempted to justify the differential wage rate by noting that the Americans were superior workers, that they had higher living costs, and that when they frequented the brothels they were charged more than the Mexicans for the same services. Despite these soothing arguments, from late afternoon until sundown various groups of American residents and cowboys exchanged shots with the Mexicans.[55]

Finally, at about seven o'clock in the evening, Colonel Kosterlitzky, the "Eagle of Sonora," soared into town with thirty-one gendarmes and twenty-five federal *rurales*. His rugged troops immediately went to work, and in cooperation with Izábal and Torres he issued an order establishing martial law. Again, some Mexicans were killed, and over thirty were arrested, as Kosterlitzky put down the last of the disorders in Ronquillo. Meanwhile, Greene, accompanied by the company's private police commander, Chief Rowen, and about thirty *rurales*, patrolled the American section of the mesa. By the next day, Sunday, more than fifteen hundred Mexican troops had arrived and the weekend strike was over.[56]

[54]Ibid., pp. 298–300, 311; Pletcher, *Rails, Mines, and Progress*, pp. 245–246; Brown, "The Mexican Liberals," p. 336.

[55]Pletcher, *Rails, Mines, and Progress*, pp. 246–247.

[56]Ibid., p. 248; Greene, "Brief resumé," CM files; Cornelius C. Smith, *Emilio Kosterlitzky: Eagle of Sonora and the Southwest Border*, pp. 127–151.

Naturally enough, the enemies of Díaz, like Gutiérrez de Lara, said that "ten thousand miners went out on strike" (more than were employed by Greene) and "hundreds of miners were massacred in cold blood upon the streets." On the other hand, Barroso's official figures reported twenty-three deaths (four Americans, seventeen Mexicans, and two so badly burned that they could not be identified). Greene reported five American dead, but noted with some incredulity that "the number of Mexicans killed has been reported at about twenty and stands at that figure, although the burial squad was at work three nights after reporting twenty as the number killed." Barroso also listed the number wounded as twenty-two, with fifty-four persons arrested as of 5 June on various charges ranging from robbery and rioting to arson and murder. Others not arrested were threatened by Torres with impressment, a situation that would force them to participate in the war against the Yaquis.[57]

On 5 June, Torres summoned Diéguez, Calderón, Ibarra, and five others to his office under the pretext of wanting to hear the complaints of the workers. Once there, they were all arrested. Izábal wanted to apply the *ley fuga* and shoot them, but was restrained from such action by Corral, who sent him a telegram on 8 June, explaining that the agitators could not be shot because it would cause a national scandal. Instead, they should be sent to the federal prison of San Juan de Ulúa, off the Veracruz coast. However, the following day he did suggest to Izábal that they could be executed under article 47 of the penal code, but it would have to be done on the recommendation of the court. This, at least, gave the prisoners a breathing spell.[58]

Lázaro Gutiérrez de Lara was also arrested. He was placed in the Cananea jail with about thirty other strike leaders. Then his brother, Dr. Felipe Gutiérrez de Lara, an influential physician who lived in Mexico City, inquired of Díaz as to why his brother had

---

[57]Lázaro Gutiérrez de Lara and Edgcumb Pinchon, *The Mexican People: Their Struggle for Freedom*, p. 329; Greene, "Brief resumé," CM files. The Barroso data is from Francisco Medina Hoyos, *Cananea: Cuna de la Revolución Mexicana*, pp. 82–84, 91–95.

[58]Brown, "The Mexican Liberals," pp. 337–338; Luna, *Ramón Corral*, p. 118.

been imprisoned. Díaz forwarded the inquiry to Izábal. The governor, fearing for his political life because of the Bisbee army incident, assumed that Díaz, in questioning the arrest, was not in favor of it. Thus, Izábal ordered the release of Gutiérrez de Lara, and, in the latter's own words:

> . . . he [Izábal] then answered Díaz. "At your request I have released De Lara." And then Díaz telegraphs him again and said, "I did not ask you to release De Lara; I asked you simply for information." Then my friends told me to skip out from there.[59]

Which he did, first going to Arizona, and later joining the PLM in Los Angeles.

Diéguez, Calderón, and Ibarra were originally held incommunicado for several days while the authorities tried to determine what to do with them. Then they were placed in the Cananea jail, where they stayed throughout the long, hot summer of 1906. In September they were joined in the Cananea jail by Plácido Ríos, a man who had been active in both the *Club Liberal* and the strike. He had been arrested after authorities in Douglas, Arizona (including, once again, Tom Rynning), had arrested members of the Liberal club there, finding correspondence on Bruno Treviño that linked Ríos to the Cananea strike. Most of the Arizona group was eventually deported, and Izábal sought the extradition of José Bermúdez and the others who had escaped deportation. From Cananea, Diéguez, Calderón, Ibarra, Ríos, and the others were sent to Hermosillo for trial and sentencing. The three Liberal leaders were found guilty of sedition and sentenced to fifteen years at San Juan de Ulúa. In August 1909 they were transferred there, being shipped with Yaqui captives first to the Belem prison in Mexico City before passing on to San Juan de Ulúa.[60]

---

[59]"Statement of Mr. L. Gutiérrez de Lara," U.S. Congress, House, *Alleged Persecutions,* pp. 22–23.

[60]"Testimonios de Plácido Ríos," *Huelga de Cananea,* pp. 27–33; Calderón, *Juicio sobre la guerra,* pp. 115–124. Calderón states that of three hundred political prisoners sentenced to Ulúa after 1906, only eighty were alive in 1911. As for Diéguez and Calderón, like Juan Sarabia they were released from Ulúa when Madero took over from Díaz in 1911. After 1913, both took up arms against Huerta, eventually becoming *carrancista* generals in Obregón's Division of the Northwest. After 1929, Calderón was governor

When one surveys the aftermath of the Cananea strike, it appears that the event was unique in at least two respects. First, there was the presence of Americans, volunteers or not, involved in a police action on Mexican soil. Independent newspapers were especially critical of Izábal and the Arizona Rangers, especially Catholic and labor publications. The Catholic *El Tiempo* angrily declared that the Americans should be punished for provoking violence at Cananea and that Governor Izábal should be prosecuted for soliciting American aid. The labor newspapers were especially enraged over Izábal's statement that the Americans were better workers and so deserved higher wages. The *Correo de Sonora* noted that a mining proprietor in Baja California hired Japanese workers and that, even though they were not good workers, he paid them more than the Mexican workers because in Mexico "the price of labor is not dependent upon the quality of work done, but upon the nationality of the worker." Thus, the Izábal blunders provoked nationalistic sentiments throughout Mexico, sentiments that were surprisingly in favor of the Mexican strikers.[61]

The arrival of Rynning and his friends also involved Díaz in diplomatic problems. He would have preferred to have treated the matter as a local strike, punishing the regional bandits and going on with business as usual. But Rynning was good copy, and the event had been too well publicized in the United States to allow Díaz to use the *ley fuga* freely and openly. Diplomatic entanglements also restricted his actions. For President Díaz, Governor Kibbey, and the State Department, the Bisbee volunteers elicited all kinds of questions about Mexico's sovereignty and the meaning of American neutrality laws. As for consul Galbraith, Ambassador

---

of Nayarit, and was eventually honored after his death with the Decoration of Belisario Domínguez. Diéguez (who, ironically, was *presidente municipal* of Cananea from 1912 to 1913) was governor of Jalisco between 1917 and 1919. He supported the *delahuertista* revolt in 1923, only to be apprehended by the authorities and shot in 1924. See both Salvador Azuela, "Un miliciano de la Revolución," *El Universal* (Mexico City), 12 November 1955, pp. 3, 5, and Jesús Romeo Flores, "Maestros y amigos. Esteban B. Calderón: Precursor de la Revolución, maestro de escuela y constituyente," *El Nacional* (Mexico City), 11 October 1955, pp. 11, 19.

[61]Brown, "The Mexican Liberals," pp. 339–340; González Navarro, *El Porfiriato*, pp. 320–321; González Ramírez, *Fuentes*, III, 88.

David E. Thompson was pleased to announce to Díaz on 25 August 1906 that the State Department had replaced him with another consul, one "whose conduct, I hope, will be more prudent and acceptable than that of his predecessor."[62]

Díaz's solution for the problem was to whitewash the affair and to provide a reasonable defense and explanation for Izábal's behavior. Fortunately for the Sonoran governor, he had a good friend in Ramón Corral. Corral secretly wrote Izábal's public statement, which first appeared in the government press and was published later as an official *Informe* of the Ministry of Domestic Affairs. Rynning's volunteers were described as armed individuals with no uniform or insignia. According to the *Informe*, they were not even organized volunteers, but simply a group of people who had gathered out of curiosity and were concerned because they had friends and family in Cananea.[63]

Díaz was not about to admit the obvious: that Rynning and his friends had a long history of breaking strikes and Mexican heads, going back to the Morenci strike of 1903; that the Arizona Rangers worked closely with the Arizona Cattle Growers' Association and had as their principal task the protection of the livestock industry, including Colonel Greene's extensive empire along the San Pedro valley;[64] that the Bisbee volunteers were in Mexico to protect Greene's interests; and that, whatever the individual motives of the American forces, Díaz's governor was using them to protect American capital in a struggle with Mexican labor. Díaz could make a show out of the grand jury investigation of the governor (which eventually absolved him of any guilt), and he could force the governor's resignation after 1907. But the mother country had been violated, Díaz appeared to be Greene's lackey, and the PLM and Francisco Madero would not let him off the

[62]Rynning, *Gun Notches*, p. 312; Thompson to Díaz, 25 August 1906, CPD, leg. 31, doc. 010501.

[63]"Informe del Señor Gobernador de Sonora relativo á los disturbios ocurridos en Cananea, June 12, 1906," *Memoria de la Secretaría de Gobernación*, 1 December 1904–30 June 1906 (Mexico City, 1909, doc. no. 17), pp. 45–46, held by Fundación Cultural de Condumex, Archivo Carranza, Mexico City.

[64]Jay J. Wagoner, *Arizona Territory, 1863–1912: A Political History*, pp. 374–385.

hook.[65] Thus, in this way, Cananea was a catalyst of revolution in the history of Mexico.

The other unique dimension of the Cananea strike that distinguished it from earlier labor conflicts of the Porfiriato was the obvious presence of the PLM and of other agitators and socialists from the United States. The presence of the latter was due to the proximity of Cananea to the United States, the casualness of frontier crossings at that time, and the obvious cultural, geographical, and economic interdependence of Arizona and Sonora. As for the PLM and the local Liberal clubs, they were radical and revolutionary, their ends were political, and their actions, at least indirectly, helped to bring about the strike.

To ask the question, as most historians have done, as to whether the Cananea strike was an organized revolutionary uprising or simply a spontaneous labor conflict, is to embrace logical fallacies. First, the question reflects the fallacy of the excluded middle. The strike was not an either-or situation but the result of many variables, including the organizing efforts of the PLM and the W.F.M. as well as the "spontaneous" outbursts of the angry mob. Again, to say that the Cananea strikers thought of themselves as "working Mexicans rather than Mexican workers" is to assert that nations are "more real" than classes and to deny the possibility of a nationalist, working-class struggle. From the PLM point of view, the strike was a political weapon, and "simultaneous" revolts were the materials from which social revolutions were made.[66] The other fallacy is that of question-framing. The wrong question is being asked, since the results of the strike, and the strike as a causative factor itself, are probably more meaningful matters than the question of the cause(s) of the strike.

From Díaz's perspective, the degree of the PLM involvement in the strike was irrelevant. The presence of the PLM in Cananea was obvious, both through the circulation of *Regeneración* and

[65]Madero, in his criticism of Díaz, called Cananea a national scandal. See *La sucesión presidencial en 1910*, pp. 206–208.

[66]For a different interpretation see Anderson, "Mexican Workers and the Politics of Revolution," pp. 101–105, 110–113. Also see Anderson's *Outcasts in Their Own Land: Mexican Industrial Workers, 1906–1911*, especially pp. 110–117. See, too, Stephen C. Crawford, "El Partido Liberal Mexicano y la huelga de Cananea," *Latinoamérica* 5 (1972): 138–164.

through the activities of the local Liberal clubs. The workers' cause was being articulated in the larger context of revolutionary ideology. It was an organized attempt to politicize the Mexican worker, develop class consciousness, and unify labor against capital and its ally, the Díaz state. Whatever the cause, the PLM was now identified with the violence and conflict of striking workers, and Díaz was not about to renounce his policy of protecting the privileged positions of foreigners in Mexico.

Those with a stake in the system had no academic questions to ask about the causes of the strike. Fenochio, Kosterlitzky, Izábal, Torres, Corral, Creel, Fall, Díaz, and Greene—all saw it as a combined W.F.M.–PLM conspiracy. The solution was obvious: jail or execute the local leaders; extradite, deport, kidnap, arrest, and harass PLM members in the United States; and, by all means, solicit the aid of the U.S. government in stopping the activities of Ricardo Flores Magón, *Regeneración*, and the St. Louis Junta. Thus it was the "unique" features of the specter of Cananea that aroused fears on both sides of the border and that made of Cananea a catalyst of *both* revolution and suppression in the history of Mexico and the United States.

The Lord said to Moses, 'Send men to spy out
the land of Canaan. . . .'

Numbers 13:1–2

4. Pursuing Rebels in the Land of Canaan

WHILE the fires of Cananea were still smoldering, the PLM began
its summer assault on the Díaz dictatorship. In a supplement to the
1 June edition of *Regeneración*, the editors issued the charges that
would be echoed by the critics of Díaz throughout the summer of
1906. First, Mexico's workers had been insulted by Greene and
treated unfairly because of their nationality. And, second, Díaz had
supported Izábel in his call for foreign help. According to the PLM,
Díaz was a traitor who had "asked that the feet of foreign legions
trample our soil and step over our brethren." It was he who had
petitioned the White House to protect "the Yankee Company
threatened by the indignation of those who have been fleeced."
Thus, the PLM asserted, the Mexicans' duty was clear—"convert
apathy into enthusiasm and fear into rage," resurrect the past hero-
isms of Ayutla and La Reforma, preserve the nation, step forward
and make "them stop in their work of treason!"[1]

The apparent failures of the Cananea strikers, as well as the
official repression that immediately followed, led the PLM to reap-
praise its situation. The local Cananea leaders had failed to initiate
and maintain a successful strike or to create a successful political
revolution. There had been problems of communication both between the Junta and the clubs and between the Liberals and the
workers. The major problem was one of inadequate resources—
funds, arms, ammunition, and fighting men. The need now was for

[1]*Regeneración*, 1 June 1906, translated copy enclosed in David E.
Thompson to the Sec. of State, 19 June 1906, Records of the Department of
State, Record Group 59, Diplomatic Despatches from U.S. Ministers in Mexico,
1823–1906, microcopy 97, vol. 183, roll 178, National Archives, Washington,
D.C. (hereafter cited as Dip. Des.), despatch no. 96.

more energetic leadership, propaganda, and organization. Thus the PLM, beginning with its patriotic appeals of 1 June and continuing through the summer, increased the level of propaganda, violence, and conflict with the hope of unseating the dictator by the end of the year.

In early June a circular entitled "General Instructions to the Revolutionaries" was sent out, followed by the aforementioned "Program and Manifesto of the Mexican Liberal Party" of 1 July. Both documents had been undergoing formulation for several months, but neither was issued until after the outbreak of the Cananea strike. They outlined general strategy and tactics as well as ideology and goals. The "Instructions" called for the *revoltosos* to rise up in arms if and when an uprising occurred at Cananea or at any other PLM center. Another signal for revolt was the eventuality of the arrest of any Junta member, since it was assumed that a government attack on the Junta would indicate that secret PLM plans had fallen into the hands of the enemy and that a general governmental assault on the entire organization was to follow. Finally, if these events did not materialize, the Junta would announce a future date for a general insurrection throughout Mexico. Although Mexican authorities and American businessmen thought that that day would be 16 September, Mexico's Independence Day, the Junta's leaders were evidently not eager to begin a revolution on a day when the authorities would be alert to signs of revolt. Thus the initial outbreaks did not occur until late September and early October.[2]

All during the summer of 1906 the American-based Liberals were most active in making preparations for the forthcoming revolution. Liberal clubs were organized in Brownsville, Eagle Pass, Laredo, Morenci, and Metcalf.[3] The major centers for revolutionary work and organization were the three border towns of Douglas, Del Rio, and El Paso. Munitions were obtained and smuggled across the Arizona and Texas borders into Mexico, and plans were laid for the invasion of Mexico via Agua Prieta, Jiménez, and Ciudad Juárez respectively.

[2]Fabela, *Documentos históricos*, X, 36–68.
[3]For the Morenci and Metcalf clubs see Isidro Romero to Sec. de Rel. Ext., 12 September 1906, AREM, L–E–1241, 3rd pt.

By the summer of 1906, Tomás Espinosa had replaced Lázaro Puente as president of the *Club Liberal Libertad* of Douglas, even though Puente continued as editor of the *revoltoso* newspaper *El Demócrata*. Through the Douglas club, PLM emissaries maintained contacts with Liberals in Solomonville, Clifton, Metcalf, Mowry, Morenci, and Cananea, as well as with the St. Louis Junta. Many of the Douglas leaders were experienced "agitators" like Abraham Salcido, who had been arrested for inciting riots during the Morenci strike of 1903 and had served three years at the territorial penitentiary at Yuma. After his release, Salcido had gone to Cananea and was active with Bruno Treviño and Plácido Ríos in the labor unrest there. Treviño was also active in the Mowry area. Under the leadership of these men the Douglas club had grown in membership to over three hundred by late August 1906.[4]

During August the Douglas group met almost nightly at a secret meeting place called the Half-way House, a restaurant between Agua Prieta and Douglas. There, plans were made for raiding stores, acquiring arms and ammunition, cutting telegraph wires from Douglas, blowing up railroad lines on both sides, and invading Sonora via Agua Prieta. Also meeting with the Douglas Liberals, unknown to the *revoltosos* at that time, was a spy in the pay of the Arizona Rangers. Intelligence obtained through this source was forwarded by Rynning to the Sonoran authorities, including Governor Izábal, General Torres, and Colonel Kosterlitzky.[5]

At Del Rio the leaders of the Liberal club were Pedro N. González, president, and Crescencio Villarreal Márquez, secretary. González was a perennial revolutionary, having smuggled arms as early as 1892. Márquez, who had been with Flores Magón in Laredo in 1904, was, in 1906, chief of the Texas-Coahuila district. Working through a political front known as the *Amantes de la Libertad*, and promoting PLM propaganda through two newspapers, *1810* and *El Mensajero*, Márquez smuggled arms and propaganda to Liberals in Jiménez, Coahuila, and Eagle Pass, Texas.[6] Márquez also maintained communications with Francisco Madero in San Pedro, Coa-

[4]Myers, "The Mexican Liberal Party," pp. 106–107; "Testimonio de Plácido Ríos," González Ramírez, *Fuentes*, III, 141–142.

[5]H. C. Wheeler to Joseph H. Kibbey, 14 August 1906, NF, case 283/1–3.

[6]Griner to Boynton, 13 May 1907, NF, case 5028/8.

huila; at this time, Madero was becoming disillusioned with the PLM and was forming his own Democratic Party movement.[7] In September 1906 and again in the summer of 1908 the Del Rio club would launch raids on Jiménez and Las Vacas respectively.

El Paso became the center of PLM activity during the latter part of 1906. By early September, Ricard Flores Magón and Juan Sarabia had joined Antonio Villarreal and Lauró Aguirre in El Paso. Even before Flores Magón arrived, several Liberal newspapers were being published there, including *La Bandera Roja, La Democracia, El Clarín del Norte*, and Aguirre's *La Reforma Social*.[8]

El Paso was strategically important for several reasons. First, there were many unemployed migrant workers in the area who would join the movement in the hope of receiving food and money. Second, El Paso was a railroad center with links to the prosperous ranches of Chihuahua (a source of provisions) and the mines and villages of Sonora and Coahuila. Most important, across the border was the city of Ciudad Juárez, a perfect revolutionary stronghold with a large population, a federal garrison, a wealthy customshouse, a few important banks, and several munitions stores. Control of Cuidad Juárez not only meant confiscated goods, munitions, and revenues for the revolution; it would also provide the PLM with a commercial center that would eventually have to be recognized by U.S. treasury and customs authorities.[9]

For several months before the Junta arrived in El Paso, Aguirre had been acting as the front man for the PLM (with Prisciliano G. Silva being the actual contact between the exile leaders in Canada and their followers elsewhere). Aguirre was a free-thinking socialist who did not always privately agree with the Junta but who went along in public to maintain solidarity. As a propagandist, he not only edited his own newspaper but also provided the printing press for *La Voz de la Mujer*. And he smuggled copies of *Regeneración* to railway workers across the border who then transported them to the interior of Mexico.[10]

[7]Madero to Márquez, 17 August 1906, in Fabela, *Documentos históricos*, X, 73–75.
[8]Francisco Mallén to Creel, 29 October and 20 November 1906, STC, box 26, folder 2b, and box 27, folder 9c, respectively.
[9]Myers, "The Mexican Liberal Party," pp. 113–114, 153–154, 161–163.
[10]Ibid., p. 113.

Aguirre also served as a kind of unofficial public spokesman for the PLM. Not one to shun publicity, he helped to stir public fears about anti-Americanism in Mexico with his open statements about PLM hopes and aspirations. For example, during the middle of August he was interviewed by a reporter for the *New York Herald*. In the article, which appeared with a 3″ x 4″ photograph of Aguirre, he spoke of the graft and corruption of Díaz's government, especially noting the tax evasions and concessions of the Terrazas clan of Chihauhua and the progress of the Liberal Party movement in Mexico. To an El Paso and American audience of Creel's and Terrazas's friends, he readily publicized the 1 July "Program" and outlined several of the PLM's educational, political, and economical goals.[11]

That the United States might intervene in Mexico to protect American interests was a PLM nightmare. To curtail such a possibility, the Junta's propaganda campaign included a direct public plea to Roosevelt and the American people. On 12 September the Junta sent an eleven-page statement to Roosevelt cautioning him about intervening in the forthcoming revolution. The Junta readily acknowledged their revolutionary goals and outlined the causes, characteristics, and objectives of the revolution. The anti-revolutionist theme was emphasized, with the Junta arguing that

> . . . armed intervention of the United States will not reestablish peace; on the contrary it will make war more terrible and more prolonged. . . . What would have been a simple revolution against Porfirio Díaz, of short duration and which would not threaten American interests, would be converted, by the intervention of the United States into an international war that would occasion enormous losses to the two countries in the struggle.[12]

The Junta, blending threats with pleas, sought to reassure Roosevelt that their revolution was exclusively against Díaz, not foreigners.

Yet Roosevelt's concern about anti-American uprisings in Mexico was shared by most of the American business community. After the violence at Cananea, many Americans were alarmed at the pos-

[11]*New York Herald*, 19 August 1906, encl. in Thompson to Robert Bacon, 28 August 1906, NF, case 100/14–16.

[12]Ricardo Flores Magón to Roosevelt, 12 September 1906, NF, case 100/88–89.

sibility that the uprising in Sonora was only the beginning of a determined effort to bring about the overthrow of Díaz and the expulsion of foreigners from Mexico. In spite of the Junta's assurances, their July "Manifesto" and subsequent press releases, as well as the news of the Douglas "conspiracy," served only to increase American fears. As was noted above, rumors then circulating in Mexico and the United States said that a revolt was to break out on Mexico's Independence Day, 16 September.

During the months of July and August, rumors of anti-American plots circulated in the United States. Most of the reports were generated by the Associated Press. Newspapers picked up the stories and ran articles declaring that Mexico's railway employees were attacking American workers and that General Bernardo Reyes, governor of the state of Nuevo León and a traditional rival of Díaz, was to lead the revolution. The Reyes story was given more credence when the reputable *Harper's Weekly* repeated the story in its August issue.[13]

During late July and early August the Department of State was inundated with inquiries from American citizens, most of them actual or potential investors concerned about the rumors of revolt. These letters ranged from simple inquiries about the credibility of the reports to questions about investment opportunities and the security of American investments in Mexico.[14] One individual preoccupied himself with a lengthy condemnation of Cananea's consul Galbraith for not raising the American flag over his office during the Cananea riots.[15]

As 16 September approached, the headlines became more hys-

[13]John A. Valis to Porfirio Díaz, 25 July 1906, CPD, leg. 31, doc. 008193 (encl. of clipping from *St. Louis Globe Democrat*); Broughton Brandenburg, "The War Peril on the Mexican Border," *Harper's Weekly* 50 (25 August 1906): 1198–1200, 1217.

[14]See the following, all from National Archives Microfilm Publication, Washington, D.C., Domestic Papers of the Department of State, Record Group 59 (microcopy 40, vol. 292, roll 171): Huntington Wilson to F. W. Wetmore, 26 July 1906; Alvey Adee to A. W. Faithfull, Esq., 28 July 1906; Robert Bacon to Dr. George C. Millikan, 2 August 1906; Bacon to Tabasco Land and Development Company, 2 August 1906; Bacon to J. H. Lindenberger, 9 August 1906; Wallach McCathran to Chief of Dept. of Justice, 14 August 1906; Bacon to Edward L. Hamilton, 14 August 1906.

[15]Ibid., Bacon to George Sytherland, 3 August 1906.

terical. Referring to troubles in Aguascalientes, the *St. Louis Post-Dispatch* declared in a front-page headline: "BULLETS DRIVE AMER-ICANS FROM TOWN IN MEXICO." On 14 September, it was reported by the *St. Louis Republic* that Douglas Liberals would kill twenty Americans for every Mexican deported to Mexico. Most newspapers reported in September, as did the St. Louis press, that "RIOTS ARE FEARED ON INDEPENDENCE DAY."[16]

On 24 July, Acting Secretary of State Robert Bacon informed Ambassador David E. Thompson of a report about an organization of Mexican railway workers in northern Mexico who planned the expulsion of foreign workmen on 16 September. Because of the obvious danger to American persons and property, Bacon sought assurances from Thompson concerning the security of American na-tionals.[17] On 31 July, the ambassador responded, indicating to Bacon that Díaz had assured him of the falsity of the report and that the chief officers of the *Gran Liga de Empleados de Ferrocarril* (Grand League of Railway Employees) were incensed over the great injus-tice the American press was doing to their order. Thompson then urged Bacon to take steps to silence the Associated Press, which was the main source of the rumors.[18]

That same day, 31 July, Thompson sent telegrams to all Amer-ican consuls in Mexico, ordering them to report on conditions in their areas of jurisdiction, especially the purportedly "sensational-ized" notices of anti-American revolts being published in the United States. Having been clued to the proper responses, it was not sur-prising that by 2 August twenty-four consuls had provided Thomp-son with dutiful testimony about the false nature of the American newspaper accounts. These consular reports were forwarded to both Díaz and the State Department on 3 August.[19]

[16]*St. Louis Post-Dispatch*, 2 and 13 September 1906; *St. Louis Republic*, 14 September 1906.

[17]Bacon to Thompson, 24 July 1906, U.S., Department of State, *Papers Relating to the Foreign Affairs of The United States*, pt. 2, 1906 (1909), p. 1125.

[18]Thompson to Sec. of State, 31 July 1906, CPD, leg. 31, doc. 010475.

[19]See the following, all from CPD, leg. 31: Thompson to U.S. consuls in Mexico, 31 July 1906, doc. 010477; the various consuls to Thompson, 31 July–1 August 1906, docs. 010472–010474, 010477–010484; Thompson to Sec. of State, 3 August 1906, doc. 010476; Thompson to Díaz, 3 August 1906, doc. 010471.

Deputy Consul General Edward Conley echoed these sentiments when he later reported that stories about a "Mexican Boxer
uprising" hurt Mexico but "do even more harm to American interests in that country [since] anything affecting the prosperity or
standing of Mexico becomes of more than mere neighborly interest
to Americans."[20] Although neither the consuls nor Thompson could
have known it at the time, the reports had some substance, for the
Gran Liga, in 1908, sponsored a major national strike on behalf of
the "Mexicanization" of the railroads.[21]

By the end of August, several complaints about the press in
general, and *Harper's Weekly* in particular, were being sent to the
State Department from citizens and officials in Mexico. On 28 August, sixty "prominent" Americans, residents of Chihuahua, wired
Thompson "to contradict the many false and sensational statements
in the press of our country and particular in HARPERS WEEKLY
of August 25th regarding uprisings against Americans."[22] Díaz himself complained to Thompson about the "yellow journalism" of
Harper's Weekly and the *New York Herald*, and suggested that the
editors were being most unfair in not allowing Vice-President Corral
to publish a response in their journals.[23] Finally, Thompson, once
again angered by the *New York Herald* article, told the State Department that the American reports were creating unrest among
Americans in Mexico and giving dangerous ideas to the "lower
classes." The only truth in all of these stories, asserted Thompson,
were the reports about the St. Louis Junta, whose newspaper definitely should be suppressed.[24]

These threats of a Liberal revolt and an anti-American uprising
were of great concern to the American financial and business community. Since the financial stability of the Díaz regime depended
on foreign investors, the PLM's plans for rebellion represented an
economic hazard as well as a political problem for Díaz's govern-

[20]Edward M. Conley, "The Anti-Foreign Uprising in Mexico," *The World
Today* 11 (October 1906): 1059.
[21]Ruiz, *Labor and the Ambivalent Revolutionaries*, p. 13.
[22]W. W. Mills to Sec. of State, 28 August 1906, NF, case 100/13 and
17–18.
[23]Díaz to Thompson, n.d. (late August 1906), CPD, leg. 31, doc. 010504.
[24]Thompson to Bacon, 28 August 1906, CPD, leg. 31, docs. 010505–
010507, or NF, case 100/14–16.

ment. As early as 2 June, New York papers ran headlines declaring: "Greene Copper Stock Drops on Riot News."[25] After the Cananea strike and the July "Manifesto," foreign investors became less willing to purchase Mexican securities.

Aware of the problem, American investors urged Díaz to issue a proclamation to the Mexican people showing what Americans and other foreigners had done for Mexico and the importance of American capital for Mexican development.[26] Díaz and the state governors hired public relations experts to promote an image of a tranquil Mexico. For example, even though PLM activity was very great in Veracruz, that state's "PR man" assured Boston investors that Americans were in no danger there and that Cananea was only a local labor incident of little importance.[27] Daniel Guggenheim, president of the American Smelting and Refining Company, joined Colonel Greene in issuing press releases stating that American property was safe in Mexico and that President Díaz was in control of the situation.[28]

Yet the rumors persisted, and by the second week of September the financiers of Wall Street definitely had the jitters. On 14 September, the *Mexican Herald* bureau in New York reported:

> . . . the investing public is disturbed by the reiterated rumors printed in American papers regarding a threatened anti-foreign movement and revolutionary outbreak.
>
> If trouble of any kind develops, no matter how comparatively trivial, the large interests which thus far have been able to keep the market of Mexican securities steady in the face of rumors should find it difficult if not impossible to hold up prices through the heavy selling movement which would be bound to follow.
>
> During the past week the movement of all Mexican securities has been unprecedentedly light, investors refusing to place their money in Mexican securities, preferring to wait. . . .[29]

Evidently, the statements by Greene and Guggenheim had little effect on the market.

[25]"Special" from New York to the *St. Louis Post-Dispatch*, 3 June 1906.
[26]E. H. Osborn to Díaz, 6 August 1906, CPD, leg. 31, doc. 010374.
[27]Alexander M. Gaw to A. W. Faithful, Esq., 2 August 1906, CPD, leg. 37, doc. 008742.
[28]Guggenheim, "American Property Safe in Mexico," *New York Herald*, 12 September 1906, CPD, leg. 31, doc. 010791.
[29]As quoted in Brown, "The Mexican Liberals," p. 351.

Then the fated hour arrived. It was 16 September, and the security forces were out in large numbers. The *Gendarmería Fiscal* was in waiting at Cananea. Federal troops were stationed at Nogales. Arizona Rangers and soldiers from Fort Huachuca were patrolling the line. But all was quiet. The Clifton raiders did not ride into Cananea. It was a celebration, so people were disorderly. It was a festival, so people were drunk. But there was no revolution.[30] W. W. Mills, consul at Chihuahua, summed up the general view when he noted: "Celebration passed peaceably and quietly as a Quaker meeting. 'Uprising' talk absurd."[31]

On 17 September, Cananea Consolidated Copper Company shares led all other Mexican stocks with a gain of 3 1/4 points. *The Mexican Herald* expressed the relief of the financial community, remarking that investors would no longer take such reports of anti-American uprisings so seriously.[32] The Latin-American Club and Foreign Trade Association of Mexico City was so thrilled that its members passed a resolution in support of Díaz stating "that there is not the remotest possibility of an outbreak against any foreigners."[33] That was on 19 September. Seven days later, Juan José Arredondo led his PLM rebels into the village of Jiménez, Coahuila, and the *magonista* revolt was underway.

A review of the various accounts of the summer of 1906 makes it clear that most American officials, in hopes of maintaining a desirable climate for foreign investments, chose to follow the official Mexican government line. This was partly due to the close working relationship between Thompson and Díaz and to Thompson's influence over the consular corps. Only after September did the actual extent of PLM activity become obvious to United States officials in Washington. Until then, official Washington had only been concerned about a few agitators in Arizona and an even smaller group of radicals in St. Louis.

Perhaps Consul General Alfred Gottschalk gave the most astute analysis, when, on 10 September, he reported to the State Depart-

[30]Fenochio to Díaz, 17 September 1906, CPD, leg. 65, doc. 002225.
[31]Mills to Thompson, 17 September 1906, NF, case 100/90–95.
[32]Brown, "The Mexican Liberals," pp. 352–353.
[33]James F. Coyle and James Arbuckle to Ignacio Mariscal, 19 September 1906, AREM, L–E–1241, 3rd pt.

ment that the rumors had already hurt United States trade relations with Mexico. Observing the political climate in Mexico, he
stated, somewhat prophetically,

> . . . that once General Díaz dies—and he is aging fast and not
> nearly so vigorous physically today as popular legends lead one to
> suppose—some political upheaval will take place which may, for a
> time, seriously threaten the peace of the country and the interests
> of foreigners pursuing moneymaking avocations here.[34]

Although Díaz was hardly on his deathbed, Gottschalk rightly
noted the relationship of Díaz's rule to the security of American
capital, and was aware of the obvious political threats to that rule.

Like Consul Gottschalk, Díaz knew that political conditions
were threatening, and even though a public profile had to be maintained, behind the scenes it was necessary to move against his PLM
enemies in the United States. The *magonistas* may have been portrayed as "bandits" and "local agitators" for popular consumption,
but privately Díaz knew (as did Thompson) that he was in a class
struggle with authentic revolutionaries. The specter named "Cananea" was not to be denied.

Although Mexico's spokesmen persistently declared that all was
peaceful in the country, Díaz was sufficiently concerned about the
growing unrest to call a series of special cabinet meetings. For
Díaz, rumors of unrest always meant the possibility of American
intervention, and, in any case, the distrust and increasing violence
in Cananea, Aguascalientes, and Chihuahua could undermine his
own government. From these meetings the decision was made to
commission the poet laureate Rafael de Zayas Enríquez to make a
thorough and confidential study of the situation. Zayas Enríquez,
a long-time Díaz supporter, had extensive experience and maturity
as a writer, lawyer, army officer, and deputy to Congress. In researching his study he traveled to the mines of Cananea and the
factories of Orizaba, and talked and lived with the workers.

A preliminary study on the troubles in Veracruz was sent to
Díaz on 17 July 1906. It was soon followed by the major report,
entitled "Confidential Notes Regarding the Political and Social Situation Which has been Brought About in the Country; its Causes

[34]Alfred L. M. Gottschalk to Bacon, 10 September 1906, NF, case 100/56.

and the Way to Ward off the Danger," submitted to Díaz on 3 August 1906.[35] In surveying the causes of the PLM movement, Zayas Enríquez concluded that the "Socialists" were exploiting the general discontent of the country in order to attack "industrialism" and the government. Politically, many groups were unhappy with regional bosses and the elite rule of the *científicos*. The "Socialists" had been able to gain political victories by manipulating industrial labor and articulating genuine grievances through the opposition press. The uprisings in Cananea and Aguascalientes were merely "forerunners of what is being worked up in other cities under the cover of the labor question." He concluded the first section of his study by saying, "I perceive that there is agitation below and alarm above."[36]

His recommendations were simple and direct. First, repression was not the answer; persecuted editors become martyrs. Second, "Nothing is so fatal in politics as the *laissez faire* doctrine. . . . The silence of kings is the justification of the charges made against them by the people." The solution was simple. Díaz must break his silence and demonstrate to the people that the government was justified in its actions at Cananea. Since the government press, *El Imparcial*, was already discredited in the eyes of the people, other voices and supporters would have to counter the propaganda of the "Socialists." To calm the immediate agitation, public opinion would have to be considered and modest actions instituted to relieve the grievances of labor. According to Zayas Enríquez, positive reforms would inspire confidence in the government—Díaz could overcome the revolution by leading it.[37]

Díaz was more than willing to improve the government's techniques of counterpropaganda (today called "disinformation"). *El Imparcial*'s editors were told to change their image. In 1907, the ministries of domestic and foreign affairs authorized Mexico's

[35]This report was unknown to the public until it was reproduced two years later in Zayas Enríquez's study of the life of Díaz, *Porfirio Díaz: La evolución de su vida*. An English version of this book was printed in the same year. Translated by T. Quincy Browne, Jr., it was called simply *Porfirio Díaz*. The "Confidential Notes" are found on pp. 224–243. Excerpts quoted from the report can also be found in Barrera Fuentes, *Historia*, pp. 194–197.

[36]Zayas Enríquez, *Porfirio Díaz*, pp. 224–237.

[37]Ibid., pp. 237–243.

consuls in the United States to hire "friendly agents" to use the American press to combat the "libelous and insidious publications" of the PLM. The consuls were also encouraged to make more creative use of the press by issuing news releases and interviews that discredited the *magonistas*. The St. Louis consul became an expert, portraying the PLM leaders in the local press as "swashbucklers," "fugitives from justice," and swindlers engaged in petty crimes against the poor.[38]

As for leading the revolution, Díaz preferred repression to reform. Enrique Creel was selected to direct a binational espionage system, and by November 1906 private detectives of the Pacific Cooperative Detective Association of Los Angeles and the Furlong Secret Service Company of St. Louis were in the pay of the Mexican government. In addition, the secret police were "modernized," customs officers were given greater authority, and Díaz's agents received new training in the modern science of cryptography.[39]

Concerning the workers, Díaz warned them after Cananea that he meant to maintain public order at any price. Future revolts (like Río Blanco) would be met with force and repression. Workers could plead their cases, but only with hats, not guns, in their hands. They would not be allowed to organize or strike.[40] As for the St. Louis Junta, the object was to suppress their publication and extradite them from the United States, whereupon they would join their Cananea comrades in the dungeons of San Juan de Ulúa.

Immediately after the outbreak of the Cananea strike, Díaz had in his possession evidence linking Flores Magón in St. Louis with confederates in Cananea. Some of these materials, such as the request by Guadalupe Mendoza for arms and ammunition from the Junta, dated back as early as November 1905.[41] Others connected Calderón and Diéguez with the PLM. For example, in Calderón's

[38]For examples of counterpropaganda, see M. E. Diebold to Sec. de Rel. Ext., 7 January 1907, and Miguel Macedo to Mariscal, 18 April 1907, in AREM, L–E–1243, 7th pt.

[39]Anonymous, "Como se descifran todos los documentos en clave; la clave del General Díaz era sensillísima," *El Demócrata* (Mexico City), 30 August 1924, p. 14.

[40]Ruiz, *Labor and the Ambivalent Revolutionaries*, pp. 24–25.

[41]Guadalupe Mendoza to Ricardo Flores Magón, 2 November 1905, CPD, leg. 31, doc. 006229.

abode Cananea authorities discovered his 6 April 1906 letter to Villarreal. Again, on inspecting the offices of the Oversight mine, company officials uncovered a letter written from Flores Magón to Diéguez.[42]

On 31 May, even before the strike, Díaz received a letter from Kosterlitzky in which was enclosed a 29 May statement by company manager A. S. Dwight. This memorandum contended that a Liberal revolution was brewing in Cananea with the ultimate objective of expelling all foreigners and overthrowing the government.[43] After the strike, several issues of *Regeneración* were found circulating among the workers by Commandant Juan Fenochio.[44] Thus, from the beginning, Díaz had few doubts that the Cananea strike was political in nature and had been precipitated and financed by the St. Louis Junta with the aid of their socialist allies in the United States.

As indicated, Díaz was complemented in his thinking by the views of Cananea company managers. James H. Kirk, an old mining companion of Greene and manager of the company's mining division, testified that the Cananea trouble could properly be "attributed to a Socialist club which has been in existence for a considerable time called 'La Junta'."[45] Greene and the other managers supported Kirk in his views of the strike's causes.

On 8 June, General Manager A. S. Dwight, in recalling the events prior to the strike, said that he had been informed on Tuesday, 22 May, that

> . . . there was a movement on foot among certain discontented people in camp to get up a strike among the Mexican employees of the company in order to assist in the propagation of a political movement which was being fomented by a party calling themselves Liberals, who took as their platform the principles enunciated by a certain group of individuals calling themselves a 'junta' who were located in St. Louis, Missouri, and who published a paper called *Regeneración*. I immediately took steps to verify the truth of this rumor, which at first seemed absurd and beyond belief. I was sur-

[42]Medina Hoyos, *Cananea*, pp. 39–40; Brown, "The Mexican Liberals," p. 337.

[43]Kosterlitzky to Díaz, 31 May 1906, CPD, leg. 31, docs. 006183–006184.

[44]Fenochio to Díaz, 12 June 1906, CPD, leg. 65, doc. 001203.

[45]"Testimony of James H. Kirk," n.d., CM files.

prised to find confirmatory evidence from all quarters of the camp and soon began to realize the necessity of making serious preparations for possible trouble.[46]

Thus, management's views aided greatly in shaping the thinking of Díaz and his lieutenants about Cananea.

In addition to the company's managers, an important source of information about Cananea came from the *Gendarmería Fiscal* in Sonora. Its most important officer was Colonel Emilio Kosterlitzky, who was stationed at Magdalena but roamed the greater part of Sonora. His immediate superior was Commandant Fenochio, and Kosterlitzky reported to both him and Díaz. Fenochio operated between Nogales and Cananea. Because of his bravery and audacity, Kosterlitzky became a living legend in Sonora and the Southwest.

Kosterlitzky had deserted the Czar's navy in the 1870s when the Russian fleet was in a Venezuelan port. From there he made his way to Mexico, where he eventually joined Lerdo de Tejada's army. In Mexico he worked his way through the ranks to become a full colonel. He was known as a tough, harsh disciplinarian who commanded the finest body of mounted troops in Mexico. "Stern eyed, erect, slender, and jut-jawed," he was in the best of Cossack traditions, with close-cropped hair and a sword for a swagger stick. He directed an espionage network second to none in Sonora—with an intelligence chief appropriately called *El Zoro* (The Fox). Although Kosterlitzky had fought Yaquis and *bandidos*, his main fame came with the Cananea affair.[47]

As early as 1 June, Kosterlitzky reported to Fenochio that "Gutiérrez de Lara is the principal leader of the revolt aided by that ex-Inspector of the Inconsequential ["ex-Vista de la Motita"], [Enrique] Bermúdez, and others of little account (like Bermúdez) who were writers of that filthy scurrilous sheet (*Regeneración*)." Fenochio, in turn, along with the editor of the Cananea *Herald*, reported to Díaz that the strike was the work of several socialist groups in the United States, including agitators from the Denver office of the

[46]"Testimony of A. S. Dwight," 8 June 1906, CM files.

[47]Clark A. Cubley and Joseph A. Steiner, "Emilio Kosterlitzky," *Arizoniana* 1 (Winter 1960): 12–14.

Western Federation of Miners.[48] Acting on this intelligence, Díaz did not hesitate to request from Ambassador Thompson and the State Department assurances that the U.S. government would assist in curtailing *magonista* activities, especially the military and propaganda efforts of the PLM.

In June 1906 the State Department was composed of highly competent individuals, and Mexico was the cornerstone of America's Central American policy. Elihu Root, formerly secretary of war, was secretary of state. As such, he had close personal relations with Mexico's ambassadors, first Joaquín Casasús and later Enrique Creel. Root's understudy at State was Robert Bacon, the first assistant secretary. Bacon had come to the department as a former Harvard graduate and partner in J. P. Morgan's banking firm. Alvey *"Semper Paratus"* Adee (as John Hay called him) and Huntington Wilson were second and third secretaries respectively. James Brown Scott was solicitor for the Department of State, a position that required him to advise the department on matters of international law, claims, and extradition of criminals.[49]

State's man in Mexico was, of course, David Eugene Thompson. Born in Bethel, Michigan, in 1854, he began his livelihood in 1872 as a laborer in the employ of the Burlington Railway in the state of Nebraska. A self-made man, he demonstrated conspicuous ability as a manager, and by 1881 he was superintendent of the Burlington lines west of the Missouri. After 1890 he left the railway to become an investor, and by 1902 he owned and managed various enterprises, including the Columbia Fire Insurance Company of Nebraska, the *Lincoln Daily Star*, and a number of restaurants along the Burlington route. Between 1892 and 1899 he occupied a mansion that was the show place of Lincoln; it was later purchased by the Board of Public Lands and Buildings for use as the governor's mansion.[50]

[48]Kosterlitzky to Fenochio, 1 June 1906, CPD, leg. 31, doc. 006187; W. T. O'Donnell to Fenochio, n.d. (June 4?), with a duplicate copy to Díaz, CPD, leg. 31, docs. 006201–006202.

[49]Philip C. Jessup, *Elihu Root*, I, 514–515; Graham H. Stuart, *The Department of State: A History of its Organization, Procedures, and Personnel*, pp. 202–205; Bertram D. Hulen, *Inside the Department of State*, p. 26.

[50]David E. Thompson ms., Vertical File, Nebraska State Historical Society, Lincoln. See also, the *Lincoln Star*, 13 November 1950.

In 1900, Thompson, espousing both Populist and Republican issues, entered state politics. After a fierce struggle for control of the Lancaster county delegation to the Republican State Convention, he emerged victorious as the county's candidate for U.S. senator. Between 15 January and 28 March 1901, a major contest took place in the Nebraska Senate, where the principal business was the selection of the state's two U.S. senators. During the fifty-four ballots, the most formidable candidate was David Thompson. By 15 March, political boss Marcus Hanna was aroused enough to sue openly for peace. Finally, on 28 March, Thompson withdrew his name. Unable to gain the prize himself, he did have enough strength to dictate the election of the two successful candidates, Charles H. Dietrich and Joseph H. Millard.[51] In return, the two senators and Hanna persuaded Roosevelt to reward Thompson with the post of Envoy Extraordinary and Minister Plenipotentiary to Brazil, a position he accepted in October 1902, much to the relief of local Nebraska politicians.[52]

In spite of an incident in Rio de Janeiro in which the American consul general brought misconduct charges against him, Thompson, exonerated by Secretary Root, was raised to the grade of ambassador and allowed to retain that rank on his transfer to Mexico.[53] The appointment to Mexico generated much controversy. His political enemies alleged that he only wanted the post so that he could be closer to his business interests and that his scandalous personal life (a reference to his divorce and his marriage to his much younger stenographer) made him unfit for such a position. In spite of the

---

[51]Thompson's "Populist" platform included opposition to imperialism, entangling alliances, and military growth, as well as an appeal for "free silver." See "My Credentials," Thompson ms., Vertical File, Nebraska State Historical Society, Lincoln. Also see *Nebraska State Journal*, 5 January to 29 March 1901.

[52]Millard to Roosevelt, 11 August 1902; Hanna to John Hay, 11 September 1902; Dietrich to Roosevelt, 5 October 1902; Roosevelt to Hay, 9 October 1902—all from Records of the Department of State, Record Group 59, Service Applications and Recommendations, 1906–1924, National Archives, Washington, D.C. (hereafter cited as FSAR), David E. Thompson, 1902–1909, letters, news clippings, etc., 87 pp.

[53]"Thompson Under Fire," 6 December 1905 (news clipping), and Root, "Memorandum," 27 December 1905, FSAR.

critics, the two senators from Nebraska were once again able to persuade Roosevelt to deliver the political plum.[54]

As ambassador to Mexico, Thompson attracted a competent and faithful embassy staff and developed a close, personal working relationship with the aging dictator. William Franklin Sands (a perennial "trouble-shooter" for the Department of State) and Joseph C. Grew (later ambassador to Japan) worked as secretaries and found their boss "rugged, tough, powerful, intelligent, and shrewd." As the only ambassador accredited to Mexico, Thompson, like Henry Lane Wilson after him, was the dean of the diplomatic corps—an honor don Porfirio recognized when he offered Thompson a permanent escort of cavalry (which was refused—after all, Thompson had the services of the finest chauffeured car in all of Mexico City). Having the complete confidence of Díaz, trusted and well liked by the cabinet, he became a major power in Mexico and was greatly in demand at all the important social and political functions.[55] His only enemies in the American colony were business rivals (and their lawyers) who envied Thompson's access to Díaz and his business successes in and out of Mexico. It was these rivals who were eventually to force Thompson's resignation on 30 November 1909.[56]

Thompson's friendship and cooperation with Díaz (and the cientifico clique around Díaz) did not go unrewarded. As ambassa-

[54]D. Wright to Roosevelt, 9 November 1905; F. A. Harrison to Root, 22 January 1906; Thompson to Roosevelt, 2 April 1904; Dietrich to Roosevelt, 29 August 1904; Millard to Roosevelt, 17 March 1904; Joseph B. Foraker to Roosevelt, 26 November 1904; Thompson to Root, 24 January 1906—all from FSAR.

[55]William F. Sands and Joseph M. Lalley, Our Jungle Diplomacy, pp. 123–129, 133–149; Joseph C. Grew, Turbulent Era: A Diplomatic Record of Forty Years, 1904–1945, pp. 30–31.

[56]Thompson's major error was in angering Lebbeus R. Wilfley, an American claims lawyer who specialized in getting the American Embassy to act as his collection agent. Wilfley represented some wealthy American rubber plantation interests who blamed their capital losses on Thompson, who allegedly influenced Díaz in litigation to invalidate their titles. After Thompson's resignation, Wilfley found a powerful alley in Ambassador Wilson. See the anonymous "confidential" letter to Thompson from the U.S. Senate, 7 May 1909, FSAR. See also Thompson to Taft, 17 May 1909, and Taft to Philander Knox, 28 June 1909 (with encl. of Wilfley to Carpenter, 22 June 1909), FSAR. Also see Wilfley to Taft, 15 May 1911, in Gene Z. Hanrahan, ed. and comp., Documents on the Mexican Revolution, II, pt. 2, 388–390.

dor, Thompson, in spite of his denials and those of his supporters, did make use of his public office for private gain. On receiving a leave of absence in March 1908, he traveled to the Isthmus of Tehuantepec to explore business prospects. In May 1909 he appealed to President Taft to allow him to stay on as ambassador, at least until January 1910. It now appears that he was motivated by a desire to use the authority of his office and the influence of Díaz to conclude a major business transaction before leaving his post. At the end of 1909, shortly before leaving office, Thompson formed a partnership with George I. Ham of the United States Banking Company. The company acquired the Pan-American Railway and organized the Pan-American Construction Company. The transaction involved the cooperation of Díaz and Minister of Finance Limantour, since it included a concession to the Pan American highway.[57]

In December 1910, Thompson, acting on behalf of his partner as an intermediary, sold the Pan-American Railway to the Mexican government, which merged it into the National Railways of Mexico. Although Ham's banking operation soon became defunct, Thompson made a very substantial profit from the transaction, estimated by Ambassador Wilson to have been between $350,000 and $500,000 (U.S.). After this deal, Thompson, much to the annoyance of Henry Lane Wilson, stayed in Mexico City until May 1911, a strong and loyal supporter of Porfirio Díaz to the end.[58]

Thompson's special services for Díaz began shortly after his arrival in Mexico and were focused on the troubles at Cananea. Two days after the outbreak of the strike, Ambassador Thompson met personally with Díaz. At that meeting he was informed by Díaz that the strike had been initiated by at least twenty revolutionaries at Douglas and Cananea who were inspired from headquarters in St. Louis. This information the ambassador dutifully reported to the State Department the same day.[59] On 19 June, Thompson, having

[57]"Leave Records," David E. Thompson, FSAR; Thompson to Taft, 17 May 1909, FSAR; Henry Lane Wilson to Knox, 10 May 1911, Hanrahan, Documents, II, pt. 2, 359–366 (with encl. of Thompson-Ham contract).

[58]Wilson to Knox, 10 May 1911, RDS, file 812.00/1803. See also Hanrahan, Documents, II, pt. 2, 357–366, 388–390, and "Testimony of Sherburne G. Hopkins," U.S., Congress, Senate, Investigation of Mexican Affairs, II, 2559.

[59]Thompson to Díaz, 3 June 1906, CPD, leg. 31, doc. 007217. See also Thompson to Díaz, 5 June 1906, and Thompson to Sec. of State, 3 June 1906 (copy to Díaz), CPD, leg. 31, docs. 007221–007222.

received several copies of *Regeneración* from President Díaz, forwarded them to the State Department. In the accompanying dispatch he said that Díaz "has told me the publishers of the paper are anarchists in all that they advocate and on his expressed sentiments, I venture to suggest that if these men could be dealt with as such men should be, the President would feel a deep gratitude."[60] Throughout the summer, with rumors of impending anti-American uprisings on all sides, Thompson continued to provide the acting secretary of state with data and information about the editors of *Regeneración*, each time indicating, as he did on 28 August, that "President Díaz would be most grateful if these individuals were treated as anarchists" and their publication suppressed.[61]

On 5 July, having been urged to act by Thompson, and following the advice of the State Department's solicitor, the acting secretary of state ordered copies of *Regeneración* forwarded to the attorney general's office. Referring to the "alleged Mexican anarchists" living in St. Louis, Assistant Secretary Adee indicated that "the [State] Department would be glad to have your views [the attorney general's] as to what measures, if any, can be taken against the newspaper in question."[62]

By 12 July, the U.S. attorney for eastern Missouri, David P. Dyer, was ordered by the Justice Department to begin an investigation of the St. Louis Junta, and by 16 July copies of *Regeneración* had been forwarded to Dyer's office. After examining the copies, Dyer concluded that the Junta members could be punished under both civil and criminal law. In addition, he noted that "if the Editor of this publication is an alien and an anarchist, it seems that he can be deported" under the provisions of the Immigration Act of 1903. In order to expedite the investigation, Dyer requested that a secret service agent be assigned to his office. By the end of August, operative Joe Priest was ordered by the Treasury Department to report to U.S. Attorney Dyer.[63]

[60]Thompson to Sec. of State, 19 June 1906, Dip. Des.

[61]Thompson to Bacon, 28 August 1906 (copy to Díaz), CPD, leg. 31, docs. 010505–010507.

[62]James Brown Scott to Bacon, 2 July 1906, Dip. Des., no. 79; Adee to the Acting Attorney General, 5 July 1906, Records of the Department of State, Record Group 59, Domestic Letters, microcopy 40, National Archives, Washington, D.C. (hereafter cited as Dom. Letters), vol. 291, roll 170.

[63]See the following, all 1906: Act. Att. Gen. to Dyer, 12 July; Act.

During the same period, Díaz had asked the United States to curtail the movement of arms and munitions into Mexico. In July, Roosevelt created a special posse to patrol the border in cooperation with Arizona Rangers, customs officers, and U.S. marshals.[64] In August, after the Nogales collector of customs had noted the folly of trying to stop arms while Mexican officials were allowing Mexicans to cross the border with arms and ammunition, Díaz issued a decree that restricted the legal movement of munitions into Mexico to only those individuals specifically authorized by the federal government.[65] Finally, from September through November, members of the Fifth Cavalry were assigned border duty to enforce the embargo. American troops were withdrawn at the end of the year, having successfully completed their mission.[66]

Concerned about the constitutional and legal questions that enforcement of the embargo elicited, on 31 August the solicitor of the State Department requested a legal opinion from the Department of Commerce and Labor. Secretary Lawrence Murray answered that the joint resolution of Congress of 22 April 1898 restricted to seaports the president's power to prohibit the export of war materiel. He suggested that since the current legislation was inadequate, both departments should initiate new proposals to the next Congress to strengthen the law. Without another law, Murray argued, the shippers could be advised against the movement of contraband, and of the possible risks involved, but could not be stopped. Eventually a new law was passed, but it did not happen until Senator Elihu Root introduced the idea to Congress in 1912.[67]

Meanwhile, the rumors circulating that summer about an im-

Att. Gen. to Dyer, 16 July; Dyer to Act. Att. Gen., 24 August; Act. Att. Gen. to Act. Sec. of Treasury, 27 August; Act. Sec. of Treas. to State, 29 August—all from RG 60, file no. 43718.

[64]Loeb to H. M. Hoyt, 24 July 1906, RG 60, file no. 43718; Bacon to Kibbey, 21 July 1906, Dom. Letters, vol. 292, roll 171.

[65]Bacon to Sec. of Treas., 9 August 1906, Dom. Letters, vol. 292, roll 171; Thompson to Díaz, 21 August 1906 and Thompson to Sec. of State, 18 August 1906 (copy to Díaz), CPD, leg. 31, docs. 010497–010498.

[66]Acting Sec. of War to Commander, Dep't. of Colorado, 8 September 1906, NF, case 283/6–7.

[67]Lawrence O. Murray to Sec. of State, 4 September 1906, NF, case 283/20.

pending anti-American uprising in Mexico came to fruition during the first week of September. Ambassador Thompson, forwarding information Díaz had received from Kosterlitzky, reported that an army of five hundred to eight hundred men were planning to move against Cananea from Arizona before 10 September. Another group of fifty were reportedly marching from Sierra Los Ajos.[68] Reacting to this news, Roosevelt instructed the State Department to "go to the utmost limit in proceeding against these so-called revolutionists," and placed on alert the departments of War, Justice, Treasury, and Commerce and Labor.[69]

On 5 September, at the request of Izábal, thirty Arizona Rangers, accompanied by immigration officials and the local sheriff, raided a meeting of the *Club Liberal Libertad* in Douglas. Seventeen members of the revolutionary junta were arrested by the federal attorney for Arizona and held under section 5286 of the Revised Statutes (relating to hostile expeditions). Most had been under surveillance for weeks. Although seven of them were soon released for lack of evidence, the others were detained for deportation hearings.[70] Around the same time, immigration inspector J. J. Murphy accompanied other Arizona Rangers in the arrest of "agitators" in the Mowry and Patagonia mining camps north of Nogales. Murphy feared that these *revoltosos* were planning to lead an army of miners into Nogales, Sonora, to attack the customhouse and arsenal.[71] These persons were also to be deported.

In reporting these events to Dyer, J. L. B. Alexander, the U.S. district attorney for Arizona, noted that the arrests had led to the acquisition of a large amount of correspondence between Ricardo Flores Magón in Toronto and the officers of the Douglas club. These letters instructed the rebels on invasion plans and provided commissions for revolutionary officers. All of this directly implicated the St. Louis Junta. For attorney Dyer this meant that the stakes were now much higher. This was not simply an obscure immigra-

[68]Thompson to Bacon, 5 September 1906, NF, case 100/20.

[69]Roosevelt (Loeb) to Bacon, 6 September 1906; Bacon to Roosevelt, 6 September 1906, NF, case 100/26.

[70]W. F. Nichols to Sec. of State, 7 September 1906, NF, case 100/37; Alexander to the Attorney General, 8 September 1906, NF, case 100/32.

[71]Brown, "The Mexican Liberals," pp. 347–349; *St. Louis Post-Dispatch,* 4 September 1906.

tion violation or a libel case being initiated by an irate citizen; this was the big time—a violation of the neutrality laws of the United States of America.[72]

Dyer was about to initiate action against the St. Louis editors of *Regeneración*, but events were moving too quickly from another direction. On 12 September, before the St. Louis attorney had completed his investigation, a group of deputy sheriffs and private detectives seized the office of *Regeneración* on Lafayette Avenue. The sheriff took charge of the property under provisions of an attachment and libel suit for $2,500 filed in the circuit court by Norton Chase, the New York lawyer who represented Cananea's copper magnate, William C. Greene. The suit charged that on 15 July 1906 the defendants were guilty of libel when they published in *Regeneración* the allegation that Greene had bribed Governor Izábal of Sonora as part of a cover-up scheme to disguise "Yankee" violence at Cananea.[73]

Greene, well aware of the Arizona arrests and fearing a new series of revolutionary uprisings on 16 September, had decided to strike a fatal blow at the central Junta before the revolution could begin. On 4 September, his personal secretary requested from A. León Grajeda, Mexico's vice-consul in New York City, a letter of introduction for Chase to present to the consul in St. Louis. The next day, Chase traveled to Washington and talked to Bacon at the State Department and to Balbino Dávalos at the Mexican Embassy. The Mexican chargé d'affaires, obviously impressed by Chase's senatorial ambitions and personal determination, assured him of the cooperation of the St. Louis consul in their common cause against the Junta.[74]

From Washington, Chase went to St. Louis, where he conferred with consul Rafael de P. Serrano and St. Louis immigration inspec-

[72]Alexander to the Attorney General, 9 September 1906, NF, case 100/33; Alexander's telegram to St. Louis authorities is quoted by Dyer in his letter to the Attorney General, 16 September 1906, RG 60, file no. 43718. Canadian authorities were surprised to learn that the PLM headquarters was probably in either Toronto or Montreal. See *The Montreal Daily Star*, 6 September 1906.

[73]*St. Louis Globe-Democrat*, 13 September 1906.

[74]León Grajeda to Sec. de Rel. Ext., 4 September 1906, and León Grajeda to Serrano, 4 September 1906, AREM, L–E–1240, pt. 2; Dávalos to Sec. de Rel. Ext., 5 September 1906, AREM, L–E–1240.

tor James R. Dunn. Although Bacon had been most sympathetic to him, showing Chase Roosevelt's orders, and although federal attorneys and immigration inspectors had provided him with useful information, he had been advised by State that the federal courts had no jurisdiction in the matter. Therefore, on 11 September he instituted a civil suit in the Missouri State Court, naming Manuel Sarabia, Librado Rivera, Antonio Villarreal, and four others as defendants.[75]

While Chase was in St. Louis preparing his suit against the PLM, the State Department was involved in its own discussion about the proper actions to take. As indicated, Bacon had been briefed by Chase on 5 September concerning Greene's decision to take legal action against the Junta. Chase had urged the State Department to initiate criminal proceedings against the *magonistas*. A few days later the department received from the St. Louis Junta and Lauro Aguirre letters that had been addressed to Roosevelt. The Junta denied allegations about being "anarchists," and Aguirre urged Roosevelt to curtail the actions of Governor Kibbey with regard to the Douglas group.[76]

Adee and Scott quietly exchanged notes on Greene's concerns and the PLM's situation. Adee cautioned that " 'Suppression' may be risky unless on legal grounds." Then, in order to reduce that risk, he outlined for Scott some possible measures, including prosecution for neutrality violations, a conviction for fraud or obscenity under the postal laws, a possible state action for incitation to the commission of a crime, or the initiation of a criminal libel suit. Scott was more cautious, asserting that it "is not customary for governments to prosecute for libels on foreign potentates." Observing the language of Thompson's dispatches, he noted that the "terms 'anarchist' and 'assassin' . . . naturally occur to the lips of those intrenched in power who fear others seeking their place."[77]

Later after reading the July "Program and Manifesto," Scott

[75]Greene to Bacon, 12 September 1906, NF, case 100/39.
[76]Editors of *Regeneración* to Roosevelt, 7 September 1906, NF, case 100/31; for Aguirre's letter see Arizona *Daily Star*, 7 September 1906, encl. in Arturo Elías to Sec. de Rel. Ext., 8 September 1906, AREM, L–E–1241, pt. 3.
[77]"Memorandum," Adee to Scott, 11 September 1906, and Scott to Adee, 12 September 1906, both NF, case 100/31.

concluded that the document contained no incitation to a felony and that it was not against the libel laws of the United States to advocate the overthrow of the government of Mexico. Unimpressed with either Chase's or Dyer's arguments, Scott considered it inadvisable to request proceedings of a criminal nature, that is, to act as Díaz's second. Thus, on 12 September and immediately afterwards, Adee and Scott agreed not to make any specific legal recommendations to either the attorney general of the United States or the governor of Missouri. Instead, all that was done was to forward copies of Thompson's dispatches to them, and it was left to the Justice Department and the attorney general of Missouri to decide if a legal case existed.[78]

Although the federal attorney for Missouri had suggested to Greene the possibility of a civil suit, Governor Joseph W. Folk and Attorney General Herbert S. Hadley were not likely to take steps against *Regeneración*. Folk was a well-known "Progressive" reformer, a student of international law, and a friend of organized labor. Hadley, a Republican serving a Democratic governor, was a "trustbuster" unfriendly to and preoccupied with Standard Oil's monopolies in Missouri. He too was in the best of "Progressive" traditions and was sympathetic to labor, saying publicly that the laws and the courts were there to protect labor as well as the rights of property. Thus, it came as no surprise when Folk reported to the State Department that the laws of Missouri did not provide for any summary possession of the *Regeneración* office.[79]

Yet the Junta's office had been closed by a "private" citizen. The sheriff's action was of dubious legality, but it was not ineffective. Flores Magón's publication would not appear again until June 1907, when the Junta resurrected it under the new name of *Revolución* from their headquarters in Los Angeles. And even though the PLM leadership, with the exception of Villarreal, was not in St. Louis at the time of the seizure (being scattered between Canada and Texas), the few remaining members of the PLM in St. Louis

[78]Scott to Adee, 27 September 1906, NF, case 100/89; Adee to Taylor, 12 September 1906, NF, case 100/31.

[79]Louis G. Geiger, *Joseph W. Folk of Missouri*, XXV, 3–15, 90; Herbert S. Hadley papers, collection no. 6, folders 50–64; ms. collection, University of Missouri, Columbia; Folk to Bacon, 17 September 1906, NF, case 100/81.

were eventually arrested or forced to flee from official harassment.[80]

As for Ricardo Flores Magón, Chase confided to the St. Louis consul that he was in Toronto (he was actually in El Paso at the time) and that extradition could be easily facilitated.[81] Attorney Dyer was also still willing to help, completing his initial investigative report in late September and reporting to the attorney general as late as November that "every effort has been made by the officers of the department of Justice and of the Postoffice department at this place in conjunction with the mexican consul and furlong secret service company to locate magon."[82] No statement could better testify to the intergovernmental and intragovernmental assault on the *magonistas* than this one by the St. Louis attorney.

The questionable legality of the St. Louis operation did not prevent the authorities from acting similarly in the future. Within two weeks of the St. Louis action, Ambassador Thompson requested the suppression of *La Reforma Social*, Aguirre's *revoltoso* publication in El Paso. Again the wheels of "justice" were set in motion, with Thompson's request being forwarded to the attorney general of the United States and the governor of Texas.[83] Between 1906 and 1910, at least ten *revoltoso* publications were seized by American officials, the properties attached, and the editors arrested. The more infamous of these acts included the suppression of the aforementioned *Revolución* in Los Angeles and Práxedis Guerrero's *Punto Rojo* in El Paso.[84]

Greene's activity in St. Louis was neither the beginning nor the end of his crusade against the PLM and their American allies. His cause was one with that of the Mexican government, which was in a serious struggle for political survival. After the suppression of *Regeneración*, his friend Luis Torres told him:

[80]See the *St. Louis Post-Dispatch*, 21 November 1906, and the *St. Louis Globe-Democrat*, 3 December 1906.

[81]Serrano to Sec. de Rel. Ext., 14 September 1906, AREM, L–E–1241, pt. 3.

[82]Dyer to Hoyt, 6 November 1906, RG 60, file 90755.

[83]Adee to Thompson, 29 September 1906, NF, case 100/106.

[84]Bartra, *Regeneración*, pp. 51–64. These practices also violated certain judicial interpretations that held that "the U.S. government has no power, under our Constitution and laws, to interfere with publications in the states criticising foreign governments or encouraging revolts against such governments." From John B. Moore, A *Digest of International Law*, VII, 980.

I know my dear Mr. Greene, that you are doing all your best to aid in every way the prosecution of the revolutionists, and I repeat here what I have said to you before, that never were interests more close-ly running on the same channel, searching for the same end, as are the interests of the Mexican Government and the interests of your company in trying to suppress radically all intent of disturbance along the frontier for the sake of Cananea. . . . To put an end to their evil doings . . . I have behind me all the protection of General Díaz and you have the aid of President Roosevelt and the backing of your company.[85]

And this kind of joint campaign would have to continue if the "po-litical agitators" were to be stopped.

When the PLM struck Cananea, they hit the very flesh and marrow of Greene's being, and nothing less than a blood feud could satisfy the injury. Greene was persuaded that high-ranking mem-bers of the St. Louis Junta had actually engineered the strike from Ronquillo. To State Department officials, Greene alleged that Manuel Sarabia, an editorial writer for *Regeneración* and a found-ing member of the Junta, had been in Cananea during the last days of May and had left only two hours before the strike started. Sa-rabia, Greene contended, had published handbills, made inflamma-tory speeches, and aided in organizing the mob. Although he later rationalized his vendetta against Manuel Sarabia on the grounds that he had confused Manuel with his cousin Juan, in 1907 he did not hesitate to defend the Mexican government's attempted kid-napping of Manuel Sarabia.[86]

Greene was particularly disturbed by the activity of Lázaro Gutiérrez de Lara. Speaking of Gutiérrez de Lara's role in the Cananea riot, company manager A. S. Dwight said that "De Lara's part in this uprising was that of a virulent local agitator, who did all he could to stir up race hatred against the Americans." Of all the local strike leaders, only Gutiérrez de Lara succeeded in fleeing from his captors, eventually going to Los Angeles. When Greene learned of his presence in Los Angeles, he arranged for Gutiérrez de Lara's arrest and had charges brought against him for stealing firewood from Greene's Mexican property. The case, which was in-itiated in 1907, referred back to an incident that had taken place in

[85]Torres to Greene, 21 September 1906, NF, case 100/103.
[86]Greene to Bacon, 5 July 1907, NF, case 7418/5.

1903 when Gutiérrez de Lara, a practicing lawyer, had advised his client to cut wood on disputed land in order to establish the client's claim of ownership. Because Greene could not demonstrate his case to the court's satisfaction, the hearing was dropped and Gutiérrez de Lara escaped extradition.[87]

After the closing of the St. Louis office of *Regeneración*, Greene and his lawyer Norton Chase continued to pursue the radicals. According to the testimony of Senator Albert Fall, Chase delivered a large portion of the materials seized at St. Louis to U.S. border authorities. They in turn shared their information with Corral and the Mexican secret police. These materials included PLM membership lists and a directory of revolutionary agents. The seizure of these documents was a drastic blow to the PLM, since this information directly aided the Mexican and American authorities in their mid-October arrests of Juan Sarabia in Ciudad Juárez and Antonio I. Villarreal in El Paso. It further led to the arrest of dozens of Liberals in Mexico.[88]

On 1 December, Greene was in El Paso as a government witness in the indictment against Villarreal. Shortly thereafter he joined Chase in San Antonio, from where they jointly traveled to New York City. Before going to New York, Greene and Chase helped to persuade Vice-President Corral to hire Judge J. G. Griner of Del Rio, Texas, as a special assistant and informer. Judge Griner was charged with investigating the Jiménez rebels. Both Chase and Corral hoped to extradite the sixty-five persons who had followed Juan José Arredondo in the raid on Jiménez during the past September.[89]

One reason for Greene's persistence in these matters was his conviction that representatives from the Western Federation of Miners had been involved in the Cananea strike. In his memorandum to company officials on 11 June 1906 he stated "that a socialist club had three meetings at midnight on the night of the 30th of May . . . [and] that agitators of the Western Federation of Miners had been through the mines inciting the Mexicans, and that they

[87]For both Dwight's and Gutiérrez de Lara's account, see U.S., Congress, House, *Alleged Persecutions*, pp. 20–22, 95.

[88]Fall to President Woodrow Wilson, 30 July 1913, Fall Papers.

[89]Norton Chase to Ramón Corral, 1 December 1906, AREM, L–E–854, 118–R–5. For the hiring of Griner see Enrique Ornelas to Ignacio Mariscal, 6 December 1906, AREM, L–E–854, 118–R–5.

had been furnishing money for the socialistic club that had been established at Cananea."[90] Greene's views about W.F.M. participation were supported by all of the important company managers, auditors, and engineers, such as Dwight, Kirk, Young, and A. B. Wadleigh.

Atherton Wadleigh was a mechanical engineer, inventor, and efficiency expert. From 1899 to 1902 he was employed by Bethlehem Steel, where he became good friends with Frederick W. Taylor, a man who was then developing a solid reputation as a systems analyst (and who would become a famous efficiency expert with his own scientific theories). In 1902, Wadleigh came to the attention of Greene while contracting workers in Denver for strike-breaking assignments in Arizona and Sonora. He soon joined Greene's operation at Cananea as a supply manager, minor stockholder, and unofficial consultant—adopting many of the ideas of "Taylorization" for Cananea. In the June strike of 1906, he commanded a group of deputized employees who guarded the Greene mansion.[91]

In describing the strike a few weeks later to Taylor, he testified that Greene's bravery and tact had saved the plant and that the strike and violence had been caused by members of the American Miners' Union, who had used the Mexicans as tools to achieve their own ends. Wadleigh's reference was undoubtedly to the American Labor Union, which was called the Western Labor Union at the time of its formation in 1898 in Salt Lake City by the Western Federation of Miners. The A.L.U., a part of the W.F.M., had affiliates consisting of Colorado railway workers, coal miners' locals, and western hotel and restaurant workers. Its official organ, *The Voice of Labor*, featured socialist writers. In 1905, some of its delegates were involved in launching the I.W.W. Thus, Wadleigh's testimony complemented that of Greene and the other managers.[92]

To investigate the links between the W.F.M. and the PLM, Greene had the services of a hired labor spy, the Cananea com-

[90]Greene, "Brief resumé," 11 June 1906, CM files.

[91]See Wadleigh to Taylor, 5 June 1902; Wadleigh to Taylor, 10 March 1902; Taylor to Wadleigh, 8 October 1902; Wadleigh to Taylor, 5 June 1902; Wadleigh to Taylor, 9 March 1904—all from Frederick W. Taylor Collection (Correspondence), A. B. Wadleigh File, 1899–1908, folder 106B, Stevens Institute of Technology, Samuel C. Williams Library, Hoboken, New Jersey.

[92]Ibid., Wadleigh to Taylor, 25 July 1906.

pany's police commander, Chief Rowen. He also had the intelligence services of the Manufacturers' Information Bureau of Cleveland, Ohio. Rowen actually worked his way into the inner circles of the W.F.M. leadership in Denver. By July, he could report that, for several months, funds originating with the local in Butte, Montana, had been redirected through the Denver headquarters to a W.F.M. organizer in Bisbee, Arizona. From Bisbee, the organizer, Joe Carter, distributed money and literature to "agitators" in Nacozari and Cananea. From the Information Bureau, Greene received copies of the "Official Proceedings" of the May 1906 convention of the W.F.M. in Denver—the convention that had passed a resolution in support of the Cananea workers' strike for higher wages.[93]

As late as December 1906, Greene maintained the services of a special agent in Denver. At this time his informant reported that Greene's New York City business rivals were financing the W.F.M. with the hope of undermining his operations in Mexico.[94] With these kinds of alarming reports, it was no wonder that the colonel, whose business and health were both beginning to fail, was so preoccupied with *revoltoso* fever. By February 1907, Greene Consolidated Copper Company exchanged shares with Greene Cananea Copper Company, an action that took the company out of Greene's hands. Suffering a nervous breakdown in 1908, Greene finally died on 5 August 1911, having lived long enough to witness Madero's revolt and the occupation of Cananea by *revoltoso* Juan Cabral. Ironically, Cabral, a Cananea boy, had been educated in the United States, where he came under the influence of Greene's old enemy, Lázaro Gutiérrez de Lara.[95]

In October 1906 the Junta, now operating on Texas soil, issued a new set of "Revolutionary Instructions," calling for all revolutionists to attack the Mexican government but, in the process, to respect the rights of "neutral" foreigners.[96] Before these plans could go into effect, however, the PLM's plots were foiled by the joint actions of

[93]Rowen to Greene, 20 and 23 July 1906, Fall Papers; H. J. Temple to Greene, 25 June 1906 (with encl. of M. G. Turner to H. J. Temple, 19 June 1906), Fall Papers.

[94]David Cole to Greene, 12 December 1906, Fall Papers.

[95]Sonnichsen, *Colonel Greene*, pp. 253–257.

[96]"Instrucciones," 15 October 1906, in González Ramírez, *Epistolario y textos*, pp. 64–66.

U.S. and Mexican authorities. By appealing openly to Roosevelt, and by operating publicly with declarations of intent and guarantees of protection for foreigners, the PLM may have aided in its own undoing. Although they were not anarchists in 1906, the suppression of that year not only radicalized them but made them go further underground. The next round would be characterized more by guerrilla warfare than by revolts designed to ignite mass insurrection. It was no accident that, in 1907, the editors changed the name of *Regeneración* to *Revolución*.

As has been indicated, the greatest setback had been the October arrests of Villarreal and Aguirre in El Paso and of seventeen Liberals in Ciudad Juárez, including the Junta's vice-president, Juan Sarabia, and the PLM general-in-chief, César Canales. These arrests, testimony indeed to the efficiency of Creel's binational police and espionage network, had been facilitated by the undercover work of double agent Adolfo Jiménez Castro, a captain of the federal soldiers stationed in Ciudad Juárez.[97] Thus, even though 1906 witnessed PLM uprisings in Sonora, Coahuila, Veracruz, and Tamaulipas, planned revolts in Cananea, Nogales, Agua Prieta, Sierra Los Ajos, Nacozari, Parral, Matamoros, and Ciudad Juárez failed to take place because of official opposition. The apex of PLM activity was over; many Mexican Liberals were in jail in Mexico, Flores Magón was in hiding, and the forces of suppression were rapidly ascending.

A binational police system was taking shape. The voice of Díaz for Americans was David Thompson, whose businessman's values complemented those of Enrique Creel and William Greene. In fighting the *magonistas*, the colonel had both the resources of his own company and those of two governments. Roosevelt, unafraid to interpret the constitution broadly and expand his presidential powers if the situation demanded it, aided Díaz by using the police and military authority of the nation to curtail *revoltoso* activity. In this matter he was aided by local, federal, and territorial authorities, including Rangers, cavalry, customs officials, immigration officers, federal attorneys and marshals, and even private detectives.

True, a few small, legalistic, and libertarian voices were heard

[97]Silvano Montemayor to Creel, 20 October 1906, STC, box 27, folder 12a.

at the departments of State and Commerce and Labor. Yet the solicitor's office was a very small part of the bureaucracy, most of which
was hostile to the *revoltosos* and in support of Díaz. And when
Greene and Chase came to Washington, they made appointments
with Roosevelt, Root, and Bacon, not with Scott and Adee. In Mexico, Juan Sarabia joined dozens of other rebels from Cananea, Ciudad Juárez, Nogales, Veracruz, and elsewhere in the cells at San
Juan de Ulúa. Now Thompson (Díaz) wanted American-based
revoltosos brought into Mexican prisons—and thus began the campaign of deportation.

> . . . the United States has delivered its military
> and civil resources into the hands of the Ty-
> rant.
>
> John Kenneth Turner

5. The Deportation Campaign

IN surveying the plight of Mexico's rebels in the United States between 1906 and 1911, John Kenneth Turner described what he
called Díaz's "campaign of deportation"—the practice of carrying
numerous refugees across the border to face the summary methods
of Mexican "justice." He listed the various schemes as, first, to institute extradition proceedings under charges of "murder and robbery"; second, to deport through the Bureau of Immigration under
charges of being "undesirable aliens"; third, "to kidnap outright
and feloniously carry across the line." As a PLM partisan, Turner
was not likely to be an objective source, but his observations, although lacking details in some cases, were generally correct, especially for the period between the closing of the St. Louis office of
Regeneración in September 1906 and the arrest of Ricardo Flores
Magón in Los Angeles in August 1907.[1]

Extradition occurred under the provisions of the 22 April 1899
treaty between Mexico and the United States (as supplemented by
the agreement of 25 June 1902). The original treaty contained nineteen articles, with article II listing twenty extraditable crimes and
offenses—including murder, rape, bigamy, piracy, arson, burglary,
robbery, forgery, counterfeiting, embezzlement, kidnapping, larceny, mayhem, and the "malicious and unlawful destruction of railways." Article IX allowed extradition to be initiated on either the
state or federal level for crimes committed in the frontier states.
Article X stipulated that the accused could be detained no longer
than forty days while awaiting the production of evidence upon
which the extradition claim was founded.[2]

[1]Turner, *Barbarous Mexico*, p. 235.
[2]Charles I. Bevans, comp., *Treaties and Other International Agreements*

Two provisions were especially important for the *revoltosos*. Article III, section 2, excluded individuals from extradition "when the crime or offense charged shall be of a purely political character." Although the definition of "political" was unclear, all extraditable crimes, with the exception of an attempt against the life of a head of state, could legally be declared political offenses (depending on the temperament and "politics" of the magistrate, the motivation of the defendant, and the circumstances of the crime). If and when this happened, the accused escaped extradition. Article III also excluded those individuals who had previously undergone punishment for the crime or offense for which extradition was being demanded.[3] Thus, the language of article III limited the scope of extradition to exclude those PLM radicals and aliens whose prior acts were either political or had been punished in Mexico.

One of the earlier and more celebrated extradition cases was that of Librado Rivera in 1906. Because Díaz had failed to apprehend Ricardo Flores Magón in the El Paso arrests and because the revolutionists appeared to be on the run, the Mexican government instituted extradition proceedings on 26 October against Rivera and several other Junta leaders and *revoltosos*.[4] By the end of October, after a warrant had been issued for the arrest of Rivera, David P. Dyer, the U.S. attorney at St. Louis, was informed by the attorney general as to the street address of Librado Rivera and other suspects.[5] Dyer, in turn, contacted the local postal and immigration authorities, and consulted with the Mexican consul and the office of the deputy U.S. marshal.[6]

The Mexican colony lived in the impoverished DeKalb and Convent Street area of St. Louis. The Villarreal sisters (Andrea and Teresa) and their sixty-one-year-old father, Próspero, inhabited a dismal upstairs apartment at 123 Convent. Next door, at 125 Convent, were three women and three small children—a Señora Sau-

---

of the United States of America, IX, 900–907 and 918–919. See also U.S. Department of State, *Papers* (1908), pp. 595–597.

[3]Bevans, *Treaties*, pp. 902–903.

[4]Bacon to the Attorney General, 30 October 1906, RG 60, file 90755.

[5]Balbino Dávalos to Bacon, 29 October 1906, and Attorney General to Dyer, 31 October 1906, both RG 60, file 90755.

[6]Dyer to the Attorney General, 1 November 1906, and Dyer to Hoyt, 6 November 1906, both RG 60, files 90755/92649 and 92809 respectively.

cedo and her child; Felice Sarabia (mother of Juan Sarabia); the wife of Librado, Evarista Concepción A. de Rivera; and the two Rivera infants. On 6 November, two men disguised as gas company employees came to the house at 125 Convent. When a man who called himself Herber Koro answered the door he was arrested, even though the detectives carried no warrant and were uncertain as to the true identity of the man. Koro, who claimed to be from Argentina, was turned over to immigration inspector James R. Dunn, who sent him to the city hospital for "observation." There the arrested man was identified by another Mexican as Librado Rivera.[7]

A few days later another resident of the Rivera household ran into trouble with the authorities. Although his Anglo associates called him A. L. Apple, the Mexican community in St. Louis knew him as Aaron López Manzano (a man known to his intimates and the Mexican authorities as A. L. Saucedo).[8] López Manzano had been a typesetter in the *Regeneración* office at the time of the September raid and, believing himself to be immune from arrest, had remained in St. Louis after that date.[9]

On 13 November, after having been followed for several days, López Manzano was arrested at the general delivery window at the St. Louis post office. He was taken into custody by Deputy U.S. Marshal W. W. Noll on the charge of taking mail addressed to another. In custody, López Manzano soon joined Rivera at a preliminary hearing held behind closed doors before U.S. Commissioner Chase Morsey. After the hearing the two men were secretly placed aboard a train heading south toward Mexico.[10]

Although a cloak of secrecy surrounded the arrest, hearing, and forced departure of the men, the two Villarreal sisters eventually learned of the men's fate and declared to the local press that the two were "being 'railroaded' to Mexico to be shot for opposing the administration there."[11] The *St. Louis Post-Dispatch*, which had reported as early as September 8 that, "as a matter of international comity, Díaz would like to have Roosevelt's Big Stick used on the

---

[7]*St. Louis Post-Dispatch*, 18, 20, and 21 November 1906.

[8]M. Diebold to Sec. de Rel. Ext., 20 November 1906, AREM, L–E–1245, pt. 9.

[9]*St. Louis Post-Dispatch*, 21 November 1906.

[10]*St. Louis Post-Dispatch*, 21 November 1906.

[11]Ibid.

regenerationists as soon as possible," was most sympathetic to the plight of the Mexican aliens. By the third week of November their writers were drawing historical parallels between the *magonistas* and Missouri's Civil War heroes who had been forced to flee to Mexico in the 1860s, and were openly denouncing the "Spanish American methods" being introduced from Mexico City to Washington "in open violation of American precedents, constitution and laws."[12]

As the whole affair began to come to light, the St. Louis newspapers continued to run stories about the dreadful living conditions of the women and children of Convent Street. They publicized their abject poverty, dire financial straits, and dependence on charity.[13] That is, the publicity was favorable to the aliens, whereas the federal officers were viewed as unfeeling men who did not play fair. Sometimes the authorities hurt their own image, as when an immigration inspector said that "he had been looking for a legal excuse to deport the Mexicans, and if they were put in the poor house or became public charges they could be deported under the law."[14]

As the St. Louis press began reporting the story of Rivera and López Manzano in full, a public reaction against the authorities set in. With the secrecy surrounding the exiles shattered, the authorities altered their plans. When the train transporting the two *revoltosos* pulled into Ironton, Missouri, some seventy-five miles south of St. Louis, their captors were ordered by telegram to place the exiles in custody in the local jail.[15] A short time later the two Mexicans were returned to St. Louis by U.S. marshals.

Back in St. Louis, López Manzano was given a hearing before Commissioner Morsey on the charge of violating the postal laws. On 1 December, López Manzano was released on his own recognizance, promising to return on 3 January 1907 if the grand jury returned an indictment.[16] Instead, he quickly fled to Monterrey (Nue-

---

[12]Ibid., 24 November 1906.

[13]Ibid., 18 November 1906; *St. Louis Globe-Democrat*, 21 November 1906.

[14]*St. Louis Globe-Democrat*, 21 November 1906. Also quoted in Axelrod, "St. Louis and the Mexican Revolutionaries," p. 106.

[15]Fuentes, *Historia*, pp. 206–207; Axelrod, "St. Louis and the Mexican Revolutionaries," pp. 106–107.

[16]*St. Louis Post-Dispatch*, 1 December 1906.

vo León). In April he was arrested by Mexican officials, who were assisted by none other than Thomas Furlong, the famous St. Louis private detective. López Manzano was eventually sent to Belem prison in Mexico City, an unhappy victim of Díaz's highly effective police system.[17]

In the meantime, Rivera, having been charged by the Mexican authorities with murder and robbery for his alleged participation in the Cananea strike, was brought before U.S. Commissioner James R. Gray for a preliminary extradition hearing in St. Louis. On 30 November, the commissioner released to the press the statement that "it appeared from the proofs that the offense complained of was entirely of a political nature, [thus] the said defendant, Librado Rivera, was discharged."[18] On his release, Rivera wisely withdrew from sight, eventually emerging with Flores Magón in California.

The reputation of the federal authorities had been slightly tarnished as a result of the short-lived *cause célèbre*. Although the *Globe-Democrat* called the release of Rivera "an act of justice," the *Post-Dispatch* was more explicit:

> The developments of the week make it seem likely that the plan arranged between somebody in the City of Mexico and somebody in Washington will fail at least of its main object of getting possession of the "Junta" at wholesale. It would be undiplomatic to say that the whole proceeding, regardless of pretexts of the immigration laws, was in the nature of an attempt at kidnapping.[19]

James Brown Scott and others at the State Department had been ignorant of the entire Rivera affair, but it is obvious that the local federal officials—Dyer, the U.S. marshals, the immigration inspectors, and even Commissioner Morsey—had been involved in a kind of conspiracy. Unlucky in this instance, yet undaunted, the Mexican government would try again in January, when a request for the extradition of Rivera on the charges of attempted robbery, murder, and "damage to the property of others" (the latter was not an extraditable offense, as Scott reminded the Mexicans) was filed with the

[17]González Ramírez, *Epistolario y textos*, pp. 108, 174–175. López Manzano's Belem correspondence can be found on p. 107.

[18]*St. Louis Post-Dispatch*, 30 November 1906.

[19]As quoted by Axelrod, "St. Louis and the Mexican Revolutionaries," p. 107. See also *St. Louis Post-Dispatch*, 2 December 1906, and *St. Louis Globe-Democrat*, 3 December 1906.

office of the secretary of state.[20] Meanwhile, the "extraditionists" were initiating another offensive at Del Rio, and Juan José Arredondo was to be the major attraction.

After the Jiménez uprising of 26 and 27 September, Díaz sent orders to Governor Miguel Cárdenas of Coahuila demanding the arrest of the revolutionists in northern Mexico and Texas. He was most insistent that the Jiménez outrage called for the use of the death penalty as an example to others. In sending these orders, Díaz made it clear that if *revoltoso* heads were not produced, his state officials would be obliged to lend him their own—with drastic changes in official circles being threatened as the price of failure.[21] Since the consul at Eagle Pass had reported in early October that Del Rio was the southwest Texas headquarters of the St. Louis Junta and the center of operations for revolution in Coahuila, an extradition dragnet was ordered for the entire region.[22] By 24 October, the Mexican government requested the provisional arrest of Arredondo and sixty-five others, who were charged with robbery, assault, and murder in connection with the disturbances at Villa Jiménez. Cárdenas sought their extradition from the governor of Texas under article IX of the treaty of 1899.[23]

To prepare the Mexican government's case against the Jiménez rebels, Corral, on the recommendation of Norton Chase, hired J. G. Griner. Griner, the Val Verde county judge, was originally employed to prosecute Arrendondo and five others in the extradition hearings of 1906, but was later retained as a legal representative and informant for the Mexican government in Texas.[24] In preparing his case, Griner was assisted by San Antonio consul Enrique Ornelas; secret service agent Joe Priest; the U.S. attorney for western Texas, Charles A. Boynton; the U.S. district commissioner; and officials of the local immigration office. Developing a broad strategy, Griner reported to the consul that complaints had been filed before a variety of federal governmental agencies and that, if extradition were denied, they would try again under the Bureau of Immigra-

[20]Godoy to Sec. of State, 26 January 1907, RG 60, file 90755.

[21]*St. Louis Globe-Democrat*, 22 November 1906.

[22]Francisco de Villasana to the Governor of Texas, 5 October 1906, AREM, L–E–1241, pt. 5.

[23]Dávalos to Sec. of State, 24 October 1906, RG 60, file 90755.

[24]Hanrahan, *Documents*, I, pt. 1, 88–89.

tion. And, he noted, "those that we cannot get under the Immigration Department or under the Extradition Proceedings, as now on trial, we will have tried for violating the United States Neutrality laws."[25]

Arredondo and five other alleged revolutionists underwent extradition proceedings in San Antonio from the last part of December to 5 January 1907. In spite of the best efforts of Griner and Boynton, the U.S. commissioner, though indicating that the evidence was sufficient to show "probable cause," held that the acts complained of were of a "purely political character" and excluded under article III of the Extradition Treaty. The defendants were then discharged. However, in a practice that was to become all too common, Arredondo was immediately served with a warrant by immigration inspector R. G. Callahan and taken into custody on the grounds that he was an alien in the United States without inspection.[26]

Although the board of inquiry recommended the deportation of Arredondo, Judge Walter Gillis, Arredondo's Del Rio attorney, appealed the decision to the secretary of commerce and labor, who, in agreement with the secretary of state, discharged the order.[27] With the failure to extradite or deport Arredondo, proceedings against the sixty-five others were eventually withdrawn, even though the San Antonio immigration inspector was willing to make applications for warrants against them for illegal entry (an especially peculiar charge for the Mexican Americans among them).[28]

With Arredondo free, Enrique Creel became even more nervous about conditions along the Texas frontier, especially at Eagle Pass, where Arrendondo and the *revoltosos* were allegedly preparing for another invasion.[29] By the end of April, it was obvious to Creel that neither Boynton nor Griner could develop sufficient evidence

[25]Griner Report, December 1906, 6 pp., AREM, L–E–854, 118–R–5.

[26]All of the major San Antonio newspapers covered the Arredondo hearings between 17 December 1906 and 7 January 1907, including the *Daily Gazette*, and the *Daily Light*. See also Boynton to the Attorney General, 23 March 1907, NF, case 5028/4–6, and Luther C. Steward to F. P. Sargent, 6 January 1907, RG 60, file 90755.

[27]U.S., Congress, House, *Alleged Persecutions*, p. 56.

[28]Steward to Sargent, 6 January 1907, RG 60, file 90755.

[29]Creel to Sec. de Rel. Ext. 28 March 1907, AREM, L–E–1243, pt. 7.

to warrant criminal proceedings, secure indictments, or justify convictions against Arredondo and the others.[30] Momentarily dropping the idea of a neutrality case, Creel induced Root to request from the secretary of war the stationing of troops at Del Rio and Eagle Pass. Root also requested the assignment of a special military investigator for the frontier. By late June, Captain William S. Scott, a cavalry officer from Fort Sam Houston, was assigned to special army intelligence duty to investigate "the doings of Mexican emigrados on the American side of the boundary line."[31] Meanwhile, Arredondo was decoyed across the line into Mexico on the promise of immunity. There he was arrested and taken to Belem prison, where later he "conveniently" died.[32]

Although the Mexican government had not been successful in extraditing the Jiménez rebels, its officials had gained valuable experience for the future. With the services of Griner, Boynton, and now Scott, a binational espionage structure was taking shape. Mexico's lawyers were becoming more adept in dealing with the subtleties of American law. And, in spite of the limitations of the Treaty of Extradition, it was obvious that extradition proceedings could be used to harass and detain the *magonistas* and provide authorities with additional information that could be used later in deportation and criminal cases. Throughout it all, the cooperation of U.S. marshals and immigration officials with Mexico appeared to be certain.

Thus, in 1909, the Del Rio grand jury had no trouble in delivering several indictments against *revoltosos* who had been involved in the Las Vacas uprising of June 1908. One lifetime resident of Del Rio, Calixto Guerra, was detained for sixteen months on extradition and neutrality violation charges before his release in January 1910. Although he was never found guilty of any of the charges, his detainment had been most effective. Another Las Vacas *revoltoso* and long-time resident of Texas was Guillermo Adán. Adán had escaped from the Ciudad Porfirio Díaz jail and was arrested in Texas and confined at Eagle Pass for an extradition trial. U.S. Commissioner Joseph O. Boehmer refused the extradition and ordered Adán dis-

[30]Creel to Sec. de Rel. Ext., 25 April 1907, AREM, L–E–1243, pt. 7.
[31]Root to Sec. of War, 8 June 1907, NF, case 5028/9–10; Bacon to Robert Shaw Oliver, 21 June 1907, NF, case 5028/7–8.
[32]U.S., Congress, House, *Alleged Persecutions*, p. 60.

charged. Then, as had been the case with Arredondo, he was immediately rearrested by immigration inspectors for entering the United States at night without inspection. Adán was kept in jail for fifteen months before finally being freed.[33]

The practice of detaining aliens beyond the forty-day period stipulated by article X of the treaty became common. Inez Ruiz, who had been a political prisoner in Mexico for seven years, escaped to the United States, only to be arrested by a U.S. marshal in October 1909. He was held for forty days awaiting extradition charges. At the end of that period, he was released, rearrested, and held for a second forty-day period. He, too, was finally released in January 1910, when the commissioner determined that his crime was of a political nature.[34] Ruiz's case was not unlike that of Gutiérrez de Lara, who was held in the Los Angeles county jail in 1907–1908 for three consecutive forty-day terms.[35]

Thus the general tactics first outlined by Griner in 1906 were used in the years immediately prior to the Revolution of 1910. Although extradition convictions were rare (due not only to the language of the treaty but also to the legal services provided aliens by the aforementioned League for the Protection of Political Refugees), detentions and harassment were politically as effective as convictions. It is apparent that in too many of these cases extradition was simply a prior condition of deportation. This was true of Arredondo, Adán, and Gutiérrez de Lara. It was also the case with Antonio Villarreal in late 1906 and early 1907.

As was indicated previously, Villarreal was captured in a raid in El Paso shortly after midnight on the morning of 20 October. The success of this action was due to the efforts of a government spy, Adolfo Jiménez Castro, a captain in the federal garrison at Ciudad Juárez. On the evening of 19 October, Jiménez Castro accompanied a force of young revolutionaries across the international bridge from El Paso into Ciudad Juárez. The group thought they were going to seize the municipal jail. Instead, Jiménez Castro led them into a police trap near the customs office, where they were arrested. He then returned to El Paso to lead American authorities in the capture

[33]Ibid., pp. 53–56.
[34]Ibid., pp. 56–57.
[35]Ibid., pp. 23–27.

of seven *revoltosos* who were meeting in a house near the river. Of those captured the most important were Lauro Aguirre, editor of *La Reforma Social*, and Pedro González, better known as Antonio Villarreal.[36]

A few hours after their capture, Villarreal and Aguirre were charged by the U.S. marshal for the western district of Texas with violating the neutrality laws, that is, with launching a military expedition into a country at peace with the United States. Steps were taken to hold the men for a forty-day period in order to permit the Mexican government to make its case for extradition. By the end of October, both Villarreal and Aguirre had the familiar extradition charges of murder, robbery, and assault brought against them. In Aguirre's case, the charges harked back to offenses allegedly committed in Chihuahua in 1896 and 1897 during the *teresista* phase of his political life.[37]

Realizing in advance the weakness of its extradition case, the Mexican Embassy was soon persuaded by Greene's lawyer, Norton Chase, to institute immigration deportation proceedings against Villarreal in lieu of extradition. On 6 November, the Department of Commerce and Labor transmitted a warrant to the El Paso immigration inspector for the arrest of Villarreal. Six days later the extradition charges were dropped. So as to clear the way for deportation, Boynton was ordered by the Justice Department, which was acting on the advice of the Mexican Embassy, to dismiss all neutrality violation charges. Thus, by the end of November, Villarreal's fate was in the hands of a Special Board of Inquiry of the Immigration Service meeting in El Paso.[38]

Villarreal had been specifically charged under sections 2 and 21 of the Immigration Act of 1903. Section 2 excluded any person

[36]W. Tovar y Bueno, "Los precursores de la Revolución," *La Prensa* (Mexico City), 11 October 1932; El Paso *Herald*, 20 October 1906; El Paso *Times*, 20 October 1906.

[37]Boynton to the Att. Gen., 20 November 1906, RG 60, file 90755; James Rudolph Garfield to the Att. Gen., 10 November 1906, RG 60, file 90755/91997; Dávalos to Sec. of State, 28 and 29 October 1906, RG 60, file 90755.

[38]Chase to Root, 5 November 1906, NF, case 1741/9; Dávalos to Sec. to Sec. of State, 6 November 1906, NF, case 1741/10; Garfield to T. F. Schmucker, 6 November 1906, RG 60, file 90755; Att. Gen. to Boynton, 12 and 23 November 1906, RG 60, file 90755/91997.

who had been convicted of a crime involving moral turpitude; section 21 provided for the return of all aliens within a three-year period after the date of their illegal entrance into the United States. It was demonstrated to the board that Villarreal had been convicted of the crime of manslaughter in Monterrey in 1901 and that he had not been in the United States over three years. Two out of the three members of the board originally voted against deportation, but on 20 November, after further evidence had been received, the board reversed itself and voted unanimously for Villarreal's deportation.[39]

In the meantime, Villarreal's sisters in St. Louis were launching a national campaign in support of their brother. Hundreds of petitions from workers in Texas and California and from socialists in St. Louis were sent to the State Department and to President Roosevelt. Most either argued against Villarreal's extradition on political grounds or pleaded with Roosevelt to grant the defendant's lawyers sufficient time to present their case. Teresa and Andrea Villarreal told Roosevelt:

> All the accused have the right to defend themselves. Please grant to our brother Antonio I. Villarreal time enough to present his proofs. Let not him in [to] the hands of the tyrants of Mexico, where death awaits to [sic] the prisoners. It is not the land of Jefferson and Washington: that is a land of liberty, Justice! Justice![40]

The campaign on behalf of Villarreal was the first significant awakening of the radical community in America to the Mexican aliens' plight.

It is ironic that a letter from Andrea Villarreal to Roosevelt would eventually be used as evidence against Villarreal in his deportation case. After the El Paso Board of Special Inquiry had made its recommendation, its decision was forwarded to Secretary of

[39]Garfield to Att. Gen., 10 November 1906, RG 60, file 90755/91997; Boynton to Att. Gen., 20 November 1906, RG 60, file 90755; Dávalos to Sec. of State 6 November 1906, NF, case 1741/10; Garfield to Schmucker, 6 November 1906, RG 60, file 90755.

[40]Villarreal González sisters to Roosevelt, 26 November 1906, RG 60, file 90755. See also Andrea and Teresa Villarreal González to Roosevelt, 24 January 1907, NF, case 1741/34–35; Aurelio N. Flores et al., to Roosevelt, 27 November 1906, NF, case 1741/22; Boynton to Att. Gen., 11 February 1907 (with an attached petition), NF, case 1741/43–45.

Commerce and Labor Victor H. Metcalf for review. He in turn sought an opinion from the Department of Justice. W. H. Moody, the solicitor, provided that opinion.

Moody held that although Villarreal as a political offender could not be extradited to Mexico, that fact had no bearing on his status as a violator of the immigration law. He also ruled that even though "this alien may be unjustly dealt with by the Mexican authorities," this in itself was not a proper excuse for not enforcing the deportation order. Concluding that Villarreal had not acted in good faith when presenting his testimony before the board, Moody recommended to Commerce and Labor that the decision of the Board of Special Inquiry be upheld. His only reservation concerned the question of the identity of the alien, who claimed to be Pedro González, not Villarreal. On this matter he entered evidence that had not been available to the board, a letter written from Villarreal's sisters and father in St. Louis on 18 November 1906—the authenticity of which conclusively established Villarreal's true identity.[41]

Thus, by 11 January 1907 the deportation order had been delivered by Villarreal's captors. At this point Villarreal's lawyers sought and received a thirty-day extension to produce evidence as to his right to remain in the United States. His lawyers now attempted to have Villarreal arrested on the earlier charge of violating the neutrality laws, in hopes of delaying deportation. Villarreal, as was his right, requested a special hearing on this matter. He desired to give evidence against himself that would bind him over to a grand jury—a jury that, incidentally, could not possibly deliver an indictment before April. A trial would further delay deportation. Villarreal was obviously a desperate man, preferring three years in a U.S. penitentiary on a neutrality violation to returning to Díaz's Mexico.[42] Villarreal's hearing took place on 25 February 1907. The U.S. commissioner at El Paso dismissed the government's original complaint charging Villarreal with violating the neutrality laws, and

[41]Moody to Metcalf, 8 December 1906, RG 60, file 90755.

[42]Oscar Straus to Root, 11 January 1907, NF, case 1741/26; Root to Att. Gen., 4 February 1907, NF, case 1741/36–37; Scott to Bacon, 4 February, 1907, NF, case 1741/39; Boynton to Att. Gen., 11 February 1907, NF, case 1741/43–45.

the immigration authorities at El Paso immediately took him into custody.[43]

On the way to the county jail, the charming Villarreal, who had been a model prisoner all along, was allowed the privilege of sending a last telegram to his family in St. Louis before departing for Mexico. His guard, a Texas employee named Tony Sierra, waited outside the Western Union office. Villarreal entered the building and immediately exited through the back door. He then caught a trolley to east El Paso and went into hiding at the home of an El Paso merchant and sympathizer. He eventually rejoined Flores Magón and Rivera in Los Angeles.[44] Alas, the "trials" of Villarreal had become a "trial" for Díaz, whose patience was wearing thin— not having had a deportation "victory" since early October in Douglas, Arizona.

The Arizona episode began in early September, when several *revoltosos* were arrested at Douglas, Mowry, and Patagonia by immigration inspectors accompanied by Arizona Rangers. Some of these individuals, like Bruno Treviño, Carlos Humbert, and Genaro Villarreal, were placed in the Nogales jail, where they joined many Mexicans who had been held incommunicado for several weeks. At this time the Arizona border was in a frenzy of excitement, with rumors of war, revolution, and jailbreaks on all sides. On 4 September the population of Agua Prieta became hysterical over the report that two thousand soldiers were marching on the town. American merchants in the Mexican towns of Nogales, Naco, and Agua Prieta packed their valuables and fled across the border, even though no one seemed to know if the troops were friendly or hostile.[45]

Meanwhile, Arizona Rangers concentrated at the line were making several arrests. Troops from Fort Huachuca were placed on alert and dispatched to Douglas as a "moral" act of support for the Mexican government. Phoenix authorities apprehended suspicious individuals and seized dynamite and explosives. The Mexican consul at Tucson, Arturo Elías, was directing arrests and sending warrants to Nogales, Douglas, El Paso, Laredo, and Eagle Pass. Most

[43]Boynton to Att. Gen., 2 March 1907, RG 60, file 90755.

[44]W. Tovar y Bueno, "Los precursores," *La Prensa*, 14 October 1932.

[45]Tucson *Citizen*, 3 and 5 September 1906; *Washington Times*, 4 September 1906.

American authorities and businessmen were certain that an anti-American uprising was about to begin in Mexico. It was not a good time for the Mexican community in Arizona, especially those who were dependent on the American government and constitutional traditions for their protection and well-being.[46]

Although many of those arrested had to be released for lack of evidence, several leaders and members of the *Club Liberal Libertad* were detained at Douglas and Nogales. Among those arrested were the present and past presidents of the club, Tomás de Espinosa and Lázaro Puente. Espinosa, "the biggest fish of all," was separated from the rest for special treatment. After being held in the Douglas jail for two weeks, he was assigned to a Douglas grand jury, which eventually delivered an indictment under section 5286 of the neutrality law. Espinosa was found guilty of the charge, fined one thousand dollars, and sentenced to two years' imprisonment at the territorial prison at Yuma. As for Puente, he and three comrades, Abraham Salcido, Luis García, and Gabriel A. Rubio, were transferred to the Tucson county jail. There they were joined by Treviño, Humbert, and G. Villarreal, who had been escorted by immigration inspector George W. Webb from Nogales to Tucson. All had deportation charges brought against them.[47]

Information found on the persons of Treviño and Rubio implicated Ricardo Flores Magón in the revolutionary activities of the Douglas club. One letter, written on 18 August and addressed to Treviño, indicated that the Douglas club should show extreme prudence because Flores Magón was "sure that Roosevelt had to do all in his power to prevent the fall of Díaz, his ally, who is delivering to him all the property of the nation."[48] Other correspondence to

[46]Bacon to Thompson, 7 September 1906; Guillermo Macalhín to Sec. de Rel. Ext., 3 September 1906; Elías to Sec. de Rel. Ext., 4 September 1906; Antonio Maza to Sec. de Rel. Ext., 4 and 8 September 1906—all AREM, L–E–1240.

[47]Corral to Sec. de Rel. Ext. 22 September 1906; AREM, L–E–1241, pt. 4; Pietro Ferrua, "Sources of Study on the Mexican Revolution, II: The Archives of the U.S. District Court of Southern California," *Bulletin Centre International de Recherches sur l'Anarchisme*, 31: 7; Malcalhín to Sec. de Rel. Ext., 5 September 1906, AREM, L–E–1240.

[48]R. Flores Magón to Treviño, 18 August 1906, encl. in Antonio Lozano to Sec. de Rel. Ext., 6 September 1906, AREM, L–E–1240, pt. 2.

Rubio spoke of revolutionary centers in Mexico, the planned uprising at Cananea, Greene's resources and the Cananea garrison, and the need to capture customshouses to obtain arms.[49] In addition, other incriminating evidence was obtained by the Mexican consul at Tucson, who intercepted all mail coming out of the county jail that was written by Treviño, Humbert, and Garcia.[50]

With this information, U.S. attorney J. L. B. Alexander assured Webb that deportation would be no problem, as it would not be necessary to apply all the technicalities of the law in these cases. With this advice, Webb, through the local consul and the Mexican Embassy, sought an opinion from the Department of State as to whether or not those detained could be deported in conformity with the immigration laws.[51] The solicitor's office rendered an opinion on 10 September.

Alvey Adee and James Brown Scott shaped the State Department's position on this matter. Adee noted that it had long been the practice of the United States that immigration laws could not be used in lieu of extradition, and that this principle was even stronger when the immigrants in question, like those at Arizona, were charged with political offenses. He also observed that deportation of criminals depended on evidence of actual conviction of some criminal, non-political offense (that is, to be charged, rather than convicted, was not sufficient). Scott, as the international legal expert, surveyed American immigration legislation back to the act of 1875 and concluded that the law exempted not only all political offenders (excluding anarchists) but all crimes "growing out of the result of such political offenses."[52] Meanwhile, on 10 September (without waiting for the State Department's advice), Webb initiated

49Ibid. Also see R. Flores Magón to Rubio, 31 May and 27 July 1906, encl. in Mariscal to Corral, 1 October 1906, AREM L–E–1241, pt. 5.

50Elías to Sec. de Rel. Ext., 10 and 13 September 1906, AREM, L–E–1241, pt. 3.

51Mariscal to Señor Enc. de Neg. *ad. int.* de México, 7 September 1906, and Maza to Sec. de Rel. Ext., 7 September 1906, both AREM, L–E–1240. See also Dávalos to Sec. de Rel. Ext., 8 September 1906, AREM, L–E–1241, pt. 3.

52Adee to Scott, "Memorandum," 8 September 1906; Scott to Adee, "Memorandum in regard to the expulsion of certain Mexican citizens now held as prisoners at Nogales by Immigration Inspector Webb of Arizona,"— NF, case 100/27.

immigration hearings before a Board of Special Inquiry at Tucson for six of the immigrants (not including Salcido, who had already provided the consul with a written confession).[53]

The investigations were conducted by Webb, who was acting in the absence of Arizona inspector J. J. Murphy. The interrogations were designed to bring out the connection between *revoltoso* activity on the frontier and the troubles at Cananea, and evidence was produced that demonstrated that all of the immigrants had at one time entered or re-entered the United States from Cananea—with Rubio and Treviño having been there during the June strike. Of all the questions asked, those directed at Humbert and Treviño were the most blatantly political, designed as they were to elicit "revolutionary" responses and root out heresy.[54]

After all the testimony had been taken, it appeared that a strong case in favor of deportation could not be made. As Puente's attorney noted, none of the accused fell under the "excluded persons" category of section 2 of the Act of 1903 (that is, idiots, insane persons, paupers, beggars, persons with loathsome and contagious diseases, persons convicted of a felony, anarchists, polygamists, prostitutes, contract laborers, and so forth). All were employed and honorable individuals with no previous arrest records in Mexico or the United States. All had passed over the line in the open, and had brought money with them. Most had not seen any inspectors when they crossed, although a few were inspected, including Puente, who had his luggage checked. Most were not strangers to Arizona— Puente had been in the United States for seventeen months and Rubio had lived in the country continuously (with the exception of five months in Cananea) for fifteen years.[55]

In order to recommend deportation the board had to rely on a technicality in the law. As has been mentioned, immigrants could be excluded from entry for physical or mental reasons. Therefore,

[53]Elías to Sec. de Rel. Ext., 11 September 1906, AREM L–E–1241, pt. 3 (with enclosures of Salcido's confession and Webb's interrogations).

[54]"Statements of Aliens and Related Findings of Board of Special Inquiry, 1905–1908," Records of field offices, District no. 15 (El Paso, 10 and 11 September 1906 [Tucson]), Records of the Immigration and Naturalization Service, Record Group 85, National Archives, Washington, D.C. (hereafter cited as RG 85), pp. 252–286.

[55]Ibid., "Statement by J. F. Ross," 10 September 1906, pp. 261–262.

a physical examination by the U.S. Marine Hospital surgeon was required of all applicants. Because the accused, ignorant of the requirement, had not made application for admission and were not inspected by the Public Health and Marine Hospital surgeon, they were considered to be in the United States in violation of the immigration laws.[56] Thus, although precedent and tradition exempted political offenders from the immigration acts, the Tucson board was more concerned with frontier conditions than legal principles. Obviously, "radicalism" in Arizona was a loathsome and contagious disease requiring inspection, isolation, and radical surgery.

Initially the Department of Commerce and Labor appeared to approve the board's deportation order. On 15 September, Abraham Salcido, who had readily admitted his revolutionary intentions to his captors, was taken to Nogales and turned over to the Mexican authorities by Inspector Webb. (It should be remembered that Salcido was greatly disliked by the Arizona Rangers, who remembered his strike activities in Morenci in 1903 and who knew him only as a convicted felon who had served time at the Yuma penitentiary.) From Nogales, Salcido was taken to the state prison at Hermosillo.[57]

The others were also notified of their impending deportation and told to prepare themselves for the trip. On learning of the deportation order on 17 September, Puente sent a last farewell to his son then living in Douglas. In a moving statement he told him: "I am a victim of the hatred and persecution of prominent people. These are men without honor—when the word 'justice' comes from their lips, it is always spoken sarcastically."[58]

Then, on 20 September, much to the consternation of the Arizona and Mexican authorities, the Department of Commerce and Labor reversed itself. The department had obviously been influenced by the opinions of many citizens who had been flooding the government with letters and telegrams arguing that "to deport is to execute." The secretary of commerce and labor, after having reviewed the board's evidence, was more impressed by the immigration officers' failure to inspect and attend to their duties than by the

[56]Ibid., "Action by Board," 10 and 11 September 1906, pp. 269, 286.
[57]Washington *Post*, 15 September 1906.
[58]Puente to his son, 17 September 1906, AREM, L–E–1241 (encl. in Elías to Sec. de Rel. Ext., 18 September 1906).

supposed guilt of the *revoltosos*. He curtly ordered Webb to have the immigrants medically examined and the results reported. Fearing that their prisoners would be released, Webb and Elías immediately prepared a new brief, attaching to it this time English translations of the confiscated letters as well as written assurances from Díaz that the deported *revoltosos* would be guaranteed their rights under Mexican law.[59]

Two days later, Webb sent the commissioner-general of immigration a lengthy argument in favor of the *revoltosos'* deportation. In shaping his discourse, Webb had the support of district attorney Alexander, who had earlier called the Douglas group "plotters" and "conspirators." Alexander, like Webb, was more concerned with their political behavior than with specific immigration violations.[60]

Webb began his letter with a defense of the boundary officers, noting that it was very easy for a well-dressed Mexican to cross the border at points where there was a town on both sides. Then he made his major point:

> It is a very serious thing and treated very seriously by the residents of these towns, so near the Mexican border, that these parties have been stirring up strife and revolution against Mexico and the United States. A large percentage of the inhabitants of the Mexican interior are United States citizens, who have vast amounts of capital invested there, and many of them have their families with them, and the matter of the embryonic revolution affects American interests very seriously—as much as it does the Mexican government.

Webb summarized his views by arguing that the rumors about deportees being shot were groundless, that the affair affected lives and American property in Mexico, and that deportation would prove to be a "deterrent to others of a similar class."[61] Thus, like the board's earlier recommendation, Webb's purely political thinking did not make the legal case for deportation under the terms of the Immigration Act of 1903.

Yet the arguments and assurances of Webb, Alexander, Elías,

[59]Elías to Sec. de Rel. Ext., 21 September 1906, AREM L–E–1241, pt. 4.
[60]J. L. B. Alexander to Webb, 14 September 1906 (encl. in Elías to Sec. de Rel. Ext., 18 September 1906), AREM, L–E–1241, pt. 4.
[61]Webb to Comm.-Gen. of Immigration, 22 September 1906 (encl. in Elías to Sec. de Rel. Ext., 23 September 1906), AREM, L–E–1241, pt. 5.

and Díaz succeeded. On 2 October, the Mexican consul received a telegram from the secretary of commerce and labor ordering the deportation of the six *revoltosos*. On the night of 3 October they were taken to Nogales and forced across the border by the immigration authorities. As they crossed the line a force of Mexican *rurales* arrested them, handcuffed them one to the other, and escorted them to the state prison. From Hermosillo they were eventually sent to San Juan de Ulúa to join Salcido and the other Cananea martyrs. It would be almost five years before the young Puente would see his father again.[62] Four days after the deportation, Greene was once again lobbying the government on behalf of General Torres, requesting additional apprehensions and deportations—and Manuel Sarabia was about to leave Chicago for the "hotbed" of Douglas, Arizona.[63]

By early summer 1907, Sarabia was in Douglas working as a reporter for the *International American*. On the morning of 30 June he was waiting at the train station for the mail car going to El Paso. While there he was intercepted by a large, red-faced man who ordered him to go to the city hall. Although Sarabia did not know the identity of this man in plain clothes, the stranger's two-hundred-pound frame and blue-barreled revolver were highly persuasive arguments. The man, who turned out to be Sam J. Hayhurst, an Arizona Ranger, arrested Sarabia without either filing a complaint or issuing a warrant. At the city hall he was placed in custody by the local jailer, Lee Thompson.

There he was personally guarded by the city marshal, James Dowdle, until about ten o'clock at night, at which time he was spirited out of jail into a waiting automobile. He was joined in the car by Dowdle and the Douglas constable, A. J. Shropshire. When Sarabia attempted to shout for help, he was handcuffed, gagged, and blindfolded. Then the chauffeur, Henry Elvey, sped through the dark streets of Douglas to the adjoining border community of Agua Prieta (what Sarabia called the "town of a hundred adobe houses"). There Sarabia was turned over to a group of Kosterlitzky's

[62]Elías to Sec. de Rel. Ext., 6 October 1906, AREM L–E–1241, pt. 5; San Francisco *Chronicle*, 5 October 1906.

[63]Metcalf to Sec. of State, 12 October 1906, NF, case 100/133.

mounted soldliers. Sarabia now found himself a victim of the ultimate kind of deportation tactic, an official kidnapping.[64]

At Agua Prieta, Sarabia was tied to the back of a mule, which was led by one of the mounted horsemen. Placed on the mule "like a bag of potatoes," he was forced to ride all night on the trotting animal before arriving, sore and injured, at Naco the next morning. The horsemen taking Sarabia to Naco were escorted by the Agua Prieta chief of police as well as by Kosterlitzky—both of whom rode comfortably in a carriage at the head of the column. From Naco, fifteen officers took Sarabia to Cananea, where he was placed in a cell until 3 July. While at Cananea his captors told him he was headed for Hermosillo and would be lucky if he were not shot on the way. From Cananea six soldiers took him on an eighteen-hour ride to Imuris, from where he was sent to the prison at Hermosillo. In jail with Yaqui Indians, Manuel was certain that he would soon be joining cousin Juan at Ulúa—an expectation that was reinforced by the visits of Greene and Torres to his cell.[65]

Fortunately for Sarabia, his kidnapping did not go unnoticed. On the day of the kidnapping, President Roosevelt received a telegram purportedly sent by Sarabia saying: "Sir—I have been arrested for political causes. I ask for my rights according to law."[66] Apparently some Mexican members of the community had heard Sarabia's cries for help and had immediately gone to Mother Jones. The good Mother quickly got involved in the cause, sending telegrams to both Roosevelt and Governor Kibbey and then calling a public protest meeting.

The publisher of the local paper, the Douglas *Examiner*, George H. Kelly, angry over an attempt by consul Maza to silence the story, published many details of the kidnapping between 1 and 3 July and

[64]Ward Albro narrates the Sarabia kidnapping in his article "El secuestro de Manuel Sarabia," *Historia Mexicana* 18 (January-March 1969): 400–407. See also González Ramírez, *Epistolario y textos*, pp. 113–118. Sarabia's account, "How I Was Kidnapped," originally appeared in the December 1908 issue of *The Border*. The same account appears as a six-page pamphlet in NF, case 1741/104. For primary documents of the incident see NF, case 7418/1–24 ("Arrest of Arizona Resident in Mexico").

[65]"How I Was Kidnapped," pp. 11–12, NF, case 1741/104; W. A. Chamberlin to Sec. of State, 19 July 1907, NF, case 7418/20.

[66]Sarabia to Roosevelt, 1 July 1907, NF, case 7418/1.

sent telegrams to the president encouraging governmental action. A citizens' committee, headed by the influential Judge D. A. Richardson, established the basic facts of the kidnapping and demanded federal action from Roosevelt, Attorney General Bonaparte, and Secretary Root. Very quickly, petitions, letters of protest, and telegrams started to inundate the departments of State and Commerce and Labor. Messages were received from hundreds of irate citizens in Douglas, Del Rio, St. Louis, Albuquerque, El Paso, and Denver.[67]

Within a few days the facts had been fairly well established and were reported to the territorial governor and the Department of Justice by Alexander. Hayhurst had arrested Sarabia at the request of Harry Wheeler, captain of the Arizona Rangers. Wheeler had ordered the arrest after Captain Ramón Ramos Barreras, an officer in the Mexican federal army stationed in Sonora, had brought charges of murder against Sarabia. The homicide charge was merely a pretext to allow Ramos and consul Maza to "spirit" Sarabia out of Arizona. It was later established at a hearing at Tombstone that Dowdle, Shropshire, and Elvey were all in the pay of the Mexican consul at Douglas.[68]

All the unwanted publicity soon forced the authorities to act. The local Citizens' Committee had been most critical of the inaction of the Cochise county marshal and attorney, and the demands for federal action finally shamed them into moving against the kidnappers. On 5 July, several individuals were detained by Douglas authorities for questioning, including Maza, Shropshire, Thompson, and Hayhurst. Two days later, Captain Wheeler and a public investigator, W. C. Foster, arrived in Hermosillo with orders from Governor Kibbey to retrieve Sarabia. Torres agreed to the arrangement, and Sarabia was brought back to Arizona by 12 July and released of all charges. On his return, Sarabia received a hero's welcome from the local community. Although Dowdle fled the territory, Maza and Shropshire were arrested for kidnapping and held for the

[67]Douglas *Examiner* to Roosevelt, 5 July 1907; Citizens' Committee to Roosevelt, Bonaparte, and Root, 3 July 1907; "Amantes de la Libertad" to Commerce and Labor; El Paso citizens to State; Scott to Dip. Bureau, 25 July 1907—all NF, case 7418/2, 3, 12–15, 20.

[68]J. L. B. Alexander to Att. Gen., 18 July 1907, NF, case 7418/17; "How I Was Kidnapped," p. 14.

next grand jury at Tombstone. However, the kidnapping charges were eventually dropped and the authorities were happy to simply let the incident fade away.[69]

The Sarabia episode had several consequences. It was such a celebrated event that the PLM now became well known nationally, and this brought about a new alliance between American radicals and the PLM. In this respect the participation of the famous Mother Jones had been helpful to the Liberal Party. The incident also hurt Díaz's public image, for now the American press and people became aware of the validity of many of the PLM's anti-Díaz charges. The Sarabia case served as an excellent example of Díaz's repressive police system and gave new impetus to the *magonista* movement in the United States. Finally, it also served as a warning to the enemies of Díaz. Thus, after Flores Magón, Rivera, and Villarreal were arrested in Los Angeles on 23 August 1907, their attorneys vigorously resisted their extradition to Arizona for fear of their clients being kidnapped in the same fashion.

The Los Angeles arrest, by far the most important occurrence in the early history of the "diplomacy of suppression," was the climactic battle of Díaz's deportation struggle. As was proper for such an important occasion, this event was characterized by all three dimensions of Turner's "campaign of deportation"—kidnapping, extradition, and deportation through the immigration service.

At the least, a circumstantial case can be made to support the contention that Thomas Furlong and the city detectives who arrested Flores Magón, Rivera, and Villarreal in Los Angeles were initially planning a kidnapping, not an arrest. As has been seen in the earlier Rivera and Sarabia incidents, kidnapping was not out of the question as a technique to be used by local authorities and private detectives. Sarabia had testified that a private detective (whom he called a "Pinkerton") had been involved in the kidnapping attempt on him. Cooperation in this kind of venture was easy to obtain, since a $20,000 reward had been offered for assistance in the capture and arrest of Flores Magón. Sworn testimony given in the Los Angeles courts indicates that the city detectives who accom-

[69]"How I Was Kidnapped," p. 14. See also González Ramírez, *Epistolario y textos*, p. 113.

panied Furlong were motivated by and received their share of the reward money.[70]

Other evidence points toward a kidnapping plot. First, the officers, had they been planning an arrest, had sufficient time to file a complaint and obtain a warrant. Yet the arrest took place without either. At the courthouse, when they had to present charges, there was initially a delay, and then Rivera was finally charged with "resisting an officer" and Flores Magón and Villarreal were accused of being "fugitives from Missouri justice." Second, Furlong had secreted an automobile in the vicinity but did not use it after the arrest. Third, in the skirmish that followed their confrontation the outcries of Flores Magón attracted a crowd of witnesses—in itself a deterrent to any potential kidnapping plot. Somewhat unprepared for this development, the officers overreacted by beating the Mexicans brutally with their pistols. In an affidavit later sworn to by W. F. Zwickey, it was alleged that Furlong was more interested in getting the defendants to Arizona and across the line than in the case or the charges for which they were being tried. Finally, like Captain Ramos Barreras during the Sarabia affair at Douglas, Ambassador Creel was on the spot in Los Angeles the night before the "arrest."[71]

A few days later, the original charges were changed. Flores Magón and Rivera were placed under provisional arrest and detained to await extradition hearings. This charge dated back to October 1906, when the Flores Magón brothers and Rivera were accused of "murder, robbery, and attempted destruction of railway tracks," and when Flores Magón was thought to be in El Paso. By December, the extradition order was forwarded to officials in Smithville, Texas, the town where Flores Magón was supposed to be at that time. In January, a new extradition warrant was telegraphed to secret service agents in New York City, it then being believed that the Flores Magón brothers were about to arrive there from Canada. As for Villarreal, his case was referred to the Department

[70]Turner, *Barbarous Mexico*, pp. 245–249.

[71]Ibid. See also Bonaparte to Sec. of State, 28 August 1907, NF, case 1741/54, and "Affidavit of W. F. Zwickey," 27 January 1980, U.S. v. Flores Magón, Antonio I. Villarreal, and Librado Rivera, Criminal 23 (U.S. Dist. Ct., So. Cal. Div., 1908), U.S. Federal Archives and Records Center, Laguna Niguel, California (hereafter cited as FRC Laguna Niguel).

of Commerce and Labor, and he was detained for deportation hearings—it being recalled that he had been under the charge of immigration officials when he had escaped from custody in El Paso in February.[72]

In early September, Creel decided to change the charges once again. As Jesús Flores Magón had pointed out to Roosevelt, it was unlikely that the leading *magonistas* in the United States could be extradited or deported to Mexico, especially when such procedures had failed in the cases of Rivera, Arredondo, and Villarreal. Another concern, of course, was the growing support that the Los Angeles leaders were receiving from organized labor, especially from Samuel Gompers, who was publicly opposed to the extradition and deportation of Flores Magón. Meeting with U.S. Attorney Alexander in Los Angeles (who "just happened to be" in southern California on vacation), Creel told him confidentially that the Mexican government did not have the evidence needed to hold the men for extradition, or even to prosecute them for the alleged crimes committed in California and Missouri.[73]

Alexander then shared with Creel his recollections about the Douglas junta arrests and the successful conviction of Espinosa on neutrality violation charges. He was certain that with the materials acquired from the defendants in St. Louis, Douglas, El Paso, and Los Angeles, there was ample evidence to prove that the St. Louis Junta conspired to set on foot a military expedition from the United States into Mexico—a violation of section 5286 of the Revised Statutes. Thus, on 17 September, the U.S. attorney for the southern district of California was instructed by the Justice Department to cause the arrest and removal of the defendants to Arizona on conspiracy charges.[74]

The failures of extradition and the limitations of deportation had led to a new strategy. Extradition and deportation could be used to get at the "small fry," but Ricardo and his friends de-

---

[72]Adee to Att. Gen., 28 August 1907, NF, case 1741/54; Root to Att. Gen., 23 October 1906, RG 60, file 90755; Bacon to Dávalos, 23 January 1907, and Bacon to Sec. of Treas., 24 January 1907—NF, case 1741/28–29.

[73]J. Flores Magón to Roosevelt, 26 August 1907, NF, case 1741/60; J. L. B. Alexander to Att. Gen., 10 September 1907, NF, case 1741/65.

[74]Alexander to Att. Gen., 10 September 1907, and Act. Att. Gen. to Sec. of State, 17 September 1907—NF, case 1741/65.

manded a different approach. Convicting the *magonistas* under the neutrality laws would contain the revolutionaries and be as effective a tool of harassment as the campaign of deportation had been. Although local officials, as well as postal, immigration, and Justice Department authorities, had been most helpful in the deportation struggles, that battle had been hindered by the American tradition of fair play and constitutional rights. The situation had not been aided by the kidnapping ploy, a tactic that rightly hurt Díaz's image in the United States (and came at a time, it should be noted, when American businesssmen in Mexico, suffering from the impact of the stock market drop of 13 March 1907 and the mid-year recession, were first becoming disillusioned with don Porfirio's leadership). All of this had created more sympathizers for the PLM.

Thus a new approach would be instituted. The new strategy would be in the mainstream of America's legal traditions and, it was hoped, would be applauded by the libertarian minority—in the magistrate's courtroom, the solicitor's office of State, and the editorial room of the St. Louis press. It was time for Mexico to step out of the limelight and allow "Uncle Sam" to face the insurgents directly.

All the gringos were against him,
even the referee.

Jack London, "The Mexican"

6. "Uncle Sam" and the Insurgents

IT was 5:13 on the morning of 18 April 1906. Suddenly a vibration
was felt; then a major tremor traveled from the bay through the
downtown section of Market Street. San Francisco was in the beginning of her death throes. Buildings began to crack. A chimney
fell into the square below. Flames, fanned by a breeze, spread
north to Broadway, illuminating the sky for five miles. The Valencia
Hotel, a magnificent four-story wooden structure, sank into its own
basement, a pile of splintered timbers—pinning many dead and dying occupants, drowning others as the cellar filled with water.
Then several buildings collapsed in succession: the Hearst Building,
the five-story Palace Hotel, the Grand Opera House, and the Merchants Exchange Building. The Cliff House Resort slid into the
ocean.

San Francisco's inhabitants wandered aimlessly. Hundreds of
inmates from the Agnews insane asylum roamed the streets in a
state of panic. Streetcars and ferryboats became temporary homes
for others only temporarily mad. Prisoners from the fifth floor of
the Hall of Justice marched with the men from the Presidio. People
emerged from their apartments to be greeted with showers of fall-
ing bricks, cornices, and walls. Van Ness millionaires, still in their
night attire with silver money belts in hand, circulated with the
drunk-crazed rioters of Mission Street.

Then the mayor declared war. Many were made homeless and
some were killed when the army bombarded the sixteen-block area
between Van Ness and the Golden Gate Park with artillery shells.
But the attempt to establish a fire line failed, the dynamite and
bombs only adding to the total terror. And when it was almost over
a Naval Reserve officer discovered a looter digging in the ruins of a

jewelry shop. Law and order was restored with the bayonet that pierced the thief's back. Then the 13th Infantry arrived from Angel Island for patrol duty. In a few days all was over: no food or water, only flames, smoke, gales, famine, disease, refugees, corpses, and martial law. Gomorrah's battlefield appeared to be empty of life and meaning.[1]

Still the almost destroyed city persisted, a refuge for the wicked and the disinherited. It was to this city that Ricardo Flores Magón had come after fleeing from almost certain arrest and imprisonment at El Paso in October. In despair, without any funds or organization, he sought the natural camouflage of the urban guerrilla. He, the impoverished political refugee, now joined San Francisco's other fugitives in a common struggle for survival against nature and society. Here he would remain for several weeks before rejoining his comrades in Los Angeles later in the year. It was here, in San Francisco, that his personal tragedy merged with that of the fallen and razed city.

He recalled this experience several years later when he wrote from Leavenworth:

> San Francisco ought to be beautiful now. I was there in 1907, when a large part of the city was in ruins—just as my revolutionary plans for Mexico were in ruins. In my sorrow I was forced to go into hiding among the ruins, with a $20,000 reward on my head and the secret service of two countries pursuing me from this place to that, from city to city. Often many days would pass without a piece of bread touching my lips, and then I would think of those wretched and miserable people who must kill for a piece of bread. I would entertain such thoughts myself, until my ideal separated me from my instincts. It was literally a time of life or death for me. My arrest would mean immediate passage to Mexico and death without any pretensions to justice. You see now, my dear friend, why I have many good reasons to remember San Francisco.[2]

In his recollections about California, Flores Magón could also not forget Los Angeles, where the arrest he feared so much took place on 23 August 1907—an action that depleted his revolutionary energies and curtailed his radical ambitions.

[1]This account of the San Francisco earthquake has been reconstructed from the *New York Times*, 19 and 20 April 1906.
[2]Translated by the author from Ricardo Flores Magón to Nicolás T. Bernal, 30 October 1920, in *Epistolario revolucionario e íntimo*, p. 16.

Six days after the arrest, Consul Antonio Lozano, having initially brought libel charges against Flores Magón and the others, filed an affidavit of complaint in the U.S. District Court at Los Angeles. Flores Magón, Villarreal, and Rivera were charged with murder and larceny for actions allegedly committed on 15 September 1906 in Jiménez, Coahuila. Their detention was continued after mid-September by a temporary commitment based on a "John Doe" murder charge. On 28 October 1907, Job Harriman and A. R. Holston, noting that the forty-day time period had elapsed since the arrest and detention of the defendants, requested their discharge.[3] Even though the extradition charges were eventually dropped, the defendants remained in prison on a complaint and warrant issued from Arizona by U.S. Attorney Joseph L. B. Alexander.[4]

As he had done in the earlier Espinosa case of December 1906, Alexander charged the defendants with several violations of the neutrality laws, in particular section 5286 of the Revised Statutes of 1873. This provision related to hostile expeditions and read as follows:

> Every person who, within the territory or jurisdiction of the United States, begins, or sets on foot, or provides or prepares the means for, any military expedition or enterprise, to be carried on from thence against the territory or dominions of any foreign prince or state . . . with whom the United States are at peace, shall be deemed guilty of a high misdemeanor, and shall be fined not exceeding three thousand dollars, and imprisoned not more than three years.[5]

Under this law Flores Magón and the others were charged with conspiring from St. Louis in mid-August and early September—in conjunction with Abraham Salcido, José Treviño, Gabriel Rubio, Ildefonso Martínez, and Tomás de Espinosa—to begin and set on

---

[3]U.S. v. Magón, et al., Extradition Application Case, Commissioner's Transcript 572 (U.S. Dist. Ct., So. Cal. Div., August–October 1907), FRC Laguna Niguel.

[4]Transcript of Record on Appeal (from Cir. Ct., 9th Jud. Cir., So. Cal. Div.), Application of R. Flores Magón et al. for a Writ of Habeas Corpus, 10 February 1908–4 January 1909, Records of the U.S. Supreme Court, Record Group 267, National Archives, Washington, D.C. (hereafter cited as RG 267), pp. 21, 27–28.

[5]Quoted from John Bassett Moore, A *Digest of International Law*, VII, 908–909.

foot a military expedition from Douglas, Arizona, against the territory of Mexico on or about 1 September 1906.[6]

Alexander was confident of his chances for obtaining a conviction. After all, Espinosa had been found guilty of an identical charge involving the same circumstances. In addition, the indictment in that case named Flores Magón, Villarreal, and Rivera as co-conspirators—and the judge in the Espinosa case had held that all persons directly or indirectly involved were considered "principals" in any crime committed. Since Espinosa had been convicted and Salcido, Treviño, and Rubio had been deported, a climate of presumed guilt existed among the Anglo inhabitants of Douglas and Tombstone even before the defendants were brought to trial.[7]

In interpreting section 5286, attorneys and judges were aided by a variety of precedents, not the least being the Espinosa case itself. A "hostile expedition" was defined as a combination of individuals (citizens and aliens alike) organized on friendly soil for the purpose of conducting military operations against a friendly nation.[8] The statute created two offenses: providing means for a military expedition and setting on foot a military expedition. Thus, such groups had to have some "military" characteristics—a fighting force, with a command structure and organization, acting as a unit, with arms, to achieve a "military" purpose of attacking or defending.[9]

It was not necessary that such persons be in uniform, or have been drilled or even prepared for successful service. Nor was it necessary that they carry arms—only that arms would be available at some point in order to achieve a military objective. It was not necessary that all persons composing the enterprise be in personal contact with each other within the limits of the United States.[10] Finally, the mere act of organizing a military expedition was sufficient evi-

---

[6]See Alexander's "Complaint" in RG 267, pp. 16–19.

[7]"Instructions of the Court, Dec. 24, 1906," U.S. v. Tomas D. Espinosa, Crim. 641–A (Ariz. Terr., U.S. 2nd Dist. Ct., 1906), FRC Laguna Niguel.

[8]Ray Emerson Curtis, "The Law of Hostile Military Expeditions as Applied by the United States," *American Journal of International Law* 8 (January 1914): 8–9.

[9]"Instructions of the Court," U.S. v. Espinosa, FRC Laguna Niguel.

[10]Ibid.

dence of guilt—the expedition did not have to begin, let alone finish, to be covered under the act.[11]

Not all related military and revolutionary acts were prohibited by the law. For example, in an 1896 case it was ruled that the neutrality laws did not prohibit the shipping of arms, ammunition, or military equipment to a foreign country, nor did it forbid individuals, singly or in association, "from leaving the United States to enlist or join in military operations being carried on between other countries or different parties in the same country."[12] This meant that *revoltosos* could legally ship arms into Mexico and then enlist and participate in revolutionary movements within Mexico. Thus it was not always readily apparent from a legal standpoint whether or not *revoltoso* activity was in actual violation of the law.

Another exclusion of relevance to *revoltosos* was that relating to revolutionary agitation within the United States against other countries. In the nineteenth century, Irish and Fenian brotherhoods were notorious for their "revolutionary aid societies." Yet these groups were rarely prosecuted under the neutrality laws, since their members usually confined themselves to "moral agitation." In other words, the statute required an "overt act" to organize or set on foot a military expedition. An intention to commit a crime, "mere words written or spoken, though indicative of the strongest desire and the most determined purpose to do the forbidden act," did not constitute an offense.[13] U.S. Attorney Alexander understood this very well, and was aware of how these exclusions could make his job of prosecution more difficult. In 1908, he told the Mexican ambassador that the letters seized from the "co-conspirators" during the 1906 Arizona arrests were insufficient evidence to prove a violation of the neutrality laws.[14]

For this reason, Alexander urged that the indictment against Flores Magón and the others be expanded to include an alleged violation of the conspiracy laws, especially section 5440 of the same

[11]Ibid. See also Moore, *A Digest of International Law*, VIII, 910.

[12]Moore, *A Digest of International Law*, VIII, 914.

[13]"Instructions of the Court," U.S. v. Espinosa, FRC Laguna Niguel; Curtis, "The Law of Hostile Military Expeditions," pp. 24–25.

[14]José F. Godoy to Sec. de Rel. Ext., 17 September 1908, in González Ramírez, *Epistolario y textos*, pp. 142–143.

Revised Statutes of the United States. As quoted by the El Paso consul, that act read as follows:

> If two or more persons conspire, in order to defraud the United States or in order to commit a crime against the United States, of whatever manner or object; and if one or more of these persons execute some act in order to achieve the object of conspiracy, all the persons involved are subject to a fine of not less than one thousand dollars nor more than ten thousand dollars and imprisonment not to exceed two years.[15]

Since Flores Magón and the other defendants had not actually been in Douglas, Arizona, at the time of the alleged military expedition, it would be easier to make a case against them for conspiracy than for "overtly" organizing and setting on foot a military enterprise.

In order to improve the chances of a successful prosecution, U.S. attorneys Alexander and Oscar Lawler, representing the plaintiff (the U.S. government), decided as early as November 1907 to include conspiracy as an additional charge against the defendants. In a preliminary hearing in Los Angeles, Lawler described the government's activity as a proceeding under section 5440 charging conspiracy to violate section 5286.[16] This same attention to the conspiracy statute, that is, the planning and acting together in secret for unlawful purposes, was included in the initial grand jury indictment issued from the territory of Arizona on 28 December 1907.[17] The tactic, confusing for the defense, provided the government with a broader net with which to catch its *revoltoso* prey.

Between 26 November and 2 December 1907, a preliminary hearing was held in Los Angeles before William M. Van Dyke, the U.S. commissioner for the southern district of California. Lawler joined Alexander in presenting the government's case. As was previously noted, Holston and Harriman represented the defendants.

The hearing was important for both sides. If the government failed to establish a reasonable doubt in the judge's mind as to the innocence of the defendants, the complaint would be dismissed and

---

[15]Quoted by Antonio Lomelí to Sec. de Rel. Ext., 24 October 1908, in Fabela, *Documentos históricos*, X, 93.

[16]Transcript, RG 267, p. 48.

[17]Ibid., pp. 24–25.

Flores Magón and the others would be released. On the other hand, even if the defendants were bound over to a jury, this was the time for the defense to develop suitable grounds for a future appeal. Because the evidence and testimony at this hearing would serve as the basis for any subsequent trial, it was in the interest of both the plaintiff and the defendants to make their best arguments at this time.[18]

The government's case was presented so as to link the St. Louis Junta with Espinosa's ill-fated planned expedition of September 1906. On several occasions references were made to Espinosa's prior conviction under the neutrality laws as evidence of an illegal "overt act," the assumption being that the principal's guilt was shared by the defendants as "accessories before the fact." The government's major evidence was in the form of correspondence, mostly between Flores Magón, Villarreal, and Rivera in St. Louis and Espinosa, Martínez, Rubio, and Treviño in Douglas, Mowry, and Cananea. Although several witnesses were called to authenticate the documents (detectives Ansel T. Samuels and Thomas Furlong, Arizona Ranger W. A. Olds, and immigration inspector Charles T. Connell), only Trinidad Vázquez and Arizona Ranger Thomas Rynning provided direct evidence, the former concerning military commissions and the latter concerning arms and munitions found in the Halfway House. Most of the documentary evidence was introduced to support the charge of conspiracy. The government's case was hardly free of political overtones, with the prosecution entering into the transcript references to "anarchistic" literature and "red flags of anarchy."

The defense argued several particulars, always in the general context of the argument that the entire prosecution was inspired by the Mexican government for political rather than criminal reasons. Several of the government's witnesses were linked either directly or indirectly to the Mexican government. Thus, it was shown under cross-examination that both Furlong and Samuels were detectives in the pay of Mexico; it was alleged that Vázquez was a Mexican

[18]Information on the preliminary hearing was taken from U.S. v. Ricardo Flores Magón, Antonio I. Villarreal, and Librado Rivera, Commissioner's Transcript No. 582 (U.S. Dist. Ct., So. Cal. Div., 26 November–2 December 1907), FRC Laguna Niguel.

spy induced to testify in return for funds provided by General Luis Torres; Rynning's activity during the Cananea strike was pointed to as evidence of his pro-Díaz, anti-worker attitudes. Handwriting experts were used to question the authenticity of the documents, and even the Spanish-language skills of the court's translator were seriously questioned.

The admissibility of the government's evidence was also questioned. The defense argued that Vázquez perjured himself in testifying about a document allegedly written by Salcido and had actually forged the document himself. In addition, it was argued that the items identified by Furlong were inadmissible because they had been acquired in an unlawful search and seizure. It was further stated that the documents seized in Arizona were not valid evidence because many were written after the date of the alleged conspiracy. Finally, the defense questioned the nature of the offense itself, noting that there never were soldiers, arms, ammunition, or marching orders, that is, no hostile military expedition actually occurred (an important consideration that, ironically, was not relevant under the conspiracy statute).[19]

The most controversial witness was Vázquez. He testified that he had attended four meetings of the Douglas club at the "Oro Plata" (Half-way House) between 11 August and 1 September 1906. He said that at the 27 August meeting, Espinosa and Salcido, both of whom had been commissioned by Flores Magón, made several military appointments with the intention of leading an armed expedition into Cananea. He also testified that Rubio and Humbert had been made revolutionary officers. After viewing several documents, he identified the handwriting of Treviño, Espinosa, Salcido, and other Arizona *revoltosos*.[20]

The defense expended most of its energies in attempting to discredit Vázquez's testimony. Holston noted that his testimony was contradictory in that Vázquez was unable initially to identify the authorship of a document that he later testified was by Salcido. Noting this, Holston said somewhat sarcastically, "He [Vázquez] got a little better, of course, as he went along." To which Lawler

---

[19]Ibid. See also *Revolución*, 30 November 1907, in González Ramírez, *Epistolario y textos*, pp. 134–135.

[20]FRC Laguna Niguel, Transcript No. 582, pp. 42–72, 91–143.

retorted: "He wasn't like counsel—deteriorating with age." The defense also used handwriting experts to testify on behalf of the defendants. Their testimony, although inconclusive, did imply forgery of at least one document and did undermine Vázquez's testimony at one point. Finally, the defense put Jesús J. González, the former vice-president of the Douglas club, on the stand. His statements contradicted those of Vázquez on practically all major points, including Vázquez's denial of being in the pay of General Torres.[21]

This attack on Vázquez's credibility was not totally successful. The testimony of the two handwriting experts (one a manager of a business college, the other an auditor and accountant) was not persuasive—the result of skillful cross-examination by the government. In addition, the defense could only suggest forgery and perjury, not demonstrate it. (Today, in hindsight, it is obvious that Vázquez perjured himself when he denied his association with the Mexican government.)[22] As for González's testimony, he was not a credible witness, for he was very involved in the *magonista* cause, being affiliated with Modesto Díaz and Gutíerrez de Lara and, like the defendants, under indictment for violating the neutrality laws.[23]

The most damaging evidence against the defendants was the letters written to Espinosa from Flores Magón in August and early September 1906. Charles T. Connell, having been directly involved in the arrest of Espinosa (and a witness in the Espinosa trial), proved to be a most effective witness in identifying and authenticating this correspondence. Of special importance was the letter of 2 August 1906 (U.S. Exhibit 3-A), in which Flores Magón said:

> . . . I enclose you a commission which accredits you as Chief to organize the revolution at places you may consider more adequate and more particularly in Cananea, Douglas and Nacozari.
>
> It will be well for you in organizing the revolution as Chief, to leave [sic] other chiefs whose names you will furnish the Junta so

[21]Ibid., pp. 126–136, 250–299.

[22]Phoenix consul Arturo Elías stated that Vázquez had been hired by General Torres. See Elías to Sec. de Rel. Ext., 19 May 1909, in González Ramírez, *Epistolario y textos*, pp. 157–161. According to Myers he had been hired as a spy by Governor Izábal. See Myers, "The Mexican Liberal Party," p. 134.

[23]FRC Laguna Niguel, Transcript No. 582, pp. 140–143, 250–310. For a contrary interpretation see Turner, *Barbarous Mexico*, pp. 256–257.

as to forward them the necessary credentials. These chiefs shall be under your immediate orders for the reasons that you have made the designations. I do not know whether you are cognizant of the fact that the authorities of the United States will not permit the entering in our country people under arms. So therefore, plan the entering of compatriots under arms secretly. . . .

. . . .

. . . It is well to ascertain if it is true that there exist two thousand rifles stored in the cellar of the Cananea store. If they do positively exist, what ought to be done is to seize them at a designated hour before Green [sic] has time to arm his people. . . .

. . . It is also well for our forces to gather dynamite to be utilized in blowing up the railroads, etc. . . . The rulers are the cause of our ills and they must be hanged. . . . We ought to, therefore, direct all our blows against the tyrants.

I await your coming letter. Directly I will give you notice to prices on rifles.

. . . Do not despair. Let the citizens promptly arm themselves so that they may be ready when the hour is fixed.[24]

This letter would be used again against the defendants when, on 3 May 1909, an Arizona grand jury would make it the basis for a new indictment.[25]

At the conclusion of the hearing the commissioner decided that there was sufficient evidence of guilt to justify a final commitment in default of bail. This was done by 21 December. After an Arizona grand jury had returned an indictment for conspiracy, Van Dyke issued a preliminary order of removal to Arizona on 31 January 1908.[26] As was the judicial practice of the day, so-called "exclusionary" evidence (material seized unlawfully) was allowed to stand. With Espinosa's trial proceedings accepted as evidence, the conspiracy link between the Junta and Arizona revoltosos was made more obvious. Once again, the immigration service had performed a critical role, in the person of Charles Connell, the man who had identified Esipnosa's writings and the magonista correspondence in his possession.

[24]Flores Magón to Espinosa, 2 August 1906 (government's translated copy), in FRC Laguna Niguel, Transcript No. 582, pp. 191–193.
[25]Indictment, U.S. v. R. Flores Magón, A. Villarreal, and L. Rivera, Criminal 693 (Ariz. Terr., U.S. 2nd Dist. Ct., 1909), FRC Laguna Niguel.
[26]RG 267, pp. 24–25 and 33–39.

Juan Sarabia and the Flores Magón brothers, 1905. St. Louis *Post Dispatch*.

Left: Col. William C. Greene and daughter Eva, ca. 1899. Arizona Historical Society. *Right*: Enrique C. Creel, governor of Chihuahua, ambassador to the United States, minister of foreign relations, and unofficial director of Díaz's international spy and police system. From Lázaro Gutiérrez de Lara, *The Mexican People*.

Greene addressing workers at Cananea, 1906 (Rafael Izabel, governor of Sonora, in rear seat, wearing derby). Mrs. Joseph S. Bordwell Photo Collection, Riverside Municipal Museum, Riverside, California.

Greene mansion in Cananea under guard, 1906. Arizona Historical Society.

Left: David E. Thompson. *Evening Star* (Washington, D.C.). *Right*: Thomas Furlong, the man hired by Creel to find and report on *magonista* activity in the United States. From Thomas Furlong, *Fifty Years a Detective*.

Officers of Arizona Rangers and Mexican *rurales* at Cananea, 1906. *Left to right*: San Hayhurst, unidentified, Capt. Tom Rynning, Capt. Emilio Kosterlitzky, unidentified, O'Jada. Arizona Historical Society.

Prison and "wanted" photographs of Ricardo Flores Magón, 1906, circulated by Creel in Mexico and the United States. Bancroft Library.

The Villarreal sisters, Teresa and Andrea González (1906), *magonista* supporters who opposed Díaz from their U.S. base. St. Louis *Post Dispatch*.

Cartoon from radical feminist newspaper *La Voz de la Mujer* (El Paso, Texas), 1907; Díaz at right. Silvestre Terrazas Collection, Bancroft Library.

Outpost of *insurrectos*, with El Paso smelter in the background, March, 1911. Library of Congress.

Mexican insurgents along the Rio Grande, May, 1911. Library of Congress.

Women revolutionists, September, 1911. Library of Congress.

Francisco I. Madero receives a peace message at Cuidad Juárez, May 8, 1911 (his wife is directly behind him). Library of Congress.

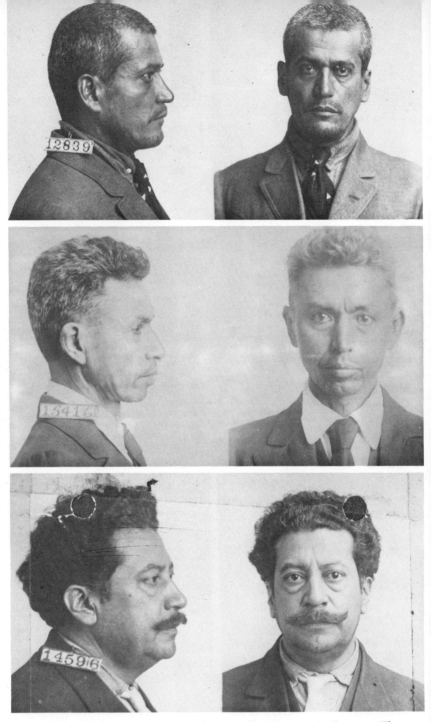

Leavenworth Penitentiary "mug shots" of (*from top*) Enrique Flores Magón, 1918; Librado Rivera, 1920; Ricardo Flores Magón, 1920. Bureau of Prisons, U.S. Department of Justice.

The defense's major assumption—that the proceedings were initiated for political reasons—was morally correct but legally irrelevant. Ironically, Rynning, a witness in this case, would have been
an ideal defendant in a neutrality violation case because of his role
in leading an army of Bisbee volunteers into Cananea on 2 June
1906. The difference between Arizona Ranger Rynning and revolutionist Flores Magón was simply one of class and status and the
relationship of class to power (political, legal, and judicial), and in
this respect the police authority of the state belonged to Rangers,
not *revoltosos*.

Meanwhile, Manuel Sarabia, who had been arrested in Los
Angeles along with Modesto Díaz and F. Arizmendí (both of whom
were associated with *Revolución*), was accused in the December
indictment of violating the neutrality laws. An affidavit of complaint
was issued in Los Angeles on 2 January 1908. In the spring of that
year his extradition to Tombstone, Arizona, was ordered. On 8 May
he was secretly removed from his Los Angeles cell and taken to the
Tucson jail. Even his counsel did not know of his removal until the
next day. Accepting his situation, Sarabia did not fight the extradition, but requested a speedy trial instead. After waiting in vain for
several months, he posted bond and was finally released from jail
in the latter part of 1908. He then jumped bail and fled to Europe.[27]

When Harriman first learned that the authorities were planning
to extradite the defendants to Arizona, he filed a formal objection.
Arguing that the United States had failed to make a *prima facie*
case, he asserted that because the defendants had not been arrested
in Arizona, and because the hearing had been in Los Angeles, the
Arizona court did not have jurisdiction. A final objection stated that
the removal was not ordered in good faith, intending only to place
these men in "the Territory of Arizona, where the Republic of Mexico and its agents and officials, may be able to kidnap and take
them out of the jurisdiction of the United States . . . by unlawful
means, there to be tried for alleged political offenses." The objec-

[27]U.S. v. Manuel Sarabia, Commissioner's Transcript No. 591 (U.S. Dist.
Ct., So. Cal. Div., January 2, 1908), FRC Laguna Niguel. See also González
Ramírez, *Epistolario y textos*, pp. 134, 146–147; Turner, *Barbarous Mexico*,
pp. 215–216; Samuel Gompers to Roosevelt, n.d., in U.S., Congress, House,
Alleged Persecutions, pp. 13–14.

tion was in vain, and the final order of removal to Arizona was issued on 4 February 1908.[28]

Undaunted, Harriman continued to fight for the defendants. In early 1908 he filed an affidavit for reduction of bond before the U.S. Supreme Court. Bail had been set at $5,000 for each defendant, and he argued that the figure was excessive and unfair, especially since bond in the Espinosa case had only been $250. The appellants were prepared to pay $500 each. In appealing for bail reduction and freedom on the defendants' own recognizance, Harriman reviewed the history of arrests, imprisonments, and rearrests since 23 August 1907. On 16 November 1908, Chief Justice Fuller, unmoved by these arguments, denied the appellants' motion with no comment or explanation.[29]

Harriman continued to delay the inevitable by filing another application with the Supreme Court, this time a writ of habeas corpus. Application was made in February 1908. Arguments were made in a 357-page brief that contained the earlier transcript, testimony, and evidence of the Los Angeles hearing as well as formal objections and post-hearing judicial orders. Because the defendants did not commit any crime in Arizona under section 5286 of the Revised Statutes, he argued, a writ of habeas corpus should be issued requiring that the prisoners be brought before the federal courts to decide the legality of their detention. On 4 January 1909 the application was dismissed on a technicality relating to the transcript of record (the so-called Rule No. 10).[30] While the appeal was pending, Flores Magón and the others had been held incommunicado in the Los Angeles county jail for sixteen months, waiting for their docket number to come up on the court calendar!

During this time the Mexican government had been busy. While the defendants were in the Los Angeles jail, the Mexican and American authorities planned a spy system that enabled them to intercept all letters and notes sent between the prisoners and their outside contacts. This system allowed the government to obtain

[28]See "Objection" and "Removal Order" in U.S. v. R. Flores Magón, A. Villarreal, and L. Rivera, Criminal 23 (U.S. Dist. Ct., So. Cal. Div., 1908), FRC Laguna Niguel.

[29]Appellant Case No. 21153, RG 267.

[30]Application of R. Flores Magón et al. for a Writ of Habeas Corpus, 10 February 1908–4 January 1909, RG 267.

additional evidence of guilt for future use in the courts. To make the system work, Flores Magón and the others were separated and held incommunicado (so they would have to write their communications). The workings of the spy system were kept quiet, so that the revolutionists never knew that *every letter* secretly sent to them while in jail had been read and photographed, with copies forwarded to U.S. Attorney Lawler and the Mexican Ministry of Foreign Relations. Messages to friends on the outside were allowed to reach their destination after being photographed, and all replies received similar treatment.[31]

In sending their communications the prisoners had hit on the device of writing messages on thin pieces of cloth and sewing these strips in the bands of their undergarments when sent out to be laundered. The Mexican consul, Antonio Lozano, would then rip open the garments, photograph the contents, and "with his own hands sew the messages back." The soiled linen would then be delivered to Librado Rivera's wife, Evarista, who, ignorant of these matters, would deliver the letters.[32]

After the defendants' appeal had been denied by the court in January 1909, plans were made to remove them to Arizona. In early March, Flores Magón, Villarreal, and Rivera were accompanied to Tucson by Deputy U.S. Marshal J. T. Durlin and two officers from the Los Angeles sheriff's office. There they were held incommunicado in the Pima county jail for two months, awaiting trial in Tombstone. Their defense was financed by the W.F.M. and the Political Refugee Defense League of Chicago, and they were represented by A. A. Worsley, of Tucson, and W. B. Cleary, the "socialist" attorney from Bisbee. Their greatest fears centered on extradition to Mexico, where they would face charges of sedition with a penalty of life imprisonment or death. In the meantime, the political climate in the United States was not conducive to a fair trial for the *magonista* leaders.[33]

---

[31]*Los Angeles Examiner*, 5 March 1909, in Lozano to Sec. de Rel. Ext., 6 March 1909, AREM, L–E–954. For examples of photographed copies of intercepted mail and messages see Lozano to Sec. de Rel. Ext., 24 February 1909, AREM, L–E–954, and other items scattered throughout L–E–954.

[32]Ibid.

[33]*Tucson Citizen*, 4 March 1909, and *Arizona Daily Star*, 5 March 1909, encl. in S. M. del Ford to Sec. de Rel. Ext., 5 March 1909, AREM, L–E–954.

On 26 June 1908 a group of Mexican revolutionists had begun an abortive insurrection by raiding Las Vacas from Del Rio. For several days the *insurrectos*, operating from an American base, made raids into Mexico. At Mexico's request, Roosevelt alerted U.S. marshals and their deputies and sent four troops of cavalry to the border. Adee, in addition, instructed the governor of Texas to send Rangers to patrol the border. Troops were specifically ordered to stop all violations of the neutrality laws between El Paso and Del Rio. A few weeks later Attorney General Bonaparte assigned a special assistant and two secret service agents to the southwestern Texas district in order to aid in investigating and prosecuting cases arising out of the violation of the neutrality laws.[34] Díaz thanked Roosevelt for his prompt aid, and the public concern over *revoltoso* violations of American laws was heightened.

Emboldened by public support and governmental concern over *revoltoso* activity, an El Paso grand jury, on 20 October 1908, returned seventeen indictments against what were alleged to be several Mexican (and Mexican American) revolutionists. Most of these indictments were made possible by the work of the attorney general's recently appointed special assistant. Fourteen were for violations under section 5286 of the Revised Statutes; the other three were for conspiracy under section 5440. Only the important *magonista* leaders were accused of conspiracy. They were, in addition to Ricardo Flores Magón and Villarreal, Enrique Flores Magón, Práxedis Guerrero, Antonio de P. Araujo, and Encarnación Díaz Guerra.[35]

The year 1908 also saw Roosevelt igniting once again the nativist, anti-anarchist campaign as he sought public support in his battle with Congress for new legislation concerning the postal and secret service agencies of the country. Having instructed the post-

[34]Roosevelt to Charles Bonaparte, 29 June 1908, *Letters*, VI, 1099–1100; Bonaparte to Bacon, 20 July 1908, NF, case 8183/107–108. At the same time Mexico located its garrisons of federal troops along the frontier at eleven points, including Matamoros, Las Vacas, Laredo, Jiménez, and Ciudad Juárez. See Creel to Bacon, 30 July 1908, NF, case 8183/115.

[35]Special Assistant Llewellyn to Bonaparte, 20 October 1908, RG 60, file 90755. Also see Lomelí to Sec. de Rel. Ext., 24 October 1908, in Fabela, *Documentos históricos*, X, 91–93, and Aureliano J. Mijares, comp., *Por la libertad de Ricardo Flores Magón y compañeros presos en los Estados Unidos del Norte*, p. 10.

master general to exclude the "anarchistic" *La Questione Sociale* from the mails, and having been advised that the printing and circulating of anarchistic materials was not an offense to the United States in the absence of a federal statute, Roosevelt appealed to the Congress on 9 April 1908 for further laws to prohibit the use of the mails for murder, arson, and treason.[36] In his now famous statement on anarchism, he said that

> when compared with the suppression of anarchy, every other question sinks into insignificance. The anarchist is the enemy of humanity, the enemy of all mankind, and his is a deeper degree of criminality than any other. No immigrant is allowed to come to our shores if he is an anarchist; and no paper published here or abroad should be permitted circulation in this country if it propagates anarchistic opinions.[37]

Even though Congress did not act, the president's comments equating radicalism with aliens were not a propitious omen for the men of *Regeneración* and red flags in the Pima county jail.

Roosevelt also raised the specter of anarchism in gathering support for his expansive use of the secret service. Prior to 1908 the secret service, although under the Department of the Treasury, had served as a general manpower pool for the other departments of government, especially Justice. Roosevelt had always made extensive use of the secret service at home and abroad. For example, after he "took the Panama," he used secret service agents there to act as *agents provocateurs* and as spies to keep American diplomatic representatives under surveillance.[38] Congress, unhappy with the use of secret service agents by the Department of Justice to spy on congressmen and businessmen, voted in 1908 to prohibit their use by departments other than Treasury. In lobbying against this prohibitive amendment (which he often ignored in practice), Roosevelt said that "the Secretary of State, for instance, reports to me that this provision will hamper him seriously in dealing with anarchists

---

[36]Roosevelt to the Dept. of Justice, 20 March 1908, *Letters*, VI 977–978.

[37]U.S. Congress, Senate, Committee on the Judiciary (Message from the President of the United States), *Transmission through the Mails of Anarchistic Publications*, Senate Doc. No. 426, 60th Cong., 1st Sess., 2 December 1907–30 May 1908, p. 1.

[38]Sands and Lalley, *Our Jungle Diplomacy*, pp. 33–36.

when he receives notice that such are in the country; that, for instance, it would have hampered him in the past in giving protection to foreign visitors when he learned anarchists meditated outrages upon them."[39] A similar line of argument was used by Roosevelt in his annual message to Congress later in the year.[40] Like Roosevelt's other acts that year, from mobilization to postal reforms, the publicity generated by the secret service argument did not improve the general plight of alien Mexican radicals in the United States.

On 5 May 1909, in this climate of opinion, the federal trial of Flores Magón, Villarreal, and Rivera finally began. Although the local Mexican community was most sympathetic to the *magonistas*, "proper Anglos" tended to side with Roosevelt's personification of the "Big Stick" at home, Attorney General Bonaparte. The prosecution included, along with Alexander and Lawler, Horace H. Appel, a man who was reputed to be the most celebrated criminal lawyer west of the Rocky Mountains. The trial took place before Judge Fletcher M. Doan in the district court of the second judicial district of the territory of Arizona. Although Arizona law provided for defendants to be tried separately in "felony" cases of this kind (Arizona law defined a "felony" as a crime punishable by death or by imprisonment in the territorial prison), the motion by the defense for a separate trial was overruled.[41]

As in the Los Angeles hearing, the trial was not removed from political considerations and influences. The Los Angeles transcript was allowed as evidence, as were copies of the politically volatile 1 June 1906 "Manifesto and Program," the 9 September 1906 "General Instructions to the Revolutionists," and the 14 March 1907 "General Instructions to the Followers" (the latter two having been seized illegally by Furlong). Trinidad Vázquez was once again the star witness, contradicting some of his earlier Los Angeles testimony and absurdly testifying that "he could tell a man was a socialist by simply looking at him [laughter]." Other witnesses subpoenaed by the government included Arizona Rangers Harry Wheeler,

[39]Roosevelt to Joseph Gurney Cannon, 29 April 1908, *Letters*, VI, 1019.

[40]*Annual Message of the President*, 8 December 1908, U.S., Congress, Senate, *Papers*, 1908, pp. xxxviii–xl.

[41]Cleary to Hon. William B. Wilson, 4 May 1910, in U.S., Congress, House, *Alleged Persecutions*, pp. 15–17.

Thomas Rynning, and W. A. Olds, immigration inspector Charles Connell, and private detectives Ansel Samuels, H. C. Loehr, and Thomas Furlong.[42] The jury of twelve included no Mexican Americans, at least none with Spanish surnames.[43]

The case went to the jury a few minutes before midnight on Saturday, 15 May. At about one-thirty Sunday morning, according to Cleary, the Furlong detectives and government officials began to fire off their weapons as in a celebration. By seven o'clock that morning all the detectives, Mexican government officials, and prosecution witnesses had left town, evidently informed in advance of the jury's verdict. At 10 A.M. a verdict of "guilty" was delivered to the crowded courtroom, now filled with the friends and relatives of the defendants, including the Villarreal sisters, *revoltosa* María Talavera (Flores Magón's *compañera*), and the wife and children of Rivera. The men of Juárez in the land of Lincoln were genuinely surprised and shocked by the verdict.[44]

Cleary immediately moved for a new trial and was overruled. He then sought to get the judge to agree to a notice of an appeal, which the judge refused to do. Thus, the judgment was not stayed, and the defendants were not admitted to bail. By Wednesday, 19 May, sentencing took place. The defendants were found "guilty of the crime of conspiring to commit an offense against the United States" and sentenced to eighteen months in the territorial prison at Yuma, Arizona.[45] Again, as the irony of history would have it, the warden of the Yuma penitentiary was now none other than the former captain of the Arizona Rangers, Thomas Rynning.

The Yuma prison had originally been constructed from adobe

[42]Ibid. See also Elías to Sec. de Rel. Ext., 19 May 1909, in González Ramírez, *Epistolario y textos*, pp. 157–161; Transcript, RG 267, p. iii; "Subpoenas," U.S. v. R. Flores Magón, A. Villarreal, L. Rivera, and M. Sarabia, Criminal 669 and 671 (Ariz. Terr., U.S. 2nd Dist. Ct., 1907 and 1909), FRC Laguna Niguel.

[43]Elías to Sec. de Rel. Ext., 13 May 1909, in González Ramírez, *Epistolario y textos*, p. 155.

[44]U.S., Congress, House, *Alleged Persecutions*, p. 17; González Ramírez, *Epistolario y textos*, pp. 158–159.

[45]U.S., Congress, House, *Alleged Persecutions*, p. 17; "Judgment and Commitment, May 19, 1909," U.S. v. R. Flores Magón, A. Villarreal, & L. Rivera, Criminal 693 (Ariz. Terr., U.S. 2nd Dist. Ct., 1909), FRC Laguna Niguel.

bricks by Spaniards on a small hill near the banks of the Yuma river. During the end of the nineteenth century it had been used as a fort in the war against the Apaches. By 1909 its outcast inhabitants consisted mostly of Mexican and Negro prisoners, surviving on a diet of coffee, oats, and bread. Those detained for long periods were forced to work as stonecutters in a quarry in the neighborhood of the prison; others were employed as skilled workers within the prison. Flores Magón and Villarreal, after serving a one-week apprenticeship, went to work in a tailor shop. Because of the excessive heat (even Madero lamented their imprisonment, saying that "el clima de Yuma es abrasador"—the climate of Yuma is searingly hot)[46] they worked from five to eleven in the morning. Because of illness, Rivera spent most of his time in the infirmary.[47]

After eight months they were transferred to the prison at Florence. Here Rivera spent ten days in the "dungeon," an underground hole off the patio that was eight feet high and five feet wide. The experience so weakened him physically that he was ill for the rest of his life. On 3 August 1910, afer serving fifteen months of the original sentence, the men were released. Greeted at the prison gates by John Kenneth Turner and spokesmen for the W.F.M., they returned to Los Angeles two days later. There, after speaking to a large gathering of supporters at the Labor Temple, they went back to the business of revolution. By September a new edition of *Regeneración* was being published.[48] But the three-year detention had been a severe setback for Flores Magón, enabling Madero to eventually replace him as Mexico's revolutionary hope of the future.

The successful conviction and imprisonment of Flores Magón spurred the Mexican authorities to new heights in their war against the *revoltosos*, and, as usual, their concerns were facilitated by the U.S. government, especially the Department of Justice. Plans were made for the rearrest of Flores Magón and Villarreal under the El Paso indictments as soon as they were released from the Arizona prison. Although this never did occur, several other individuals in-

[46]Madero to S. Medrano, 9 October 1909, *Archivo de Francisco I. Madero*, II, p. 446.
[47]José C. Valadés, "Memorias del General Antonio I. Villarreal—en la penitenciaría de Florence," *La Prensa* (San Antonio), 1 December 1935.
[48]Ibid.

volved in the 1908 revolts were indicted and rearrested under the neutrality laws. Tomás Sarabia and José M. Rangel were arrested in San Antonio on 10 August 1909 on a charge of breaking the neutrality laws. Sarabia was held for over five months awaiting the action of a grand jury. With no indictment forthcoming, he was finally released on 10 January 1910. Rangel, like Antonio de P. Araujo, was convicted under the neutrality laws and sentenced to two and one-half years at Leavenworth. A similar fate overtook Priciliano Silva and Encarnación Díaz Guerra. American enforcement of the neutrality laws soon proved to be Díaz's most successful weapon, reinforcing the tactics of kidnapping, extradition, and deportation. Even if individual *revoltosos* were not convicted, they were detained and rearrested on other charges. In other words, they were politically neutralized.[49]

Another example of the Mexican government's increasing audacity was its attempt to influence judicial proceedings by surreptitiously obtaining information from attorneys for the defense. In this, the example of John Murray is illustrative. As secretary of the Political Refugee Defense League, he was personally responsible for organizing and assisting in the legal defense of the *magonistas*, including that of the Tombstone defendants. During most of 1909, from March through December, San Antonio and El Paso detectives in the pay of the Mexican government and in cooperation with American postal authorities tampered with his mail, opening and resealing envelopes and forwarding copies to the Mexican minister of foreign relations. Suspecting this, Murray and two eyewitnesses prepared "test letters" that were mailed to themselves. By so doing they were able to prove that the letters had been opened and resealed. This practice of the Mexican and American governments was finally exposed in the congressional hearings of 1910, after several *revoltosos* had already been convicted and imprisoned.[50]

As has been suggested, violations of the rights of Mexican aliens became the norm during the pre-revolutionary years of 1907–1910. The public became aware of most of these persecutions when

[49]U.S., Congress, House, *Alleged Persecutions*, pp. 57–62.

[50]Ibid., pp. 75–78. A copy of Murray's correspondence to Trowbridge, in the possession of the Mexican government, can be found in Lomelí to Sec. de Rel. Ext., 30 March 1909, AREM, L–E–954.

they were exposed by Congressman William B. Wilson of Pennsylvania during the House debate of 1910. One problem for most aliens was the public assumption that aliens were second-class "citizens" not protected by the Constitution and laws of the United States. This was partly understandable, given the confusion that then existed in legal and judicial circles over the status of the alien. The extent of application of the Bill of Rights to aliens had been a complicated legal problem for the courts, and the legal status of aliens, illegal immigrants, and naturalized citizens had been debated on several occasions.

Beginning with *Yick Wo* v. *Hopkins*, 118 U.S. 356 (1886), the courts generally held that aliens (and by implication all "persons," including illegal immigrants) had constitutional rights and were covered by the "equal protection" clause of the Fourteenth Amendment. However, in spite of a vigorous tradition of minority dissents, the Supreme Court reaffirmed on several occasions the original decision of *Fong Yue Ting* v. *U.S.*, 149 U.S. 711 (1893), in which the congressional powers of exclusion and deportation were considered plenary; this power was not limited in any way by the Bill of Rights. In other words, an alien enjoyed constitutional rights in ordinary civil and criminal cases but not in exclusion and deportation hearings.[51]

As has been indicated, the American government's legal rationale for its activities against the *revoltosos* was its public responsibility to enforce the existing laws on immigration and neutrality and its agreement with Mexico under the terms of the 22 February 1899 Treaty of Extradition. Yet, in spite of the rationale, many of the government's activities were of questionable legality. This was especially the case on the local level, where the immigration officials, accustomed to summary methods, excluded aliens on political grounds and forced deportations without hearings. These same officials, in collusion with private detectives and local police authorities, often facilitated the political kidnappings that occurred from time to time.

More subtle were the violations of the civil and political rights of aliens. Arrests and seizures were often made without complaints

[51]See Konvitz, *Civil Rights in Immigration*, pp. 44–49, 103–109; Green Haywood Hackworth, *Digest of International Law*, III, 555–562.

and warrants. Charges were unclear, often changed, and at times never even brought forward. Excessive bail was charged, which in turn meant prolonged detentions, usually incommunicado. Detainment while the accused were awaiting trial could last several months (at times without any evidence being brought against them). Rearrests were common; speedy and just trials were rare. In addition, the climate of opinion, fostered in part by the nativist, anti-radical views of Roosevelt, made the ideal of a fair trial for aliens difficult to attain. Government witnesses, not always the most trustworthy or credible of individuals, were often in the pay of the Mexican government, whose officials were more often motivated by political concerns than legal offenses. Police misconduct was common, both during arrests and imprisonment. In and out of prison the aliens' rights of privacy were violated by postal authorities, private detectives, and consular officials intercepting the mails.[52]

Issues of privacy rights often overlapped with those of freedom of speech and of the press, especially when use of the mails was involved. In 1910, acting on a complaint of the Mexican ambassador that articles in *Regeneración* were malicious and anarchistic, the State Department requested a legal opinion from Justice as to whether or not it was illegal to send anarchistic literature through the mails. The attorney general reported that it was not against the federal laws to send such literature, but that sections 211 and 212 of the Penal Code prohibited the sending through the mails of "indecent, obscene, filthy, or immoral matter."[53] Second-class mailing privileges were denied to the editors of *Regeneración*, and, by World War I, political propaganda would be considered "indecent, obscene, filthy, and immoral."

The most obvious violation of freedom of speech and press came with the closing down of alien newspaper offices, the seizing of their properties, and the harassing of the writers and editors. As the St. Louis incident of 1906 showed, the laws of the state and

[52]Several examples of persecutions of Mexican citizens by the government of the United States came out during the House debate of 1910. See U.S., Congress, House, *Congressional Record*, 61st Cong., 2d Sess., 21 April 1910, 45, pp. 5135–5138.
[53]F. E. Hutchings to J. A. Fowler, 17 January 1911, RG 60, file 90755/383.

federal governments did not authorize the suppression of newspapers, and libel suits had to be based on criminal, not political, offenses. Later, in 1910, again in response to the Mexican ambassador, the State Department ruled that "inflammatory newspaper propaganda" did not constitute a violation of the neutrality laws.[54] Yet Justice and immigration officials, in conjunction with consuls and local authorities, continued to curtail the publication and circulation of *revoltoso* newspapers. This practice not only was contrary to constitutional traditions but was also in violation of neutrality laws that specifically disallowed the government from moving against editors critical of a foreign government.[55]

In addition, both Roosevelt and Taft, in spite of the latter's alleged legalism, pursued a most liberal interpretation of the neutrality laws that allowed search and seizure missions in order to stop arms, munitions, and persons from going into Mexico. This commerce in arms was not a violation of the neutrality laws until the Arms Embargo Act of 1912. Moreover, customs regulations were often confused with neutrality statutes, with illegal embargos being instituted along the border by officers of the U.S. Army, customs officials, and immigration inspectors.

Finally, the propriety of the U.S. government's activities in these matters must be questioned. Even though it was against the law for government agencies to hire and use private detectives, government investigators and secret service agents cooperated closely with detectives who were in the employ of a foreign country—a country whose leaders, naturally enough, had no constitutional scruples (at least in terms of the U.S. Constitution) when it came to confronting the *revoltosos*. The entire practice of using secret service agents at home and abroad for political purposes was not a part of the humanitarian traditions of the past, especially when it affected America's self-image as a refuge for religious and political outcasts. The conclusion is unavoidable: the U.S. government aided and abetted Mexico's leaders in their struggle with the

[54]Hackworth, *Digest of International Law*, II, 140–142.

[55]"The U.S. government has no power, under our Constitution and laws, to interfere with publications in the states criticising foreign governments or encouraging revolts against such governments." From Moore, *A Digest of International Law*, VII, 980.

magonistas, even to the extent of breaking and ignoring American laws. The practice of governmental violation of the constitutional rights of aliens and citizens did not begin with World War I, the Red Scare, or even with the modern CIA. Its antecedents date back to the turn of this century, if not before.

Essentially, the problem was sociological rather than legal. Procedural guarantees, even if not violated, could not fairly resolve what was in effect an unfair struggle between the rich and the poor, between capital and labor. Civil libertarians could argue legal and constitutional rights, but in the end it was really a question of the class interests of the state, which, in turn, had a monopoly on police and judicial power and authority. The proceedings against the *revoltosos* were political, not criminal, the result of an effective binational police and espionage system.

THREE
The Machinery of Suppression
in Don Porfirio's Mexico

> All professions have their parasites and crooks.
> Thomas Furlong, detective

7. The Creel International Detective Agency

It was 7 January 1907, one day before the bloody massacre at the Río Blanco textile mills, and Juan Sarabia was "on trial" in Chihuahua.

"You are the *bandido* Juan Sarabia?"

"I am not a *bandido*," answered Sarabia. "*Los bandidos* are the others."

"Who are these 'others'?" the don asked.

Sarabia paused, smiled bitterly, and looked directly at the old patrón, Luis Terrazas. He replied, "Porfirio Díaz, Corral, Creel, Terrazas and many others."[1]

Díaz's orders were executed. The workers were executed. Guilty! All parties were guilty of class consciousness. Sarabia was sent to San Juan de Ulúa and ordered to stay there for seven years in order to erase his guilt and his consciousness.

Then it was 24 January 1907, seventeen days after Juan Sarabia's "trial" in Chihuahua, sixteen days after the deaths of the Río Blanco strikers. Earlier, in December, Enrique Clay Creel had been officially named "Embajador Extraordinario Plenipotenciario de México en los Estados Unidos de América." Don Enrique was now in El Paso, on his way to his new post in Washington. A banquet was to be held in his honor that evening at the Hotel Sheldon.

Francisco Mallén, the Mexican consul at El Paso, had made all the arrangements down to the smallest detail. The banquet program had been engraved in gold, and included, appropriately, a quotation from Mexican Secretary of the Treasury José Liman-

---

[1]Sarabia quotation translated from the anonymous author of "Cómo fracasó el movimiento revolucionario de 1906," *El Demócrata* (Mexico City), 10 September 1924.

tour about "commerce, friendship, order, justice, and progress." The toasts and responses had been rehearsed, including Judge Peyton F. Edwards's fervent praise of the immortal Lincoln and the immortal Díaz. The audience, well orchestrated, knew that timing was important, with "tremendous applause" to follow the judge's final superlative: "I believe that President Díaz is the greatest statesman in the world today." The champagne, liqueurs, and cognac were ready to be served ("J. & F. Martell, or does the señora prefer Marie Brizard?").[2]

It was nine o'clock, the Regimental Band of Fort Bliss struck up the music, and el jefe político and director of the "Friends of Enrique Creel," Señor don Silvano Montemayor, had just arrived from the dimly lit streets of Ciudad Juárez. Don Enrique and his wife, Señora Angela Terrazas de Creel—the daughter of the wealthy Chihuahua patrón don Luis Terrazas—were quartered on the entire first floor of the Sheldon. From there they easily made their way to the banquet hall. Greetings, toasts, dry martinis, responses, "tremendous applause," Moët and Chandon wines, and a menu: "Blue Points Sur coquille; Tortue Verte; Pate de foie gras en bellevue, Amandes Salees Jeu; Aiguilettes de Black Bass en papillotte, Salade de Concombres; Filet de Boeuf Richelieu; Asperges Sauce Mousseline; Punch des deux Nations; Salades de laitue; Becassines Anglaise; Ice Cream en Moules Varies; Gateaux de Soiree."[3]

South of El Paso it was also time "to supper." Sarabia emerged from the blackness of his cell into the dimly lit prison courtyard. He joined a brown line of ragged, bare-limbed figures. They moved slowly across the stone-flagged pavement to the copper cauldron in the corner. When the trusty called his number, Sarabia, holding a large earthen cup in his hands, passed before the big pot. An iron ladle greeted him with warm, two-day-old soup—"tremendous applause," for it was once again atole, the corn-flour gruel of fallen gods and mortals. It was getting late, the señora was tired of dancing, and don Enrique was satiated. Consul Mallén called it good, the judge went home, and the banquet was declared over. The

---

[2]AREM, L–E–422, Enrique Creel, su expediente personal.
[3]Ibid.

prisoners were returned to their cells, located on the entire first floor.[4]

At the time of the banquet, Creel was fifty-three years old and was just reaching the apex of his political and business careers. He had been born in Chihuahua, the son of a Kentuckian, the first American consul in that city, and his education and experiences made him bilingual and bicultural. Having married into the fabulously wealthy Terrazas clan, he became the family's main contact with the financial and political centers of Mexico City, New York, London, Paris, and Washington.[5]

Between 1903 and 1907, while his father-in-law was governor of Chihuahua, Creel served as interim governor and as *regidor* on the Chihuahua City council. In these capacities he furthered the wealth and prestige of the family's holdings in the state, granting timber concessions to William Greene and Albert Fall and mineral rights to Guggenheim's American Smelting and Refining Company. With his younger brother Juan he managed and directed the Banco Minero de Chihuahua and the Mexican Central Railway. In addition, he served on the corporate boards of the Banco Mercantil de Monterrey and the Banco Nacional Refaccionario, and wrote several books on banking, commerce, trade, and agriculture.[6]

To facilitate the development of the Terrazas estate, in 1903 Creel arranged for a rapprochement between Porfirio Díaz and don Luis. Their combined political power allowed Creel to pacify labor in Chihuahua and attract foreign capital for developmental purposes. Part of that pacification involved the centralization of state power. By October 1907, Creel was inaugurated constitutional governor of Chihuahua for a four-year period. As governor, Creel appointed *jefes políticos* who had executive and judicial authority over the cities and villages in their districts. A power triad was eventually developed that included Díaz (as well as Corral and Subsecretary of Foreign Relations Rosendo Pineda), the Terrazas

[4]This description was inspired in part by John Murray's "San Juan de Ulua," *The Border* 1 (February 1909): 2.

[5]*The Mexican Herald*, 15 October 1908, NF, case 8183/185.

[6]William H. Beezley, *Insurgent Governor: Abraham González and the Mexican Revolution in Chihuahua*, pp. 7–9; Ceceña, *Mexico en la órbita imperial*, p. 82.

clan, and important foreigners like Greene, Guggenheim, Lord Cowdry (Weetman Pearson), and William Randolph Hearst. Creel's world view complemented that of the foreign elites and embraced the ideas of modernization, industrial progress, international law, and global capitalism.[7]

As a financier and banker, Creel had many international contacts. He was president of the French-controlled Banco Central Mexicano, the second largest banking firm in all of Mexico (only the Banco Nacional de México was larger). He was also president of the joint Mexican-French Banco Hipotecario de Crédito Territorial and the British-owned Mexican Eagle Oil Company. As a board member of the American-operated Kansas City, Mexico and Orient Railway Company, Creel had many business colleagues in the United States. His biculturalism served him well in financial circles and also facilitated his political career (it was not surprising that he served as official translator and host when Taft met Díaz at El Paso and Ciudad Juárez in 1909).[8]

Between 1907 and 1911, Creel served variously as state governor, Mexican ambassador to Washington, and finally, minister of foreign relations. He was ambassador from 18 December 1906 until his resignation on 25 September 1908. Most of that time was spent on leave from Washington handling political and clan matters in Chihuahua. For example, during 1908 he was only in Washington for one month, between 8 July and 12 August, leaving most of the government's work in the hands of the *chargé d'affaires*. On 25 April 1910, Creel was named minister of foreign relations, a post he retained until 23 March 1911.[9]

Toward the end of the Porfiriato he was excluded from office as Díaz made several compromises in hopes of retaining power. With her husband having been shuffled aside, Mrs. Creel spoke most bitterly of Díaz, saying that

> Don Porfirio asked Enrique to come to Mexico, as Secretary of Foreign Relations, but he did not care to do so. Yet, on the urgent re-

[7]Beezley, *Insurgent Governor*, pp. 8–9.
[8]Ceceña, *México en la órbita imperial*, pp. 81–82.
[9]For Creel's credentials and a list of career activities see E. Garza Pérez to Manuel Berlanga, 14 February 1919, AREM, L–E–422, E. Creel, su expediente personal.

quest of Don Porfirio, at a great sacrifice of his personal business interests and a loss of a great deal of money, he came and now Don Porfirio has kicked him out.[10]

Forced from power, he went into exile into the United States, a reluctant *revoltoso* who supported Orozco against Madero in 1912 and later, in 1915, as spokesman for the San Antonio refugees, urged Huerta's revolt against Carranza.

Between 1906 and 1911, as governor, ambassador, and minister, Creel was the essential man who directed and coordinated Porfirio Díaz's attack against, first, the *magonistas*, and, subsequently, the *maderistas*. Creel, as informal head of Díaz's espionage service, secured the cooperation of U.S. authorities and employed several detective agencies in the United States to assist in the arrest and prosecution of revolutionary exiles. The most important detective agency was the Furlong Secret Service Company of St. Louis, Missouri, owned and managed by Thomas Furlong. Furlong's investigators worked throughout Canada, the United States, and Mexico in what was truly an international operation. Creel coordinated the activities of the Furlong detectives with those of governmental authorities, forwarding intelligence reports from Furlong to Vice-President Corral, the U.S. Department of State, and the various consulates in the United States (especially Los Angeles, Tucson, St. Louis, El Paso, Eagle Pass, San Antonio, and New York City).[11]

In order to expedite investigations, Creel, by arrangement with Corral, would often authorize key individuals to receive Furlong's secret reports. These individuals included such special legal advisers and informants as Judge Griner of Del Rio, John W. Foster of San Antonio, the Creager and Hudson law firm of Brownsville, and, of course, William Greene's attorney Norton Chase. To facilitate intelligence on the Mexican side, Creel, as governor, circulated wanted posters, interrogation instructions, and general directions to the Mexican secret police, to the state and military governors of Sonora, Nuevo León, and Coahuila, and to important *jefes políticos*

[10]As quoted in Arnold Shanklin to Wilber J. Carr, 27 April 1911, in Hanrahan, *Documents*, II, pt. 2, 303.
[11]See Creel's correspondence in STC, box 26, folder 72 & box 27, folders 11d and 13a.

in the border districts.[12] U.S. consuls, such as Luther Ellsworth, a special Justice and State Department agent, were also part of Creel's espionage system.[13]

Military intelligence was also important in Creel's operations. Kosterlitzky's reports were forwarded by Torres to Creel, and the district chiefs or *jefes* had access to information gathered by the local *acordadas* (private fighting forces). On another level, Creel's fellow banker, General Manuel González Cosío (president of the Banco de Londres y México), the minister of war, received intelligence from Creel and forwarded most of the relevant troop and military police data to Corral and the Foreign Relations Ministry. Corral, in turn, as head of Gobernación's *policía secreta,* as well as those federal rovers, the *rurales,* furnished Creel with operatives' reports and photographs, which were then circulated among the district chiefs.[14]

Creel's sources of information were in no way limited to Mexico. American postal authorities cooperated with local consuls and private detectives in censoring and intercepting the mails. Spies and informers, in the pay of the Mexican government, infiltrated Liberal Party ranks. In at least one instance a U.S. customs collector was suspected by Treasury Department officials of being a secret agent of the Mexican government.[15] And, of course, the U.S. military, the secret service, and the Bureau of Investigation (after 1909) cooperated with Creel and the Mexican consuls. Finally, American entrepreneurs, especially Greene, shared their own intelligence with their colleague and friend, don Enrique.

Throughout this period the consular corps, Mexican and American, proved to be a most vital part of Creel's spy and police network. By this time there were thirty-one Mexican consulates in the United States, more than half of them west of the Mississippi. They were usually staffed by a consul, vice-consul, and secretary. Most of the duties and responsibilities of the consuls were outlined in the *Reglamento* of 1871 as revised in 1905 (and in 1910–

[12]Ibid.

[13]See Dorothy Pierson Kerig, "A United States Consul on the Border During the Mexican Revolution: The Case of Luther T. Ellsworth" (thesis).

[14]See the Corral-Creel correspondence for 1906 in STC, box 26, folder 7a.

[15]Robert Dowe to Luther Ellsworth, 24 December 1910, RG 60, file 90755/395.

1911). The consul's formal duties were primarily centered on the promotion of trade and commerce. Under the law of Mexico the consul was restricted from involvement in the political affairs of the country in which he was stationed. Making conditions more difficult for consuls along the frontier was the presence of a large Mexican community whose members often interpreted the consul's duties in terms of their own ethnic and political concerns, a unique situation that did not face Mexico's consuls elsewhere.[16]

Of special significance in the history of the *revoltosos* were the consulates of Los Angeles, Phoenix, Tucson, El Paso, St. Louis, San Antonio, and New York City. Of secondary importance were the consulates and vice-consulates of Calexico, Nogales, Del Rio, Douglas, Naco, Kansas City, Denver, Brownsville, Eagle Pass, Laredo, Rio Grande City, Atlanta, and Cincinnati. In addition, the consul-general at Montreal and the Toronto consul were important sources of information about *magonista* activities. At Montreal the consul-general developed a close working relationship with the Canadian secret police, at times communicating with them to the exclusion of the Canadian foreign service. In Europe the consulates and legations at Hamburg, Vienna, and Trieste were also occupied with forwarding local newspaper reports about rumored PLM uprisings in Mexico.[17]

Along the frontier, conditions pushed the consuls toward espionage and away from their normal commercial duties. Although their intelligence roles and special duties as secret police agents were never formalized into law, it is obvious that the consuls were assigned these roles when dealing with the *revoltoso* problem. The presence of a large community of Mexicans and Mexican Americans sympathetic to the goals of the *revoltosos* (by April 1911, U.S. marshall Eugene Nolte estimated that 90 percent of the

---

[16]Juan Gómez-Quiñones, "Piedras contra la Luna, México en Aztlán y Aztlán en México: Chicano-Mexican Relations and the Mexican Consulates, 1900–1920," in *Contemporary Mexico: Papers of the IV International Congress of Mexican History*, ed. James Wilkie, et al., pp. 496–497. See also AREM, L–E–1669, Asunto: Correspondencia recibida por el consulado de México en Phoenix, Arizona, EEUU de A.—durante los años de 1904 a 1909.

[17]AREM, L–E–1244. See also D. A. Ansell to Sec. de Rel. Ext., 7 September 1906, and O. W. Vieer to Sec. de Rel. Ext., 5 and 6 September 1906– AREM, L–E–1241, pt. 3; Gilberto Martínez to Sec. del Rel. Ext., 6 September 1906, AREM, L–E–1241, pt. 4.

residents along the border sympathized with the Madero movement),[18] politically hostile to Díaz, and in organized revolt, meant that the consul could hardly remain apolitical. Practically all the smaller towns along the border had a personage who "enjoyed" the title of consul or vice-consul. Some of these towns were quite remote, having little or no trade and commerce, yet supporting a consulate that could only be maintained at a cost to the Díaz government of thousands of dollars a year. Obviously these individuals were not simply consuls: they were spies, legal advisers, investigators, and special police agents.[19]

In the supression of the *revoltosos* a general pattern developed among the consuls. As a rule, both Creel and the Ministry of Foreign Relations facilitated much of the correspondence between and among consuls. When the *revoltosos* were threatening the peace in Douglas, for example, much correspondence took place between Antonio Maza (Douglas), Arturo Elías (Tucson), and Francisco Mallén (El Paso). Not only did the consuls cooperate with each other, they developed close working relations with the local authorities as well, especially state and territorial officials, Texas and Arizona Rangers, and U.S. marshals, attorneys, and customs and immigration officials. The Ministry of Foreign Relations always kept related government agencies informed of the content of consular reports, forwarding copies and memorandums to the Treasury (Hacienda), Interior (Gobernación), and War departments. Although the early efforts of the consulates to curtail *magonista* actions were direct and crude, involving local officials in physical assaults and harassment, the later efforts were more sophisticated and made more use of U.S. federal police and judicial authority in suppressing the rebels.[20]

The *magonistas* were quick to develop a political issue out of the role of the consuls. After the Arizona Rangers broke up the Douglas Liberal club, Aguirre wrote to Roosevelt, complaining that the group had been disbanded by order of the consul in violation

[18]Nolte to Att. Gen., 25 April 1911, in Hanrahan, *Documents*, I, pt. 2, 336–337.
[19]Gómez-Quiñones, "Piedras contra la Luna," p. 500; Turner, *Barbarous Mexico*, p. 240.
[20]AREM, L–E–1240; Gómez-Quiñones, "Piedras contra la Luna," p. 507.

of the U.S. Constitution, and requesting his benevolent intervention because the "Mexicans do not have the protection of their consuls, only their persecutions."[21] Later, in 1911, Flores Magón wrote an article in *Regeneración* called "In Defense of the Mexicans" in which he publicized the irresponsibility of the Calexico consul for not investigating the death of a Mexican laborer.[22] He concluded his article by saying that the consuls

> . . . are excellent police for the despots and the bourgeoisie, but are worthless when some poor Mexican comes before them in need of help.
>
> The Mexicans have been abandoned to the forces of luck in this country—akin to the way they are treated in Mexico. They are excluded from the hotels and restaurants; in the so-called courts of justice they are found guilty and sentenced in the twinkling of an eye; the penitentiaries arc full of Mexicans who are Absolutely Innocent. In Texas, Louisiana, and other states they live without hope simply because of a stupid prejudice against our race.[23]

Flores Magón's charges were echoed by other *revoltosos* who rightly viewed the consular staff as foreign representatives more friendly to Anglo and upper-class interests than to those of the Mexican community in the United States.

The specific assignments of the consuls ranged from general surveillance of the *revoltosos*, especially the PLM, to outright intimidation and harassment. Following Creel's instructions they hired private detectives. The Pacific Co-operative Detective Association and the I. S. Hurst Detective Agency worked in conjunction with the Los Angeles consul. A private detective by the name of Manuel Peña del Pino was hired by the Mexican consul in Phoenix. The Furlong Secret Service Company, hired by the St. Louis consul, worked on a national and international scale. In New York City, the Burns and Sheridan National Detective Agency was employed to investigate the activities of the *revoltosos*, especially those attempting to send arms and finance to *maderistas* in Texas and

[21]*Arizona Daily Star*, 7 September 1906, encl. in Elías to Sec. de Rel. Ext., 8 September 1906, AREM, L–E–1241, pt. 3.

[22]Flores Magón, "En Defensa de los Mexicanos," *Regeneración* (n.d.), in AREM, 12–7–2, 1241 (73–1), Expediente: "Mexicanos en Santa Rita, Albuquerque," 1911.

[23]Ibid.

Mexico. Burns and Sheridan also had detectives on assignment in Chicago. Creel employed this company on the recommendation of Attorney General George Wickersham, who noted that they "have supplanted the Pinkerton Agency in all national bank work." Creel also hired individual detectives for specific jobs, like E. J. Thavonat, head of a secret police company in San Francisco. To aid the consuls, several legal advisers were hired to act as informants, including Judge Griner, T. M. Paschal, Thomas Foster, and Creager and Hudson in Texas and Norton Chase in Missouri and New York City. Finally, some secret service personnel, nominally working under the directions of the departments of Justice and Treasury, had their travel and living costs paid for by the Mexican government.[24]

The consuls also hired undercover agents to infiltrate the juntas and clubs of the *revoltosos*. Mention has already been made of Trinidad Vázquez's pivotal role in spying on and testifying against the Douglas Liberals. Vázquez was also used in the prosecution of Flores Magón, Villarreal, and Rivera—and it is likely that the consuls manufactured false evidence for his use. Others included Ansel Samuels, who infiltrated the St. Louis Junta in 1905, and Jiménez Castro, who was used to set up the arrests of the El Paso group. In addition, Norton Chase arranged with Corral and secret service agent Joe Priest to place Eduardo Ruiz in the San Antonio county jail to pose as a Liberal sympathizer. While there, Ruiz spoke with Trinidad García, who revealed his activity in Jiménez and told how Ricardo and Enrique Flores Magón directed the uprising. He also implicated Villarreal and other Arredondo rebels in the Jiménez uprising.[25]

The consuls became experts in intercepting the mails. Mail

---

[24]Hurst to Lozano, 4 February 1911, AREM, L–E–627, R–10–2; Creel to Cayetano Romero, 7 February 1911, AREM, L–E–627, R–10–3; C. C. Crowley to Lozano (var. letters for 1906), AREM, L–E–1244; for Peña del Pino see AREM, L–E–954; Creager and Hudson to Alberto Leal, 29 December 1906, AREM, L–E–1244; Wickersham to the Mex. Amb. (Francisco de la Barra), 17 November 1910, RG 60, file 90755; Enrique Ornelas to Mariscal, 17 June 1907, AREM, L–E–855, 118–R–5.

[25]Mariscal to Ornelas, 6 December 1906, and Ornelas to Mariscal, December 1906, in Fabela, *Documentos históricos*, XI, 32–35.

to and from *revoltosos* and their sympathizers was opened in Los Angeles, Tucson, St. Louis, El Paso, and San Antonio. Antonio Lozano not only intercepted the mail of *magonistas* in the Los Angeles county jail, but of American citizens and radicals who aided and were friendly with the prisoners. Like Lozano, Arturo Elías, the consul in Tucson, intercepted all mail going to Treviño, Humbert, and García in the Tucson county jail. Between 1906 and 1909 the Mexican consul in St. Louis estimated that he intercepted about three thousand letters. Most of these were seized and copied by Furlong agents, who then forwarded copies to the consul, who in turn sent them on to Corral, Mariscal, and Creel. Copies of all the intercepted communiques were forwarded to Corral at Gobernación, where information was shared with Mexico's secret police.[26]

When conditions demanded it, the consuls were willing to use bribery to induce illegal ends, which included kidnapping and murder. Bribes, theft, and robbery were used to obtain information on *magonistas*. Deception was commonly practiced to lure people into Mexico, as when the old, gray-headed Colonel Redondo was promised a commission in the regular army of Mexico, plus a salary and pension, as a reward for turning over to the government the names of Liberal sympathizers. In December 1908, on his return to Mexico, instead of being greeted by his family he was welcomed by the prison guards at Belem. The most notable case of refugee kidnapping was that of Manuel Sarabia, who was originally arrested under the direction of consul Maza. Later, the consul attempted to cover up the plot by muzzling a string of Arizona newspapers. Consul Lozano, also in the kidnapping business, ran fake employment offices whose staff attempted to hire *revoltosos* and lure them to Mexico, where they could be captured by the police. Finally, Luis Alberto, a Mexican agent in Del Rio operating in conjunction with the consul at Eagle Pass, offered

[26]U.S., Congress, House, *Alleged Persecutions*, pp. 78–80; González Ramírez, *Epistolario y textos*, pp. 172–173; Mallén, "Indice compendiado de la correspondencia adjunta," 22 October 1906, STC, box 27, folder 9b; Furlong to Diebold, 17 March 1908, AREM, L–E–954 Bis (also see Furlong to Diebold, 8 January 1907, and various other examples of mail interceptions in L–E–954 Bis); Miguel Macedo to Sec. de Rel. Ext., AREM, L–E–1243, pt. 7.

two "hit men" one thousand dollars for each Las Vacas revolutionist killed.[27]

An interesting example of the various espionage and intelligence tasks of the Mexican consuls is the case of A. V. Lomelí, the consul at Laredo in 1906 and the man who replaced Mallén at El Paso in late 1907. From Laredo, Lomelí reported to the minister of foreign relations on a variety of *revoltoso* matters. He observed the commerce of the region, reporting on the clandestine movement of arms and munitions across the border. Lomelí complained that his information was limited by a lack of "means of vigilance," the timidity of honorable Mexicans, and the hostility of the majority of the Mexican community.[28]

Lomelí noted the actions of the local community, and concluded that the workers in the workshop of the National Railways of Mexico appeared to be planning a strike or revolt (a conclusion that proved to be accurate). He went on to describe secret meetings that the labor leaders were attending, and suggested that the potential for a riot or an armed expedition was extremely high, given the propensity of the poor for "socialism." After naming several troublemakers, he noted "A. L. Apple's" fraudulent use of the mails, and encouraged his superiors to get the post office to deny the use of the mails to the *magonistas*. Finally, he pleaded for a more efficient spy service, maintaining that it "would be better for the Secretary of Gobernación to send here a skillful and loyal secret agent, since the American and Mex-Tex detectives here cannot be employed with any confidence because of their absolute lack of honor."[29]

The consulate operations succeeded in a number of ways. The consuls suppressed several *revoltoso* newspapers and, with the aid of local American authorities, prevented the *revoltosos* from exercising their constitutional rights of free speech. The threat of Creel's international police force was usually enough to get the

---

[27]U.S., Congress, House, *Alleged Persecutions*, pp. 21, 82–89; Turner, *Barbarous Mexico*, pp. 238–241.

[28]Lomelí to Sec. de Rel. Ext., 8 September 1906, AREM, L–E–1240, pt. 2, pp. 105–106.

[29]Ibid.

more timid to engage in self-censorship. The consuls also directed most of the major arrests, including those in Douglas, St. Louis, El Paso, Del Rio, and Los Angeles. The border arrests usually involved the coordination of police raids on both sides. It was also the consuls who managed the campaign of deportation and facilitated the American enforcement of the neutrality laws.

The consul's role as a spy would continue throughout the post-revolutionary period, from Madero through Carranza. Terrorism, threats, and violence all intimidated the *revoltosos*. In the end the PLM adherents and leaders were left confused, distrustful of one another, and in prison. And these successes had to be shared with their American counterparts across the border, for U.S. consuls in Mexico were also a part of the "Creel International Detective Agency."

By 1911 the United States had twenty-five consulates in Mexico, many of which reflected the traditional concern of consuls in protecting the rights of American seamen by being located along the Mexican coasts, in La Paz, Mazatlán, Manzanillo, Acapulco, Salina Cruz, Tapachula, Progreso, Frontera, Veracruz, Tampico, and elsewhere. Frontier stations included Ensenada, Nogales, Ciudad Juárez, Ciudad Porfirio Díaz (today Piedras Negras), Nuevo Laredo, and Matamoros. The important Spanish colonial towns of Puebla, Oaxaca, and Mérida did not then have consulates.[30]

Like those of their Mexican counterparts, the American consuls' primary duties were commercial in nature. As Huntington Wilson noted, the object of consular service was

> . . . the extension and increase of American business by opening up, widening, and developing fields for our export trade. . . . [The consul] must know what the country needs or would take in raw materials, in commodities, and in manufactured articles. . . .
>
> Our consular service, then, exists to facilitate and promote the material and personal interests of the American people in foreign countries.[31]

[30]Philander Chase Knox Papers, Library of Congress Manuscript Division, Washington, D.C. (hereafter cited as Knox Papers), Dept. of State File, "Disorders in Mexico," Information Series "A", Box 40, No. 73, 15–30 March 1911.

[31]Huntington Wilson, "The American Foreign Service," *The Outlook* 82 (3 March 1906): 499–500.

As the American empire expanded, so too did the consular service and the consuls' responsibilities. It was only a small step from supplying economic data for American exporters to that of developing information on *revoltosos* for State and Justice agents.

Since the consul also had to regulate customs in his district and collect duties, he was concerned with the movement of equipment and people. Illicit trade and commerce were legitimate consular concerns, and then as now drugs and guns were linked to the business of smuggling munitions and cheap labor to and from the United States. With no other American espionage agents on Mexican soil (with the exception of a few secret service agents and army intelligence officers), it is no wonder that the consuls stepped in to fill the intelligence gap. In 1911 they were a main source of military intelligence on Mexico, as well as important allies of the Bureau of Investigation and Treasury's secret service.[32]

A classic case study of a U.S. consul on the border is that of Luther T. Ellsworth. Ellsworth officially assumed his duties at Ciudad Porfirio Díaz on 31 December 1907 after a ten-year foreign-service career at posts in Venezuela, Colombia, and Chihuahua City. Beginning in 1908, he played a major role in developing a network designed to prevent *magonistas* and *maderistas* from committing neutrality violations and otherwise disrupting the rapport between Mexico and the United States. By June 1908 he had been appointed "special representative of the Departments of Justice and State in all neutrality matters." Because he preferred undercover work, the routine business of running a consulate office was left to the vice-consul and the consul's clerk.[33]

Ellsworth's first assignment came in 1908 with an investigation at Del Rio into the origins of the Las Vacas uprising. He soon joined Eagle Pass customs collector Robert W. Dowe, U.S. marshal Eugene Nolte, U.S. attorney Charles Boynton, as well as several American cavalry troop officers, in a general undercover assignment. Out of this investigation came several recommendations on

---

[32]For a history of the expansion of the consular service see Chester Lloyd Jones, *The Consular Service of the United States*.

[33]See NF, case 2787, "Personnel File of Luther T. Ellsworth."

how to improve American enforcement of the neutrality laws, including the idea of a special frontier secret service and the employment of "former" Furlong detectives to assist Joe Priest and other special agents in Texas, Arizona, and California.[34]

Throughout 1909, Ellsworth cooperated with Nolte and Priest in developing a police network from Brownsville to Nogales. It was Ellsworth's hope that the new system would be instrumental in suppressing the trend toward "socialism." He constantly urged the hiring of extra secret service men, marshals, and customs officers, and encouraged immigration inspectors to engage in spying. Ellsworth also argued for more Spanish-speaking officials and investigators, to be assigned to the important port of entry cities like El Paso and Nogales. To improve enforcement in the Del Rio area, he suggested to the Mexicans that they upgrade that city to consular status (which was done). Fluent in Spanish and at home with Mexican officialdom, he was assured by Corral that the Mexican secret police in Arizona would inform him of any important findings.[35]

From 1910 to 1911 he was active in containing the *maderista* movement. He worked especially closely with Thomas Foster and Stanley W. Finch (chief of the Bureau of Investigation) in intercepting Madero's mail and in maintaining surveillance over the Francisco Madero family in San Antonio. This latter assignment was carried out at the behest of Consul-General Ornelas of San Antonio.[36] In fulfilling his duties he developed an intragovernmental structure of the first magnitude, as illustrated by the following note he sent to the State Department in 1910:

> There is evidence on both sides of the border line of serious unrest and intrigue. Have situation on American side of border well in hand and with assistance of federal officers of Customs, Immigration, etc., United States Marshals, Bureau of Investigation Agents,

[34]Kerig, "A United States Counsul," pp. 21–37; "Brief Combined Report of the Investigation," Boynton et. al., NF, case 8183/82.

[35]Kerig, "A United States Consul," pp. 38–51.

[36]Ellsworth to Knox, 9 November 1910, RG 60, file 90755; Foster to Creel, 1 February 1911, AREM, L–E–627; also see the anonymous (intercepted) letter to F. Madero, Sr., 13 December 1910, in RG 60, file 90755/378.

United States Secret Service men, and United States Cavalry will keep it so.[37]

The only branch of Creel's spy service that was more important than Ellsworth's activities and the consular services of both countries was that of private detectives in the United States, the group that Ellsworth failed to mention in the above quotation.

As for private detectives in the pay of Mexico, much confusion has been generated by historians about this aspect of the "diplomacy of suppression"—an indication that some of the dust from the Cananea uprising has still not settled! Most authors assert that the famous Pinkertons were hired by the Mexican government to trace the everchanging paths of the *revoltosos*. Díaz's enemies of yesterday, like writers today, used the term "Pinkerton" in a generic way to mean "private detective" in general, a use that was misleading and is historically inaccurate.[38]

Thus the Flores Magón brothers spoke of the Pinkertons who followed them to Canada and compromised Manuel Sarabia in St. Louis. John Kenneth Turner stated that during the Cananea strike "Greene's Pinkertons were sent about the streets for another shootup of the Mexicans," and the socialist editors of the *St. Louis Labor* referred to "The Blood-Stained Pinkerton Agency" that sent operatives to Cananea in order to incite the Mexicans into rebellion.[39]

---

[37]Quoted from Ellsworth to Sec. of State, 19 November 1910, RG 60, file 90755/285. Also see Ellsworth to Sec. of State, 15 February 1911, in Hanrahan, *Documents*, I, pt. 1, 162.

[38]James Cockcroft has Pinkertons running through his narrative, crediting them with the arrest of Enrique Flores Magón in San Antonio in 1905 and of Ricardo Flores Magón in Los Angeles in 1907. He even refers to that "Pinkerton detective Thomas Furlong." Other writers who refer to Pinkertons in this sense are Gómez-Quiñones, Bernard Axelrod, and William Beezley. In a letter to the author from New York City (17 August 1973), W. C. Linn of Pinkerton's Inc. states: "We have heard from many sources that we are involved in the investigation of the activities of a Mexican revolutionary group in the years cited in your letter. Nevertheless, we have no records to substantiate the allegations."

See the following: Cockcroft, *Intellectual Precursors*, pp. 121, 125–129, 134, 146; Gómez-Quiñones, *Sembradores*, p. 25; Axelrod, "St. Louis and the Mexican Revolutionaries," p. 97; Beezley, *Insurgent Governor*, p. 11.

[39]Enrique Flores Magón, "Añoranzas. La Pinkerton," *El Nacional* (Mexico City), 17 May 1946, pp. 3, 7; Turner, *Barbarous Mexico*, p. 184; *St. Louis Labor*, 4 August 1906.

But the *magonistas* were mistaken. As has already been indicated, a variety of detective agencies were involved, the most important being Furlong's company, which worked for Creel between 1906 and the eve of the Revolution,[40] and the available evidence indicates little if any Pinkerton involvement.

One of the earlier firms to be hired by Creel was the Pacific Co-operative Detective Association of Los Angeles, which worked for Lozano between November 1906 and the middle of March 1907. C. C. Crowley, the company manager, supervised operatives in Los Angeles, Carlsbad (New Mexico), El Paso, and Ciudad Juárez ("between the smelter and across the river"). In Los Angeles, Crowley himself intercepted PLM mail and posed as a hiring agent for the labor bureau of the Western Pacific Railway. At one time he attempted to hire Gutiérrez de Lara to act as a hiring agent who would unwittingly send his PLM associates to nonexistent jobs in Mexico. Once in Mexico they would be arrested. Unfortunately for Lozano, Gutiérrez de Lara refused the offer.[41] Crowley's operatives in Carlsbad and El Paso concentrated on the PLM members in the mining camps—often spending more time and money getting drunk with their *revoltoso* suspects than in obtaining information. Carlsbad was not an easy place to stay sober in even then. Because of Crowley's limited successes, Creel suspended his services after 16 March 1907.[42]

In southern Arizona during 1908 and early 1909, the Mexican consul at Phoenix, Arturo Elías, had the services of private detective Manuel Peña del Pino. This detective was also in the pay of Miguel López Torres, the vice-consul of Clifton, Arizona. Peña del Pino was originally from Oaxaca, but by 1909 he had lived in Tucson for over eleven years. He was mainly active in the Arizona and New Mexico area (Tucson, Morenci, Metcalf, Nogales, Yuma, Globe, Clifton, and Albuquerque), although at one time he re-

[40]Furlong's own faulty memory records 1907 as the year when he was first hired by Creel. See his *Fifty Years a Detective*, p. 138.

[41]AREM, L–E–1244, contains several examples of correspondence between Crowley and Lozano.

[42]Crowley to Lozano, 25 October 1906, AREM, L–E–1244; Crowley to Lozano, 16 October 1906, encl. in Lozano to Mariscal, 16 October 1906, AREM, L–E–1245, pt. 9; Creel to Sec. de Rel. Ext., 16 March 1907, AREM, L–E–1243, pt. 7.

ported on the activities of Práxedis Guerrero in El Paso and Chihuahua. Most of his accounts were character descriptions of *magonistas* in the mining camps of Arizona. At the end of March 1909 he was transferred from Arizona, having been recommended for service with the Mexican Bureau of Immigration.[43]

The exact date when Furlong first went to work for Creel and the Mexican government cannot be determined with accuracy. In November of 1906, the Mexican consul at St. Louis, M. E. Diebold, was ordered by the minister of foreign relations to employ the services of Furlong's Secret Service Company. Shortly thereafter, Furlong himself went to Toronto and Montreal in search of Ricardo Flores Magón. On 16 December 1906 Furlong was in Mexico City being briefed by the authorities.[44] At that time the abundance of information collected by Creel and Corral after the El Paso arrests was made available to Furlong. Shortly after his return to the United States in January 1907, Furlong suspected that Flores Magón was in Los Angeles.

It was also at this time that the Mexican government was experiencing its first major failures in extraditing the *revoltosos*, first the release of Librado Rivera and Aaron López Manzano in St. Louis and later the Arredondo rebels in Texas. Because of this, Furlong was instructed to return to St. Louis and not arrest Flores Magón. The government wanted more evidence—of the type that could be used in a neutrality case—and needed more time. In the meantime, Furlong traveled to Monterrey, Nuevo León, and aided in the arrest of the same Aaron López Manzano. In June 1907 he was ordered to Los Angeles by Creel, where he subsequently arrested Flores Magón, Villarreal, and Rivera. He remained in Los Angeles until February 1908 to help in the preperation of the government's case.[45]

During 1908 Furlong sent several agents to operate in Texas, Arizona, and Oklahoma. He also testified against Flores Magón and aided the Tombstone authorities in developing their case

[43]For Peña del Pino see the following: Miguel López Torres to Sec. de Rel. Ext., 15 February and 2 and 16 March 1909; Elías to Sec. de Rel. Ext., 2 and 31 March 1909—all AREM, LE–954.

[44]González Ramírez, *Epistolario y textos,* pp. 173–174.

[45]Ibid., pp. 174–175. See also Furlong's *Fifty Years a Detective,* pp. 140–148.

against the *magonista* leaders. In September 1908 a Furlong agent arrested Antonio de P. Araujo in Waco, Texas. Araujo, it will be remembered, was accused and convicted on neutrality violation charges in 1909 for leading the Las Vacas attack of June 1908.[46]

Furlong continued his operations for the Mexican government during 1909, appearing as a witness at the Tombstone trial in the early part of the year. Toward the end of 1909 he and his employees were shadowing Aguirre in El Paso. In October, Furlong agents aided a group of Mexican detectives and secret police in the arrest of "socialists" who, it was feared, threatened the security of presidents Díaz and Taft, who were meeting in Ciudad Juárez and El Paso. Most of these arrests took place in Mexico after Furlong's detectives had lured their suspects across the international bridge. The joint operation had been designed by Furlong and Corral, with consul Lomelí acting as an intermediary between the American detectives and the Mexican secret police under the command of Pedro Zúñiga, a *jefe político* from the Laguna district. After El Paso, Furlong, at the urging of the Mexican government, went to San Antonio. There he discovered Práxedis Guerrero, who was meeting with John Murray at the time.[47]

From San Antonio, Furlong was ordered to New York City. He went there on the personal order of Díaz, who wanted to be certain that Bernardo Reyes and his son Rodolfo caught the boat for their "voluntary" exile in Europe. In New York Furlong had a pleasant time, following Bernardo and his family to and from the tourist attractions, from Central Park to Grant's Tomb. Furlong then left New York City at the end of the year to travel back to Los Angeles to deal with a scandal that had erupted with the recent rearrest of Gutiérrez de Lara.[48]

Throughout 1910, Furlong's services were retained in order to locate and arrest that new threat to Díaz rule, Francisco Madero. As late as 29 December 1910, Furlong reported that Madero was not in San Antonio but had not, as yet, entered Mexico. He also sadly noted that as of December 1910 "all the Mexicans near El

[46]González Ramírez, *Epistolario y textos*, pp. 175–176.
[47][José C. Valadés], "Siguiendo la pista a políticos mexicanos," *La Opinión* (Los Angeles), 23 and 30 April and 7, 14, and 21 May 1939.
[48]Ibid., 4 and 11 June 1939.

Paso are in favor of the Liberals."[49] Thus, during the four years of his employment for Mexico, he had been Creel's essential ally. Furlong's major success had come, of course, with the arrest of Ricardo Flores Magón and Villarreal in Los Angeles in 1907. And although the exact figure cannot be obtained, Los Angeles newspaper writers have credited Furlong and his agents with having succeeded in seizing over 180 Mexican revolutionaries who were turned over to the government of don Porfirio Díaz.[50] Whatever the precise figure, there can be no doubting the terrible effectiveness of the old railroad detective from St. Louis.

As important as Furlong and the private detectives were, Creel was often dependent on the public detective forces of the Mexican and U.S. governments, the former consisting primarily of the aforementioned *policía secreta* of Corral's Ministry of Domestic Affairs. In the United States, before 1911, there were at least seven governmental organizations involved in detection work in cooperation with the Mexican government. These were as follows:

Division of Post Office Inspectors.

Treasury Department, Secret Service Division.

State Department, Special Agents (special emissaries to Mexico for the conduct of clandestine diplomacy—what has been called "spying in striped pants," a favorite device of Woodrow Wilson).[51]

Treasury Department, Customs Agents.

Justice Department, Bureau of Investigation (created in 1909; later known as the Federal Bureau of Investigation, the FBI).

Navy Department, Office of Naval Operations.

War Department, Military Information Division (MID to 1908; afterwards known as War College Division), including the military attaché in Mexico.

In addition, on an infrequent basis, federal attorneys, marshals, and immigration inspectors also performed intelligence roles.

[49]Furlong to Creel, 29 December 1910, AREM, L–E–622. See also John U. Menteer to Creel, 29 and 31 December 1910, AREM, L–E–622.

[50]Anonymous, "Cómo fracasó el movimiento revolucionario de 1906," *El Demócrata*, 6 September 1924.

[51]For Wilson's clandestine diplomacy in Mexico see Larry D. Hill, *Emissaries to a Revolution*.

Although mention has been made of all of these organizations, a special comment is in order concerning the customs, Bureau of Investigation, and military intelligence agencies. It is of some interest to note that after 23 September 1908 a number of prominent citizens of Eagle Pass filed several charges against Robert W. Dowe, the collector of customs there. The most serious charge was that Dowe was a secret agent of the Mexican government, receiving compensation in violation of paragraph 7, section 9, article I, of the U.S. Constitution, which forbids officeholders from profiting from any "king, prince, or foreign state." Nolte, Ellsworth, and others were witnesses to the facts behind the charge, a charge that eventually led to a Treasury Department investigation. Although Dowe was initially dismissed from the service, the charges were eventually dropped and he was reinstated.[52] It is quite likely that Dowe was not the only customs officer to be compromised by Díaz; in any case, customs officers always provided important information to State, War, and Treasury.

Between 1909 and 1911, the Bureau of Investigation joined Treasury's secret service agents in maintaining surveillance over the *revoltosos* and shared its information with the Mexicans. At times, however, relations became strained between the two countries as their spies began spying on each other. In 1911, it was rumored that the bureau was creating a branch office in San Antonio in which would be centered all information gathered by American and Mexican secret service agents. This allegation was dismissed by Ellsworth as being *"absolutely without foundation"* [italics Ellsworth's]. As he noted, the idea of a combined secret service would create too many international complications. Ellsworth and Finch apparently had a very low opinion of the Mexican secret police and their detectives, noting that Mexican secret service agents were suspected of burglarizing the San Antonio office of the Bureau of Investigation and that Mexico's detectives were "impeding the sincere, conscientious, hardworking U.S. Special Agents of the Bureau of Investigation" by their constant vigilance of such agents. In spite of these misunderstandings, the Mexican secret service and the Bureau of Investigation continued

[52]U.S., Congress, House, *Alleged Persecutions*, pp. 18–19.

their close cooperation, a critical factor that helped to cause the failure of the *orozquista* rebellion in 1912.[53]

As for the army, military intelligence became important in the history of United States–Mexican relations after 1891. In that year the Military Information Division (MID) sent officers into Mexico to aid in preparing tactical and strategic maps of that country. By 1895, the MID had dispatched a military attaché to Mexico City. The attaché, assigned to the embassy and having access to consular and diplomatic sources, became an important part of the U.S. intelligence network in Mexico by 1911. In that year Captain Girard Sturtevant, the military attaché in Mexico, provided the War College Division with a brilliant analysis of the underlying causes of the Madero insurrection, listing several popular grievances, such as Ramón Corral's role, the monopolization of "graft" by the *científicos*, the direct appointment of *jefes políticos* by state governors, and the general sense that the Díaz regime had lasted too long.[54]

The year 1907 was especially important in terms of the U.S. military's awareness of the *revoltosos*. That year an aggressive reconnaissance and clandestine program was initiated by the MID for Latin America, especially Central America and Mexico. At the same time, somewhat independently, Creel had sent to Root a Furlong field report suggesting that the revolutionaries could be discouraged by the stationing of a small number of soldiers at Del Rio and Eagle Pass. The Furlong report also suggested that trouble would be serious in the event of Díaz's death, and noted certain assassination threats that had been made on the life of don Porfirio. Root, alarmed by this information, forwarded the Furlong report to the Department of War and requested that an "Inspector

[53]Ellsworth to Sec. of State, 28 February 1911, Records of the War Department General and Special Staffs (WCD, War College Division; MID, Military Intelligence Division), Record Group 165, National Archives, Washington, D.C. (hereafter cited as RG 165), file 5761–39. Also see Ellsworth to Sec. of State, 7 March 1911, in Hanrahan, *Documents*, I, pt. 1, 223–224. For the Orozco strategy and its failures see Charles H. Harris III and Louis R. Sadler, "El Paso, 1912, in the Mexican Revolution" (unpublished ms.).

[54]Marc B. Powe, *The Emergence of the War Department Intelligence Agency, 1885–1918*, pp. 20–25; Sturtevant to Chief, WCD 20 February 1911, RG 165, file 5761–12.

General" be sent into the area. On June 12, the War Department selected Captain William S. Scott to investigate the "doings of the *emigrados*."[55]

The Scott report is an excellent example of early military intelligence. Scott traveled through several frontier towns, including San Antonio, Eagle Pass, Del Rio, El Paso, Douglas, and Laredo. In these towns he interviewed consuls (Ornelas, Villa Sana, Mallén, Lomelí, and others), customs officials, postmasters, immigration inspectors, and U.S. marshals. He also received information from Mexico's two legal advisers in Texas, T. M. Paschal and Judge Griner. Scott described the political activities of Aguirre, Araujo, Tomás and Manuel Sarabia, C. Márquez, and a host of lesser-known *revoltosos*. He concluded that the Mexicans along the frontier could not organize for a revolution but could cause considerable annoyance for the United States. Scott suggested that the local authorities at Douglas were the example to follow—that is, he suggested a campaign of deportation and prosecution. Scott, a hardliner, would be a most persuasive influence in shaping the thinking of the Justice and War departments from 1907 to 1911.[56]

In 1908 the MID followed up on the Scott mission by sending an officer into Mexico. The man chosen was Second Lieutenant Joseph W. Stilwell, a language instructor at West Point. His mission was coordinated with both the War and State departments. Before departing he received explicit instructions—not to take anything which would reveal his true identity; to use an assumed name and employ code words to indicate his arrival; to memorize the information gathered; and to correspond through an address not associated with the government. As in all "Mission Impossible" assignments, the War Department warned Stilwell that it would disclaim any knowledge of him and the mission if he were caught, and that "discovery would be greatly to the prejudice of your military reputation."[57] Evidently the mission was a success, for Stilwell eventually became a general in the U.S. Army.

By 1911, military intelligence about Mexico was becoming an

<hr/>

[55]Powe, *Emergence*, p. 48; Creel to Root, 29 May 1907, and Root to Sec. of War, 8 June 1907—both NF, case 5028/9–10.

[56]Scott to Adj. Gen., 26 August 1907, RG 60, file 43718.

[57]Powe, *Emergence*, pp. 48–49.

established governmental business. Because of the need to revise and develop its 1911 "Contingency General War Plan For Mexico," the War College Division telegraphed all American consulates in Mexico requesting political, economic, and military information. Because the initial responses were too vague and did not include data on the *rurales*, another request for information was sent out. With this information the War College Division was able to develop several lengthy studies: "Location of Certain American and European Interests in Mexico," "Survey of American Business Interests in Mexico," and "Estimate of Military Forces in the Field (Both Sides)." These reports, the result of combined consular and military intelligence, prepared the U.S. Army for an invasion of Mexico in the event of any revolutionary threats to American capital interests.[58]

Thus the "Creel International Detective Agency" was the machinery of the "diplomacy of suppression" in the early history of the *revoltosos*. The machinery's basic components consisted of consular spies and private and public detectives, and involved both espionage and "dirty tricks." Espionage was big business for both the private and public sector, and "private" Americans were very much a part of the network, as detectives, labor spies, operatives, legal advisers, informants, and "concerned businessmen." It was a binational operation designed to protect domestic and foreign elite interests in Mexico—to promote capital, control labor, and stop "socialism."

The machinery would withstand the revolutionary strains of 1911, with the Mexicans moving away from the use of private detectives to a reliance on an institutionalized secret police. As for the Americans, espionage would become more bureaucratized and technological—away from the daring exploits of legal thugs in the secret service to the paraphernalia of wigs, false teeth transmitters, invisible ink, and spy satellites. From the Bureau of Investigation

[58]See the following: Contingency War Plans, 16 March 1911, file 5761–21; telegram to consulates, 7 March 1911, 5761–49; military intelligence request, 24 March 1911, 5761–40; estimate of Mexican forces, 30 March 1911, 5761–69; "Location of Certain American and European Interests in Mexico," by Majors Johnson and Pence, 21 March 1911, 5761–35; "Survey of American Business Interests in Mexico," 5761–19—all RG 165.

would spring the FBI, America's spy agency for Mexico and Latin America in the 1930s and during World War II. After that date the CIA, allied with those "spies in striped pants" at State, would keep the Mexican connection alive.

FOUR
Señor Madero, Mr. Taft, and
the *Insurrectos*, 1910–1913

Por último, tengo también fé en la Democracia.
Francisco I. Madero, 1911

8. The *Maderista* Movement

On the evening of 18 May 1910, Halley's Comet brushed the earth with its long, spreading tail. At various points, intermittent flashes were seen "resembling an arch of glowing white surmounted by a crest of crimson." It took less than fifteen seconds for the comet to travel from Veracruz to Mexico City, only sixty-six seconds to cross the North American continent. American tourists traveled to fancy Alpine resorts to view it; "comet picnics" were organized in Berlin and Potsdam. Thousands of immigrant workers in Pennsylvania refused to enter the coal mines, fearing that the earth would be destroyed. Indiana's poor squandered their savings on a Last Judgment party. In Colorado, Mexican and Italian workers at the Leadville and Cripple Creek mines remained underground to avoid possible contact with the tail of the comet.[1]

Near El Paso, hundreds of Mexicans from villages along the border gathered about crucifixes erected on the hills, awaiting the appearance of the comet they feared would destroy the world. For ten days they sought to avert the impending disaster with music, incantations, and prayers. They searched for refuge in caves and canyons in the mountains. When the comet passed without catastrophe, dancing and feasting replaced the religious ceremonies. Yet all knew that this glare, which had destroyed the quiet of night and had made the cattle uneasy, was an announcement. Elders told the young that the coming of the comet meant famine and plague.[2]

The village shamans understood the signs of nature. Had not the eruption of Mt. Colima the year before been correctly seen as a promise that the powerful Old Ones were to come and sweep the

[1] *New York Times*, 19 May 1910.
[2] Ibid.

wicked away? Even in the city the scribes and historians knew that significant events always accompanied the coming of Halley's Comet. In 44 B.C., Halley's Comet blazed for seven days after the assassination of Julius Caesar—the time it took for the soul of Caesar to be received into heaven. In A.D. 30 the comet signaled the crucifixion of Christ; in 1066 the comet blazed a trail followed by the Norman conquerors of England. For Mexico the meaning of the portent was clear—civil war, death, and a new life were at hand.[3]

Later the *corridos*, Mexico's popular folk ballads, would retell the story. In "De Madero" the villagers sang:

> Oh comet, if you had but known
> What it was you prophesied,
> You never would have come out that way,
> Lighting up the sky;
> It is not your fault, God knows
> That you were ordered to do it.
> Oh, what a man this Madero,
> How good are his deeds!
> He commands all the wrong-headed ones
> To free and release their prisoners.
> O Lady of Guadalupe
> Bestow blessings upon him![4]

The world of don Porfirio and doña Carmelita was coming to an end. The Day of Judgment was at hand, and the Lord had sent an Apostle of Democracy called Madero to act as judge and deliverer.

Francisco Ignacio Madero[5] was thirty-six years of age at the time of Halley's Comet. The child of wealthy creole landowning families in Coahuila, his grandfather, don Evaristo Madero, was a personal friend of Minister of Hacienda José Limantour. At the age of fourteen, he and his younger brother sailed for France, where they attended classes in Versailles and Paris, studying economics and commerce. On his return, Francisco departed for the United

[3]Ibid., 18 May 1910; Anita Brenner, *The Wind that Swept Mexico*, plate no. 43.

[4]Translated by the author from Vicente T. Mendoza, comp., *El corrido mexicano*, p. 25.

[5]Most sources give his middle name as Indalecio. Madero's marriage license and other primary documents give it as Ignacio. See Johnson, *Heroic Mexico*, p. 37.

States, where he spent a year at the University of California at Berkeley studying agriculture. He later incorporated many North American techniques and practices in the management of his father's hacienda, including the introduction in 1894 of a high-yield type of American cotton. Between that year and 1905 he was active as an aristocrat-farmer-and-rancher in Coahuila.[6]

Madero's personal philosophy, a result of his stay in France, was mystical, idealistic, and humanistic—a kind of "spiritism" that taught that man's sufferings were due more to human imperfection than divine ire. Madero's ethical humanism held that materialism, as represented by man's ego, would have to be overcome so that the spiritual purposes of life could be realized. Spiritism meant to Madero that individuals were responsible for the common good, that individual greed and self-satisfaction must be sacrificed for the welfare of society. His attitudes were shared by other intellectuals, like Antonio Caso, who later developed their own "personalistic" ideas into a more systematic belief known as Christian Dualism.[7]

Madero's philosophy partly explains his actions as a benevolent *patrón* and political reformer. On his hacienda he built schools and paid for the food and clothing of students and teachers. Imbued with the "progressive" notions of North American reformers, as early as 1905 he was active as a liberal innovator in state politics, initiating nominating conventions and electoral platforms. A man of conscience, he was personally brave and honest, a believer in the idea that personal morality was the essential political virtue. Opposed to Flores Magón's anarchism, after 1906 Madero held that liberty must be established on a foundation of law. Mexico's salvation could only be achieved through reforms in public education, which would lead to an enlightened populace, popular democracy, and honest government. As Madero said in 1911: "In the final analysis, I too have faith in democracy; a type of government (such as

---

[6]Charles C. Cumberland, *Mexican Revolution: Genesis Under Madero,* pp. 30–32.

[7]Ibid., pp. 33–35; Raat, "Ideas and Society in Don Porfirio's Mexico," p. 51.

mine) which can be strong, and is strong, because this type of government is the people and the nation."[8]

With the exception of his flirtations with the *magonistas*, Madero's first attempt at openly articulating his political philosophy came with the publication in 1908 of his book *La sucesión presidencial en 1910*. This was in response to an interview that James Creelman, an American journalist, had had with Porfirio Díaz. The interview, published first in *Pearson's Magazine*, appeared in Mexico in the official government newspaper *El Imparcial* as well as several provincial papers.[9]

In the interview, which took place at Chapultepec Castle, Díaz said, for the first time in public, "I do not want to continue as president. This nation is ready for a definitive life of liberty." Concerning Mexico's future, Díaz went on to say:

> It is an error to suppose that the future of democracy in Mexico has been placed in jeopardy by the lengthy period that I have occupied the position of president. . . . I can sincerely say that the office has not compromised my political ideals, and that I believe that democracy is a true and just principle of government, even though its application is only possible for people who have advanced to a high stage of political development.

And, from Madero's point of view, the clincher was: "I welcome an opposition party in the Mexican Republic. If it appears, I will regard it as a blessing, not an evil." Madero needed no further invitation.[10]

The Creelman interview was news of the first magnitude. Throughout 1909 there was a flurry of political activity. Backers of Bernardo Reyes, the *caudillo* of Nuevo León, formed the Nationalist Party (*Partido Nacionalista Democrático*—PND) to promote Reyes's candidacy in the 1910 election. The *científicos* looked to

---

[8]Cumberland, *Mexican Revolution*, pp. 32–35; Womack, *Zapata and the Mexican Revolution*, p. 55, n. 4; Madero to the Junta . . . del Partido Liberal, 28 December 1911, Archivo General de la Nación, Mexico City, Ramo Revolución, Libros Copiadores de Madero, Copiador núm. 1.

[9]Johnson, *Heroic Mexico*, p. 41.

[10]Translated by the author from Germán List Arzubide, *Madero: El México de 1910*, pp. 23–24.

Limantour as their candidate. *Magonistas* continued their plotting. And Madero released his *La sucesión presidencial*, sending a complimentary first copy to Enrique Creel in Chihuahua—a book whose message was "Down with *reyismo* and militarism, no more boss rule, and honest elections," all under the banner of the new Anti-Reelectionist Party.[11]

Madero's appeals were well received, especially among upper- and middle-class hacendados and industrialists disenchanted with Díaz's perpetual rule. Despite its bland message, the book was popular. Before long, Anti-Reelectionist clubs were being formed all around the country. Straining his family's resources, Madero established several political newspapers, including a daily, *El Antireeleccionista*, in Mexico City. Later in the year he went on a speaking tour through northwestern Mexico.[12]

In spite of Madero's moderation—for example, he had no objection to the reelection of Díaz if it were a free election and if Anti-Reelectionists were represented in the legislature, state governorships, and vice-presidency—and in spite of the promise of the Creelman interview, Madero and other opposition *políticos* were soon being harassed by Corral's police system. Secret agents from the Ministry of Domestic Affairs filed reports on the activities of the *maderistas* and the *reyistas*. On 23 September 1909 the police occupied the office of *El Antireeleccionista* in Mexico City, arresting several *maderistas*. In January 1910, Samuel Espinosa de los Monteros, secretary of the *reyista* party, and the entire PND executive board were arrested by secret police and jailed in Belem on charges of sedition. On 6 June, after winning his party's nomination for the presidency, Madero was arrested in Monterrey and held under house arrest in San Luis Potosí; a while later, his brother Gustavo was arrested and detained in the offices of the Mexico City *policía secreta*. Before the July 1910 elections, thousands of Anti-Reelectionists, *reyistas*, and *magonistas* were in jail, most of whom had

---

[11]Johnson, *Heroic Mexico*, pp. 41–42; Madero to Creel, 31 January 1909, *Archivo de Francisco I. Madero*, II, 312.

[12]Johnson, *Heroic Mexico*, pp. 42–43.

been arrested by members of the Creel-Corral spy and police network.[13]

On 4 October 1910 the election results were officially declared in favor of Díaz and Corral by a congressional committee. That night Madero escaped his captors in San Juan Potosí and boarded a northbound train, eventually arriving in San Antonio. By 25 October, Madero had issued a *Manifiesto al Pueblo Americano* and a political program called the "Plan of San Luis Potosí" (deliberately backdated to 5 October to avoid any allegations of violating U.S. neutrality laws). The "Plan" declared the June and July elections void and named Madero provisional president. In addition, the principles of effective suffrage and no reelection were reaffirmed, and all citizens were called on to take up arms at 6 p.m. on Sunday, 20 November 1910, to overthrow the "illegitimate" government of don Porfirio Díaz. In a strategic gesture to his American hosts, Madero called attention "to the duty of every Mexican to respect the persons and property of foreigners."[14]

When Madero arrived in San Antonio in October, he joined a *revoltoso* movement that had been developing for five years under Flores Magón and had been intensified by *magonistas*, *reyistas*, and others during the first nine months of 1910. Early in that year, Mexican intellectuals, writers, and opposition party politicians began to drift into exile in sanctuaries above the U.S. border. Most refugees relocated in Los Angeles, Tucson, El Paso, and San Antonio. Their dissatisfaction was voiced through the publication of Spanish-language newspapers, especially the Los Angeles–based *Regeneración* and Paulino Martínez's *Monitor Democrático* in San Antonio. Many editions were smuggled across the border; others found their readership among the more than one million Mexicans in the United States. By November 1910 the *revoltosos* had formed political clubs, recruited Mexican dissenters and American adventurers, and purchased arms and munitions. Smugglers were working

[13]Ibid., pp. 44–45; *Archivo de F. I. Madero*, II, 328, 435; Anthony T. Bryan, "Mexican Politics in Transition, 1900–1913: The Role of General Bernardo Reyes," (dissertation), p. 271; Fabela, *Documentos históricos*, V, 79.

[14]An English version of the "Manifesto" and "Plan" of 1910 can be found in U.S., Congress, Senate, *Papers* (*1911*), pp. 351–352. Also see "Al Pueblo Americano," in Fabela, *Documentos históricos*, V, 82–84.

both sides of the border. When Madero crossed the border at Eagle Pass the night of 19 November to join his comrades in Mexico, he did not initiate the Mexican Revolution—he joined it.[15]

Although military failures soon forced a disappointed Madero to return to San Antonio, his call for rebellion was carried out without his presence on the field. Pascual Orozco, José de la Luz Soto, and Doroteo Arango (alias Francisco ["Pancho"] Villa) sparked rebellions in Chihuahua. *Magonistas* like Práxedis Guerrero and Prisciliano Silva soon joined them. Across Mexico self-constituted *jefes* of the revolution strapped cartridge belts across their chests and entered the fray, followed closely behind by their faithful *soldaderas*. By February 1911, Mexicali had fallen and the northern two-thirds of Mexico had become the scene of several bloody skirmishes. The *federales* were being forced to split their forces and move in several directions. Seven thousand rebel troops were proving to be too much for Díaz's twenty thousand federal soldiers.[16]

After spending December in New Orleans, Madero returned to San Antonio. By 13 February 1911 he had returned to Mexico, crossing the border a few miles southeast of El Paso. His return had been forced both by the threat of his impending arrest by American officials and the need to regain control over a rebellion that was advancing without him. By 10 May, Orozco, nominally under Madero's command and aided by Villa and a brass cannon stolen from the lawn of the El Paso City Hall, defeated the *federales* at Ciudad Juárez, the first major military success of the Madero revolution. The Treaty of Juárez that followed provided for the resignation of Díaz and Corral and for the succession of Fran-

---

[15]Hanrahan, *Documents*, I, pt. 1, i–ii.

[16]Paul Vanderwood estimates the size of federal and rebel troops in April 1911 as 20,000 for the former and 10,000 for the latter. He further states that rebel forces quadrupled to 40,000 by May 1911. U.S. Army estimates for March 1911 indicate that the federals numbered 22,532 and that the rebels were over 7,100. Whatever the exact number, it is obvious that Díaz was never able to achieve the ten-to-one ratio considered ideal for successful counter-guerrilla warfare. See both Vanderwood, "The Counter-Guerrilla Strategy of Díaz," *Hispanic American Historical Review* 56 (November 1976): 558–559, and War College Division Map of Mexico, Knox Papers, Dept. of State File, Information Series "A", "Disorders in Mexico," Box 40, No. 73, 15–30 March 1911.

cisco León de la Barra (recent ambassador to the United States) as interim president. De la Barra then turned over the office of president to the constitutionally elected Madero on 6 November 1911—the day of the coming of the Apostle of Democracy. Contrary to the scientific predictions of the day, the comet's tail had indeed scorched the Mexican earth below.

As Mexico's Revolution developed, the elements of class division and civil war came to the front. Although all fighting groups were nominally united in the struggle to overthrow Díaz, the objectives of the revolutionaries were often in conflict with one another. The primary tactical difference was between those who advocated a violent revolution for radical socio-economic goals and those who sought nonviolent change for political purposes. The former, the position of Flores Magón, reflected the views of discontented lower-class and lower-middle-class groups, and envisioned a workers' and peasants' struggle against the ruling bourgeoisie. Madero, who did not advocate revolt until the "Plan of San Luis Potosí," represented the latter view—the position of discontented bourgeois groups unhappy with the political repression of Díaz and the government's inadequacy in dealing with the problems of a modern capitalist economy. The *maderistas* sought to reform the bourgeois state—to cure the ills of recession, abandon government and private monopolies, control and shape the development of organized skilled labor, and modernize agriculture, mining, commerce, talize the nation with liberty, freedom, and political democracy, and trade, banking, and industry. In short, the new regime would revidevelop the already existing economic order—including the interests of the Madero family.

Initially, Madero had supported the PLM. Early in 1905 he had sent a money order to Flores Magón in San Antonio, and he had aided in the circulation of *Regeneración*. This was at a time when the political rhetoric of liberal democracy and anti-clericalism had disguised the class interests of the various participants. Yet, as early as November 1905, Madero was beginning to edge away from the *magonistas*. At that time he initiated a project to develop a local *Club Democrática* that, though not antagonistic to the PLM, would not operate in secret and would advocate an evolutionary process of gradually elevating the public spirit through education, a process that would eventually make for "effective suffrage." Thus, Madero's emphasis on nonviolent, political objectives was very clear from the start.[17]

Even before the Cananea strike of 1906, Madero had become disillusioned with the PLM, telling Antonio Santos in March that "I myself have not remained affiliated with them [the PLM] believing that there can be no victory for that side." In writing to *correligionario* Crescencio V. Márquez in August 1906, Madero argued that fomenting revolution was "antipatriotic" and counterproductive. In September, Madero refused arms and other aid to Prisciliano Silva, saying that Díaz was not a tyrant and that he himself would not be a party to useless bloodshed.[18]

More than anything, though, it was the PLM's use of violence that angered Madero and prevented any future *magonista-maderista* coalition. After the Jiménez uprising in 1906, Madero told don Evaristo, his grandfather and the patriarch of the clan: "I deplore with all my heart the useless blood that was shed by the brave men of the frontier and all the actions that were prejudicial to the nation—actions carried out, it would appear, only for the exaltation of those ambitious bastards in St. Louis." He later referred to both the Viesca and Las Vacas raids of 1908 as farces. Evidently Madero, who had started his political career later than Flores Magón and with greater caution, had not as yet suffered any disillusionment with peaceful means of protest.[19]

As the left wing of the *magonistas* moved toward anarchism after 1908, Madero sought to become the moderate and progressive alternative to the radicals. Initially he supported the pro-Reyes

[17]Madero to R. Flores Magón, 17 January 1905; Madero to P. N. González, 3 November 1905; Madero to Jesús Martínez Carrión, 20 December 1905—all *Archivo de F. I. Madero*, II, pp. 109–110, 141, and 144–146 respectively.

[18]Madero to Santos, 14 March 1906; Madero to C. V. Márquez, 17 August 1906—*Archivo de F. I. Madero*, II, pp. 150 and 165–166. See also Cockcroft, *Intellectual Precursors*, p. 159.

[19]Madero to don Evaristo Madero, 1 October 1906; Madero to Eulario Treviño, 25 February 1907; Madero to Raúl Madero, 13 July 1908—all *Archivo de F. I. Madero*, II, pp. 172–173, 183, and 213–214 respectively.

Partido Democrático, but with Reyes's forced exile in November of 1909, Madero became the bourgeoisie's most important progressive spokesman. In early 1910 he began to receive both *reyista* and *vaz-quista* backing, eventually being named candidate of the PND as well as the Partido Antirreeleccionista. By political maneuvering Madero hoped to achieve a political accommodation with the Díaz regime that would gradually move power away from the *porfiristas*. Madero knew a PLM revolution would be destructive of vested economic interests, including Madero's own. Thus, he had to oppose not only Díaz but also the *magonista* Left.

With Madero's call for a 20 November uprising, several *revoltosos* took to the field—including *magonistas* who were instructed to take advantage of the fighting but not to make common cause.[20] Spontaneous revolts and conspiracies developed that were not directed by Madero. For example, the Mexican secret police unearthed an extensive plot in which a group of rebels had contemplated the assassination on 20 November of the entire inner circle of the *científicos*.[21] Between November 1910 and February 1911, several PLM commanders collaborated with Orozco and others in a common effort against Díaz. At the end of February, Flores Magón openly declared that he had withdrawn his assistance from the Madero revolution. By that time, PLM chieftain Prisciliano Silva had been arrested by Madero, and both Gutiérrez de Lara and Villarreal had gone over to Madero, taking their forces with them.[22] With Flores Magón's arrest in June, a further split developed within PLM ranks when the recently released Juan Sarabia was read out of the party.[23] Before Madero took over the presidency at the end of 1911, he had inherited the support of ex-PLM moderates, some *zapatistas* and *villistas*, the American radical and labor community (especially Mother Jones and Samuel Gompers), and a variety of upper- and middle-upper-class hacendados, industrialists, and bankers.

---

[20]Cockcroft, *Intellectual Precursors*, p. 176.

[21]Henry Lane Wilson to Sec. of State, 21 November 1910, Hanrahan, *Documents*, II, pt. 1, 93–94.

[22]Ellsworth to Sec. of State, 2 March 1911, in ibid., I, pt. 1, 198–199.

[23]See "Manifiesto de los Flores Magón," 23 September 1911, in González Ramírez, *Fuentes*, IV, 369–375.

After Díaz's flight, *magonista* forces fought *maderistas* in Baja California. The June imprisonment of Flores Magón meant that the field was momentarily clear of rivals. Ironically, Díaz had engineered his own destruction by his failure to compromise in 1909 and 1910. Political suppression, dishonest elections, and government censorship encouraged many of the upper class to question the legitimacy of his regime. Yet Díaz stubbornly refused to make any genuine reforms. Banishing Reyes only created a vacuum that Madero's followers rushed to fill. His refusal to cooperate with Madero until it was too late, in fact his suppression of Madero and his supporters, finally led to Madero's disillusionment with nonviolent politics. When Madero announced his "Plan de San Luis Potosí," he enlisted the support of many military leaders, urban intellectuals, angry peasants, and industrial workers. By so doing he conceded to them a kind of political legitimacy. When Madero failed to satisfy their expectations, the coup and later developments precipitated the social revolution Madero feared so much.

Madero's successful coup was due not only to Díaz's intransigence but also to Madero's skill as a politician and revolutionary manager. When Furlong and his sleuths began pursuing Madero, they faced a challenge much greater and a group more skilled than that of the *magonistas*. Madero had resources not available to Flores Magón. Some of the wealthiest men of Mexico supported him. He also had the backing of sympathizers along the border. Because the *magonistas* had demonstrated time and again the duplicity of Mexican consuls and border authorities, the Mexican community in the United States was supportive of the *revoltosos*. Having ample finances and the sympathies of the border population, Madero was able to develop a revolutionary apparatus far more efficient and successful than that of the *magonistas*.

Madero, unlike Flores Magón, was not seeking a broadly-based social revolution. His purposes and program were most narrow, being nothing more than a traditional coup d'etat. Thus Madero's organization was small and compact, with all resources being directed at overthrowing the dictator. As a child of the upper class, Madero had access to the tools of that stratum. Madero's organization shaped and used its resources to develop a clandestine espionage operation not unlike that already being used against him by the Mexican government (of course, of a smaller magnitude). This included the services of competent lawyers, a revolutionary secret police, hired detectives, paid informants, and "turncoat" consuls.

One of Madero's lawyers was Sherburne G. Hopkins, of the Washington firm of Hopkins and Hopkins. From Washington and New York City he acted as counsel and director of Madero's secret service in the United States. Hired by Gustavo Madero, he worked closely with the secretary of the *maderista* mission to Washington, Juan Sánchez Azcona. For his services over a seven-month period, from 1 November 1910 to 1 June 1911, he was paid $50,000 (U.S.).[24]

As Madero's legal adviser, Hopkins performed a variety of duties. One of his major responsibilities was that of countering Díaz's propaganda campaign against Madero in the United States. It was in this capacity that he worked with Sánchez Azcona. He also was hired to protect Madero's followers from the Mexican government's continual "campaign of deportation." For example, Hopkins succeeded in getting extradition charges dropped against Sánchez Azcona, who had been arrested and confined for forty-five days without bail on a charge of embezzlement. Hopkins provided similar services for other *maderista* rebels, keeping many out of jail and arranging for the release of others. Again, in his role as counsel, Hopkins enabled the *maderistas* to get military materiel into Mexico without violating the neutrality laws.[25]

As secret service director, Hopkins funneled monies to the various operatives and supervised their many activities. As a legal adviser to the Guatemalan government, he was able to make use of that government's consular network to facilitate the movement of Madero's secret agents. Hopkins dispatched agents to Mexico on sabotage and espionage missions, sending them by way of New Orleans and other American cities. It was his responsibility to pay the travel and operating costs of the agents and provide for their salaries.[26]

[24]See S. Hopkins's testimony, U.S., Congress, Senate, *Investigations of Mexican Affairs*, II, 2520–2574.

[25]Ibid., pp. 2528–2530.

[26]De la Barra to Gobernación, 2 December 1910, Fabela, *Documentos históricos*, V, 112.

Hopkins also acted as an intermediary in arranging for the transportation of arms and munitions from New York City and St. Louis to Texas. Early in 1911 he hired Harvey Phillips, a former secret service agent, to transport a shipment of rifles and ammunition purchased from the Francis Bannerman and Sons surplus company of New York. Phillips, using the alias A. C. Funks, disguised the first consignment as furniture and shipped it to Frank Cody in El Paso. Although Bureau of Investigation officers arrested Phillips in March in El Paso, they could not legally hold the munitions, which eventually found their way to caches on the Mexican side.[27]

Many of Madero's secret service agents worked in conjunction with established private detective firms, such as the Thiel Detective Service Company of El Paso. Thiel's manager, Henry C. Krump, who had earlier uncovered data on revolutionaries in Douglas, Arizona, was hired by Gustavo Madero to work for the *maderista* cause. Revolutionary leader Abraham González brought Krump into the revolutionary circle and arranged for him to have free access to work with the revolutionists in Ciudad Juárez. Krump sent daily reports not only to the *maderistas* but also, after May 1911, to the Bureau of Investigation. One of Krump's lesser duties included delivering mail to the revolutionaries, not the least of whom was Giuseppe Garibaldi, grandson of the famous Italian patriot and soldier of fortune.[28]

After the initial failure of 20 November, Abraham González directed Madero's revolutionary movement from El Paso. There he was a source of inspiration to wavering *maderistas* during the time of troubles between November and February. Disarming observers by operating openly, he rented offices in the Caples Building for Madero's provisional government and gave regular interviews to the local press corps, who, in turn, magnified reports of Madero's victories and reported unfavorably on Díaz. Well known in the border community, González made use of his acquaintances to promote the *maderista* cause. Some local authorities, like El Paso cus-

[27]Michael Dennis Carman, "United States Customs and the Madero Revolution" (thesis), pp. 96–97.

[28]See both the photographic evidence of Henry Krump in the Aultman Photo File, El Paso Public Library, and the Citizens Vertical File, H. C. Krump, El Paso Public Library. See also Harris and Sadler, "El Paso, 1912, in the Mexican Revolution," p. 6.

toms collector Luke Dowe, became close personal friends of the likable González and furthered, at least indirectly, Madero's insurrection.[29]

González directed a most accomplished campaign to provision rebel forces. To facilitate the movement of men and equipment, he created a communications network through which military reports and supplies were relayed. To isolate his adversaries, González channeled monies and equipment to José Perfecto Lomelín, *jefe* of the revolutionary forces of Chihuahua, who in turn intercepted communications and rail shipments between Chihuahua and Torreón. In February, González hired Dr. I. J. Bush to establish a hospital and medical corps for the care of the revolutionists. An *insurrecto* hospital was organized in El Paso and Dr. Bush trained several Mexican girls to be nurses. To smuggle arms into Mexico, González organized a virtual ring of contraband artists to assist him in getting munitions from small border towns in Texas to the guerrillas in the Chihuahua mountains.[30]

Smuggling arms and ammunition into Mexico was evidently quite simple. Dr. Bush recalled that he and a small group of sympathizers stole a cannon from the El Paso City Hall and hid the three-inch field piece for several weeks in a hole dug in the back yard of a suburban El Paso home. While the group waited for an opportunity to move the piece, gunpowder was ordered and cannisters were manufactured. Meanwhile, González and the rebel council circulated rumors that the cannon was already in Mexico. Finally, at the appropriate time, a Mexican family hired by the rebels loaded the cannon into a farm wagon and drove thirty-five miles downriver from El Paso, past American army patrols, and across the Rio Grande without incident.[31] While U.S. secret service agents watched each other watching González from their head-

<hr/>

[29]Beezley, *Insurgent Governor*, pp. 44–45; Peter V. N. Henderson, "Mexican Rebels in the Borderlands, 1910–1912," *Red River Valley Historical Review* 2 (Summer 1975): 211.

[30]Beezley,. *Insurgent Governor*, p. 45; Madero to J. P. Lomelín, 6 November 1910, *Archivo de F. I. Mandero*, III, p. 307; Henderson, "Mexican Rebels in the Borderlands," p. 211; Mardee Belding de Wetter, "Revolutionary El Paso: 1910–1917," *Password* 3 (April 1958): 54.

[31]Carman, "United States Customs and the Madero Revolution," pp. 99–100.

quarters at the Sheldon Hotel in El Paso, rebel sympathizers moved arms and equipment inconspicuously across the border.

González also directed recruitment efforts, receiving volunteers at his El Paso office. Agents were sent along the border in search of expatriate Mexicans sympathetic to the *revoltoso* cause. Other recruiters were sent to major cities like Denver, Kansas City, and Chicago seeking men for the *maderista* armies. Many "desperados" and colorful soldiers of fortune were attracted to Madero's campaign. In addition to the aforementioned Garibaldi, there were "Dynamite Slim" from Arizona (known in more polite circles as "Death Valley Slim"), "Bloody Mahoney," the fighting Irishman, "Rapid Fire" Crumb, "Red" Stratton, Tom Mix, Sam Dreban, "the fighting Jew," and Captain Oscar Creighton, "the dynamite Devil" from the foreign legion.[32]

González was also influential in attracting to Madero's cause a shadowy figure by the name of C. F. Z. Caracristi. Caracristi, a lawyer and sometime business associate of Creel, acted as diplomatic agent and legal counsel. He provided valuable service to Madero by subverting the Mexican consul in El Paso, Antonio Lomelí. Lomelí bartered useful information about federal troop movements in Chihuahua in return for a three thousand dollar payment in installments of three hundred dollars a week.[33]

Lomelí's services also included the spreading of false information to U.S. authorities about rebel activities. For example, Lomelí reported, without any evidence, that armed revolutionaries from the Flores Ranch had entered Mexico (in reality they were peaceful woodcutters); that armed rebels were operating at Presidio in the Big Bend country of the Rio Grande (an area inaccessible to both rebels and authorities); and that Antonio Villarreal and Práxedis Guerrero were in El Paso (at a time when Villarreal was in Los Angeles and Guerrero in Chihuahua). The consul also charged the Bureau of Investigation with laxity and incompetence.[34] All of

[32]Beezley, *Insurgent Governor*, p. 46; Belding de Wetter, "Revolutionary El Paso," p. 55.

[33]Beezley, *Insurgent Governor*, p. 47.

[34]For these examples see the following: Eugene Nolte to the Att. Gen., 31 December 1910 (in which is enclosed a letter from El Paso Deputy Marshal H. R. Hillebrand to Nolte; and a letter from Lomelí to Hillebrand), RG 60, file 90755/394; C. M. Foraker to Att. Gen., 31 December 1910, RG 60,

these activities were undertaken by Lomelí to divide the authorities (redirecting them from Madero's trail to that of Flores Magón), generate confusion, undermine credibility, and overtax the manpower resources of the U.S. Department of Justice.

In acting as a "turncoat" consul, Lomelí was being consistent with his career goals. For the thirty-four years that he served in the consular corps, between 1884 and 1920, Lomelí distinguished himself as a "careerist" and opportunist. He succeeded in keeping himself in a consular post throughout the administrations of Díaz (consul at Tucson, Laredo, El Paso, and San Francisco), Madero (as director general of consulates), and Huerta (consul general in Barcelona, Spain, and Havana, Cuba). In late 1910 and early 1911, Lomelí sensed the future trends, assessed his chances correctly, and began undercover work for Madero while in the pay of the Díaz government. Having ingratiated himself with Madero, the payoff was his appointment in October 1911 (after the election of that month) as *Director General de Consuldados*. Never trusted by Carranza, Lomelí, after 1914, had to wait until 1920 before offering his services to the Mexican government once again.[35]

Lomelí was not the only consul successfully purchased by Madero. Madero's agents succeeded in enticing four employees of the consulate in San Antonio to act as revolutionary spies. Since two of the four had brothers fighting in Madero's ranks in Mexico, it would appear that Díaz was getting careless in the management of his consular spy and police system. Not only were consular employees bought out but, if the authority of Judge Griner can be trusted, San Antonio consul Enrique Ornelas himself was suborned. Again the "double-crossing" services of Ornelas were made possible with the aid of Gustavo Madero's checkbook.[36]

Another accomplishment of González and the exiles was the

---

file 90755/397; Cole to Att. Gen., 23 December 1910, RG 60, file 90755/371; Nolte to Lomelí, 31 December 1910, Hanrahan, *Documents*, I, pt. 1, pp. 110–114.

[35]These generalizations are derived from materials found in AREM, L–E–1784, H/131/178, A. Lomelí, su expediente personal.

[36]Wickersham to Sec. of State, 5 December 1910, RG 60, file 90755/331 (same letter appears in Hanrahan, *Documents*, I, pt. 1, pp. 88–89 and RDS, 812.00/535); Franklin Macregla to Sec. of State, 7 February 1911, RDS, 812.00/759.

solicitation of funds necessary to finance the revolution. Unfortunately for the historian, the question of the sources of Madero's financing poses a variety of problems. The issues surrounding the question have been made more obscure by allegations concerning the role of Rockefeller's Standard Oil Company. Some of the earliest rumors of Standard Oil involvement in the Madero revolution were published in England, especially in the early March 1911 issues of the *London Star*. These newspaper items alleged that Standard Oil financed Madero's revolt in return for concessions, and by so doing were outmaneuvering their British competitors in Mexico. Shortly thereafter, Vice-President Ramón Corral released a statement from Spain to several international newspapers containing similar charges.[37]

In 1912 these allegations were revived, first as part of the anti-American, anti-Madero passages of the *Plan orozquista* and later by the testimony of some of the witnesses who appeared before the [William Alden] Smith Committee on Foreign Relations of the U.S. Senate. These hearings, in which Senator Albert Fall participated, were intended to ascertain if Madero's revolt (and subsequent uprisings) had been financed from American sources. One witness, Juan Pedro Didapp, a writer, publicist, and former Mexican consul in Spain, Turkey, and the United States, testified emphatically that Standard Oil and Sherburne Hopkins had given the *maderistas* five million dollars. The reason, according to Didapp, was to enable the Waters Pierce Oil Company to win concessions from Madero's revolutionary government at the expense of British-owned interests.[38]

Although much of the Senate testimony was conflicting, a circumstantial case was made linking the fortunes of Standard Oil with the successes of the Madero forces. This argument has been strengthened by recent Justice Department evidence indicating

[37]The best account of the Standard Oil issue is Peter Calvert's *The Mexican Revolution, 1910–1914: The Diplomacy of Anglo-American Conflict*, pp. 73–84. For the specifics about the London press and Corral see the news release by H. C. Folger of Standard Oil, 4 April 1911, and Knox to John D. Archbold, 10 May 1911—both Hanrahan, *Documents*, I, pt. 2, pp. 433 and 425–428 respectively.

[38]U.S., Congress, Senate, *Revolutions in Mexico;* for Didapp's testimony see pp. 458–472.

that contacts were made between alleged representatives of Standard Oil and Madero's spokesmen. Although not conclusive, the circumstantial case is argued along the following lines. First, Standard Oil lost many important concessions to Lord Cowdray (W. D. Pearson and Son) in the last years of the Díaz era. Second, Waters Pierce Oil Company was a Mexican subsidiary of Standard Oil of New York. Third, Sherburne G. Hopkins, who was legal counsel and director of Madero's secret service in the United States, represented the Waters Pierce interests and was hired by Gustavo Madero to expose the graft of Cowdray and his friends on the National Railways board. Fourth, Hopkins was in an excellent position to be an intermediary—shifting funds from the St. Louis office of Henry Clay Pierce to the revolutionary junta. Finally after Madero's successful rise to the presidency Standard Oil received a governmental concession that gave to the company control of Cowdray's crude oil interests.[39]

The evidence, as recorded in State Department files, is sufficient to establish certain facts. On 18 April 1911 a certain C. R. Troxel approached an unnamed informant in the Sheldon Hotel in El Paso. The informant, an employee of the Bureau of Investigation, identified Troxel as a representative of the Standard Oil Company. At this meeting Troxel allegedly stated that his company was willing to furnish the *insurrectos* with from $500,000 to $1,000,000 on the condition that the *insurrectos* would issue to his company 6-percent gold bonds and certain commercial concessions. Troxel then supposedly offered the informant money in return for setting up a meeting between Madero's agents and himself. The informant then introduced Troxel to J. V. Smith, a revolutionary agent in El Paso. Later Smith told the informant that Troxel revealed his credentials and that they included a letter from John D. Archbold of Standard Oil authorizing him to make contracts.[40]

Negotiations continued through the rest of April and into the first week of May between Madero's financial agents in El Paso,

[39]Kenneth Grieb, "Standard Oil and the Financing of the Mexican Revolution," *California Historical Society Quarterly* 50 (1971): 59–71.

[40]Hanrahan, *Documents*, I, pt. 2, pp. 411–440, contains a special appendix of nine documents relating to the Standard Oil case; for Troxel's initial contact see Finch to Att. Gen., 26 April 1911, pp. 411–413.

Alfonso Madero and Luís Hernández, and Troxel. One of the first drafts of the agreement was composed by Smith and Hernández among the comforts of the Turkish Bath and Massage Parlors on San Antonio Street near the Toltec Club, under the watchful eye of Justice Department detectives. After Madero had tentatively agreed to a contract, Gustavo met with Troxel in the El Paso public park on 2 May to conclude the deal. In that meeting it was agreed that Madero's government would be able to cancel all concessions when the loan had been repaid after a five-year period.[41]

However, before the loan was concluded the battle of Ciudad Juárez was over, Madero was victorious, and the loan was no longer necessary. On 15 May, John Archbold wrote to Secretary Knox denying his company's involvement in the scheme. On 17 and 19 May, a company representatve, William H. Libby, met with the attorney general and later provided him with a dispatch that he claimed had been the only contact the directors ever had with Troxel—a relatively unimportant letter from Troxel to Archbold, dated 13 January 1910, concerning oil and gas rights in Mexico. In other words, Troxel was unknown to company officials.[42]

In hindsight it is obvious that certain facts tend to invalidate the circumstantial case of Standard Oil involvement. First, there is the testimony of Didapp and the question of the reliability of the Senate's evidence. Didapp was not a credible witness—he was an opportunist who had served under both Díaz and de la Barra, having been dismissed by the latter. In addition, he was a notorious anti-*maderista*, having been a public apologist for the military and the *reyistas* for over nine years at the time of the hearings. It should be remembered that Bernardo Reyes had launched his own revolt against Madero only a few months before the Senate hearings began. As for the hearings themselves, the several witnesses contradicted each other concerning Standard Oil's role, and much of the testimony, including that of Didapp, was internally inconsistent. Finally, the two senators most active on the subcommittee were Smith and Fall, individuals hostile to Madero's constitutional

---

[41]Wickersham to Sec. of State, 8 May 1911, ibid., pp. 429–430.
[42]Archbold to Knox, 15 May 1911; Libby to Att. Gen., 22 May 1911; Troxel to Archbold, 13 January 1910–all ibid., pp. 431–432, 435–438.

government and friends of Orozco and the Terrazas family of Chihuahua, that is, Madero's political enemies.[43]

As for Hopkins, it was not surprising that he should deny any involvement as an intermediary in his public testimony before the Senate. What is surprising were his *private* statements made in confidence to Madero's private secretary in 1912. At that time Hopkins reported to Azcona that he had been reading published reports from Mexico accusing Madero of compromising his government by having received money from the Waters Pierce and Standard Oil interests. Hopkins was genuinely shocked by the charge and was convinced that the accusations were false, a product of Madero's enemies in the United States. Before reacting publicly, he advised Azcona that he intended to telegraph Madero to ask him personally about the validity of the allegations.[44] This was hardly the language of one conspirator talking to another. Although Hopkins had been involved in an embezzlement scheme with Gustavo, and had been in the center of many Central American revolutions, it would appear that in the Mexican case his only role as an intermediary between Gustavo Madero and Henry Clay Pierce came with his investigation of the National Railways—an inquiry designed to enable Madero to get the *científicos* (or *porfiristas*) off the board "as expeditiously as possible."[45]

Finally, there remains the question of Troxel's motives and role. It is possible that he was a concealed agent for either Standard Oil or Waters Pierce, unknown to one party or the other. However, if the Troxel letter to Archbold of 13 January 1910 is authentic, then another clue to Troxel's true identity has been uncovered.[46] In that letter Troxel refers to his business partner in Chihuahua and gives his name as Albert Terrazas. This Terrazas was the son-in-law of Governor Enrique C. Creel of Chihuahua. Could it be that Troxel, a man with business and social contacts with the Terrazas-Creel family, was part of the Corral-Creel spy system? That he was in El Paso as an *agent provocateur?*

[43]Calvert, *The Mexican Revolution*, pp. 74–76; Raat, "Ideas and Society in Don Porfirio's Mexico," p. 50; Hopkins to Juan Sánchez Azcona, 29 December 1912, AGN/RRV, carta 367.

[44]Hopkins to Azcona, 18 December 1912, RGN/RRV, carta 359.

[45]U.S., Congress, Senate, *Investigation of Mexican Affairs*, II, 2553.

[46]See above, n. 42.

It will be recalled that Corral was one of the first of the Mexican officials to associate Standard Oil with Madero's movement. What better way for Corral and Creel to discredit Madero than to link the unpopular Standard Oil Company with Madero's cause? The identities of U.S. secret agents in El Paso would have been known to Creel, and it would not have been difficult for Creel to have steered Troxel, posing as a Standard Oil representative, to Bureau of Investigation informants who would then report their findings to higher authorities. Although the evidence is far from conclusive, the *agent provocateur* theory fits the historical circumstances, is in agreement with the methods of the Porfirian system, and is a plausible hypothesis.

Standard Oil's image tended to provoke public hostility in both Mexico and the United States. In Mexico, of course, the company was an object of attack for nationalists, anarchists, Marxists, *magonistas*, and Yankeephobes. In the United States a generation of "progressives" and "liberals" raised on Ida Tarbell and the polemics of Roosevelt's "trust-busting" had no love for the giant corporation and its "robber baron" owner. Any *maderista* involved in a conspiracy with Standard Oil would have to be suspect. The result would be a loss of credibility for Madero's movement, especially among his middle-class backers in Mexico and the United States. It is not surprising that the individuals and groups who kept the rumors alive after 1911 concerning Standard Oil's link to Madero were anti-*maderistas*, that is, *reyistas*, *orozquistas*, and *científicos*, along with Creel's friend and Greene's ex-partner, Senator Fall, and Madero's foe, Ambassador Henry Lane Wilson.

All of this is not to say that Standard Oil did not benefit from Madero's revolt or that Anglo-American international oil rivalries were not a part of the Mexican Revolution. All that is being asserted here is that, in the final analysis, it is unlikely that Standard Oil financed Madero's 1911 revolts and that the Standard Oil rumors were, in all probability, provoked and kept alive by Madero's enemies in Mexico and the United States.

If all this be correct, the question still remains: Where did the funds for Madero's revolution come from? Most historians agree that Gustavo Madero was the principal source of money, acquiring $500,000 (U.S.) in an embezzlement scheme involving a

French construction company. In addition, the rest of the Madero clan obtained between $300,000 and $400,000 for the cause. Madero himself raised another $100,000 from wealthy contributors in Mexico and San Antonio. According to Francisco Madero, Sr., twenty-six Mexican senators and several Mexican millionaires supported his son's campaign. Finally, as with the *magonistas*, thousands of undocumented contributions came from Mexican exiles in the form of small amounts of cash, arms, cattle, horses, hides, food-stuffs, and cheap or free labor. All of this, of course, does not take into consideration forced loans and the fruits of war obtained on the battlefield. If Hopkins's estimate of the aggregate cost of Madero's revolution is taken seriously (and Hopkins was certainly in a position to know), then it would have been no problem for Madero to raise the $1 million to $1.5 million (U.S.) needed to finance his revolt.[47]

Thus, part of Madero's success was due to the efficiency of his organization. Madero's movement, drawing on the organizational and legal skills of González, Caracristi, Gustavo Madero, and Hopkins, was a professional one—an operation that had none of the amateurism characteristic of other *revoltoso* groups. In struggling against American authorities and Porfirio Díaz, Madero was always able to hire his own secret agents, private detectives, and informants. Unlike Flores Magón, he had the wealth and talent to successfully fight fire with fire.

Not surprisingly, after Díaz was gone Madero kept the "Creel International Detective Agency" intact as a weapon to be used against other *revoltosos*. Some of the names changed—Manuel Calero replaced Creel at the embassy—but Hopkins was retained to affect publicity and politics in Washington and the institutionalized police and spy network remained.[48]

Madero, like Díaz before him, solicited Taft's support in extraditing and arresting *reyistas*, *orozquistas*, *vazquistas*, and *magonistas*. It was partly Calero's efforts that brought about the new

[47]Calvert, *The Mexican Revolution*, pp. 82–83; Henderson, "Mexican Rebels in the Borderlands," pp. 211–212. For the comments of Madero, Sr., see F. L. de la Barra to Knox, 10 December 1910 (encl. of San Antonio *Light and Gazette*, 20 November 1910), RG 60, file 90755/362.

[48]For Hopkins's role see Hopkins to Azcona, 29 December 1912 and 4 January 1913, AGN/RRV, cartas 367 and 373.

embargo act of 1912—promoted by Senator Elihu Root and signed into law by Taft. The embargo on arms to Mexico, naturally enough, aided Madero and hurt Orozco. As for the *magonistas*, Madero's commercial agent in New York City, that old *reyista* Heriberto Barrón, advised Madero to seek Flores Magón's extradition in October 1911 after Mother Jones and several American labor leaders had broken their ties with the *magonistas*. Although Knox declined to extradite for legal reasons, as late as February 1913 alleged anarchists in Tampa, Florida, were being deported on grounds that they were involved in an assassination plot led by Araujo, Flores Magón, and Anselmo Figueroa (in spite of the fact that at the time, Araujo was in Canada and the others were in prison in McNeil, Washington).[49]

In October and November 1911, Madero had little difficulty in curtailing the *reyistas*. The Corral-Creel system worked well in their absence. Mexican immigration authorities were instructed to report the movement of *reyista* agents. Postal authorities were ordered to intercept all *reyista* mail. Consuls in Eagle Pass, Laredo, Rio Grande City, and San Antonio employed private spies and engaged the assistance of local officials (district attorneys and Texas Rangers). Mexico's secret police were also active. Secret service agents penetrated the *reyista* inner circle and reported their findings to the Ministry of Domestic Affairs and the San Antonio consul.[50]

Somewhat ironically, de la Barra and Madero employed both the Thavonat Secret Police Company and the Furlong Secret Service Company to aid the *maderistas* in their struggle against the pro-Díaz *científicos*. After June 1911, the *científicos* formed a central junta in New York City with regional centers in Chicago, St. Louis, San Antonio, Laredo, Brownsville, and New Orleans. In St. Louis, Madero's consul hired Furlong to send agents to Chicago to locate arms allegedly deposited there. In September, Furlong reported to the minister of foreign relations that Chicago

---

[49]Berta Ulloa, *La Revolución intervenida. Relaciones diplomáticas entre México y Estados Unidos* (*1910–1914*) pp. 19–21; Heriberto Barrón to Madero, 30 October 1911, AGN/RRV, carta 76; AREM, L–E–1440, Asunto: Pres. Madero, 1911–1913, III/515/1, Anarquistas que intentan atentar contra la vida del Presidente Madero.

[50]Bryan, "Mexican Politics in Transition," pp. 314–315.

was very large, that he did not know any of the conspirators, and that his agents could not even locate Agustín Piña, the Mexican consul in that city.[51] It was no wonder that Creel's old colleague failed in his first mission for the *maderistas*, given his past friendship with Díaz and the *científicos*. After this experience Madero wisely tended to rely more on his consular corps and the secret police than on American private detectives.

Thus, throughout the era the espionage and police system first developed by Creel remained intact; first being used against Madero as a *revoltoso*, later by Madero, the successful revolutionary, against other *revoltosos*. Madero's reliance on the Díaz system may have been his undoing. As the example of Furlong shows, Creel's allies knew the system better than Madero and were of questionable allegiance. Madero refused to dismantle the Porfirian state, relying on the federal army, judges, senators, secret police, and the American Bureau of Investigation. In the end that mistake in judgment cost him his post and his life, as ambitious soldiers came to the fore. In the meantime, President Taft was at the border, engaged in watchful waiting.

[51]Ulloa, *La Revolución intervenida*, pp. 18 and 295, n. 90.

The revolution did not triumph by force of arms.

Porfirio Díaz, 1911

9. Taft's "Neutrality" Diplomacy

On 31 May 1911, Díaz had been forced to flee from Mexico. While he was enroute to Spain, seven days later, Madero entered Mexico City in triumph. Díaz watched the development of Mexico's revolution, first from Madrid, later, by the middle of summer, from his residence-in-exile in Paris. Having received a note of "sympathy and sorrow" from the American president, he responded to Taft by saying:

> The revolution did not triumph by force of arms; I could have restored order, and it would not have been the first time; but it would have stifled the industry, commerce and credit of Mexico, exposing her politics to international controversy, and as it was said that my presence in the executive chair was the sole cause of insurrection, I made the last sacrifice for peace, that of my personal pride, and may this peace soon be restored in order that my country may return to the way of prosperity.[1]

Thus Díaz went into exile believing himself to have been a national martyr—the self-sacrificing leader who relinquished power out of, to use Taft's words, a "disinterested love of country."[2]

Díaz's account of Madero's victory is too self-serving to be credible. It is obvious that circumstances forced the old dictator's hand and that his fall from power was something other than the act of an unselfish national hero. With the federal army and state still intact as of late May 1911, could there be another explanation other than Díaz's to support his statement that "Madero did not

[1]Díaz to Taft, 20 July 1911, William Howard Taft Papers, Library of Congress Manuscript Division, Washington, D.C. (hereafter cited as Taft Papers), Doc. 5, Reel 376, Series 6, no. 241.
[2]Taft to Díaz, 7 June 1911, Taft Papers, Doc. 4, Reel 376, Series 6, no. 241.

triumph by force of arms"? Perhaps Díaz's allusion to the politics of "international controversy" is not without meaning in this context. This very likely could have been a reference to the potential threat of American military intervention and the constant presence of Yankee influence in indirectly shaping and supporting the Madero revolt. It is possible that Díaz was forced to resign, not by Madero's troops, but by circumstances engineered against him and in favor of Madero by the American government.

This interpretation is supported by many contemporary historians who argue that Taft's legal training and judicial experience led him to follow a more cautious, restrained neutrality policy than that of his predecessor. As applied to neutrality diplomacy, Taft's "legalism," it is asserted, had the effect of aiding Madero and hurting Díaz. Thus, William Beezley states that there was "a change in the enforcement of neutrality laws . . . [that] followed the transition in the White House from the stick-waving Roosevelt to the gavel-swinging Taft." P. Edward Haley argues that the diplomatic and commercial policies of the Taft administration were shaped by the State Department, and that these policies reflected the legal training and background of the upper level of the department. He concludes by saying: "On balance, the formal neutrality of the United States benefited the Maderistas and undermined Díaz." And, finally, Edward Berbusse, in an article on the neutrality diplomacy of the United States at this time, concludes, like Haley, that "the United States Secretary [of State] interpreted our 'neutrality laws' with strong sympathy for the followers of Madero."[3]

There is nothing seriously wrong with these statements if neutrality policy is considered only as a problem of diplomacy, with the focus on the State Department—specifically, the actions and attitudes of Taft's secretary of state, Philander Chase Knox. However, the assumption that neutrality policy was interpreted and enforced primarily by Knox, acting in concert with the president, is a narrow view of history, only partially correct. To begin with,

---

[3]Beezley, *Insurgent Governor*, p. 56; P. Edward Haley, *Revolution and Intervention: The Diplomacy of Taft and Wilson with Mexico, 1910–1917*, pp. 24–25; Edward J. Berbusse, "Neutrality-Diplomacy of the United States and Mexico, 1910–1911," *The Americas* 12 (1956): 283.

neutrality policy was not simply the product of presidential proclamations and legislation (which was sparse—for this period, primarily the congressional codification of 1873 known as the Revised
Statutes) but also of legal precedents, international concerns,
federal court decisions, and the opinions and actions of the U.S.
attorney general, military authorities, customs officials, immigration
officers, and local and state authorities. Given the "hard-headed"
approach of Attorney General George W. Wickersham on neutrality
matters, the rigorous enforcement role of special agent Ellsworth,
the availability of a new manpower pool known as the Bureau
of Investigation, and the improved telephonic communications of
the police and army services of the state and federal governments,
it could be argued that enforcement of the neutrality laws was
potentially more effective after 1909 than before. And this was
as true for *maderistas* as for other *revoltoso* groups.[4]

Knox, a former Pennsylvania lawyer and U.S. attorney general, was Taft's secretary of state from 1909 to 1913. Because Taft
was not nearly the activist in foreign policy that Roosevelt had
been, Knox was far more in control of the apparatus of policy
making than Elihu Root or John Hay had been. Because immigration from and trade with Latin America, especially Mexico and
Cuba, increased greatly after 1909, the department's work load on
Latin American matters was greater than before. Taft was especially concerned with U.S. interests in Mexico, Cuba, Nicaragua,
and Panama. Apart from this, there was little to distinguish Taft's
Latin American policy from Roosevelt's. Continuity was maintained in the Department of State with the appointment of Huntington Wilson, the former third secretary, as assistant secretary
of state, while good old reliable Alvey Adee was retained as
second assistant secretary. Scott stayed on as solicitor until March

[4]Most historians in the United States derive their accounts of Taft's
neutrality diplomacy from either Berbusse or Haley. Both these interpretations
rely exclusively on State Department sources, that is, decimal file 812.00. Both
accounts fail to ascertain the attorney general's concept of neutrality as contained in his letter of 13 February 1911 to Knox (RG 60, file 90755/516).
Although Haley simply states that the letter is missing, Berbusse says: "Unfortunately, this letter cannot be found in either the State Dept. or Justice
Dept. files" (see above, n. 3, Berbusse, p. 275). Again, Treasury Department
materials relating to the Customs Service were overlooked by Haley and
Berbusse.

1911. Wilson himself noted the continuity, saying, "If Knox's policy towards the southern republics differed from Root's, the difference was only in emphasis."[5]

It was understandable that under Knox the department would continue the civil libertarian and "legalistic" traditions that had characterized it under Root. Scott's concern for the constitutional rights of free speech, whether exercised by the author of *Barbarous Mexico* or a *maderista* editor in Texas, was echoed in the statements of Knox, Adee, and others. In these matters, as in many affecting the *revoltosos*, the State Department was in opposition to the "hardliners" at Justice.

Even before the scheduled revolt of November 20, the Mexican government appealed to the U.S. government to suppress the *maderista* movement. Messages were forwarded from Díaz and Creel (now as minister of foreign relations) to Mexico's ambassadors in Washington, initially Francisco León de la Barra, then, after April, Manuel de Zamacona (at which time de la Barra had replaced Creel at Foreign Relations). Joaquín D. Casasús also served as a special ambassador to Washington during part of this period. Most of these messages sought to persuade the U.S. government that the *maderistas* were violating America's federal statutes prohibiting the enlistment of *revoltosos* (R.S. 5282) and the arming of military expeditions (R.S. 5286) by their anti-Díaz activities in Texas, Arizona, and California.[6]

Until February 1911 the Mexican government usually sought American action against both *magonistas* and *maderistas*, allowing the American government to assume that *magonistas* were acting in concert with *maderistas*. On 4 January 1911, Roberto Ruiz, a lawyer in the office of the Mexican Ministry of Foreign Relations, released an extensive study in which Francisco Madero, Ricardo Flores Magón, Abraham González, Práxedis Guerrero,

[5]Francis M. Huntington-Wilson, *Memoirs of an Ex-Diplomat*, p. 208. See also Richard D. Challener, *Admirals, Generals, and American Foreign Policy, 1898–1914*, p. 266, and Stuart, *The Department of State*, p. 212.

[6]See, for example, de la Barra to Sec. de Rel. Ext., 17 November 1910; Creel to Mex. Amb., 20 November 1910; de la Barra to Sec. de Rel. Ext., 19 January 1911; Creel to Sr. Encar. de Neg. ad-inter. de Mex., 8 February 1911–all Fabela, *Documentos históricos*, V, 91–92, 97, 173, and 233–234 respectively.

and other *correligionarios* were charged with a variety of "documented" violations of section 5286 of the U.S. Revised Statutes. The approach evidently worked, for the American ambassador, the Department of State, and the adjutant general's office all adhered to the notion that Madero and Flores Magón were working together. Not until early March were Ellsworth and his superiors at the Justice Department completely aware of the schism between the two *revoltoso* forces. By then the identification of *magonismo* with *maderismo* had not aided the latter in the eyes of the "hardliners" at Justice and War.[7]

Knox first publicly disagreed with Mexico's interpretation of neutrality on 1 December 1910 in a note to de la Barra. In response to Mexico's assertion that González and Lomelín were violating the neutrality laws in their operations at Presidio, Texas, the secretary found that since no state of war existed in Mexico, the individuals named were not in violation of the rules of international law regarding armed rebellions. He further observed that "mere propaganda in and of itself" was protected under the liberty of speech and press provisions of the Constitution and therefore was not punishable under the statutes.[8] By mid-December, Knox had instructed Ambassador Wilson that "it appears to be a general rule of international law, long established and well settled, that even in a state of war mere trade in arms, ammunition, and other articles of contraband is considered legal and subject to no penalty save the loss of the goods if captured in the trade."[9] Thus it was held that the actions of Madero's agents in purchasing arms in the United States and operating out of San Antonio were excluded from both international and American laws on neutrality.

By the end of January, Knox had definitely developed a most

[7]Ruiz to Min. de Rel. Ext., 4 January 1911, ibid., V, 141–146. See also Henry Lane Wilson to Sec. of State, 16 November 1910 (encl. Memorandum), Hanrahan, *Documents*, II, pt. 1, 87–90; Adee to Att. Gen., 19 November 1910, RG 60, file 90755/285; "Memorandum for the Adj. Gen.," November 1910, Records of the Adjutant General's Office, 1780s–1917, Record Group 94, National Archives, Washington, D.C. (hereafter cited as RG 94), AG 1716354D; Ellsworth to State, 2 March 1911, Hanrahan, *Documents*, I, pt. 1, 198.

[8]Knox to de la Barra, 1 December 1910, Knox Papers, State Dept. File, Information Series "A," Box 39, No. 72, p. 1.

[9]Ibid., Knox to Wilson, 14 December 1910, No. 72, pp. 4–5.

formal and "legalistic" position on neutrality, one that, if followed, would enable Madero to operate with impunity. His views were summarized in a note to the Mexican ambassador:

> It is not an offense against the United States to transport arms, ammunition, and munitions of war from this country to any foreign country, whether they are to be used in war or not; nor is it an offense against the United States for individuals to leave this country with intent to enlist in foreign military service; nor is it an offense against the United States to transport persons out of this country and land them in foreign countries, although such persons have an intent to enlist in foreign armies; nor is it an offense against the United States to transport from this country persons intending to enlist in foreign armies and munitions of war in the same ship.[10]

The neutrality statute only prohibited the organizing of a military or hostile expedition in the United States to be carried on against foreign powers with which the United States was at peace.

To clarify the difference between a commercial and a hostile expedition in the minds of border officials, Knox subsequently communicated a similar point of view to the director of the consular service, Wilbur J. Carr. Knox's position and interpretation were then forwarded to Ellsworth and several American consuls in Mexico, with the additional comment that "the policing of the Mexican border is a matter for the Mexican Government, and not for this Government."[11]

By February, the actions and opinions of Knox had produced strains within the president's cabinet. Most angry and disillusioned with Knox's "legalism" was Attorney General George W. Wickersham. Offended that he had not received prior notice of State's instructions of 25 January to Ellsworth, Wickersham asserted that Knox's position contradicted the president's instructions on neutrality enforcement and, if unqualified, would impede any cooperation between the departments of Justice, War, and Treasury in carrying out the president's desires. Wickersham, in a particularly goading note to State, suggested that Knox, in holding to his

[10]Knox to de la Barra, 24 January 1911, Hanrahan, *Documents*, I, pt. 1, 126–128. Also see U.S., Congress, Senate, *Papers* (*1911*), p. 397.

[11]Carr to Ellsworth, 25 January 1911, RDS, 812.00/672a. Also see Haley, *Revolution and Intervention*, pp. 22–23.

broad, unqualified statements on commerce in contraband, was not in accordance with the rule of law as it was understood in the Department of Justice and as it had been interpreted by "Attorney General Knox" in 1902.[12]

Wickersham refused to accept Knox's views concerning the differences between a commercial and a hostile expedition. Citing the authority of former Attorney General Harmon (1895), Wickersham held that persons supplying arms and munitions from the United States and affiliated in any way in a hostile plot or with hostile purposes were involved in a military, not commercial, enterprise and were therefore in violation of international law and American statutes. Thus, the department's obligation was clear: "The President's direction has been that we shall undertake to police the Mexican border as effectively as our forces will permit, and endeavor to prevent the importation of arms and ammunition into Mexico and the exclusion from Mexico of Mexican citizens going to Mexico with hostile intent against the existing government."[13] And even though Huntington Wilson called Wickersham's letter "extremely outrageous," and Knox's rebuttal included the forwarding of Wickersham's letter to Taft, there is no evidence to suggest that the attorney general changed his mode of operation vis-à-vis the *maderistas* to please either Knox or Taft, at least not prior to May 1911. Neutrality enforcement against Madero would remain vigorous, the chief of police would continue to debate the lawyer, and Taft would reign above the confusion and chaos of cabinet politics.

Wickersham's views were reflected in his orders to the federal attorneys and marshals along the frontier. As early as 20 November the Justice Department ordered the U.S. attorney at San Antonio to cause the immediate arrest of Madero. A few days later, similar orders were sent to officers in the Western District of Texas and Southern California. By early December, de la Barra assured Creel that both Taft and Wickersham were seeking the arrest of Madero for purchasing and transporting arms in violation of American neutrality laws. By the end of January, federal officers in San Antonio, operating under orders from Wickersham and the Bureau

12Wickersham to Knox, 13 February 1911, RG 60, file 90755/516.
13Ibid.

of Investigation, were preparing for Madero's arrest there. As American authorities began to close in on him, Madero found it expedient to return to Mexico on 13 February to take up the leadership of a revolution that was proceeding without him.[14]

Yet effective enforcement was no easy task, whatever Wickersham's intentions. Assistance from Mexico was not always forthcoming. Because Díaz needed to retain troops to protect Mexico City, they were not always available for frontier duty. Ellsworth noted in February that "the American side of the Border is a solid, living mass of troops, marshals and officers of every description [whereas] the Mexican side is *one vast blank spot*" [italics Ellsworth's].[15] By March, the U.S. attorney for Arizona could report only five cases under the neutrality laws, complaining that, due to the pro-Madero sympathies of the border population and his own manpower shortages, it was practically impossible to get sufficient evidence for violations of either the enlistment or military enterprises statutes.[16] Yet several *maderistas* in Texas and Arizona were eventually arrested and held for grand jury examinations during the spring and summer of 1911, in spite of the fact that Madero's revolt had been successfully concluded in May.[17]

Although limited in number, the successful arrests and convictions that did occur were the result not only of Wickersham's vigorous direction but also of the actions and views of government officials on the local level. These individuals held to a view of neutrality enforcement much broader in scope than that being pronounced by Knox at State. R. W. Dowe, the Eagle Pass customs collector, was of the opinion that he had the right to seize all shipments of rebel rifles and cartridges, even when the rebels controlled Ojinaga, a sub-port of entry across from Presidio, Texas.[18]

Likewise, Luther Ellsworth not only used military and customs

[14]Fowler to U.S. Att. in San Antonio, 20 November 1910, RG 60, file 90755/300; Att. Gen. to Sec. of State, 28 November 1910, RG 60, 90755/305; de la Barra to Creel, 8 December 1910, AREM, L–E–616, R–4–1; Wickersham to State, 26 January 1911, RDS, 812.00/673.

[15]Ellsworth to Sec. of State, 18 February 1911, Hanrahan, *Documents*, I, pt. 1, 164–167.

[16]J. E. Morrison to Att. Gen., 31 March 1911, ibid., pt. 2, 287–291.

[17]Ellsworth to Sec. of State, 11 May 1911, ibid., pp. 365–368.

[18]Ibid., pp. 365, 309.

authorities to enforce the neutrality laws but also told the secretary of state that "American soldiers have instructions to arrest and turn over to the U.S. Marshal any armed bodies of men found on American side of the border line."[19] This, of course, was a position far in excess of Knox's formal declarations, many of which were either never heard, never understood, or simply ignored. Unlike Knox, Ellsworth and his army of soldiers, secret agents, and customs officials were more concerned with stopping the smuggling of arms and men into Mexico than with either protocol or legal niceties.

Ellsworth was as vigilant in watching *maderistas* after November 1910 as he had been with the *magonistas* before that date. Still an important part of the "Creel International Detective Agency," he directed and coordinated an efficient corps of Bureau of Investigation agents, U.S. marshals, military commanders, mounted customs inspectors, and immigration officials. In cooperation with private detectives, customs authorities, and postal workers he intercepted *maderista* mail, including letters addressed to Madero's father in San Antonio. His agents, some of whom were paid Mexican spies, maintained surveillance over the revolutionary junta in San Antonio. By studying bills of lading for all freight and express shipments, his men were able to frustrate many attempts by the rebels to move munitions from San Antonio and other border points into Mexico. Because of excellent telephone, telegraph, and mail service between Ciudad Juárez and San Antonio, he was able to relay and send instructions to consuls and viceconsuls throughout Texas and northern Mexico. In his struggle against the *maderistas*, he was well aided by Texas authorities, especially Governor Colquitt and his Texas Rangers.[20]

More than any other group, customs officials assigned to the Mexican border vigorously attempted to prevent the smuggling of arms to rebels and to inhibit the return of Mexican citizens who

[19]Ellsworth to Sec. of State, 4 February 1911, RDS, 812.00/728. Also see Dowe to Ellsworth, 24 December 1910, RG 60, file 90755/395.

[20]Ellsworth to Sec. of State, 13 December 1910, RG 60, file 90755/378; Ellsworth to Sec. of State, 25 December 1910, Knox Papers, Series A, No. 72, p. 7; Ellsworth to Sec. of State, 10 February 1911, and O. B. Colquitt, "Proclamation," 11 February 1911, Hanrahan, *Documents*, I, pt. 1, 148–152 and 154–156 respectively.

were assumed to be potential *maderistas* to their homeland. Approximately 150 customs officers performed their duties along the 1,900 miles of frontier. Although their normal responsibilities primarily involved the collection of import duties, they were also required to prevent illegal exports, such as guns and ammunition, that were not sent through the normal channels of customs ports. Because they were instructed to enforce neutrality laws (which, according to Knox, did not outlaw contraband) and to prevent the export of illegal munitions, many customs officials came to believe that the two overlapped and that all munitions exports to the rebels were illegal. Part of this confusion was generated by Ellsworth, who directed much of the enforcement of the neutrality laws after 1909.[21]

To contain the Madero insurrection, customs officials sought to intercept and detain the smuggling of horses, cattle, arms, and munitions by *insurrectos*. By January 1911 deputy collector Luke Dowe of Del Rio was instructing his officers to "detain any consignments except those in the hands of Mexican federal officers."[22] To get at gunrunners and smugglers, customs officials acted as guides and scouts to the cavalry. Roving patrols of mounted riders also aided in the task. Finally, customs collectors were instructed to reject legitimate applications to export arms and ammunition.

The effective curtailment of illegal munitions exports from the United States was a task that the border customs service was not prepared to handle. The service lacked the experience, manpower, and legislative muscle. Few arrests occurred, because smugglers were well informed by sympathetic collaborators—including local officials, dealers, and grafters—of the location and movement of customs officers.[23] Even the weather and terrain worked against them. A drought that lasted from 1907 through 1910 meant that the range was lacking in natural forage, a condition that prevented

[21]Carman, "U.S. Customs and the Madero Revolution."

[22]Luke Dowe to Deputy Collector (Langtry, Texas), 31 January 1911, Records of the Bureau of Customs, Record Group 36, Letterpress Volume, Eagle Pass, Texas, 1909–1913, Federal Archives and Record Center, Fort Worth, Texas (hereafter cited as FRC Fort Worth), p. 166.

[23]Carman, "U.S. Customs and the Madero Revolution," pp. 32–34.

scouting forces from staying in the field any longer than four or five days at a time.[24]

To aid the customs service in its struggle against the *maderistas*, troops were mobilized along the frontier. Although the initial authorization occurred as early as 21 November 1910, it was not until March 1911 that Taft surprised the American public by ordering twenty thousand soldiers to the border, ostensibly to engage in training maneuvers and enforce the neutrality laws. Taft's announcement provided a screen for another objective—to use the army to interdict arms and ammunition to the rebels in Mexico, that is, to enforce the customs laws. Although Taft could not order army commanders to enforce customs regulations, he could tell them to enforce neutrality. Believing that the curtailment of gun smuggling was a part of neutrality law enforcement, army officers did not hesitate to pursue and arrest gunrunners headed for Mexico.[25]

Taft evidently had several objectives in mind in ordering the March mobilization, the least important of which was that of a training maneuver for the army. To newspaperman Talcott Williams he confided that he could not take the public into his confidence since to do so would amount to a *casus belli* with the existing government of Mexico, which had minimized the danger of Madero's insurrection. Instead, Taft reported, "I allowed the War Department to report that the going of the troops was for maneuvers."[26] A different explanation was provided the Mexican ambassador, who was assured that the troops were not mobilizing or holding maneuvers on the boundary, but were detached in order "to patrol the boundary and prevent insurrectionary expeditions from American soil against the Mexican government."[27] As has

[24]Luke Dowe to Eagle Pass customs collector, 27 December 1910, FRC Fort Worth, p. 143.

[25]McCain, Adj. Gen., to Com. Gen. San Antonio, 21 November 1910, Hanrahan, *Documents*, I, pt. 1, 68; Carman, "U.S. Customs and the Madero Revolution," pp. 73–86. Initial mobilization orders for November 1910, can be found in RG 94, AG 1716354 F, G, I, W, A123–124, J, L, and A18.

[26]Taft to Talcott Williams, 28 March 1911, Taft Papers, Series 6, Reel 365, case no. 95A.

[27]State to Mex. Amb., 13 March 1911, RG 165, 5761–26, encl. 3.

been seen, this explanation, at least in the context of customs and neutrality laws, was partly true.

The primary objective was explained in full in a confidential note to the army chief of staff, General Leonard Wood. Taft told Wood that he had acted after learning from the American ambassador that Mexico was about to explode like a volcano with a general insurrection that would injure or destroy "American investments of more than a billion dollars" as well as endanger the lives of forty thousand or more Americans. Troops were to be positioned so that, if revolutionary conditions demanded it, they could be sent into Mexico to "save American lives and property." In the meantime, it was hoped that the presence of American troops would prevent insurrectionary expeditions from American soil and provide encouragement to Díaz and his backers. In other words, it was designed to enable Díaz to stem the tide of insurrection. Taft hoped that a show of force would stop the revolution, preserve the Porfirian peace, and make military intervention unnecessary. If the demonstration did not work, the troops would be better trained and best situated for action in Mexico.[28]

Around the time of the mobilization, several minor matters were beginning to lead to the disillusionment of certain U.S. businessmen and officials with Díaz. Rockefeller and Doheny became unhappy when Díaz began to favor British petroleum interests. American mining groups wanted more concessions than Díaz was willing to give. Limantour angered New York's bankers by introducing new nationalistic financial policies and by seeking loans and credit in Europe instead of the United States.[29]

The most serious diplomatic problem was Díaz's refusal to provide the United States with a permanent lease on Magdalena Bay, Baja California, site of an American naval station. It was feared in some U.S. naval circles that Díaz, or a subsequent Mexican government, would lease this site and Turtle Bay to the Japanese. Intelligence reports added to the fears of America's military establishment, as when the American military attaché in Mexico City reported that the chief of the Mexican secret service had been quoted as saying: "Wait until Mexico and Japan get together;

---

[28]Taft to Wood, 12 March 1911, Hanrahan, *Documents*, I, pt. 1, 225–229.
[29]Johnson, *Heroic Mexico*, p. 47.

then with Japan to attend to the naval work while we attack by land, we'll make short work of the 'Gringos'." The rumors were well established, especially in Europe, where as late as 1915 the German *Tages-Zeitung* was reporting that the Magdalena Bay incident was one of the principal causes of the fall of Porfirio Díaz.[30]

Although relations between Díaz and the United States became more strained after February 1911, it appears that Taft did not abandon Díaz until after the 10 May victory of Orozco's troops at Ciudad Juárez. On 12 May, after a meeting with the secretary of state and the attorney general, Taft issued an order to the Department of the Treasury. His instructions called for the passage without obstruction of guns and ammunition from El Paso to Ciudad Juárez, stating that the mere sale of supplies in El Paso to Mexicans, "whether insurrectos or supporters of the Government," was not a violation of international law or U.S. statutes. To this critics who argued that this policy favored the *maderistas* who held Ciudad Juárez, he answered that it was probably true but was a situation that grew out of the weakness of the Díaz government, for which the United States was not responsible.[31]

Thus, Taft had finally come around to Knox's view that "international law favors the continuance of commercial transactions and holds them innocent in a neutral country until those transactions become really a part of a military operation against a friendly government."[32] Taft was now ready to accept the inevitability of Díaz's fall and was aware that he could no longer maintain the status quo. Díaz, the friend of American businessmen and presidents, was on the way out. Taft had aided him within the limits of American law. However, the objective of protecting American lives and property was greater than that of supporting the aging dictator. The chaos of revolt and rebellion had to be brought

---

[30]Knox to Sec. of War, 4 March 1911, RG 165, 1766–156. Also see Sturtevant to Chief, WCD, 3 January 1911; Wilson to Sec. of State 10 February 1911; *Deutsche Tages-Zeitung* (Berlin), 17 April 1915 (navy translation-FV, 26 May 1915)—all Records of the Office of the Chief of Naval Operations (ONI, Office of Naval Intelligence), Record Group 38, National Archives, Washington, D.C. (hereafter cited as RG 38), C–9–b908.

[31]Taft to Sec. of Treas., 12 May 1911, RG 165, WCD, 5761–222.

[32]Ibid.

under control. Within two weeks of Taft's message Díaz resigned the presidency.

It was now time for Taft to pursue a policy that would favor Madero as American capital's best chance for peace in Mexico. Madero, a reformer in the American "Progressive" mold, was acceptable as the least of all evils. He was the obvious alternative to radical revolution, especially the *magonista* revolution of class warfare. Taft's "neutrality diplomacy" would protect American lives and property by denying to Madero's *revoltoso* enemies the use of American soil as a base for "revolution" and "counterrevolution," by dropping federal charges against *maderistas* in American jails, and by threatening U.S. intervention if Madero did not promote American capital interests over those of European and Japanese competitors.[33]

Not surprisingly, Flores Magón and his followers did not stop their participation in the Baja revolution with the exile of Díaz. From the *magonista* point of view, the only significance of 25 May 1911 was that the *federales* now included *maderista* as well as *porfirista* officers. By 22 June, Flores Magón's socialist army was forced to flee from Tijuana and leave the Baja to the forces of Madero. Yet *magonista* campaigns were not limited to Lower California, and the fighting continued through the remainder of the year. Several hundred *magonista* guerrillas ensconced themselves in the Burro mountains of Coahuila, five hundred miles south of Eagle Pass, Texas. In September, PLM veteran José Inés Salazar led a group of twenty-five armed *magonistas* from Columbus, New Mexico, into Chihuahua. As late as January 1912, Texas Rangers were reporting that organized bands of *magonistas* were making raids from Mexico across the Rio Grande in order to steal horses and cattle.[34]

After Madero's victory, and in accordance with his Mexican policy, Taft continued the well-established practice of suppressing

[33]Berta Ulloa refers to this as "Madero entre la espada y la pared" in *La Revolución intervenida*, pp. 26–27. Gastón García Cantú lists eight incidents during 1911–1913 in which Taft threatened armed intervention into Mexico in his *Las invasiones norteamericanas en México*, pp. 272–275.

[34]Ellsworth to Sec. of State, 16 June 1911, Hanrahan, *Documents*, I, pt. 2, 377–382; Duncan to Adj. Gen., 22 September 1911, RG 94, AG 1716354 A842; Colquitt to Taft, 26 January 1912, RG 94, AG 1870422 A.

the *magonista* movement in the United States. Federal troops continued to act as roving patrols, often in company with Texas Rangers, whose forces had been expanded at federal expense.[35] Another practice that became routine was that of granting permission for Mexican troops to cross the border and travel on American soil in order to suppress *magonismo* and *bandolerismo*. Most often these troops were under American escort and traveled unarmed, with their arms and ammunition being shipped as baggage. To avoid delays at the border, immigration inspection requirements were usually waived. In June, Madero's troops were allowed to enter El Paso to travel eastward to Laredo and westward to Baja California; in August, a force of *rurales* was allowed to travel from Douglas, Arizona, to Tijuana, Baja California; in October, a group of Orozco's *rurales* passed over American territory from El Paso to Nogales. The government's rationale was summed up by Knox when he told the secretary of commerce that "this movement of troops is designed, among other things, to secure the adequate protection of American life and property" in Mexico.[36]

Meanwhile, the Justice Department was undertaking preparations for action against the PLM leaders. For three months, from March through May, the federal prosecutor's office in Los Angeles and Bureau of Investigation agents had been accumulating evidence with which to file a neutrality charge. After Madero (who approved of these proceedings) had been consulted in early June in El Paso, a grand jury proceeding was instituted during the second week of June. On 14 June, the four leading Junta members—Ricardo and Enrique Flores Magón, Librado Rivera, and Anselmo Figueroa—were arrested and jailed, with bail fixed for Ricardo at $5,000.[37]

The Junta's trial took place between 4 June and 22 June 1912, at which time a verdict of guilty was delivered. With U.S. district attorney Dudley W. Robinson handling the case for the federal government, the four leaders were indicted on five counts

[35]Colquitt to Taft, 26 January 1912, RG 94, AG 1870422 A.

[36]Knox to Dept. of Commerce, 11 August 1911, RG 85 (Immigration and Naturalization), 53108/71–A. From the same file see also Knox to Sec. of Commerce and Labor, 17 October 1911; Zamacona to Knox, 6 June 1911; Knox to Sec. of War, 7 June 1911; Wood to Charles Nagel, 22 June 1911.

[37]Blaisdell, *The Desert Revolution*, pp. 170–172.

of violating sections 37 and 10 of the U.S. Criminal Code (35 Stat. at Large 1088; 4 March 1909), that is, "conspiracy to hire and retain the service of foreign people as soldiers."[38] When Job Harriman abandoned the *magonistas*, the Junta leaders were left with a young and inexperienced lawyer who was unable to develop a convincing defense. Courtroom procedures on both sides left much to be desired, with the proceedings being characterized by wholesale perjury, bribery of witnesses, and inconsistent and contradictory testimony.[39]

As in the earlier Tombstone case, the times were hardly propitious for a fair trial for *magonista* radicals. Nineteen twelve was the year of the I.W.W. free speech movement, and southern California was in the center of the fray. Having been prompted by Harrison Gray Otis, the Los Angeles newspaper editor (who owned extensive properties in Baja California), the San Diego city council passed an ordinance prohibiting all public speeches. The act was obviously directed against the radicals, an attempt to prevent San Diego from becoming a base of support for the Mexican revolutionaries and their I.W.W. supporters. For six months prior to the trial the free speech controversies raged. San Diego and Los Angeles were aflame with the terror and violence of vigilante vengeance, and these conditions spilled over into the courtroom.[40]

The political dimensions of the government's case were obvious. A variety of "socialistic" materials were entered as evidence. Robinson entered as evidence the PLM "Manifesto to the Workers of the World" of 3 April 1911 and noted how the manifesto was a "clear exposition of exactly the same sort of doctrines as are contended for by the Socialists, and which find place in the literature of the Industrial Workers of the World."[41]

Although the prosecution went through the motions of proving the neutrality violation charges, the unwritten and real charge was the *magonista* alliance with American radicals, especially the

---

[38]U.S. v. Magon, et al., Crim. 374 & 375 (U.S. Dist. Ct., So. Cal. Div., 1912), FRC Laguna Niguel.
[39]Blaisdell, *The Desert Revolution*, pp. 189–190.
[40]Shanks, "The I.W.W. Free Speech Movement," p. 28.
[41]U.S., Congress, Senate, *Investigation of Mexican Affairs*, II, 2506–2508.

hated I.W.W.[42] Taft's victory sent the Mexican rebels to McNeil Island, where they served the maximum sentence, not being released until 19 January 1914. While there, Figueroa contracted the tuberculosis from which he died in 1915. The humid dungeons and glacial temperatures of McNeil Island took their toll of the others as well.[43]

Taft continued to pursue his policy against other *revoltosos*. In October 1911 the citizens of El Paso were disturbed and excited when they learned that Bernardo Reyes was going to start a revolt against Madero from that city on 1 December. The *reyistas*, according to newspaper reports, were supposedly allying themselves with *porfirista* cash and *magonista* soldiers in order to form a united front against Madero. The El Paso *Daily Times* reported that *reyista* juntas had formed in El Paso and San Antonio and that Reyes was headed for San Antonio to plan a "unified *contrarevolución*" with Enrique Creel and Emilio Vázquez Gómez. The "Plan de Bernardo Reyes" declared Madero's election null and void and named Reyes provisional president. Under the *reyistas*, order and constitutional rule would be restored and the military would be upgraded and provided with better salaries.[44]

Unlike the confusion and ineffectiveness that characterized the American government's reaction to the earlier Madero revolt, official repression of the *reyista* movement came quickly and decisively. Mexico's secret police cooperated with Justice Department agents in infiltrating the *reyista* inner circle. In early November a federal grand jury began to investigate the Reyes conspiracy. On 17 November the War Department ordered troops to be drawn

[42]U.S. v. Magon, et al., Crim. 374 and 375, "Instructions of the Court," p. 7, FRC Laguna Niguel.

[43]R. Flores Magón, E. Flores Magón, L. Rivera, A. Figueroa, in U.S. Bureau of Prisons, Department of Justice, Washington, D.C. (hereafter cited as Bureau of Prisons), McNeil Island Registers nos. 2198–2201 (7 July 1912–19 January 1914). For Figueroa in particular see Rafael Ramos Pedrueza, "Semblanzas Revolucionarias. A. S. Figueroa," *El Popular* (Mexico City), 18 May 1942, p. 5.

[44]*El Paso Daily Times*, 3 October 1911, from Archivo de la Espinosa de los Monteros, Tomo II, fol. 13 (Bib. Manuel Orozco y Berra, Chapultepec Castle annex). Also see H. L. Stimpson to Nagel, 21 November 1911, RG 85, 53108/71–B.

up along the border to prevent armed revolutionists from crossing into Mexico. The next day, Reyes was indicted by a grand jury at Laredo and immediately arrested by Eugene Nolte, the U.S. marshal at San Antonio. Reyes was charged with violating two sections of the U.S. Criminal Code pertaining to neutrality and conspiracy. Released on $5,000 bail, Reyes jumped bond and fled to Mexico, where he was soon arrested by Madero's troops and confined in the military prison of Santiago Tlatelolco to await trial for treason.[45]

Following the November arrest of Reyes, American authorities forcefully dismantled the *reyista* organization within a three-week period. Several agencies cooperated in the suppression of the *reyistas*, including the 23rd Infantry, the Bureau of Immigration, and the Texas Rangers. Governor Colquitt directed the Texas adjutant general to give notice to the revolutionists that they must leave Texas within forty-eight hours, with Rangers and immigration inspectors being authorized to arrest anyone who violated the decree. U.S. soldiers were provided with search warrants and, in the company of customs and immigration officials, made several raids on private homes in the Laredo area. The booty seized included rifles, pistols, cartridge belts, ammunition, gas pipe bombs, saddles, spurs, bridles, haversacks, lanterns, kerosene, camping equipment, and *reyista* proclamations. Several "agitators" were arrested and held for deportation proceedings under section 36 of the immigration law for entering the United States without inspection. In El Paso a carload of rifles shipped from Chicago was confiscated by customs authorities. With the December arrest of Samuel Espinosa de los Monteros, the party secretary, Reyes's rebel organization was virtually destroyed.[46]

Several factors explain why neutrality enforcement against the *reyistas* was so rigorous and so successful. It was at this time that, contrary to State Department wishes, the attorney general dropped all neutrality violation charges against the *maderistas* because Taft wished to avoid any conflict with Mexico's newly elected

[45]Bryan, "Mexican Politics in Transition," pp. 315–317.

[46]Ibid., pp. 317–319; Charles Hagadom to Adj. Gen., 24 November 1911 (5 encls.), RG 94, AG 1849275/A7; Colquitt to Taft, 29 November 1911, and F. W. Berkshire to Danl. J. Keefe, 29 November 1911, RG 85, 53108/71–B.

president. This same desire was the major dimension of Taft's Mexican policy, and the *reyista* revolt was the first genuine test of the American government's resolve. Madero was watching and Taft wanted to be convincing. Thus the American officials, supported fully by Texas authorities, moved swiftly before the *reyistas* could develop a popular base. The enforcement was so effective that Reyes himself commented somewhat bitterly that "the enmity of the United States was unleashed against me without any precedent in times past."[47]

The suppression of the *reyistas* was also testimony to the effectiveness of the binational police and espionage system under Madero, even without Creel and Corral, and the accumulated experience of the local officials on both sides of the border. Another condition that hindered Reyes was his "image" problem in the United States. Since 1909, mostly due to the reports of the then American ambassador, David Thompson, Reyes had been pictured as radical and anti-American (because he opposed America's friend, Porfirio Díaz), a State Department view that was publicized in the frontier press. In addition, the stories and reports about Reyes's links with the *magonistas*, although not substantiated, also caused grief for Reyes—especially when these views were reported to the "hardliners" at Justice. These reports had been circulating since 1909 and, as has been indicated, were still being reported by the Texas press as late as October 1911.[48]

As for Taft, in his mind he was being consistent on the matter of neutrality. After several years of never-ending border conflict, it was time for the United States to be more assertive. Syndicalism and rabid revolution were not to be tolerated at home or abroad. All of this hurt Reyes, aided Madero, and did not bode well for Pascual Orozco, who in early 1912 was planning his own revolt against Madero.

Pascual Orozco proclaimed his rebellion on 3 March. He established himself as head of the rebels of Chihuahua and boldly announced his plan to march on Mexico City and his old chieftain Madero with a force of eight thousand men. Unhappy with the slow progress of Madero's revolution, Orozco demanded several

47Bryan, "Mexican Politics in Transition," p. 331.
48Ibid., pp. 331–332.

socioeconomic reforms, most of which called for improved labor conditions and reflected the surge of economic nationalism that had begun in Mexico at Cananea in 1906. Although financed by members of the Chihuahua aristocracy, the *orozquistas* included in their rank and file many ex-*magonistas*, who, adopting as their symbol a red flag, were known as "Red Flaggers." Like *maderismo* earlier, *orozquismo* became quite popular in the United States along the border and attracted thousands of followers, especially in Los Angeles.[49]

Revoltoso control of Ciudad Juárez and the renewed fighting along the frontier created serious diplomatic and political problems for Taft. His commitment to the protection of American lives and property in Mexico meant that the "Pax Maderista" had to be restored and Orozco defeated. The violence of Ciudad Juárez threatened United States interests both there and in El Paso, and there was a popular clamor for intervention. As Governor Colquitt reminded the president, "the continued disorder and the obligation of the U.S. to the world under the Monroe Doctrine makes it now a duty for our government to intervene in Mexico."[50] Even Taft's closest advisers considered sending troops across the border to suppress violence by "return fire" as a serious option.[51] Yet intervention was not without its hazards, not the least of which was the possibility that the presence of American troops on Mexican soil might unleash a nationalist attack on American lives and property there, the very thing Taft wished to avoid. Besides, Taft rightly suspected that the *orozquistas* wanted to compel an American intervention for their own purposes.

Intervention was also a domestic political problem. Taft would not send troops into Mexico without congressional authority, and Congress was not of one mind on the matter, being divided between the pro-Orozco forces of Senator Fall (and the "Creel-Terrazas-Guggenheim crowd") and his opponents. More important, intervention was a hotly debated issue sure to generate controversy

---

[49]Michael C. Meyer, *Mexican Rebel: Pascual Orozco and the Mexican Revolution, 1910–1915*, pp. 63–65, 67–69, 87, n. 110.

[50]Colquitt to Taft, 12 February 1912, Taft Papers, Series 6, Reel 365, no. 95C.

[51]Haley, *Revolution and Intervention*, pp. 39–40.

in an election year. Although many of Taft's supporters told him that his election success would be assured if he sent the troops, most were not as blatant as N. G. Turk, a leading member of the Oklahoma headquarters of the Republican Central Committee, who told Taft:

> I am anxious that you sucseed [sic] yourself for the nomination, and I will do all in my power to bring it about.
>
> I have this suggestion to offer, and it is this; we are, and have been constantly harrassed by those Greesers to our south, and our people along the border, and in the interior, are clamoring that something be done or said, that will put a stop to the conditions which have, and are now being carried on down there. One word from you, would put a stop to Insurrectoism, and in my opinion would add new laruls [sic] to your already bedecked crown, and would prove a blessing to humanity, and assure your Nomination, and Election, to the high position that you now hold.
>
> I feel confident that when our State Convention is over, that Oklahoma, will place her approval on the present administration.[52]

On the other hand, several citizens, including investors in Mexico, wanted no intervention from the United States.[53]

One way out of the morass would be a selective arms embargo that would favor Madero by denying arms to the rebels. Its effective enforcement would involve the use of American troops, but only on the American side of the border. Agreeing with his legal advisers that "defective legislation does not relieve or excuse a nation from discharging its international obligations," Taft sought, with the aid of Senator Elihu Root, a revision of the 1898 Arms Embargo statute to allow the president to prohibit any export of war materials into Mexico. (The original act prohibited only their export from American seaports).[54]

On 14 March, a joint resolution of Congress was approved that provided

[52]N. G. Turk to Taft, 22 February 1912, Taft Papers, Series 6, Reel 365, no. 95B. For other examples see additional letters in the same file, no. 95C.

[53]See, for example, William O. Manson to Taft, 31 July 1912, Taft Papers, Series 6, Reel 365, no. 95C.

[54]Samuel Willis Spott to Taft, 11 March 1912 (encl. of quote from former Sec. of State John Foster), Taft Papers, Series 6, Reel 365, no. 95B. See also Wickersham to Taft, 13 March 1912, and Charles D. Hilles, Memorandum, 14 March 1912, Taft Papers, no. 95B.

That whenever the President shall find that in any American country conditions of domestic violence exist which are promoted by the use of arms or munntions of war procured from the United States, and shall make proclamation thereof, it shall be unlawful to export except under such limitations and exceptions as the President shall prescribe any arms or munitions of war from any place in the United States to such country until otherwise ordered by the President or by Congress.[55]

On the same day the resolution was approved, Taft issued a proclamation naming Mexico a country in which "conditions of domestic violence" existed, and Ciudad Juárez was closed as a port of entry for arms and munitions of war. By May the border town was completely sealed off.[56]

The embargo, accompanied by an effective armed patrol of the boundary and superior intelligence operations, had the desired effect. Orozco was forced to alter his strategy, and was not able to march on Mexico City after the successful first battle of Rellano because his troops did not have sufficient supplies and ammunition. Being dependent on smugglers who charged exorbitant prices for their goods and services, Orozco's campaign was soon suffering from financial insolvency. Meeting the payrolls and keeping his army of eight thousand in food and clothing became a critical problem. Weakened by the embargo, Orozco's army first met defeat on 23 May when Rellano was lost to forces led by General Victoriano Huerta. When the *orozquista* army suffered its last defeat at Ciudad Juárez in August, it divided into a number of small guerrilla bands that continued the fight until the end of the year.[57] In the meantime, *orozquistas* in the United States were being pursued by federal officers, with Orozco's father and several followers being arrested and detained by the military in October on charges of violating the neutrality laws.[58] Thanks in large part to Taft's policy, the *orozquistas* had failed in their attempt to overthrow Madero.

[55]Taft, "A Proclamation," 14 March 1912, Taft Papers, Series 6, Reel 365, no. 95B.

[56]Meyer, *Mexican Rebel*, p. 70.

[57]Ibid., pp. 71–87.

[58]Ulloa, *La Revolución intervenida*, pp. 28–29. See also Harris and Sadler, "El Paso, 1911, in the Mexican Revolution."

In spite of the demise of Orozco, Madero became ever more distrustful of Taft's motives and fearful of a military intervention as the 5 November elections in the United States approached. Even though Taft and his ambassador did not actually seek intervention (in inner circles, at least prior to February 1913, they fought the "interventionists"), they did not hesitage to use the threat of intervention to shape Madero's policies in a direction favorable to American interests in Mexico. The American ambassador, Henry Lane Wilson, was becoming more abusive all the time, inundating the State Department with pessimistic reports on Madero's inability to maintain the peace and disparaging descriptions of the Mexican president's "mental feebleness."[59]

Madero's commercial agent in New York City, Heriberto Barrón, advised him that intervention had become a part of the domestic political struggle between Democrats and Republicans and that "vicious and powerful elements of his [Taft's] party are trying to force his hands in this matter." With Congress in recess and the election around the corner, Barrón speculated that the Republicans might be tempted to ignite their campaign by focusing public interest on an intervention in Mexico. Madero's fears were not quieted after the election, for Hopkins informed him of sensationalized anti-Madero articles in Hearst's "yellow press" and of the anti-*maderista* campaign being led in the Senate by Fall and others.[60]

Although the dreaded intervention never became a reality, the threat was very real to Madero, and American domestic politics did not relieve those fears—nor did the hostile actions of the American ambassador, who became notorious for his participation in the conspiracies of the "Ten Tragic Days" of 9–19 February 1913. These events concluded with an army coup and the deaths of former *revoltoso* Francisco Madero and current *insurrecto* Bernardo Reyes. This business of *revoltoso* politics was indeed deadly. The swearing-in ceremony of Victoriano Huerta on 19 February 1913

[59]See Hanrahan, *Documents*, II, pts. 1 and 2, for the confidential despatches of Ambassador Wilson.

[60]Barrón to Gustavo Madero, 20 February 1912; Barrón to F. Madero, 1 November 1912; Hopkins to Sánchez Azcona, 29 December 1912—all AGN/RRV.

was, in effect, a funeral rite for *maderista* democracy in Mexico.[61]

Thus did Taft's Mexican policy evolve from 1909 to 1913, and, as the mobilization of March 1911 demonstrated, that policy was influenced in part by the American ambassador. Madero's successful overthrow of Díaz, although facilitated by Taft's decision of 12 May, was due more to the organizational skills, financial resources, and popularity of the *maderista* movement than to the "neutrality" diplomacy of Taft and Knox. Enforcement of the neutrality laws had been vigorous, but the Treasury and Justice departments did not have the manpower to curb what was, in effect, a popular revolution—even with the aid of the U.S. Army, the full use of which came too late to stem the tide of a *maderista* revolt that had been gaining momentum since February 1911.

After the fall of Díaz, Taft's "neutrality" diplomacy was continued, with the American government trying to maintain the status quo under Madero—as Taft had attempted to do with Díaz prior to May of 1911. This policy was pro-Madero and anti-*revoltoso*, and it succeeded in curbing the revolutionary fervor of *magonistas*, *reyistas*, and *orozquistas* in the United States. Taft's threats of intervention was another dimension of his Mexican policy —a policy that was designed to maintain Madero in power as the best means of curtailing revolutionary nationalism in Mexico and preserving American lives and property. Then, when it appeared that Taft's policy might succeed, a new round of violence was ushered in by Huerta's coup. Taft's election defeat, Madero's death, and the recalling of Henry Lane Wilson would begin another phase in the revolution that "did not triumph by force of arms" alone.

[61]For the Decena Trágica see Michael C. Meyer, *Huerta: A Political Portrait*, pp. 45–63.

FIVE
Wilsonian Hysterics, 1913–1917

The Mexicans were made the villains, and they changed the whole piece over to Mexico, so that the Japanese had Mexican names; but in the film they were still wearing Japanese uniforms [laughter].

Testimony of Captain George C. Lester, 1919

10. The Enemy Within and Abroad

WOODROW WILSON became president in March 1913. Unhappy with Huerta's inability to maintain peace, and disturbed over what he conceived to be Huerta's treacherous behavior, Wilson decided to force Huerta out of power. During his first year in office, Wilson employed a variety of tactics to rid himself of Huerta, from persuasion, loan proposals, and mediation offers to ultimatums and threats of force. Huerta's government proved to have more staying power than Wilson and his advisers had realized. In the meantime, America's potential enemy, Germany, had recognized Huerta's government and was becoming one of his most important foreign collaborators. In addition, President Huerta let it be known publicly that his government was developing strong relations with Japan, thereby nourishing the rumors that the sons of Nogi, Kuroki, and Oku were willing to send the splendid armies of the Empire of the Rising Sun against the United States from Mexico.[1]

With the failure of Wilson's earlier tactics, an incident involving what was interpreted as an insult to American naval forces visiting Tampico was used by Wilson as a pretext for more forceful measures. On 21 April 1914, U.S. military forces landed at Veracruz and occupied the port. During the occupation nineteen American sailors and several hundred Mexicans were killed. Under the threat of a U.S. invasion into the interior, and hard pressed both by the

[1]Cole Blasier's *The Hovering Giant* contains an excellent analysis of German influences on Mexico's revolution and Wilson's diplomacy; see especially pp. 105–116. Information on Huerta and Japan was taken from the Italian newspaper *Lega Navale* of 15 March 1914, trans. by "RK" of the Office of Naval Intelligence, RG 38, c–9–b 908. See also Smith, *The United States and Revolutionary Nationalism in Mexico*, pp. 34–42.

naval occupation and by his political rivals, Huerta resigned as president in July 1914, sailing from Mexico to Europe on the German warship the *Dresden*.[2]

Wilson justified his anti-Huerta policy in terms of American national honor and the philosophies of democracy, progress, and financial capitalism. Viewing Mexico through Anglo-American "Protestant" and "Progressive" lenses, he erroneously thought of Huerta as a counterrevolutionary who represented the worst of Mexico's old feudal order.[3] Wilson's morality dictated a choice other than Huerta for Mexico, a leader more in keeping with the spirit of bourgeois, democratic, and reformist America—someone like Madero, or at least in the *maderista* tradition. Thus, when Wilson said he was in sympathy with the goals of the Mexican Revolution, he was visualizing a revolt shaped and aided by the "civilized Western nations" that would be anti-feudal, democratic, and capitalistic, not the anti-capitalist, socialist, and worker's revolution envisioned by some of the more radical *revoltosos*.

During the presidency of Woodrow Wilson the twin themes of America's foreign policy remained those of containing competing empires and curtailing revolutionary nationalism, but the spector of the World War and imperial Germany's intrusions into Mexico meant that Wilson's Mexican policy would have to emphasize "containment" over "curtailment." Although Wilson initially appeared to be favoring Villa by lifting the embargo on arms shipment to him and by facilitating the marketing of cattle in the United States by *villistas*, in reality Wilson and his secretary of state, Robert Lansing, were playing one revolutionary chieftain off against another in hopes of directing Mexico's revolution into peaceful and legal channels that would respect American property rights.

By mid-1915, as with Taft in the instance of Madero, Wilson had decided that Venustiano Carranza was the least of all evils for

---

[2]Robert E. Quirk, *An Affair of Honor: Woodrow Wilson and the Occupation of Veracruz*.

[3]To suggest that Huerta's administration was something other than reactionary and counterrevolutionary is to be unconventional and to place one at odds with the pro-Revolutionary school of Mexican historians. Nevertheless, on this matter I prefer the company of Michael Meyer, whose careful scholarship amply supports his unconventional interpretations in his *Huerta: A Political Portrait*, pp. 156–177 and 229–231.

American interests in Mexico. Although Carranza was nationalistic and difficult to control, he at least represented the interests of the national bourgeoisie of Mexico and was not a spokesman for radical peasants and workers. And more important, with the possibility of American involvement in a European war Wilson was fearful of a German-Mexican coalition, perhaps even a new Triple Alliance of Germany, Japan, and Mexico. The southern flank had to be made secure, and recognition of Carranza became the only way to achieve that security.

With Huerta's exile, several rival groups competed for control over the direction of the revolution, including the *zapatistas* in the south and the *villistas* and Carranza-Obregón forces in the north. By April 1915, Villa was defeated in the state of Guanajuato at the battle of Celaya, an event that was a turning point in the history of the struggle between the rebel forces. With Villa's defeat the United States advised Carranza that it was inclined to favor his cause and formalize diplomatic relations, especially if Carranza were disposed to publish a manifesto to the nation proclaiming that his revolution would respect the lives and property of foreigners and acknowledge the legitimacy of the debt incurred by earlier governments. Wilson also urged Carranza to issue a general amnesty to his political enemies.

Although Carranza initially considered the president's message to be an affront to Mexico's national honor, and even though Wilson continued to threaten Carranza with the use of force, by 10 June 1915 Carranza did issue a *Manifiesto a la Nación*. The manifesto guaranteed protection of the life, liberty, and property of foreigners, protected all "legitimate" financial obligations, and promised that the agrarian problem would be solved without confiscations. With Carranza in control of Mexico and with the United States being pressured by German activity and European complications, Wilson finally and reluctantly extended *de facto* recognition to the nationalistic *carrancista* government on 19 October 1915. Even then, full *de jure* recognition was withheld until the new government demonstrated its "good behavior."[4]

    [4]Eliseo Arredondo to V. Carranza, May 1915; V. Carranza to Arredondo, 30 May 1915; John R. Silliman to Jesús Vrueta, 2 June 1915; Carranza, "Manifiesto a la Nación," 10 June 1915 —all AREM, L–E–1441. Also see Smith, *The U.S. and Revolutionary Nationalism in Mexico*, p. 42.

With recognition, Carranza won the reluctant support of Wilson. One manifestation of that support was Wilson's anti-*revoltoso* activity, in which the forces of the U.S. government were used to harass, detain, arrest, and eventually suppress Carranza's enemies in the United States. In 1915, *huertistas*, *orozquistas*, and *científicos* were suppressed. Late in 1915 and in early 1916 Pizaña "Seditionists" were eliminated by a combined force of federal soldiers and Texas Rangers. During 1916 the *magonista* leaders Ricardo and Enrique Flores Magón were once again tried in a federal court, with Enrique eventually being sent to the federal penitentiary at Leavenworth.

It was also during 1915–1916 that Wilson placed an embargo on arms to all other Mexican factions, including Pancho Villa's armies. In addition, Wilson aided Carranza by allowing his soldiers to be moved by train from Eagle Pass, Texas, to Douglas, Arizona, to shore up Plutarco Calles's garrison at Agua Prieta. With Agua Prieta now almost impregnable, Villa's Sonora campaign was crippled, and he soon engaged in such acts of desperation as the killing of sixteen Chinese at La Colorado and the slaughter of seventy-seven innocent noncombatants at San Juan de la Cueva.[5] These acts, along with the attacks on the persons of Americans at Santa Ysabel, Chihuahua, and Columbus, New Mexico, eventually led to General Pershing's punitive expedition, in which U.S. troops pursued Villa, albeit unsuccessfully, throughout Chihuahua. These various *revoltoso* groups were suppressed by Wilson either for diplomatic or political reasons. Thus, whereas fear of German intrigue was a decisive factor in the defeat of the *huertistas*, it was the need to make America, as well as the world, "safe for democracy," especially during the election-year compaigns of 1916, that led to the Pershing expedition and to the anti-radical campaign that eventually suppressed *villista* and *magonista* activity in the United States.

As 1916–1917 approached, security for the United States became an internal as well as a foreign and diplomatic problem. Mexico City was not the only center of German espionage, counter-espionage, sabotage, and psychological warfare. Communities as far

---

[5]Thomas H. Naylor, "Massacre at San Juan de la Cueva: The Significance of Pancho Villa's Disastrous Sonora Campaign," *Western Historical Quarterly* 8 (April 1977): 125–150.

spread as Los Angeles, New York, and Bismarck, North Dakota, were suspected of harboring German spies and sympathizers. Hysteria was widespread, with local citizens spying on their German neighbors and citizens' organizations burning books by German authors and banning the teaching of the German language in the public schools. As the hysteria spread, other aliens were suspected of anti-Americanism and bolshevism. A resurgence of nativism occurred, and Mexico's rebels in the United States were not exempt from the wrath and hatred of wartime America.

The U.S. government reacted to the local hysteria by conducting its own anti-radical and anti-foreigner campaign from 1916 into the post-war period. Using federal troops under wartime emergency powers, Wilson ordered the War Department to conduct raids on Wobblies and labor radicals throughout the country. The army raided I.W.W. halls, broke up meetings, searched boxcars for migrant workers, arrested organizers, and jailed and illegally detained hundreds of "radicals." Military detachments, disguised as local police units, joined forces with the national guard and company officials to break strikes and round up workers. Military intelligence officers engaged in counterespionage activities in order to place suspected radicals under surveillance. Operatives were used to censor mail, spy on I.W.W.'s, and gather confidential data on thousands of citizens and aliens.[6]

While the army was arresting workers and breaking strikes, Justice Department officials were busy preparing indictments, making investigations, and using the federal courts to obtain the suppression of radicals through legal prosecutions. In the fall of 1917, Bureau of Investigation agents simultaneously raided the local and national headquarters and residences of labor officials across the country. The raid led to the September indictment of the top I.W.W. leadership at Chicago and the trial of some 166 Wobblies in the infamous case of the *U.S.* v. *W. D. Haywood, et al.* The success of these and other prosecutions, including those of the *magonistas*, depended on the degree of community hysteria and the eagerness, or lack of it, of local federal attorneys.[7]

To inhibit the defense efforts of the I.W.W. and their allies, the

[6]Preston, *Aliens and Dissenters*, pp. 103–117.
[7]Ibid., pp. 118–122.

government maintained a rigid censorship policy, under which the Post Office was instructed to withhold mailing privileges from labor defense committees and to intercept, delay, and seize outright the I.W.W. defense mail.[8] By late 1917 and early 1918 the U.S. Censorship Board had arranged for all of the mail passing between the United States and Mexico to be subject to examination by federal censors located at Galveston, El Paso, Laredo, San Antonio, Nogales, San Diego, and San Francisco. The local censors worked in cooperation with representatives of the departments of State and Justice, the War Board, and the Military Intelligence Division of the U.S. Army. Telegraphs, letters, and cables were censored as the authorities sought to root out those individuals with anti-American, pro-German, and anti-war opinions.[9] Under the Espionage Act of 1917 the Post Office could declare non-mailable "indecent" materials, such as those letters containing statements obstructing the recruitment, enlistment, and other operations of the armed forces.[10]

Finally, by 1917 immigration legislation had been broadened to allow the authorities to deny naturalization to radicals and to deport suspicious aliens. Troops, trials, and deportations were the federal tools of suppression, and the more radical *revoltosos* found themselves subject not only to the federal government's hostility, but to the racial prejudice and violence of local groups as well.

On the local level, racial prejudice and fear were exploited in the struggle against the *revoltosos*. During 1915 in south Texas, racial warfare became the order of the day. Spurred on by the Texas Rangers, vigilante groups ran wild in an orgy of violence—harassing, intimidating, shooting, and killing dozens of defenseless Mexicans and Americans of Mexican descent.[11] *Revoltosos*, aliens, and loyal Mexican Americans were accused of pro-German sympathies, anti-Americanism, "socialism," separatism, and "irredentism." In Cali-

---

[8]Ibid., p. 144.

[9]Frank McIntyre to M. M. McFarland, 18 February 1918; L. S. Rowe to Collector of Customs on the Mexican Border, 22 April 1918; H. L. Hewson to Chief Cable Censor, Wash., D.C., 3 July 1918—all RG 165 (M.I.D.), file nos. 10679/2, 11, 19.

[10]Preston, *Aliens and Dissenters*, pp. 144–145.

[11]Photographic evidence of Ranger atrocities in south Texas can be found in Carlos Larralde, *Mexican-American: Movements and Leaders*, pp. 135–138.

fornia, partly because of the influence of the Otis and Hearst publications, the "Yellow Peril" image was merged with that of a "Bronze Menace," so that patriotic "Americans" (read "Anglos") could learn that it was their wartime duty to hate Mexicans as well as Japanese and that total preparedness meant that "Americans" must be ready to protect the United States from the threat of a Japanese invasion from Mexican soil.

One of the earliest of *revoltoso* groups to be suppressed in Wilsonian America was a small organization of PLM radicals who in 1913 predictably supported the *zapatistas* against both Huerta and Carranza and who were led by the *magonista* guerrilla chieftain Jesús M. Rangel. Rangel, only recently freed from Leavenworth, was serving as a PLM emissary to Zapata, carrying messages between Zapata (and Belem's political prisoners) and Ricardo Flores Magón (and political prisoners at McNeil and Leavenworth). With the aid of fellow *magonista* Fernando Palomares, Rangel organized in Texas a small band of ex-*orozquista* "Red Flaggers" into a guerrilla *foco* for service in Mexico. Most of the members of the *foco* were dedicated revolutionaries and syndicalists, and some, like Rangel and Charlie Cline, were I.W.W. members.[12]

On 11 September 1913, fourteen men led by Rangel were attempting to cross the border near Carrizo Springs, Texas (south of Eagle Pass in Dimmit County). While camped on the American side they were intercepted by Texas authorities and the U.S. Cavalry. In the scuffle that followed, two guerrillas, Silvestre Lomas and Juan Rincón (the latter a young man who had earlier worked in the *Regeneración* office), and one patrolman, a Mexican spy named Ortiz, were killed. Taken into custody, the *revoltosos* were tried for the murder of Ortiz. Despite the circumstances, the men were found guilty and given harsh sentences: Rangel and Cline were sentenced to life imprisonment, and the others received sentences ranging from twenty-five to ninety-nine years. Rangel, Cline, and two others were imprisoned at the jail in Huntsville, Texas, and the rest were sent to state farms at De Walt and Hobly Farm, Texas. Of the total

---

[12]Ethel Duffy Turner, *Ricardo Flores Magón y el Partido Liberal Mexicano*, pp. 287–290; Chaplin, *Wobbly*, p. 179.

group, six served eleven years, two died in prison, and the others escaped.[13]

The next major incident involving the *revoltosos* occurred in late 1914 and early 1915 when Pascual Orozco, tiring of the struggles taking place between the various *villista* and *carrancista* factions, decided to organize and lead his own anti-*carrancista* rebellion. Playing several roles in the revolution that was to follow, Orozco acted as a coordinator for the various exile groups in the United States. As such he spent the month of December traveling about the United States from one revolutionary center to another— San Antonio, St. Louis, Los Angeles, and New York City. Orozco was also assigned the task of acquiring arms. Thus, while in New York he conferred with *huertista* exiles and arranged for the purchase of arms and munitions. Finally, it was agreed that Orozco would serve the upcoming revolution as its supreme military commander. Because the revolt was financed by conservative *científicos* and pro-clerical *felicistas*, ex-president Victoriano Huerta was chosen to be the man to assume the presidency after victory was assured. With ample finances, a broad spectrum of support in both Mexico and the United States, and the leadership of two powerful personalities, it appeared that the pro-Huerta *revoltosos* of 1915 had every chance of changing Mexico's political destinities.[14]

While Orozco was initiating the project, Huerta, in exile in Spain, was approached by Captain Franz Rintelen von Kleist of the intelligence division of the German General Staff with an offer of financial assistance. Soon after that visit, Enrique Creel joined Huerta in Spain and convinced him of the need for his participation in the upcoming revolt, and he and Huerta decided to accept the German offer. Both men then returned to the United States, arriving in New York City on 12 April 1915. While in New York, Huerta participated in several conferences with German embassy and secret service personnel, who agreed to make several deposits for Huerta in various bank accounts and to supply and transport several thousand rifles and rounds of ammunition by German U-boats to the Mexican coast. In June, Huerta, followed by Department of Justice

[13]Turner, *Ricardo Flores Magón*, p. 293; Chaplain, *Wobbly*, p. 179; Gómez-Quiñones, *Sembradores*, p. 52.
[14]Meyer, *Mexican Rebel: Pascual Orozco*, pp. 115–124.

agents, left New York City for Newman, New Mexico, where he planned to meet his contact, Pascual Orozco.[15]

At Newman, Orozco and Huerta were arrested, charged with conspiracy to violate the neutrality laws of the United States, and placed under house arrest in El Paso. Although Orozco eluded his guards and escaped, Huerta was rearrested and placed in military detention at Fort Bliss. On the morning of 30 August, Orozco and four of his comrades were ambushed by a posse and killed. Orozco's death was explained to the public as the ultimate justice to be expected by Mexican cattle thieves. Huerta, despondent on receiving the news of Orozco's death, soon became ill of a diseased liver and died at Fort Bliss on 13 January 1916. U.S. opposition had successfully stopped the plans of Huerta and the German high command.[16]

With the deaths of Orozco and Huerta, the revolt of the exiles all but collapsed. Some of the hardier souls left El Paso and San Antonio for New Orleans, where they joined the *felicista* movement. Félix Díaz, the politically ambitious nephew of don Porfirio, was the head of this group. Intimately involved in the Huerta coup of 1913, Díaz was about as reactionary as any *revoltoso* leader on the horizon. Choosing the Catholic stronghold of New Orleans for his revolutionary headquarters, he fostered a pro-clerical conspiracy to promote U.S. intervention so that Mexico's clerics could overthrow the *carrancista* revolution and undermine the anti-clerical Laws of the Reforma.[17]

Although the central *felicista* organization, known as the *Asamblea del Movimiento Pacifista Mexicano*, was located in New Orleans, the *felicistas* had branch offices in Los Angeles, San Diego, Albuquerque, Columbus (N.M.), Nogales, Phoenix, El Paso, Laredo, Brownsville, Galveston, San Antonio, Mobile, Tampa, Baltimore, Washington, D.C., and New York City. In late February 1916, only a few weeks before Pershing crossed the border, Díaz slipped out of New Orleans for Mexico. In spite of his declaration of an all-

[15]Meyer, *Huerta: A Political Portrait*, pp. 210–229; Blaiser, *The Hovering Giant*, pp. 109, 288–289, n. 23.

[16]Meyer, *Huerta: A Political Portrait*, pp. 226–229; Meyer, *Mexican Rebel: Pascual Orozco*, pp. 131–135.

[17]Cumberland, *Mexican Revolution: The Constitutionalist Years*, pp. 236–238.

embracing manifesto of liberal reform, the twenty-thousand armed men who were supposed to greet his arrival in Mexico failed to materialize. With a limited following and faulty planning, his revolt was easily crushed by Carranza's troops.[18]

One of the most bizarre of rebel events took place in south Texas in the lower Rio Grande valley simultaneously with the *huertista* revolt of 1915. There was a series of border raids that can best be described as an irredentist movement mixed with bandit activity. In January of that year, several *huertistas*—military prisoners charged with political offenses—while confined in Monterrey, Nuevo León, issued the Plan of San Diego, a program ostensibly written in San Diego, Texas. The plan was probably released by the *huertistas* as a diversionary tactic to distract the authorities and divert their attention from the *huertistas'* scheduled revolution, but it appears that the original authors intended to initiate a social revolution in Texas and the Southwest that would bring an end to the economic exploitation and racial discrimination of non-Anglos by "white" Americans.[19]

Although the plan itself called for an uprising of Mexican Americans and Mexican nationals and for the creation of an independent Social Republic of Texas to be carved out of the states of Texas, New Mexico, Arizona, Colorado, Nevada, Utah, and southern California (territory lost by Mexico to the United States under the nineteenth-century Treaty of Guadalupe-Hidalgo), the accompanying "Manifesto to the Oppressed Peoples of America" outlined the grievances of Mexican, Latin, and black workers in Texas. The manifesto made special note of the exploitation of agricultural workers in the cotton fields and discrimination and segregation in education, transportation, and public and recreational facilities.[20]

[18]Ibid. See also Gilbert O. Nations, "Las intrigas de los clericales. Memorial a Presidente Wilson," in *México y los Estados Unidos: Opiniones de intelectuales distinguidos y de los periódicos más serios acerca de los ultimos acontecimientos*, pp. 10–11.

[19]"Plan of San Diego," U.S., Congress, Senate, *Papers* (1916), pp. 570–572; Allen Gerlach, "Conditions Along the Border—1915: The Plan de San Diego," *New Mexico Historical Review* 43 (July 1968): 195–212.

[20]"Manifesto" and "Plan Revolucionario de San Diego," 6 January 1915, Archivo "Espinosa de los Monteros," II, fol. 60–61, Bib. M. Orozco y Berra (Chapultepec Castle annex). The actual date of this copy has not been determined. The original Plan of San Diego was revised and enlarged on two

In addition to the idea of a separate country, the plan included provisions for the creation of a black republic to be carved out of six states of the American Union, as well as for the return of all lands stolen from the Apaches and the other Indians of the Territory of Arizona. Among other provisions, extreme tactics were advocated, including a war to the death against all Anglo-Americans, the killing of all North Americans over sixteen and under seventy years of age, the shooting of all prisoners, the summary execution of all armed strangers, and the enlistment only of strangers belonging to the Latin, Negro, or Japanese races. Because the authors used the language of racial warfare, many observers of the plan failed to note that ten of the twenty-eight provisions dealt with economic matters, calling for the new Social Republic of Texas to be a socialist state, with the communization of all rural lands and all transportation systems and the abolition of all forms of physical and moral exploitation of the proletariat. Finally, the plan's authors adopted as their symbol a red banner with a white stripe and bearing the inscription "LIBERTAD, IGUALDAD E INDEPENDENCIA."[21]

The first attempts at organizing under the plan were cut short in the middle of January 1915 when Basilio Ramos, a native of Nuevo Laredo and secretary of the Revolutionary Congress, was arrested in McAllen, Texas, by immigration authorities. Although papers found on Ramos at the time of his arrest linked him with General Emiliano Nafarrate, the then *carrancista* commander at Tampico, local officials took no further notice of the implications of the Plan of San Diego after the prisoner was bound over to the grand jury. Insensitive to the conditions of the non-Anglo poor in south Texas, the authorities considered the entire episode to be a meaningless and visionary scheme.[22]

---

occasions, first during the summer of 1915 and later in February 1916 by Basilio Ramos and Luis de la Rosa. It is assumed that the document cited is an authentic copy of one of the three "originals." A shorter translated version of the Plan can be found in any of the following: U.S., Congress, Senate, *Investigations of Mexican Affairs*, I, 1205–1207; Gerlach, "Conditions Along the Border," pp. 205–207; Juan Gómez-Quiñones, "Plan de San Diego Revised," *Aztlan*, 1 (Spring 1970): 128–131.

[21]"Plan Revolucionario de San Diego."

[22]"Plan of San Diego," U.S. Congress, Senate, *Papers*, (1916), p. 570; Charles C. Cumberland, "Border Raids in the Lower Rio Grande Valley—1915," *Southwestern Historical Quarterly* 57 (October 1953): 290–291.

However, during the summer months of 1915 two of the most persistent and successful leaders of the raids appeared in the persons of Aniceto Pizaña and Luis de la Rosa. Both men were American citizens who had been economically successful as south Texas *rancheros*. Both were good friends of the *carrancista* generals Pablo González, Alvaro Obregón, and Nafarrate. Pizaña and de la Rosa organized the first *magonista* clubs in south Texas after 1904. A contributor to *Regeneración*, the "realist" Pizaña was often criticized by the "idealist" Flores Magón, who remained uncharacteristically ambivalent about the entire Plan of San Diego movement. Whereas Pizaña sought immediate objectives and tactics—such as how to induce Carranza to aid him in warding off the Texas Rangers in remote regions or how to get the Germans to agree to use their submarines to conquer Texas harbors—his more visionary followers, known as *sediciosos* ("Seditionists"), wanted to create a new social order in a new south Texas republic along the lines of the Plan of San Diego. Thus, although *magonismo* was the philosophy of some of the raiders, Pizaña himself was primarily motivated by the need to stop the abuses of the Rangers.[23]

Working in unison, Pizaña and de la Rosa directed groups of from twenty-five to a hundred, organized into quasi-military companies, in raiding activities throughout the lower Rio Grande valley. During the summer the raiders attacked ranches, robbed stores, and burned bridges in south Texas between Brownsville and Raymondville. Arms, supplies, and men were smuggled in from Mexico. By late summer the fighting had expanded to include several clashes between Mexican *federales* and American troops at Progreso and Brownsville. Border raids became common, with rebels attacking and then returning to Mexico. Sympathizers were found along the entire Texas border from El Paso to Brownsville, and Carranza and Villa allowed the Plan of San Diego to be printed and circulated in Ciudad Juárez, Matamoros, Monterrey, and Tampico. By fall the fighting became even more chaotic when bandits struck at San Benito and Ojo de Agua and executed several Anglo-Americans. Peculiarly enough, with the mobilization of U.S. troops and the cooperation of Carranza, who had finally obtained U.S. recognition

[23]Larralde, *Mexican-American: Movements and Leaders*, pp. 114–115, 122–131.

(and who had used the raids as an instrument of policy), the fighting came to an end in early 1916 with Pizaña and de la Rosa both staying in Mexico.[24]

By then most of the damage had been done. Hundreds of people, primarily of Mexican descent, had been killed. Thousands had fled the valley, many into Mexico, where *carrancista* officials extorted large sums from them before permitting them to stay. Property damages and economic losses amounted to millions of dollars. More important, the raids engendered a wave of quasi-hysteria in which vigilante committees lynched and executed suspected rebels, burned the homes of Mexican Americans, and forcibly moved Mexicans out of the countryside. Many innocent people were summarily executed without trial by Rangers, local officials, and self-appointed law-enforcers.[25]

When Villa launched his anti-American raids in early 1916, most Anglos along the border from Brownsville to Los Angeles were filled with fear and hatred of all Mexicans, who were commonly believed to be lawless bandits, anti-American, pro-German and pro-Japanese, shiftless, violent, and untrustworthy radicals. The additional hysteria of wartime America only amplified and aggravated the already existing prejudice and discrimination. It was a sorry time when there was to be no justice for innocent, apolitical Mexican Americans—let alone radical, alien Mexican anarchists who were allied with the Industrial Workers of the World.

On 10 January 1916, Villa outraged the Anglo inhabitants of the border towns when "bandits" under his command shot and killed eighteen American mining engineers at Santa Ysabel. Several days later a special train was sent into Mexico to bring the corpses back to the United States. Under a special guard of Carranza's soldiers, the train bearing the dead entered El Paso one night during mid-January. Crowds gathered during the night and lynching mobs were formed to march on the Mexicans living in the part of town known as Chihuahuita. The people of El Paso even hooted and

---

[24]Cumberland, "Border Raids," pp. 285–311; "Plan of San Diego," U.S., Congress, Senate, *Papers* (1916), pp. 570–572. See also Charles H. Harris III and Louis R. Sadler, "The Plan of San Diego and the Mexican–United States War Crisis of 1916: A Reexamination," *Hispanic American Historical Review* 58 (August 1978): 381–408.

[25]Cumberland, "Border Raids," pp. 285, 301, 311.

shouted at the U.S. consul stationed in Juárez, calling him a *villista* lackey and blaming him for the deaths of the young men. As Villa continued his raids into New Mexico during the late winter and early spring of 1916, American hatred of the *revoltosos* mounted and cries were heard demanding Yankee justice for the Mexicans.[26]

The federal authorities evidently heard those cries. On 18 February 1916 an indictment was returned in the federal court at Los Angeles charging the editors of *Regeneración*—Ricardo Flores Magón, Enrique Flores Magón, and William C. Owen—with violation of section 211 of the penal code of 1910, that is, the crime of depositing indecent matter in the U.S. mails. Immediately arrested, they were brought to trial in June of that year. As the assistant district attorney for Los Angeles explained to the attorney general at that time, "we [the district attorney and his assistant] believed the late outrages along the Mexican border rendered this a most favorable time to the Government for the trial of United States versus *Magon* and *Magon*, and it was tried."[27]

Racial prejudice and fear of the actions of German agents also made 1916 an opportune time for bringing aliens and radicals to trial. For example, during that year the San Francisco newspaper magnate William Randolph Hearst, a man with considerable investments in Mexico, was busy producing a "preparedness" film called *Patria* through the International Film Service Corporation. Although the fifteen-episode "serial romance of society and preparedness" was not actually released until January 1917, for weeks the film's release had been preceded by a noisy barrage of advance publicity that included news stories, a novelized version of the photoplay for the newspapers, and advertisements in every Hearst magazine from *Motor and Motor Boating* to *Good Housekeeping*. In the film Mrs. Vernon Castle starred as Patria Channing, the heroine who had been bequeathed several million dollars to be used for "American preparedness." As the story developed, Patria assumed command of the disorganized U.S. Army and, after routing a combined force of

[26]Belding de Wetter, "Revolutionary El Paso," pp. 153–154. See also Friedrich Katz, "Pancho Villa and the Attack on Columbus, New Mexico," *American Historical Review* 83 (February 1978): 101–130.

[27]M. G. Gallaher to Att. Gen., 9 June 1916, RG 60, Straight Numerical File 16, 90755–I–22.

Japanese and Mexican soldiers who were invading California from Mexico, ended up safely in the arms of Captain Parr, a U.S. secret service agent.[28]

Although the anti-Japanese prejudices of Hearst were one motive for the film's production, *Patria's* initial popularity indicated that it reflected many of American society's social and political concerns. Episode 14 was especially revealing, for it showed Baron Huroki (Warner Oland) as a Japanese secret service agent and nobleman leading Japanese troops across Mexico in an invasion of California. Of course, the film showed the Japanese and Mexicans committing appropriate atrocities, from kidnapping to derailing trains.[29]

Although the film was farfetched, it was true that the U.S. Office of Naval Intelligence (O.N.I.) had been concerned for several years about a Japanese-Mexican naval and military alliance. From 1911 to 1918, U.S. intelligence officers and consular agents in northern Mexico had maintained surveillance on Japanese operations on the west coast, and the files of the O.N.I. for those years were filled with reports about the Japanese at Turtle Bay, the rumors of a secret treaty concerning Magdalena Bay, overtures of the Japanese government first to Madero and later to Huerta and Villa, and the participation of Japanese soldiers in the armies of Carranza. In 1916, the year of *Patria*, the O.N.I. furnished the State Department with copies of a Japanese manifesto, supposedly issued in San Francisco but found circulating in Mexico, that argued that Mexico was a victim of Yankee hatred against Japan, that is, U.S. imperial intentions in Mexico were derived from a desire to exclude Japanese commerce from western Mexico.[30]

Patria not only reflected the prejudices of American society but also nourished the fears and hatreds of hundreds of American citi-

---

[28]James P. Mock and Cedric Larson, *Words That Won the War*, pp. 143–144. See also Roger Daniels, *The Politics of Prejudice*, p. 76. The New York Museum of Modern Art has about an hour's worth of excerpts from the serial available for viewing on the premises by scholars.

[29]Mock and Larson, *Words That Won the War*, p. 144.

[30]See the materials on Japanese-Mexican relations in RG 38, c–9–b 908, especially George C. Carothers to Sec. of State, 24 June 1916. For the Japanese and Villa see "Statement of Mr. George C. Carothers," 28 February 1920, U.S., Congress, Senate, *Investigations of Mexican Affairs*, I, 1777–1778.

zens living in California and along the border. As Captain George C. Lester noted in his testimony before a Senate committee investigating German propaganda efforts during the War:

> "Patria" had a story with three barrels. Its principal excuse was "preparedness." But by the time the first episodes were released the country was already committed to that. Therefore only the other two elements, anti-Mexican and anti-Japanese propaganda, remained active.[31]

From the Mexican point of view, the film was even worse after it was revised in 1917. In order to meet President Wilson's objections, Hearst revamped the film to eliminate the anti-Japanese emphasis, removing the word "Japan" and giving the Japanese characters Mexican names. All of the sins previously charged to the Japanese villains were now dumped on Mexico, with the image of the "Bronze Menace" superimposed on that of the "Yellow Peril."

It was in this setting that the editors of *Regeneración* came to trial. The men were accused of sending "indecent" literature through the mails—"indecent" because, it was argued, *Regeneración* contained articles with "a tendency to incite murder," "stir up strife between the United States and Mexico," and "incite insurrection in the United States."[32]

During the trial the prosecution entered as evidence several issues of *Regeneración* published in the fall of 1915. All of these issues contained articles critical of Carranza and Wilson (at a time when the United States had finally extended recognition to Carranza's government) and the reformist, bourgeois societies they represented. The following excerpt reveals the thrust of Flores Magón's arguments as they appeared in the 25 September issue:

> Justice and not bullets is what ought to be given to the revolutionists of Texas, and from now on we should demand that those persecutions to innocent Mexicans should cease, and as to the revolutionists we should demand that they be not executed (shot).

[31]U.S., Congress, Senate, *Brewing and Liquor Interests and German and Bolshevik Propaganda*, II, p. 1675.

[32]"Remarks of Court Before Pronouncing Sentence," 22 June 1916, U.S. v. Enrique Flores Magón, Crim. 1071 (U.S. Dist. Ct., So. Cal. Div., 1916), FRC Laguna Niguel.

The ones who should be shot are the "rangers" and the band of bandits who accompany them in their depredations.[33]

Needless to say, the men were found guilty on two counts. Because Ricardo was ill at the time in a Los Angeles hospital, his sentence was lighter than that of his brother. Ricardo was sentenced to pay a fine of one thousand dollars and to be confined for one year and a day; Enrique was sentenced to serve three years at McNeil Island. With the finances provided by defense committees and local supporters, the Flores Magón brothers were able to remain at liberty on bond until 1918, at which time Enrique entered Leavenworth Penitentiary and Ricardo was involved in a new trial and new charges under the Espionage Acts of World War I.[34]

In reviewing the statements of federal judge Oscar A. Trippet, it is apparent that the defendants were victims of the hysteria of 1916. Had those words from *Regeneración* been printed prior to 1910, the most that would have occurred would have been an obscure libel suit. But the date was 1916, German submarines had already torpedoed the unarmed *Sussex*, Pershing was in Mexico, and war was on the horizon. As the judge said, "It seems to me that these defendants have got no right to come under the American flag. . . . They have got no right to violate our government's laws; they are aliens to this country; they are aliens to our people."[35] And, when the sentence was pronounced, the judge said that Flores Magón "was an anarchist. In other words, he expected to be always in trouble because he did not propose to obey the laws of the country."[36] Being an anarchist and an alien was most "indecent" in 1916.

[33]Quoted from a translated copy of *Regeneración* as reproduced in U.S., Congress, House, Debate on Espionage Acts, War Laws, Political Prisoners, and the Case of Ricardo Flores Magón, *Congressional Record*, pp. 685–686.

[34]Flores Magón, *Epistolario*, pp. 74–75; U.S. Congress, House, Subcommittee of the Committee on Immigration and Naturalization, Case of Enrique Flores Magón, *Communist and Anarchist Deportation Cases*, p. 110; E. Flores Magón, Bureau of Prisons, Leavenworth file, 12839–L, 21 May 1918–10 September 1920.

[35]See above, n. 33, *Cong. Record*, p. 686.

[36]U.S. v. E. Flores Magón, Crim. 1071, FRC Laguna Niguel (see above, n. 32).

SIX
The Red Scare, 1917–1923

Magon is now serving his third term in prison. He is a well educated, cunning Mexican.

W. I. Biddle, Warden,
Leavenworth Penitentiary

11. U.S. v. Magon, et al.

THE years 1917–1923 were a time of hysteria and intolerance in the United States, and even though the latter years of Wilson's administration saw a decline in *revoltoso* activity, the government's forces of suppression did not take a holiday—especially those harassing the *magonistas* in Los Angeles. As for the *revoltoso* movement, its demise reflected the strength and stability of Mexico's "revolutionary" governments as well as the *quid pro quo* arrangements between Mexico and the United States, in which "revolution" was offered up in return for "recognition." For example, once Carranza had agreed to modify the "confiscatory nature" of the Constitution of 1917, his government was granted *de jure* recognition in August 1917 and, at least during the wartime years of 1917–1918, the nominal backing of the Wilson government. Part of that support came in the form of the curtailment of anti-*carrancista* movements in the United States.

This is not to say that there was no *revoltoso* activity at this time, only that it was limited to a few radical *magonistas*, certain spokesmen for Adolfo de la Huerta, and the ineffectual followers of Félix Díaz. As for the last, a constant source of irritation for Wilson and his Mexican policy was the criticism of Senator Albert Bacon Fall. In 1919, Fall had surrounded himself with several *felicista* leaders who sought to discredit Carranza, provoke Wilson into withdrawing recognition, and eventually unseat Mexico's president. Pedro de Villar, a *felicista* leader-in-exile, rallied to Fall's cause and openly aided Fall and his Senate subcommittee in their anti-*carrancista* cause.

Between August 1919 and May 1920, Fall presided over a special Senate inquiry that held hearings in several cities along the border. This was an inquiry into the various revolutionary regimes that governed Mexico during the hectic decade after 1910. Although a profitable result of the hearings was the publication of the huge, two-volume *Investigation of Mexican Affairs* (which contains a wealth of historical material),[1] much of the testimony gathered from more than 250 witnesses was edited and compiled so as to reflect Fall's anti-*magonista*, anti-*maderista*, and anti-*carrancista* biases.

Indeed, during 1919 Fall openly tried to implicate President Carranza in a plot to provoke an uprising by Mexicans in the American Southwest. On another occasion, Fall, exploiting America's post-war paranoia, alleged that Carranza's consuls were fostering sedition in the United States by circulating "Bolsheviki" literature. Other statements and memoranda tended to link Carranza's revolution in Mexico with social unrest in the United States. Time and again Fall and his subcommittee sought to pressure the Wilson administration into withdrawing recognition from Carranza's government. Finally, in December 1919, Fall's actions and a related scheme to overthrow Carranza came to naught when Wilson publicly rebuked Fall.[2]

In spite of Fall's failure, Carranza's tenure in office was to be a limited one. In 1920, Alvaro Obregón (another Mexican too radical to suit Senator Fall) led a military coup that resulted in Carranza's death. Obregón's coup once again renewed the issue of diplomatic recognition. Harding (following the advice of his Mexican expert, the newly appointed secretary of interior—Albert Fall) demanded, as a condition for recognition, that Mexico sign a treaty of friendship and commerce that would interpret article 27 of the Mexican Constitution as nonconfiscatory and nonretroactive. [Article 27, it should be noted, had declared the ownership of lands, subsoil and water to be the exclusive prerogative of Mexicans.] In 1923, Obregón, desiring a foreign loan for the purchase of arms so as to meet the threat of a de la Huerta uprising, agreed to sign the so-called Treaty of Bucareli. This in effect affirmed the nonretroactive nature of article 27 and guaranteed to foreigners their landed property and subsoil rights. Thus by 1923 the Thermidorian phase of the Revolu-

[1]Michael Meyer, "Albert Bacon Fall's Mexican Papers: A Preliminary Investigation, *New Mexico Historical Review* 40 (April 1965): 165–174.
[2]Mark T. Gilderhus, "Senator Albert B. Fall and 'The Plot Against Mexico'," *New Mexico Historical Review* 48 (1973): 299–311.

tion had been entered—the eleventh month when Mexicans tired of revolution and revolt, of revolutionaries and *revoltosos*.[3]

Meanwhile, the "Red Scare" had been progressing in the United States. The Bolshevik or November Revolution of 1917 had added to the fears and hatred of "one-hundred-percent Americans" who were already hysterical over the supposed doings of the emissaries of the Kaiser and his Huns in the United States. "Americanism" now meant anything that represented the *status quo*, and allegations of "bolshevism" were used to counter any attempt at reform:

> You believe in votes for women? Yah!
> the Bolsheviki do.
> And shorter hours? And land reforms?
> They're Bolshevistic too.
> "The Recall" and other things like that,
> are dangerous to seek;
> Don't tell me you believe 'em or I'll
> call you Bolshevik!
> Bolshevik! veek! veek!
> A reformer is a freak!
> But here's a name to stop him, for it's
> like a lightning streak.[4]

This anti-radical public hysteria rose steadily from 1917 to 1919. In 1917, twelve hundred I.W.W.'s and suspected radicals were rounded up by the local citizenry of Bisbee, Arizona, placed on a twenty-seven-car train, and sent on a one-way trip to the New Mexico desert.[5] By 1918, immigration, sedition, and espionage legislation made widespread and simultaneous arrests possible. By 1918, mob rule was declared as Centralia Legionnaires lynched Wobblies and the rising Ku Klux Klan terrorized local preachers, teachers, and editors—anyone "infected" with Negro radicalism and bolshevism. It was a time when indifference toward violence and violations of civil liberty had become national virtues.[6]

By the end of 1919, J. Edgar Hoover of the General Intelligence

---

[3]Ruiz, *Labor and the Ambivalent Revolutionaries*, pp. 101–109.

[4]The original of this quote can be found in the Baltimore *Sun*. This version was quoted by Robert K. Murray in *Red Scare: A Study in National Hysteria, 1919–1920*, p. 169.

[5]Preston, *Aliens and Dissenters*, p. 93.

[6]Murray, *Red Scare*, pp. 179–189.

Division, Attorney General A. Mitchell Palmer, and Commissioner General of Immigration Anthony J. Caminetti had developed elaborate procedures for dealing with the Red Menace. These included sudden and simultaneous dragnet raids; secret testimony from undercover agents and informants; seizure of correspondence, mailing lists, and membership cards; cross-examination of exiles without the presence of defense lawyers; and detention of radicals in isolation, incommunicado, with excessive or no bail.[7]

The tactic of deportation reached its apex in December when 249 deportees—aliens and suspected anarchists, including the "Red Queen," Emma Goldman, and her "Red King" lover, Alex Berkman —were deported on the "Soviet Ark" from Ellis Island in New York to Finland in order to preserve "America and the human race." On 2 January 1920 the Red raids reached new heights when more than four thousand suspected radicals were rounded up in thirty-three cities, with the aliens among them being detained for deportation hearings.[8] Fortunately, the madness and persecutions of the Red Scare peaked in 1920, but the heritage of the post-war era remained in the form of cells filled with political prisoners. Execpt for those deported, interned, convicted, or killed, the country returned to the "normalcy" of Harding, Coolidge, and the Roaring Twenties (a "normalcy" that included the execution of "anarchists" Sacco and Vanzetti in 1927).

Not surprisingly, one of the more severe applications of the wartime Espionage Act took place in southern California and was reserved for the Mexican anarchists Ricardo Flores Magón and Librado Rivera. During the World War, Los Angeles, the scene of the *magonista* arrests, was a hotbed of German intrigue. This, in turn, produced widespread hysteria, with spies suspected of hiding in "every nook and cranny." As the *Los Angeles Times* editorialized:

> If the people of Los Angeles knew what was happening on our border, they would not sleep at night. Sedition, conspiracy, and plots are in the very air. Telegraph lines are tapped, spies come and go at will. German nationals hob-nob with Mexican bandits, Japanese agents, and renegades from this country. Code messages are relayed from place to place along the border, frequently passing

[7]Preston, *Aliens and Dissenters*, pp. 219–220.
[8]Murray, *Red Scare*, pp. 207–213.

through six or eight people from sender to receiver. Los Angeles is the headquarters for this vicious system, and it is there that the deals between German and Mexican representatives are frequently made.[9]

To counter the German intrigues, the Justice Department filled the city with its own spies, informants, undercover men, and counterespionage agents, not the least of whom was the now much older "Eagle of Sonora," Emilio Kosterlitzky. Kosterlitzky, who worked for the Justice Department for nine years between 1917 and 1926, had as his principal task that of keeping the government informed of the activities of Mexican political and military refugees in Los Angeles.[10]

Flores Magón and Rivera were arrested on 22 March 1918 on a charge of sedition. After they had been held for several weeks, an indictment was finally delivered by a federal grand jury. The indictment charged the defendants with violations of the Espionage Act of 15 June 1917 (specifically section 3 of Title I and section 3 of Title XII), the Trading with the Enemy Act of 6 October 1917 (section 19), and section 211 of the Federal Penal Code of 1910.

Under the Espionage Act they were accused of conspiracy to write and publish false statements that tended to interfere with the operation and success of the military and naval forces of the United States. It was further charged that these articles promoted insubordination, disloyalty, and mutiny in the military forces and obstructed the recruiting and enlistment service of the United States.[11] The charge of violating the Trading with the Enemy Act derived from the defendants' alleged failure to register translated copies of *Regeneración* with the Los Angeles Post Office as required by statute. Finally, they were accused of sending "indecent" matter through the mails, a violation of the 1910 Penal Code. (It will be recalled that a similar charge had been made against the Flores Magón brothers in Los Angeles in 1916 and that, as a result of the hearing, Enrique Flores Magón entered the federal penitentiary at Leavenworth in May 1918.) In order to prevent the release of the defen-

[9]As quoted by Cornelius Smith in *Emilio Kosterlitzky*, p. 266.
[10]Ibid., pp. 263, 284–285.
[11]"Indictment," U.S. v. Ricardo Flores Magón and Librado Rivera, Crim. 1421 (U.S. Dist. Ct., So. Cal. Div., 1918), FRC Laguna Niguel.

dants, bail was set at $25,000 each at the request of the U.S. district attorney.[12]

The government's case primarily depended on one document. This was a "Manifesto" that appeared in the 16 March 1918 issue of *Regeneración*. Because the "Manifesto" was radical in tone, published in Spanish, and sent through the mails, it was subject to a variety of wartime laws. Interestingly enough, the additional charge of having mailed "indecent" materials was not used in any of the other Espionage Act cases in southern California during the World War I era.

The "Manifesto" read, in part, as follows:

> *To the members of the party, the anarchists of the world, and workingmen everywhere.*
>
> The clock of history will soon point, with inexorable hands, to the moment in which will occur the death of a society already in agony.
>
> The death of the old society is at hand and will not be delayed much longer. This fact is denied only by those dependent upon the old system; those that profit from the injustice of the system; those that view with horror the coming of the Social Revolution, because they know that on that day they will have to work side by side with their former slaves.
>
> All the evidence indicates that the death of the bourgeoisie will come unexpectedly. The citizen, who only yesterday considered the policeman his protector and supporter, now looks upon him with a grim gaze; the assiduous reader of the bourgeois press shrugs his shoulders and with contempt throws to the ground the prostituted sheet in which appear the declarations of the heads of state; the workingman goes on strike, aware that it is no longer important that his action injures the country's interests, since the country is no longer his property but the property of the rich; . . . there are murmurs in the saloons, in the theaters, in the street cars, in the homes, especially the homes of those who are mourning the departure of a son called to war . . . to face, gun in hand, another youngster who like himself was the enchantment of his home, and whom he does not hate and can not hate, for he does not even know him.[13]

In essence, the "Manifesto" simply predicted the destruction of cap-

---

[12]Ibid. See also Sylvia Lubow, "The Espionage Act in Southern California" (thesis), pp. 128–129.

[13]A copy of the original Spanish version can be found in Bartra, *Regeneración*, pp. 531–533. An English version translated by Kosterlitzky for the government can be found in the trial records—see either "Indictment" or

italist society because of internal contradictions and class warfare. However, even though the document did not make specific reference to the United States and the war effort, the indictment still asserted that it was a "false statement" in violation of the Espionage Act.

On 15 July 1918 a twelve-man jury was impaneled to try the case, the trial lasting two days. The defense was conducted by J. H. Ryckman, Chaim Shapiro, and S. J. Pandit; the first two were labor leaders active in radical and I.W.W. defense work. The government relied on a few key witnesses, including Kosterlitzky, who, as interpreter and translator for the Department of Justice, testified to the accuracy of the translated copy of the "Manifesto." Other government witnesses included Julius Jansen, a mail superintendent at the Los Angeles Post Office; Walter M. Cookson, a Post Office inspector; and Lieutenant-Colonel William E. Purviance, a U.S. Army recruiting officer.[14]

The government's evidence was indirect and circumstantial, with no witnesses to any overt act being presented. Hoping to undermine the defendants' character, the prosecution entered as evidence a speech delivered by Flores Magón on 27 May 1917 called "See, Hear, Hush." This speech had been delivered at Italian Hall at a meeting organized by the International Workers' Defense League. The group was meeting to fight the deportation of Raúl Palma and Odilón Luna to Mexico. Flores Magón's speech was an eloquent defense of the right of free speech during wartime as well as a fervent declaration of anarchist ideals. By reading the speech to the jury, the government hoped to try the defendants for anarchism—that is, a charge more serious to the wartime jurors than any listed in the formal indictment. It made little difference to the government that not only had Librado Rivera had no demonstrable connection with the speech but also that the speech had been delivered prior to the date of passage of the Espionage Act under which the defendants were being charged.[15]

"Charge of the Court," U.S. v. R. Flores Magón and L. Rivera, Crim. 1421, FRC Laguna Niguel. Also see U.S., Congress, House, Debate on Espionage Acts, *Congressional Record*, pp. 690–691.

[14]"Bill of Exceptions," 17 January 1919, U.S. v. R. Flores Magón and L. Rivera, Crim. 1421, FRC Laguna Niguel.

[15]Ibid., pp. 9–13.

Another interesting item entered as evidence was a letter, entitled "On the Way to Golgotha," written by Emma Goldman, then a political prisoner at Jefferson Prison, Jefferson City, Missouri. This was a public appeal addressed to her "Faithful Friends" requesting all sympathizers to join the League for the Amnesty of Political Prisoners, which was based in New York City, and to aid Berkman and herself. Although published in *Regeneración*, it had originally appeared in the *Mother Earth Bulletin*. Again the government's motive was obvious: it hoped to link the *magonistas* in the minds of the jury with the open bolshevism and anarchism of the universally feared and hated "Red Queen."[16]

Judge Benjamin F. Bledsoe, involved in several other Espionage Act cases, demonstrated a deep-seated bias against the defendants in his instructions to the jury. He maintained that the defense counsel's discussions of anarchism were "childlike and bland in the simplicity with which they have been presented." Injecting a note of chauvinism into his charge, the judge said, "It is the glory of the Anglo-Saxon theory, the glory of American tradition and American vision and American determination, that in this country of ours we have a land and a government of liberty under law." Then, as if to imply that the Mexicans lacked all of these Anglo-Saxon "virtues," Bledsoe went on to say that the defendants were "entitled to have their rights measured just as though instead of being members of another nation they were of our own race." Finally, the judge set the "proper" ideological framework by flatly asserting that the jurors must rid themselves of any idea that the state was an instrument of class interests and class conflict. In Bledsoe's words, "We must relieve our minds of any suggestion at all that government in its essential attributes means the superimposing of one class upon another class." Government, according to Bledsoe, "means the joining of all classes" in a common pursuit of justice—class cooperation, not class conflict. The United States was at war and the espousal of "anarchy" and doctrines of class conflict would very easily be an "unjustifiable use and abuse of the privilege of free speech."[17]

Under cross-examination the defense elicited from inspector

<hr />

[16]Ibid., pp. 13–15.

[17]"Charge of the Court," filed 23 July 1918, U.S. v. R. Flores Magón and L. Rivera, Crim. 1421, FRC Laguna Niguel.

Cookson that he had never seen either of the defendants depositing in the Los Angeles Post Office any of the papers offered in evidence by the government. Likewise, Lieutenant-Colonel Purviance testified during cross-examination that he did not know if any of the soldiers at Fort MacArthur or at the submarine base spoke or understood Spanish, as the language of the army was English. In other words, there was no direct evidence that the defendants acted to obstruct recruitment and enlistment. Finally, the defense noted that all five counts charged against the defendants were one and the same, having been derived from the single alleged act of sending the "Manifesto" through the mails. In conclusion, the defense stated that the prosecution was condemning "mere matters of opinion," that is, "mere empty rhetoric, words,—words,—words,—words,—signifying nothing, and not false statements or false reports within the statute."[18]

All to no avail. The defense forgot that "words" did not "signify nothing" to a jury of emotional, wartime Americans. The twelve jurors only took four hours to find the men guilty on all counts. Flores Magón was then sentenced to serve twenty-one years at Mc-Neil Island; Rivera received a sentence of fifteen years. In addition, each was fined five thousand dollars. All subsequent appeals to higher courts were denied. On sentencing the two men, Judge Bledsoe allegedly said that "these men and their kind should not be allowed to hold a copy of the Constitution in one hand and a knife to stab it to death in the other." The harshness of the sentence against the two anarchists, far more severe than any pronounced by the same bench against other defendants found guilty of similar charges under the wartime acts, reflected, in part, the effect on the court of the unrestrained hysteria of the Red Scare in the streets of Los Angeles.[19]

With the leading *magonistas* in prison, the federal authorities moved against other lesser-known *revoltosos*. In late 1919, only three months before the celebrated "Soviet Ark" incident, the U.S. immigration service in Arizona was active in the arrests and deportations of several Mexican aliens. Most of the individuals concerned

[18]"Bill of Exceptions," U.S. v. R. Flores Magón and L. Rivera, Crim. 1421, FRC Laguna Niguel.
[19]Lubow, "The Espionage Act in Southern California," pp. 131, 134.

were railroad workers and miners living and working in Morenci, Arizona. They were members of a local "anarchist" club, and as such had been arrested under telegraphic warrants between 16 and 25 September 1919. In the deportation hearings that followed, the government's case was based on the link that existed between the Morenci group and *magonistas* elsewhere. Of primary importance to the immigration inspector's case were letters, pamphlets, and books found in the club, including works by Ricardo Flores Magón and correspondence between Morenci's radicals and María Talavara. Needless to say, all were recommended for deportation to Mexico as aliens who disbelieved in and opposed all organized government, that is, as anarchists.[20] Like their comrades in California and New York, the Arizona "anarchists" fell victim to the panic of the nation's Red Scare.

At this time a more celebrated deportation case was taking place at Leavenworth Penitentiary, where Enrique Flores Magón was an inmate. At Leavenworth, Enrique's language skills enabled him to work as an unofficial interpreter and to become superintendent of the Spanish school. Even though he was assigned to the mail room, and at times worked the rock pile, he did have free access to the hospital wards and was a close partner of the prison chaplain. Evidently he was treated fairly by the authorities, not complaining about his situation, being allowed to attend to the defense and necessities of other prisoners, and suffering discipline only in minor incidents involving "talking in the dining room during dinner." In October 1919, the Department of Labor requested an investigation of Enrique Flores Magón as a preliminary to a deportation hearing. On 18 March 1920, a hearing was conducted at the prison by immigration inspector Warren E. Long.[21]

During the hearing Enrique narrated his personal history as a *revoltoso*, describing his several imprisonments and his political activities from St. Louis in 1905 to Leavenworth in 1918. When

[20]U.S., Congress, House, *Communist and Anarchist Deportation Cases*, pp. 113–118.

[21]See esp. Harmon Allen to Hospital Guard, 4 December 1919, and Warren E. Long to W. I. Biddle, 29 October 1919—E. Flores Magón, Bureau of Prisons, Leavenworth register no. 12839. Also see Enrique Flores Magón, "Añoranzas. Entre Rejas," *El Nacional* (Mexico City), 19 October 1945, pp. 3, 8.

asked if he believed in "anarchy" he replied that he was a "communist anarchist":

> By communist anarchism I believe the theory of having all natural and social wealth as the property of all. . . . My form of government would be in general lines as follows: Organization of the individuals in their several works. From there in every town; from every town to every region; and from every region to what we now call national organization to form a kind of republic. When other countries follow suit, then it will be an international. . . . Every center of human activity will have its own representatives who will form a kind of congress. You may call it "soviet" or "municipality," as in Mexico.

After other evidence was introduced that linked him to his more famous brother and the Morenci club, Enrique made a final request that, if deported, he be allowed to take his family and go to Russia, not Mexico (where he was certain he would be arrested and shot). Inspector Long's recommendation to the Department of Labor was that the alien be deported because he was in the United States in violation of the Immigration Act of 16 October 1918, in that he was "a member of an organization that teaches opposition to all organized government." Interestingly, Long made no mention as to where the alien should be deported.[22]

The actual outcome of Enrique Flores Magón's case reflected the deep administrative differences within Wilson's cabinet. On 12 April 1920, immigration commissioner Caminetti, finding Flores Magón an alien anarchist, recommended his deportation to Mexico at the termination of his sentence at Leavenworth. Two days later, Caminetti's recommendation was overturned and Flores Magón's warrant was canceled by Assistant Secretary of Labor Louis F. Post, who found Flores Magón's description of government more "democratic" than "anarchistic."[23] In this instance, Post differentiated between "beliefs" and "deeds," and emphasized due process and individual liberty over the rights of the state. This case and several others like it led to a bitter disagreement between the Department of Labor and the Bureau of Immigration, and helped earn for Post the enmity of Hoover and Attorney General Palmer. In 1920, several

[22]U.S. Congress, House, *Communist and Anarchist Deportation Cases*, pp. 104–112.
[23]Ibid., pp. 119–121.

congressional investigations were made in a fruitless effort to impeach Assistant Secretary Post.[24]

On 10 September 1920, Enrique Flores Magón was released from Leavenworth. His separation from his brother for almost two years had led to some estrangement between the two. This in turn was fostered by Ricardo's common-law wife, María Talavera, who accused Enrique and his father-in-law, Rómulo Carmona, of using Ricardo for their own private ends.[25] In any case, on leaving Leavenworth Enrique continued to agitate in favor of his brother and the other political prisoners. He returned to Los Angeles, where he was under constant surveillance by Bureau of Investigation agents, and was again arrested on the pretext of being a syndicalist in violation of state law. Finally, on 4 March 1923, he was deported (with his family) to Mexico because of his libertarian and syndicalist ideas.[26]

In November 1919, Ricardo Flores Magón and Rivera had been transferred from McNeil Island to Leavenworth. Flores Magón and Rivera were included in a general transfer of prisoners, partly for reasons of Flores Magón's health and partly to remove the Mexicans from the influence of members of the radical community at Home Colony near Puget Sound. The transfer took place with the approval of the attorney general, in spite of Kosterlitzky's warnings to the Justice Department that the *magonistas* were more secure at McNeil Island, since it was further from Mexico and the Southwest and was surrounded by water (neither of the two inmates were good swimmers, according to Kosterlitzky).[27]

Ricardo became the prison librarian at Leavenworth, and appeared to outsiders to be more of a gentle philosopher or saint than a ferocious revolutionary. Rivera worked in the prison printshop

[24]Preston, *Aliens and Dissenters*, pp. 222–226.

[25]María B. Magón [Talavara] to Francisco Aonte Ocaso, 6 April 1918, p. 13 of "Indictment," Crim. 1489, FRC Laguna Niguel.

[26]Enrique Flores Magón, "Añoranzas. Libre . . . y no!," *El Nacional* (Mexico City), 16 August 1946, pp. 3a, 4a; Frank M. Sturgis to Biddle, 12 October 1921, in Enrique Flores Magón, Bureau of Prisons, Leavenworth register no. 12839–L.

[27]See Att. Gen. to O. P. Halligan, 23 September 1918; Halligan to Thomas W. Gregory, 2 October 1918; Att. Gen. to Halligan, 16 October 1918; Kosterlitzky, "Special Report," to U.S. Dist. Att.–L.A., 17 December 1918— all R. Flores Magón, Bureau of Prisons, McNeil Island register no. 2198.

and was counselor, letter-writer, and confessor for every Mexican in the compound. The Mexicans soon made the acquaintance of fellow radicals, especially members of the Leavenworth I.W.W. contingent. The Wobbly poet Ralph Chaplin became a good friend and associate of both men. At one point Rivera mockingly appointed Chaplin "Coronel" in the Partido Liberal Mexicano. Once a day for one hour, weather permitting, Chaplin, Flores Magón, and other office workers got together in the prison yard at a section of the rock pile called the "Campus" (south of "Wobbly Shed," only a few steps from "Wall Street") to engage in intellectual discussions ranging from medieval balladry to Mexican folklore. These men maintained their sanity by exchanging revolutionary poetry and encouraging one another in their daily tasks; but life was still harsh—as Chaplin said, "Flowers die and weeds flourish in prison air."[28]

By 1922, public pressures to free Flores Magón were affecting the governments of both the United States and Mexico. Although the U.S. government did its best to avoid liberating the I.W.W. contingent at Leavenworth, Harding's administration did begin offering, in December 1921, selective commutations of sentences conditioned on immediate deportation. In early 1922 several Wobblies walked out of Leavenworth as free men, leaving their comrades Flores Magón and Rivera behind. By summer, liberals and radicals were publishing articles to keep the plight of the Mexicans prisoners before the public and were continuing to write appeals to the attorney general and President Harding. Kate Crane Gartz, known as the "parlor Bolshevik," was a "socialist millionaire" and philanthropist who contributed much of her "iron-master" father's wealth and her own time to the *magonista* cause. The lawyer Harry Weinberger continued to press for amnesty and publicized the conditions of Flores Magón's failing health, especially his developing blindness.[29]

In Mexico, the amnesty campaign was more direct. Various political figures, the state legislatures of Yucatán and Coahuila, several *sindicatos*, the Mexican Federation of Labor, the Young Com-

[28]Chaplin, *Wobbly*, pp. 255–260, 277.
[29]Preston, *Aliens and Dissenters*, pp. 259–262; Gómez-Quiñones, *Sembradores*, p. 68; Mary C. Sinclair, comp., *The Parlor Provocateur, or, From Salon to Soap-Box: The Letters of Kate Crane Gartz*, pp. 33–36, 86–89, 100–103; Harry Weinberger, "Two Political Prisoners at Leavenworth," *The New Republic* 31 (5 July 1922).

munist League, and the *Partido Comunista Mexicano* pressured the regime of Alvaro Obregón to take steps to arrange for the release of all Mexican political prisoners in U.S. jails. Enrique Flores Magón, operating from Los Angeles, encouraged a general Mexican boycott of all North American goods. As a protest action on behalf of Flores Magón, Mexican workers staged stoppages, beginning in Progreso on the east coast and spreading to the ports on the Pacific side. By mid-summer, the Mexican ambassador had sought remedial action in Washington, and the attorney general's office was reviewing the cases of Rivera and Flores Magón.[30]

But for Ricardo Flores Magón the attorney general's review came too late. On 16 October 1922, Flores Magón, at the request of his lawyer, Harry Weinberger, underwent a complete physical examination. The examining physician, Dr. Simon B. Langworthy, had been hired by Weinberger to conduct the examination because Flores Magón and his friends did not trust the judgment or the motives of the prison physician. Much to Flores Magón's chagrin, Langworthy concluded that the prisoner was "standing his confinement well. His general physical condition is good." Two weeks later Flores Magón gave his own self-diagnosis to Weinberger in a letter in which he listed his many ills—chronic bronchitis, lumbago, cataracts, diabetes, irregularity, and kidney pains. Although his letter appeared to be the work of a hypochondriac, his anxieties did include a serious complaint about pains in the region of the heart. Then, at 4:15 on the morning of 21 November, the guard in Cell House "B" found Flores Magón suffering distress and pain about the heart. Fifteen minutes later, before the hospital attendant could return to his cell with medicine, Flores Magón, at the age of forty-nine, was dead. The official diagnosis was angina pectoris—death from a cardiac attack.[31]

[30]Gómez-Quiñones, *Sembradores*, p. 68; Enrique Flores Magón, "A todos los trabajadores de México, hombres y mujeres," in *Por la libertad de Ricardo Flores Magón*, comp. Aureliano J. Mijares, pp. 153–163. For Rivera's account see the following: L. Rivera to F. G. Rendón, 18 April 1922; Rivera to Gus Teltsch, 1 June 1922; Rivera to Blas Lara, 7 January 1923—all L. Rivera, Bureau of Prisons, Leavenworth register no. 15416–L.

[31]Langworthy, "Physical Examination of R. Flores Magón," 16 October 1922; Att. Gen. to Langworthy, 21 October 1922; R. Flores Magón to Weinberger, 5 November 1922; A. F. Yohe to W. I. Biddle, 21 November 1922–all R. Flores Magón, Bureau of Prisons, Leavenworth, register no. 14596–L.

Just as the question of Flores Magón's health care was a controversial political issue while he was living, so too did the circumstances of his dying become an issue after his death. Librado Rivera hinted strongly of a foul plot, noting that when he saw the cadaver of Ricardo in the prison hospital on the morning of 21 November he noticed dark marks around the neck area and a contortion of the features as if from a struggle prior to death. Eugene V. Debs, writing an article entitled "The Assassination of Magón" for the *New York Call,* declared that Flores Magón had been deliberately abandoned to death through the slow torture of neglect and mistreatment. Writing in the 1920s, the radical scholar Diego Abad de Santillán did not hesitate to claim that Flores Magón was murdered in prison.[32]

Angina pectoris is a specialized term today, but in the 1920s it meant a heart attack. Flores Magón's death was apparently due to a coronary insufficiency and resultant myocardial infarction. An infarction is simply an acute heart attack. The fact that neither Dr. Langworthy, in an extensive and complete examination one month prior to Flores Magón's death, nor Dr. Yohe, the prison physician, ever detected anything indicating disease of the heart is not in itself surprising. Even today the noted cardiologist Dr. Charles K. Friedberg says that the "EKG may be normal in 25 to 50 percent of those patients with angina pectoris."

Another theory that suggests a link between Flores Magón's alleged diabetes and the resultant blindness and heart disease has to be discarded. It is questionable that Flores Magón actually had diabetes. Although the prison physician at McNeil Island indicated that he was a diabetic in his report of 2 October 1918, subsequent tests of his urine at Leavenworth all indicated negative sugar, and any diabetes would have been so mild as to have not been likely to contribute to his death. Concerning Flores Magón's dimming vision, he was suffering eye failure of 10 and 20 over 100 because of immature cataracts. Although diabetes can be related to blindness, it is usually blindness due to retinitis (inflammation of the retina), not the opacification of the lens known as cataracts.

Much of the above information came from a conversation of the author with Charles B. Mosher, M.D., on 22 December 1976 in Fredonia, New York. Dr. Mosher has carefully studied the health records found in Flores Magón's files at Leavenworth (Register No. 14596). For additional information on the EKG and angina pectoris see Richard Spark, M.D., "The Case against Regular Physicals," The *New York Times Magazine,* 25 July 1976, pp. 11, 38.

[32]Librado Rivera, "Persecución y asesinato de Ricardo Flores Magón," in *¿Para qué sirve la autoridad?,* p. 22; Eugene v. Debs, "Prólogo a 'Rayos de Luz'," *¿Para qué sirve la autoridad?,* p. 38; Diego Abad de Santillán, *Ricardo Flores Magón, el apóstol de la Revolución Social Mexicana,* especially pp. 1–3, 129–131.

Enrique Flores Magón went further, charging outright that his brother had been assassinated by "El Toro," that is, Captain A. H. ("Bull") Leonard, head of the guards. According to Enrique, Leonard had ordered Rivera moved from an adjoining cell so as to prevent him from being a witness to the crime. In the early morning of 21 November, Leonard entered Ricardo's cell and strangled him with his bare hands. In doing this the "Bull" had simply been the instrument of Warden Biddle, Albert Fall, and Attorney General Harry M. Daugherty, all of whom were motivated by a desire to prevent the scheduled release of Flores Magón. Shortly thereafter, another Mexican inmate, by the name of José Martínez, fatally stabbed "Bull" Leonard in an act of revenge, and was himself killed in the fray—a martyr to the *magonista* (and, today, Chicano) cause.[33]

The credibility of all of these accounts is subject to question, especially that of the emotionally and politically involved Enrique. His narrative is suspect on several counts. It is true that there was an incident involving Martínez and Captain Leonard in which the "Bull" was stabbed and killed by the "maddened" and "crazed" Mexican inside the prison boilerhouse. However, as prison records indicate, the incident took place on 14 November and "Bull" Leonard then died within forty-eight hours. In other words, the alleged killer of Ricardo Flores Magón had himself been dead for at least five days prior to the reported death of Flores Magón on 21 November![34]

In addition, although Ralph Chaplin in his autobiography describes the entire Martínez-Leonard incident in a sub-chapter entitled "The Butchering of the Bull," he makes no mention of any connection between that event and the death of Ricardo, his beloved friend and comrade—a rather strange omission if Enrique's account was correct.[35] Finally, there is no evidence to indicate that

[33]For Enrique Flores Magón's account see Samuel Kaplan, *Peleamos contra la injusticia*, II, 404–412. A variation of this account is found in Gómez-Quiñones, *Sembradores*, p. 68.

[34]For the death of Leonard between 14 and 16 November and of Martínez on 30 November 1922, see G. E. Herron to Biddle, 16 November 1922; Biddle to Herron, 16 November 1922; Record Clerk to Whom it may Concern, 13 July 1925—all José Martínez, Bureau of Prisons, Leavenworth register no. 13396–L.

[35]Chaplin, *Wobbly*, pp. 275–277.

Flores Magón was about to be released in late November 1922 or that the attorney general and the secretary of the interior had entered into a conspiracy to silence forever the *magonista* hero. The conclusion is obvious: Enrique Flores Magón fabricated a story out of half-truths in order to create a martyr out of his brother to aid the *magonista* cause. Until other evidence is forthcoming, the best scholarly conclusion is that Flores Magón did indeed die of natural causes in prison, most probably of a heart attack.

Flores Magón's death precipitated a series of memorial mass meetings across the country, with pickets from the Joint Amnesty Committee carrying banners in front of the White House. These meetings in turn led to hearings and discussions in and out of Congress. Representative George Huddleston of Alabama, one of the signers of the petition for amnesty, entered into the *Congressional Record* his statement that "there are about sixty cases of men who are still in prison, not for spying, not for aiding the enemy, but for expressing opinions about and against the war or otherwise dissenting from the majority."[36]

In January of 1923 the dark funeral train made its way across Mexico, from Juárez to Mexico City, making twelve stops en route. It carried the body of Flores Magón, his casket draped with red and black flags and with bright flowers. His final homage came in the form of a renewed amnesty drive, which finally led Coolidge to unconditionally commute the sentences of the last thirty Wobblies in December 1923. Two months earlier, on October 23, thanks to the efforts of the Joint Amnesty Committee, Harry Weinberger, and Obregón's consul in Kansas City, Librado Rivera's sentence was formally commuted. He then joined a Mexican deportation party for Mexico, where he continued his political activities.[37]

It was 1923, and the radical, heroic, epic phase of Mexico's revolution was over—as was the *revoltoso* movement. It was time

[36]U.S., Congress, House, Debate on Espionage Acts, *Congressional Record*, p. 484.

[37]See all of the following: E. P. Reynolds to Biddle, 12 October 1923; Biddle to E. P. Reynolds, 15 October 1923; Consulado de México to Rivera, 15 October 1923; Biddle to Mex. Consul, 16 October 1923; Weinberger to Biddle, 15 October 1923; Biddle to Weinberger, 16 October 1923; Carl F. Zarter to J. A. Rivera, 14 June 1938—all L. Rivera, Bureau of Prisons, Leavenworth register no. 15416–L.

for a rapprochement with the United States, Henry Ford, and Standard Oil. Albert Fall had resigned in disgrace from the cabinet. Librado Rivera and Enrique Flores Magón had undergone their expulsion to Mexico. Most of the leading *revoltosos* were now dead, victims of the violence of revolution and the class struggle—Figueroa, Arredondo, Madero, Huerta, Orozco, J. Sarabia, Villa, Zapata, and Carranza. And, of course, Ricardo Flores Magón: "We know that we are destined to absorb a dagger in our flesh or to die of consumption in some prison. We accept our destiny with pleasure, satisfied with having accomplished something on behalf of the slaves."[38] It was time to return to "normalcy."

[38]As quoted by Blaisdell, *The Desert Revolution*, p. 187.

Bibliographical Essay

THE following essay contains a description of the bibliographical aids, guides, archives, manuscript collections, published documents, newspapers, and pictorial sources used in researching the subject matter of this book. A select directory of materials cited in the notes follows this essay. The directory lists in alphabetical order printed documents, memoirs, and newspapers, as well as secondary sources (books, articles, dissertations, and theses). In a few instances, some recently published items relevant to the topic but not cited have also been included. Aids, guides, and manuscripts discussed in the bibliographical essay have been excluded from the directory.

Bibliographical Aids and Guides

By far the most complete and best-organized bibliographical guide to Mexican Revolutionary history is the five-volume *Fuentes de la historia contemporánea de México* (Mexico City: El Colegio de México, 1961–1967). The first three volumes were edited by Luis González and deal with *Libros y folletos*. The other two volumes are subtitled *Periódicos y revistas* and are a collection of notes on articles in newspapers and journals prepared under the direction of Stanley R. Ross. The Ross volumes, an essential tool of research, provide the scholar with an aid to better utilizing Mexico's fine collection of newspapers and periodicals in the Hemeroteca Nacional. The fourth volume (*Periódicos y revistas*, vol. 1) is especially useful for the history of the *revoltosos*, containing both an introduction listing Spanish-language publications in the United States and a section on the "Precursores de la Revolución."

A comprehensive guide especially good for young North American scholars about to embark on historical research in Mexico is *Research in Mexican History* (Lincoln: University of Nebraska Press, 1973), compiled and edited by Richard E. Greenleaf and Michael C. Meyer. This work comprises practical information on research topics, problems, and methodology, and includes a bibliography of bibliographies, a field research guide, archival descriptions, a guide to archival collections, and an appended "scholar's map" of Mexico City. For those who hesitate to approach the somewhat overwhelming National Archives collection in Washington, D.C., Milton O. Gustafson's (ed.) *The National Archives and Foreign Relations Research* (Athens, Ohio: Ohio University Press, 1974) is highly recommended. The Record Groups of several governmental departments are described. In addition, articles by David M. Pletcher and Robert Freeman Smith treat of research problems and resources peculiar to the topic of United States–Latin American relations in the nineteenth and twentieth centuries.

For the diplomacy of the Revolution the historian has access to two extensive works: Daniel Cosío Villegas, *Cuestiones Internacionales de Mexico, Una Bibliografía* (Mexico City: Secretaría de Relaciones Exteriores, 1966); and David F. Trask, Michael C. Meyer, and Roger R. Trask, *A Bibliography of United States–Latin American Relations since 1810: A Selected List of Eleven Thousand Published References* (Lincoln: University of Nebraska Press, 1968). Only the latter volume is annotated, but both contain detailed indices. For references to the literature of the border region, see Charles C. Cumberland, "The United States–Mexican Border: A Selective Guide to the Literature of the Region," supplement to *Rural Sociology* 25 (June 1960). Equally valuable is Berta Ulloa's "Diplomacy in the Borderlands: An Analysis of Some Research Material and Opportunities in the Archivo de la Secretaría de Relaciones Exteriores de México, 1910–1920" (mimeographed paper read at the Conference on the Borderlands, 26 October 1973, at San Antonio, Texas).

Several published guides to archival collections are worth noting. An excellent and necessary work is the *Guide to the National Archives of the United States* (Washington, D.C.: National Archives and Records Service, General Services Administration, 1974). In addition to being a guide to all of the Record Groups in the National Archives, the annotations and Record Group introductions provide basic data on the origin and development of government agencies and bureaus. A more specialized aid is John P. Harrison's *Guide to Materials on Latin America in the National Archives* (Washington, D.C.: Government Printing Office, 1961). The Harrison work has recently been revised and expanded by George S. Ulibarri and appears as Ulibarri and Harrison, *Guide to Materials on Latin America in the National Archives of the United States* (Washington, D.C.: National Archives and Records Service, GSA, 1974). For information on the eleven regional branches of the National Archives, see the general information leaflet *Regional Branches of the National Archives* (Washington, D.C.: National Archives and Records Service, GSA, 1976).

Most useful of the guides to Mexican archives is Berta Ulloa's *Revolución Mexicana, 1910–1920* (Mexico City: Secretaría de Relaciones Exteriores, 1963), a descriptive guide to the 259 bound volumes in the "Mexican Revolution" section of the Foreign Relations Archive in Mexico City. In spite of the title, several *revoltoso* materials are described for the period 1904–1910. Besides the lengthy descriptions, the name index is a most helpful tool. Another useful aid for students of the Porfiriato is Laurens B. Perry's guide to the enormous Porfirio Díaz Collection housed in the library of the University of the Americas in Cholula, Puebla. This is entitled *Inventario y guía de la colección General Porfirio Díaz* (Mexico City: The University of the Americas Press, 1969). Some special collections in the United States have unpublished guides. Thus, users of the Terrazas Archive at the Bancroft Library have access to "Terrazas, Silvestre, 1873–1944: Correspondence and Papers—Report and Key to Arrangement" (University of California at Berkeley, n.d.). Michael C. Meyer's "Albert Bacon Fall's Mexican Papers: A Preliminary Investigation," *New Mexico Historical Review* 40 (April 1965) 165–174, is a general introduction to the collection, not a detailed description. For a description of anarchist and *magonista* materials in the International Institute of Social History in Amsterdam, see Raymond Buve and Cunera Holthuis, *A Survey of Mexican Materials at the International Instituut voor Sociale Geschiedenis in Amsterdam* (copies available at the institute).

Archives and Manuscript Collections

The historian interested in the Mexican Revolution and the role of the *revoltosos* along the frontier is fortunate to have access to a sizeable number of manuscript collections, both public and private, found in various places in Mexico and the United States. The most important single source of manuscripts in Mexico for this study was the Archivo de la Secretaría de Relaciones Exteriores de México. Located on the ground floor of the convent next to the Iglesia de Santiago Tlatelolco in Mexico City's "Plaza of Three Cultures," the collection contains a wealth of information on both domestic and foreign affairs. Staff personnel are very helpful in securing information from the "classified" subject index. Working space is most ample in the Biblioteca José Ma. Lafragua, located on the floor immediately above the Archive. The most valuable documents are grouped under the title "Revolución Mexicana durante los años de 1910 a 1920." It is for these documents that the researcher can best prepare himself by utilizing the previously cited guide by Berta Ulloa. Most of the information on Furlong and other private detectives in the United States came from this source (Agencias Secretas: L–E–614–L–E–616; L–E–622–L–E–627; L–E–716–L–E–724; L–E–854–L–E–855). For information on the *magonistas* on the frontier, the Pacific Co-operative Detective Agency, Furlong, and the activities of Gobernación's secret police see both "Revolucionarios en la frontera" (L–E–1240–L–E–1245) and "Flores Magón, et al., Disturbios en la frontera" (L–E–918–L–E–954). For Madero family activities between 1911–1913, see "Presidente Francisco I. Madero" (L–E–1438–L–E–1440); for Carranza, See "V. Carranza, 1913–1920" (L–E–1441–L–E–1455). Other tidbits relating to the structure, function, and development of the consular system were found in "Correspondencia recibida por el consulado de México, en Phoenix, Arizona, 1904–1909" (L–E–1669), and "Documentos relativos al sistema de vigilancia . . . por P. Ornelas, San Antonio, 1878–1886" (1–4–1601, File Series H/513.3). The Foreign Relations Archives also has a large number of personal *expedientes* of government officials. Most helpful to this study were "Antonio V. Lomelí" (L–E–1186–L–E–1189) and "Enrique C. Creel" (L–E–422).

Maderista materials can be found in the Archivo General de la Nación, which contains the Ramo Revolución–Política Interior, a small collection of correspondence to and from revolutionary figures for the 1910–1919 period. Besides Francisco Madero (2 November 1910–10 October 1912), this collection contains a few letters either to or from Pascual Orozco, Gustavo Madero, Bernardo Reyes, Evaristo Madero, Victoriano Huerta, Abraham González, Robert Lansing, and Ricardo Flores Magón. Also here are some letters from S. G. Hopkins to Madero's secretary, Juan Sánchez Azcona, relating to the Standard Oil question and American domestic politics. The entire collection has been indexed; there is an annotated card file that lists materials alphabetically and chronologically. Access to the index is by permission only. The Archivo General also has a series of Francisco Madero copybooks. These letterpress books (Libros Copiadores de Madero) are for the period 1911–1913 and are numbered, somewhat peculiarly, 1, 2, 3, and 12.

The Colección Porfirio Díaz is housed in the library at the University of the Americas in Cholula, Puebla. This archive contains 374 rolls of processed film representing 663,843 manuscripts and telegrams of the Díaz administration from 1876 to 1911. Arranged chronologically by month and year, materials used can be easily cited and found by legajo and document number. Although many of the materials from 1905 to June 1911 were reviewed in the course of this study, most attention was given to those letters and telegrams relating to the Cananea affair of 1906.

The Fundación Cultural de Condumex has some important manuscript collections for the early Revolution. The Fundación's Center of Historical Studies is located in the industrial section of the Vallejo area of Mexico City, and although difficult at first to locate, has excellent working conditions, including a most helpful staff. Of importance for this study were assorted letters from the Carranza Archive. Condumex also has a good set of government publications, especially for the Secretaría de Gobernación. Another Mexico City collection not to be overlooked is the Archivo de la Espinosa de los Monteros, located at the annex to Chapultepec Castle in the Biblioteca Manuel Orozco y Berra. Consisting of nine bound volumes, the materials (mostly newspapers) are especially good for *reyista* activities between 1909 and 1913. Volume 2 contains a copy of the "Plan de San Diego" of south Texas.

Much of the research for this book took place in the United

States in Washington, D.C., at the Library of Congress, the National Archives, and various governmental offices. Many agencies, such as the Bureau of Immigration and the Bureau of Prisons, possess important historical materials not housed at the National Archives. Many immigration materials, once stored at the National Archives, are now back under bureau control and restricted from the public. Curiously, many of the immigration deportation proceedings not available in the United States can be found as copies in the manuscript collection of the Foreign Relations Archive in Mexico. Fortunately, the Freedom of Information Act (1966) was amended in 1974 to allow scholars access to many governmental holdings previously classified. Under this act the Bureau of Prisons has made available important historical materials for the first time. Since this writing the massive files of the Bureau of Investigation have been declassified for the decade of 1910–1920, and these 80,000-odd pages of documents are available on twenty-four reels of microfilm.

Three collections were consulted at the Library of Congress Manuscript Division. Two of these, the William Howard Taft Papers and the Theodore Roosevelt Papers, are now available on microfilm through interlibrary loan. Concerning the Taft Papers, Series 5 and Series 6 contain executive office correspondence for the years 1909 to 1913 relating to the topics of intervention in Mexico, troop mobilizations, and the Mexican Revolution. For Roosevelt, see especially Series 5A, Speeches and Executive Orders, August 1904–September 1910. Another collection worth consulting is the Philander Chase Knox Papers from 1910 to 1913, especially the Department of State File (Information Series "A") on "Disorders in Mexico."

The most extensive collection of materials on the Mexican Revolution in the United States is found in the National Archives in Washington, especially Record Group 59, Records of the Department of State. For the period up to early 1906 the Despatches from United States Ministers to Mexico, 1823–1906, is available on microfilm (Microcopy 97). For the period between 1906 and 1910, State Department documents have been organized into a Numerical File (only part of which has been microfilmed to date). From this file the following were the most important for my research on the *revoltosos*: No. 100, Anti-Americanism in Mexico; No. 283, Arms and Ammunition Carried into Mexico; No. 1204, Mexican Independence

Day; No. 1741, Extradition and Arrest of R. Flores Magón, et al.; No. 2787, Personnel File of Luther T. Ellsworth; No. 3916, Mexican Labor Difficulties; No. 5028, Violations of the Neutrality Laws of the U.S.; No. 7418, Arrest of Arizona Resident in Mexico; No. 7722, Yaqui Indians in the U.S.; No. 8183, Political Affairs in Mexico; No. 9723, Closing of Cananea; No. 21057, Extradition of J. Rangel. For the period after 1910 see the Records of the Department of State Relating to the Internal Affairs of Mexico, 1910–29 (Microcopy 274, 812.00 series) and Records of the Department of State Relating to U.S.–Mexico Relations (Microcopy 314, 711.12 series). Record Group 59 also contains Domestic Letters (Microcopy 40) and several folders of Foreign Service Applications and Recommendations, 1906–1924. The latter were used to obtain letters, news clippings, and internal memoranda relating to Elihu Root, Robert Bacon, and Ambassador David E. Thompson.

From the National Archives I also obtained microfilm copies of Records of the Department of Justice. Most of these materials came from Record Group 60, file 90755 (13 reels, October 1906–1940) and Straight Numerical File 16, 90755–I, and were a valuable addition to the usually cited State Department views. Other Justice Department files consulted included nos. 43718 and 180187 and subject files 71–1–59 and 9–19–290. These dealt with the activities of *revoltosos* on the frontier, the Baja California revolt, and claims commission issues and problems. File 204091 treats specifically of the extradition trial of Antonio Villarreal.

A variety of other governmental agencies have manuscripts housed in the National Archives that relate to the topic of *revoltosos*. In spite of the fact that the Bureau of Immigration removed many of its materials from the archive, the enterprising researcher can still find deportation hearings and proceedings and related matters under Record Group 85, Records of the Immigration and Naturalization Services, files 5020, 5241–44, and 53108. Military and naval intelligence operations were found under Record Group 165, War Department, General and Special Staffs (War College Division, Military Intelligence Division, especially files 5761 and 10679), and Record Group 38, Records of the Office of the Chief of Naval Operations (O.N.I, Office of Naval Intelligence, especially c–9–b on Japanese-Mexican Relations). Related materials on war contingency plans and military intelligence can be found in the files of the Adjutant General's Office, 1780s–1917, Record Group 94 (1716354; 1849275; 1870422). Finally, Record Group 267, Records of the U.S. Supreme Court, contains Appelate Case No. 21153, R. Flores Magón v. U.S.

At least two regional offices of the National Archives house documents of interest to this study. The Federal Archives and Records Center at Laguna Niguel (formerly Bell), California, has been, until March 1975, the depository of non-current materials of the U.S. District Court of Justice of Southern California of Los Angeles. Because Arizona Territory was at one time a part of the Southern California District, the Tombstone trial records of Flores Magón, Rivera, and Villarreal are part of this collection. Although these records were (at the time of my research during the summer of 1974) unorganized and unknown to the archivists in Washington, my labors were well rewarded. Altogether there are twenty-five cases scattered through one box covering the period 1906 to 1920. The most important of these relate to the federal trials of the Flores Magón brothers, Tomás Espinosa, Manuel Sarabia, Antonio Villarreal, Librado Rivera, Antonio de P. Araujo, Anselmo Figueroa, Rhys Price, and María (Magón) Talavera (Criminal Cases Nos. 23, 64, 374, 375, 641A, 669, 671, 693, 1071, 1421, 1489, and 1508, and U.S. Commissioner's Transactions Nos. 572, 582, and 591). The other depository, the Federal Archives and Record Center at Fort Worth, Texas, contains a 500-page letterpress book containing correspondence and notes of the Office of the Deputy Collector, Eagle Pass Customs Station, and the agent at the Del Rio subport, for the period from 24 September 1909 to 20 September 1913.

Through the Freedom of Information Act, I obtained *magonista* prison records from the Department of Justice through the Washington, D.C., office of the United States Bureau of Prisons. The McNeil Island records are located at the Federal Records Center in Seattle, Washington; the Leavenworth files are stored at the Kansas City, Missouri, Federal Records Center. McNeil Island Registers 2198–2201 are for the 1912–1914 period and contain the prison records of Ricardo Flores Magón, Enrique Flores Magón, Librado Rivera, and Anselmo Figueroa respectively. Leavenworth Register 12839–L is the prison record of Enrique Flores Magón between 1918 and 1920. Leavenworth Registers 15416–L and 14596–L are those of Librado Rivera for the 1920–1923 period and Ricardo Flores Magón for the years after 1920 (the latter file continues beyond the year of Flores Magón's death in 1922 to include recent inquiries and requests for information about his life and death in prison). Finally, Leavenworth Register 13396–L is the file on José Martínez, the man who stabbed the alleged killer of Ricardo Flores Magón.

These prison files contain, for the most part, administrative records (e.g., receipts, correspondence lists, prison employment records, personal inventories, health records). However, a surprising amount of personal and official correspondence is also contained in these files, including letters and telegrams between the prisoners and their friends, relatives, and comrades on the outside, as well as correspondence between the prison warden and other governmental agencies (including special agents of the Bureau of Investigation) and interested outsiders. Because Flores Magón's health care and the circumstances surrounding his death at Leavenworth were and are controversial and politically charged issues, these records, never before available to the public, have been invaluable for the portions of this study that treat of the role of the *magonistas* in the United States.

The extensive Silvestre Terrazas Collection held by the Bancroft Library at the University of California at Berkeley was most helpful. Of special importance were the 465 letters and pieces found in three boxes (Boxes 26–28) for the period between 1899 and 1910. These boxes contain correspondence between Flores Magón and other *revoltosos* concerning their organization and revolutionary plans, and the letters of Enrique C. Creel, governor of Chihuahua (correspondence with local officials in Chihuahua and nearby states concerning apprehension of the revolutionists). This collection also contains several *revoltoso* newspapers not easily found elsewhere.

In Tucson, Arizona, I was granted access to the privately held papers of the Compañía Minera de Cananea, S.A. de C.V. This collection of company files contains business and personal correspondence, reports, letters to stockholders, telegrams, statements of company officials, and miscellaneous material relating to the affairs of the Greene Consolidated Copper Company, Cananea Consolidated Copper Company, Cananea Cattle Company, and related companies. Although the company headquarters (no longer private) is located in Cananea, Sonora, as of this writing the papers are in Tucson and are not open to the general public. Although the papers are not held, owned or located at the office of the Arizona Historical Society, individuals there were able to guide me to them.

The Cananea Company papers provide the researcher with the company view of the Cananea strike; the letters of A. B. Wadleigh, a Greene employee at Cananea, provide a different, though complementary, perspective. Copies of the correspondence of A. B. Wadleigh were provided me by the librarians of the Samuel C. Williams Library at the Stevens Institute of Technology in Hoboken, New Jersey. The Wadleigh file was folder 106B of the Frederick W. Taylor Collection (Correspondence, 1899–1908).

Limited use was made of several collections located elsewhere in the United States. Most important of these was the Albert Bacon Fall Collection, Correspondence and Miscellaneous Materials, held by the Henry E. Huntington Library at San Marino, California. Microfilm copies of the Fall Papers are available at the University of New Mexico and the University of Nebraska. Fall, it will be recalled, was an early partner of Greene and a man and politician long interested in Mexican affairs. Also at Nebraska, in the archives of the Nebraska State Historical Society located on the university campus at Lincoln, is the vertical file of David E. Thompson—one ambassador to Mexico who has been overlooked by most Mexicanists. The men who were the highest public officials in the state of Missouri during the period when the PLM had its headquarters in St. Louis were Governor Joseph W. Folk and State Attorney General Herbert S. Hadley. Their papers can be found in the Manuscript Collection at the University of Missouri, Columbia. The El Paso Public Library holds the Citizens Vertical File on H. C. Kramp, a private detective in the pay of Francisco Madero during the hectic 1910–1912 years. Finally, the Sherman Foundation at Corona-del-Mar, California, houses the Colorado River Land Company Papers (File No. 61 is the Colorado River Land Company claim against Mexico for 1911 property losses in Baja California).

Published Documents

Without any doubt the most valuable set of published documents for the Mexican Revolution remains the 27-volume *Documentos históricos de la Revolución Mexicana*. The compilation of these documents, a project of the Comisión de Investigaciones Históricas de la Revolución Mexicana, was initiated by Isidro Fabela and completed after his death by his widow, Josefina E. de Fabela. A veritable storehouse of information, the documents selected for publication came from various public archives in Mexico City (e.g., Foreign Relations, National Defense, Archivo General) and the private library of Fabela himself. Of special note for this study were volumes 5, 10, and 11, on the Maderista revolution (1964), the political activities of the Flores Magón brothers (1966), and the precursor movement, 1906–1910 (1966).

Two other valuable works published in Mexico City are Manuel González Ramírez, *Fuentes para la historia de la Revolución Mexicana*, in four volumes, and *Archivo de Francisco I. Madero*, in three volumes. In the *Fuentes* set, volume 3, *La huelga de Cananea* (1956), is indispensable for the Cananea strike, and volume 4, *Manifiestos políticos* (1957), is helpful for the 1892–1912 period. The published Madero archive includes letters for the 1900–1910 period and is available at the Nettie Lee Benson Latin American Collection, University of Texas at Austin.

Supplementing the Roosevelt Papers at the Library of Congress is Elting E. Morison, ed. and comp., *The Letters of Theodore Roosevelt*, in eight volumes. A recent and interesting collection of National Archives materials compiled by Gene Z. Hanrahan is entitled *Documents on the Mexican Revolution*, in two volumes, four parts. The first volume deals with the origins of the Mexican Revolution in Texas, Arizona, New Mexico, and California between February 1910 and October 1911. Volume 2 is about the Madero revolution as reported in the confidential dispatches of U.S. Ambassador Henry Lane Wilson between June 1910 and June 1911. Most of the documents originated with either the Department of State or the Department of Justice and include customs and immigration materials.

Some limited use was made of official Mexican government documents. Most of these were located either in Mexico City at the Fundación Cultural de Condumex or at the Benson Collection at the University of Texas. Those most helpful were: Mexico, Secretaría de Gobernación, "Informe . . . relativo a los disturbios ocurridos en Cananea," *Memoria*, pp. 45–50; Mexico, Secretaría de Guerra y Marina, *Memoria*, July 1906–July 1908; Mexico, Secretaría de Guerra y Marina, *Campaña de 1910 a 1911*; Mexico, Secretaría de Relaciones Exteriores, *Labor internacional de la Revolución Constitucionalista de México*, covering the period 1913 to 1918.

A large number of published documents from U.S. agencies were used in this study, most of which can be found in the directory following this essay. Those particularly relevant were: U.S., Congress, House, Committee on Rules, *Providing for a Joint Committee to Investigate Alleged Persecutions of Mexican Citizens by the Government of Mexico: Hearing on H. Joint Res. 201*, 8–14 June 1910; U.S., Congress, House, Subcommittee of the Committee on Immigration and Naturalization, *Communist and Anarchist Deportation Cases*, 66th Cong., 2 Sess., 1920; U.S., Congress, Senate, *Affairs in Mexico*, 62d Cong., 1 Sess., 1911, S. Doc. 25; U.S., Congress, Senate, Subcommittee of the Committee on Foreign Relations, *Revolutions in Mexico: Hearing on S. 335*, 62d Cong., 2 Sess., 1913; U.S., Congress, Senate, Committee on Foreign Relations, *Investigation of Mexican Affairs: Hearing on S. 106*, 66th Cong., 2 Sess., 1920, S. Doc. 285, 2 vols.; U.S., Department of State, *Papers Relating to the Foreign Relations of the United States, 1905–1911, 1916* (Washington, D.C.: 1906, 1909–1910, 1912, 1914–1915, 1918, 1925).

The best volume of collected *magonista* documents is Manuel González Ramírez, *Epistolario y textos de Ricardo Flores Magón*, covering the period 1904 to 1909. For the prison correspondence of Flores Magón between 1919 and 1922 see R. Flores Magón, *Epistolario revolucionario e íntimo*. Juan Gómez-Quiñones, *Sembradores. Ricardo Flores Magón y el Partido Liberal Mexicano: A Eulogy and Critique*, contains letters, and excerpts from *Regeneración*, between 1900 and 1923.

Newspapers

The Mexican government maintains one of the finest newspaper collections in the Americas. Most of the important local, state, and national newspapers are housed in the always crowded Hemeroteca Nacional in Mexico City. Here the North American researcher works side by side with retired scholars and elementary school children, undergoing socialization as well as education. Research is facilitated by a good card catalog, a competent staff, and copying facilities. In addition to newspapers contemporary with the period under study (1903–1923), I made use of later articles in *El Nacional* (1945) and *La Prensa* (Mexico City, 1932) that were either memoirs of *revoltosos* or reliable secondary accounts. Other newspapers used in this way at the Hemeroteca included *El Demócrata* (1924), *Excélsior* (1942), and *El Universal* (1938).

The most important newspaper for the period was, of course, *Regeneración*, copies of which can be found in the Hemeroteca. A large number of English translations were collected by Ambassador Thompson and appended to his despatches to the State Department (see Numerical Files). The best collection of excerpts in published form is Armando Bartra, *Regeneración*. Another collection is Ricardo Flores Magón, *¿Para qué sirve la autoridad? y otros cuentos*. *Revolución*, the 1907 edition published in Los Angeles, is available in the Terrazas Collection of the Bancroft Library.

Two articles by José C. Valadés appeared in newspapers in the United States in the 1930s. The first was a lengthy essay about Villarreal published in 1935 and 1936 by *La Prensa* (San Antonio, Texas); the second, entitled "Siguiendo la pista a políticos mexicanos," appeared in nine parts in *La Opinión* (Los Angeles). Both are valuable and rare items. *La Prensa* is on microfilm at the Eugene C. Barker Texas History Center, University of Texas at Austin; *La Opinión* can be found in the general library at the University of California at Berkeley.

Because St. Louis was a central operating zone for the PLM during 1905 and 1906, the St. Louis newspapers are an important source of information for this dimension of *revoltoso* history. Most helpful were the following newspapers housed at the office of the Missouri Historical Society in Columbia, Missouri: *St. Louis Globe-Democrat*, 1905–1906; *St. Louis Labor*, 1906; *St. Louis Post-Dispatch*, 1905–1907; *St. Louis Republic*, 1906.

Many border newspapers, often attached as clippings to official correspondence, were important for this study. Most of these clippings were found in either the Foreign Relations Archive in Mexico or the State Department materials of the National Archives. These newspapers included the *Arizona Daily Star, Arizona Republican*

(Phoenix), *The Border* (Tucson), *Douglas Examiner, El Paso Herald, El Paso (Daily) Times, San Antonio Daily Express, San Antonio Daily Gazette, San Antonio Daily Light,* and the *Tucson Daily Citizen.* In addition, the Sherman Foundation possesses a microfilm roll of the *Calexico Daily Chronicle* for 1911, and the Bancroft Library's Terrazas Collection contains excerpts from *La Reforma Social* (El Paso) for 1907 and *El Correo Mexicano* (Los Angeles) for 1907.

The most important other newspaper, for its general coverage, was the *New York Times.*

All of the newspapers used in researching this study are listed in the directory.

Pictorial

The Casasola collection of photographs is one of the best for the Mexican Revolutionary era. The original collection was first published in 1921 by Agustín Víctor Casasola. His work was continued by his son, Gustavo Casasola, who published a new, expanded edition in the 1960s. A rather unusual production, the published collection is entitled *Historia gráfica de la Revolución Mexicana, 1900–1960,* (Mexico: Editorial F. Trillas, 1960–1970). The work is a photographic history of the Revolution that integrates a wealth of photographs with an explanatory text.

For Cananea and the *magonistas,* three other published works are worth noting. First, Cornelius C. Smith, Jr., has reproduced several photographs of Kosterlitzky and the Cananea strike in his *Emilio Kosterlitzky: Eagle of Sonora and the Southwest Border.* Second, John Kenneth Turner's *Barbarous Mexico* contains several photographs of key *magonistas,* including their American comrades. Finally, for photographs of *magonistas* not available elsewhere in published form see the front section of Armando Bartra's *Regeneración.*

There are several photographic collections in the United States containing Mexican Revolutionary materials. Best for the Cananea strike is the Joseph S. Bordwell Collection in the Riverside Municipal Museum at Riverside, California. The Cananea Company files in Tucson also contain several photographs of the strike, as does the Arizona Historical Society in Tucson. One of the largest collections in the Southwest is the Otis Aultman Collection, located in the El Paso Public Library. Here one can find photographs relating to a variety of *revoltoso* activities, especially during the Madero phase of the Revolution. For Otis Aultman's photographs of the Mexican Revolution, see Mary Sarber's *Photographs from the Border* (El Paso Public Library, 1977), plates 57–100. The Library of Congress in Washington, D.C., also has a file of *maderista* materials. Although the National Archives collection was somewhat disappointing, it does have a few photographs of Mexican insurgents and *rurales* along the border, as well as an excellent collection of Mexican Army maneuvers in 1901. The Terrazas Collection at Berkeley includes a photo portfolio that has photographs of *magonistas*. These were evidently obtained by Governor Enrique C. Creel in 1906. Finally, and not surprisingly, the U.S. Bureau of Prisons has "mug" shots of all *magonistas* who did time at Leavenworth.

NOTE: Archival materials cited are discussed in the bibliographical essay and listed in "Abbreviations in Archival Citations."

Select Directory of Published Materials Cited

Abad de Santillán, Diego. *Ricardo Flores Magón, el Apóstol de la Revolución Social Mexicana.* Mexico City: Grupo Cultural "Ricardo Flores Magón," 1925.

Aguirre, Manuel J. *Cananea: Las garras del imperialismo en las entrañas de México.* Mexico City: Libro Mex Editores, 1958.

Albro, Ward Sloan. "El secuestro de Manuel Sarabia." *Historia Mexicana* 18 (January–March 1969): 400–407.

————. "Ricardo Flores Magón and the Liberal Party: An Inquiry into the Origins of the Mexican Revolution of 1910." Ph.D. dissertation, University of Arizona, 1967.

Almada, Francisco R. *La revolución en el estado de Chihuahua.* 2 vols. Chihuahua City: Instituto Nacional de Estudios Históricos de la Revolución Mexicana, 1964.

Alperovich, M. S., and Rudenko, B. T. *La Revolución Mexicana de 1910–17 y la política de los Estados Unidos.* Mexico City: Ediciones de Cultura Popular, 1976.

Anderson, Rodney D. *Outcasts in Their Own Land: Mexican Industrial Workers, 1906–1911.* Dekalb: Northern Illinois University Press, 1976.

————. "Mexican Workers and the Politics of Revolution." *Hispanic American Historical Review* 54 (February 1974): 94–113.

Archivo de Francisco I. Madero. 3 vols. Mexico City: Secretaría de Hacienda, 1960, 1963, 1966.

Arellano Z., Manuel. *Huelga de Cananea, 1906.* Mexico City: PRI, 1976.

Arizona Daily Star (Tucson), 1906, 1909.

The Arizona Republican (Phoenix), 1906.

Arzubide, Germán List. *Madero: El México de 1910.* Mexico City: Federación Editorial Mexicana, 1973.

Axelrod, Bernard. "St. Louis and the Mexican Revolutionaries, 1905–1906." *The Bulletin of the Missouri Historical Society* 28 (January 1972): 94–108.

Barrera Fuentes, Florencio. *Historia de la revolución mexicana: La etapa precursora*. 2d ed. Mexico City: Talleres Gráficos de la Nación, 1970.

Bartra, Armando, ed. and comp. *Regeneración, 1900–1918*. Mexico City: HADISE, S.A., 1972.

———. "Ricardo Flores Magón en el cincuentenario de su muerte." Suplemento de *Siempre!*, no. 565 (6 December, 1972): ii–viii.

Beezley, William H. *Insurgent Governor: Abraham González and the Mexican Revolution in Chihuahua*. Lincoln: University of Nebraska Press, 1973.

Berbusse, Edward J. "Neutrality-Diplomacy of the United States and Mexico, 1910–1911." *The Americas* 12 (1956): 265–283.

Bernstein, Marvin D. "Colonel William C. Greene and the Cananea Copper Bubble." *Bulletin of the Business Hisorical Society* 26 (December 1952): 179–198.

———. *The Mexican Mining Industry, 1890–1950*. Albany: State University of New York, 1965.

Bevans, Charles I., comp. *Treaties and Other International Agreements of the United States of America*. 12 vols. Washington, D.C.: Government Printing Office, 1968–1974.

Blaisdell, Lowell L. *The Desert Revolution: Baja California, 1911*. Madison: University of Wisconsin Press, 1962.

———. "Was It Revolution or Filibustering? The Mystery of the Flores Magón Revolt in Baja California." *Pacific Historical Review* 23 (May 1954): 147–164.

Blasier, Cole. *The Hovering Giant: U.S. Responses to Revolutionary Change in Latin America*. Pittsburgh: University of Pittsburgh Press, 1976.

Bogardus, Emory Stephen. *Immigration and Race Attitudes*. Boston: D. C. Heath and Co., 1928.

Bonine, Michael E., et al. *Atlas of Mexico*. Austin: Bureau of Business Research, University of Texas, 1970.

The Border (Tucson), 1908–1909.

Bowen, Walter S., and Neal, Harry Edward. *The United States Secret Service*. Philadelphia and New York: Chilton Co., 1960.

Brandenburg, Broughton. "The War Peril on the Mexican Border." *Harper's Weekly* 50 (25 August 1906): 1198–1200, 1217.

Brayer, Herbert O. "The Cananea Incident." *New Mexico Historical Review* 3 (October 1938): 387–415:

Brenner, Anita. *The Wind That Swept Mexico: The History of the Mexican Revolution of 1910–1942*. Austin: University of Texas Press, 1971.

Brissenden, Paul F. "The Launching of the Industrial Workers of the World." In *University of California Publications in Economics* 4 (1913), pp. 1–82. Berkeley: University of California Press, 1966.

Brophy, A. Blake. *Foundlings on the Frontier: Racial and Religious Conflict in Arizona Territory, 1904–1905.* Tucson: University of Arizona Press, 1972.

Brown, Lyle C. "The Mexican Liberals and Their Struggle against the Díaz Dictatorship, 1900–1906." In *Antología MCC.* Mexico City: Mexico City College Press, 1956.

Bryan, Anthony T. "Mexican Politics in Transition, 1900–1913: The Role of General Bernardo Reyes." Ph.D. dissertation, University of Nebraska, 1970.

Bush, I. J. *Gringo Doctor.* Caldwell, Idaho: The Caxton Printers, 1939.

Butterfield, Dolores. "The Situation in Mexico." *The North American Review* 196 (November 1912): 649–664.

Cabral, João Batista P. *O Partido Liberal Mexicano e a greve de Cananea: Breve estudo de um movimento precursor da Revolução Mexicana de 1910.* Brasília: Fundação Universidade Brasília, 1974.

Cadenhead, Ivie E., Jr. "The American Socialists and the Mexican Revolution of 1910." *Southwestern Social Science Quarterly* 43 (September 1962): 103–117.

———. "Flores Magón y el periodico The Appeal to Reason." *Historia Mexicana* 3 (1963): 88–93.

Calderón, Esteban B. *Juicio sobre la guerra del Yaqui y génesis de la huelga de Cananea.* Mexico City: Centro de Estudios Históricos del Movimiento Obrero Mexicano, 1975.

Calexico Daily Chronicle, 1911.

Calvert, Peter. *The Mexican Revolution, 1910–1914: The Diplomacy of Anglo-American Conflict.* Cambridge: Cambridge University Press, 1968.

Carman, Michael Dennis. "United States Customs and the Madero Revolution." Master's thesis, San Diego State University, 1974.

Carr, Barry. *El movimiento obrero y la política en México, 1910–1929.* 2 vols. Mexico City: Secretaría de Educación Pública (SepSetentas), 1976.

———. *The Pecularities of the Mexican North, 1880–1928: An Essay in Interpretation.* Occasional Papers No. 4. Glasgow: University of Glasgow, 1971.

Carrillo, Alejandro. "Una historia de amistad Yanqui-Mexicana." In *Antonio Villarreal: Vida de un gran Mexicano,* by Fortunato Lozana. Monterrey: Talleres de Impresora Monterrey, S.A., 1959.

Casasola, Gustavo. *Historia gráfica de la Revolución Mexicana, 1900–1960.* Mexico City: Editorial F. Trillas, 1960–1970.

Casillas, Mike. "The Cananea Strike of 1906." *Southwest Economy and Society* 3 (Winter 1977/1978): 18–32.

Ceceña, José Luis. *México en la órbita imperial.* Mexico City: Ediciones "El Caballito," 1975.

Challener, Richard D. *Admirals, Generals, and American Foreign Policy, 1898–1914.* Princeton: Princeton University Press, 1973.

Chaplin, Ralph. *Wobbly: The Rough-and-Tumble Story of an American Radical.* Chicago: University of Chicago Press, 1948.

Chisholm, Joe. *Brewery Gulch.* San Antonio: The Naylor Co., 1949.

Claghorn, Kate Holladay. *The Immigrant's Day in Court.* New York: Arno Press and the New York Times, 1969.

Clark, Victor S. "Mexican Labor in the United States." In *Bulletin of the Bureau of Labor* 17 (1908): 466–522. Washington: Government Printing Office, 1909.

———. "Social Conditions of Mexicans in the United States in 1908." In *An Awakened Minority*, edited by Manual P. Servín. Beverly Hills: Glencoe Press, 1974.

Clendenen, Clarence C. *Blood on the Border: The United States Army and the Mexican Irregulars.* New York: The Macmillan Co., 1969.

Cockcroft, James D. *Intellectual Precursors of the Mexican Revolution, 1900–1913.* Austin: University of Texas Press, 1968.

Conley, Edward M. "The Anti-Foreign Uprising in Mexico." *The World Today* 11 (October 1906): 1059–1062.

———. "The Rival of Panama: Sir Weetman Pearson's New Isthmian Railway." *The World's Work and Play* 8 (July 1906): 188–191.

Cordova, Arnaldo. *La ideología de la Revolución Mexicana: La formación del nuevo regimen.* Mexico City: Ediciones Era, 1975.

El Correro Mexicano. (Los Angeles), 1907.

Cosío Villegas, Daniel. *El Porfiriato: La vida política exterior.* 2 vols. Vols. 5 and 6 of *Historia moderna de México*, edited by Daniel Cosío Villegas. Mexico City: Editorial Hermes, 1960, 1963.

Crawford, Stephen C. "El Partido Liberal Mexicano y la huelga de Cananea." *Latinoamérica* (1972): 139–164.

Cubley, Clark A., and Steiner, Joseph A. "Emilio Kosterlitzky." *Arizoniana* 1 (Winter 1960): 12–14.

Cué Cánovas, Agustín. "El movimiento flores-magonista en Baja California." In *Memoria del Primer Congreso de Historia Regional*, pp. 741–755. Mexicali: Gobierno del estado de Baja California, Dirección General de Acción Cívica y Cultural, 1958.

Cumberland, Charles C. "Border Raids in the Lower Rio Grande Valley—1915." *Southwestern Historical Quarterly* 57 (October 1953): 285–311.

———. *Mexican Revolution: The Constitutionalist Years.* Austin: University of Texas Press, 1972.

———. *Mexican Revolution: Genesis Under Madero.* Austin: University of Texas Press, 1952.

———. "Mexican Revolutionary Movements from Texas, 1906–1912." *Southwestern Historical Quarterly* 52 (January 1949): 301–324.

──────. "Precursors of the Mexican Revolution." *Hispanic American Historical Review* 22 (May 1942): 344–356.

Curtis, Ray Emerson. "The Law of Hostile Military Expeditions as Applied by the United States." *American Journal of International Law* 8 (January and April 1914): 1–36 and 224–255.

Dambourges Jacques, Leo M. "The Anti-Chinese Campaigns in Sonora, 1900–1931." Ph.D. dissertation, University of Arizona, 1974.

Daniels, Roger. *The Politics of Prejudice: The Anti-Japanese Movement in California and the Struggle for Japanese Exclusion.* New York: Atheneum, 1968.

──────. *Racism and Immigration Restriction.* St. Charles, Mo.: Forum Press, 1974.

Deeds, Susan M. "José María Maytorena and the Mexican Revolution in Sonora." *Arizona and the West* 18 (Spring/Summer 1976): 21–40 & 125–148.

El Demócrata (Mexico City), 1924.

Díaz Cárdenas, León. *Cananea: Primer brote del sindicalismo en México.* Mexico City: Biblioteca del Obrero y Campesino, 1937; CEHSMO, 1976.

Díaz Soto y Gama, Antonio. "Valores morales de la Revolución: Santiago de la Hoz, Práxedis Guerrero." *El Universal* (Mexico City), 31 August, 1938, pp. 3, 10.

Donham, Ralph A. "Buckaroo of Wall Street." *Arizona Days and Ways Magazine* (24 November 1957): 42, 44–46.

Douglas Examiner, 1907.

El Paso Herald, 1906.

El Paso (Daily) *Times*, 1906, 1911.

Evening Observer (Dunkirk, N.Y.), 1901.

Evening Star (Washington, D.C.), 1902.

Excélsior (Mexico City), 1942 and 1956.

Fabela, Isidro, ed. *Documentos históricos de la Revolución Mexicana.* 27 vols. Mexico City: Fondo de Cultura Económica and Editorial Jus, 1960–1973.

Fain, Tyrus G., ed. *The Intelligence Community: History, Organization and Issues.* Public Documents Series. Ann Arbor: R. R. Bowker Company, 1977.

Ferrua, Pietro. *Gli annarchici nella rivoluzione messicana: Praxedis G. Guerrero.* Ragusa: Edizioni La Fiaccola, 1976.

──────. "Ricardo Flores Magón en la Revolución Mexicana." *Regeneracion* 2 (1972): 14–19.

──────. "Ricardo Flores Magón en la Revolución Mexicana." *Reconstruir*, nos. 72 and 73 (May–June 1971; July–August 1971): 40–47, 31–39, respectively.

──────. "Sources of Study on the Mexican Revolution, II: The Archives of the U.S. District Court of Southern California." *Bulletin Centre International de Recherches sur l'Anarchisme* 31 (n.d.): 7–11.

Fetherling, Dale. *Mother Jones: The Miners' Angel.* Carbondale and Edwardsville: Southern Illinois University Press, 1974.

Flores Magón, Ricardo. *Epistolario revolucionario e íntimo.* Mexico City: Ediciones Antorcha, 1975.

——. *¿Para que sirve la autoridad? y otros cuentos.* Mexico City: Ediciones Antorcha, 1976. Includes essays from earlier publications: *Sembrando ideas* (1923) and *Rayos de luz* (1924).

——. *Semilla libertaria.* 2 vols. Mexico City: Grupo Cultural "Ricardo Flores Magón," 1923.

——, and Flores Magón, Jesús. *Batalla a la dictadura.* Mexico City: Empresas Editoriales, S.A., 1948.

Foner, Philip S. *History of the Labor Movement in the United States.* 4 vols. New York: International Publishers, 1947, 1955, 1964, 1965.

The Founding Convention of the IWW: Proceedings. New York: Merit Publishers, 1969.

Furlong, Thomas. *Fifty Years A Detective.* St. Louis: C. E. Barnett, 1912.

Gamio, Manuel. *The Mexican Immigrant: His Life-Story.* Chicago: University of Chicago Press, 1931.

——. *Mexican Immigration to the United States.* Chicago: University of Chicago Press, 1930.

García, Rubén. "La llamada expedición filibustera en Baja California." In *Memoria del Primer Congreso de Historia Regional,* pp. 665–686. Mexicali: Gobierno del estado de Baja California, Dirección General de Acción Cívica y Cultural, 1958.

García Cantú, Gastón. *Las invasiones nortemericanas en México.* Mexico City: Ediciones Era, S.A., 1971.

Garis, Roy L. *Immigration Restriction: A Study of the Opposition to and Regulation of Immigration into the United States.* New York: The Macmillan Co., 1927.

Geiger, Louis G. *Joseph W. Folk of Missouri.* The University of Missouri Studies, vol. 25, no. 2. Columbia, Mo.: University of Missouri, 1953.

Gerhard, Peter.. "The Socialist Invasion of Baja California, 1911." *Pacific Historical Review* 15 (September 1946): 295–304.

Gerlach, Allen. "Conditions Along the Border—1915: The Plan of San Diego." *New Mexico Historical Review* 43 (July 1968): 195–212.

Gilderhus, Mark T. *Diplomacy and Revolution: U.S.-Mexican Relations under Wilson and Carranza.* Tucson: University of Arizona Press, 1977.

——. "Senator Albert B. Fall and 'The Plot Against Mexico.'" *New Mexico Historical Review* 48 (1973): 299–311.

Gill, Mario. "Teresa Urrea, la Santa de Cabora." *Historia Mexicana* 6 (April–June 1957): 226–244.

Ginger, Ray. *The Bending Cross: A Biography of Eugene Victor Debs.* New Brunswick, N.J.: Rutgers University Press, 1949.

Gómez-Quiñones, Juan. "Piedras contra la Luna, México en Aztlán y Aztlán en México: Chicano-Mexican Relations and the Mexican Consulates, 1900–1920." In *Contemporary Mexico: Papers of the IV International Congress of Mexican History,* edited by James Wilkie, Michael Meyer, and Edna Monzón de Wilkie, pp. 494–523. Berkeley and Mexico City: University of California Press and El Colegio de México, 1976.

————. "Plan de San Diego Reviewed." *Aztlán* 1 (Spring 1970): 124–132.

————. *Sembradores, Ricardo Flores Magón y el Partido Liberal Mexicano: A Eulogy and Critique.* Los Angeles: Aztlán Publications, University of California, 1973. (Spanish edition is *Las ideas políticas de Ricardo Flores Magón.* Mexico City: Ediciones Era, 1977.)

————, and Arroyo, Luis Leobardo. "On the State of Chicano History: Observations on Its Development, Interpretations, and Theory, 1970–1974." *Western Historical Quarterly* 7 (April 1976): 155–185.

González Monroy, Jesús. *Ricardo Flores Magón y su actitud en la Baja California.* Mexico City: Editorial Academia Literaria, 1962.

González Navarro Moisés. *La colonización en México, 1877–1910.* Mexico City: Talleres de Impresión de Estampillas y Valores, 1960.

————. *Las huelgas textiles en el Porfiriato.* Puebla: Editorial José M. Cajica, Jr., S.A., 1970.

————. *El Porfiriato: La vida social.* Vol. 4 of *Historia Moderna de Mexico,* edited by Daniel Cosío Villegas. Mexico City: Editorial Hermes, 1957.

González Ramírez, Manuel. *Epistolario y textos de Ricardos Flores Magón.* Mexico City: Fondo de Cultura Económica, 1973.

————. *La revolución social de México.* 3 vols. Mexico City: Fondo de Cultura Económica, 1960–1966.

————, ed. and comp. *Fuentes para la historia de la Revolución Mexicana.* 4 vols. Mexico City: Fondo de Cultura Económica, 1954–1957; 2d ed., 1974.

"Greene-Cananea." *The Engineering and Mining Journal* 82 (22 December, 1906): 1179, 1183.

"The Greene Consolidated Copper Mine." *The Engineering and Mining Journal* 75 (14 March, 1903) 415–416.

Grew, Joseph C. *Turbulent Era: A Diplomatic Record of Forty Years, 1904–1945.* Boston: Houghton Mifflin Co., 1952.

Grieb, Kenneth J. "Standard Oil and the Financing of the Mexican Revolution." *California Historical Society Quarterly* 50 (1971): 59–71.

Griswold del Castillo, Richard. "The Mexican Revolution and the Spanish-Language Press in the Borderlands." *Journalism History* 4 (Summer 1977): 42–47.

Guerrero, Práxedis G. *Artículos de combate*. Mexico City: Ediciones Antorcha, 1977.

Gutiérrez de Lara, Lázaro, and Pinchon, Edgcumb. *The Mexican People: Their Struggle for Freedom*. Garden City: Doubleday, Page and Co., 1914.

Hackworth, Green Haywood. *Digest of International Law*. 8 vols. Washington, D.C.: Government Printing Office, 1940–1944.

Haley, P. Edward. *Revolution and Intervention: The Diplomacy of Taft and Wilson with Mexico, 1910–1917*. Cambridge, Mass.: The MIT Press, 1970.

Hanrahan, Gene Z. *Documents on the Mexican Revolution*. 2 vols., 4 pts. Salisbury, N.C.: Documentary Publications, 1976.

Harris, Charles H., III, and Sadler, Louis R. "The Plan of San Diego and the Mexican-United States War Crisis of 1916: A Reexamination." *Hispanic American Historical Review* 58 (August 1978): 381–408.

———. "El Paso, 1912, in the Mexican Revolution." Paper read at the American Historical Association, December 1978, at San Francisco, California. Mimeographed.

Hart, John M. *Anarchism and the Mexican Working Class, 1860–1931*. Austin: University of Texas Press, 1978.

Henderson, Peter V. N. "Mexican Rebels in the Borderlands, 1910–1912." *Red River Valley Historical Review* 2 (Summer 1975): 207–219.

Herner, Charles. *The Arizona Rough Riders*. Tucson: University of Arizona Press, 1970.

Hill, Larry D. *Emissaries to a Revolution: Woodrow Wilson's Executive Agents in Mexico*. Baton Rouge: LSU Press, 1973.

Hu-Dehart, Evelyn. "Pacification of the Yaquis in the Late *Porfiriato*: Development and Implications." *Hispanic American Historical Review* 54 (February 1974): 72–93.

Hulen, Bertram D. *Inside the Department of State*. New York: McGraw-Hill Co., 1939.

Huntington, Samuel P. *Political Order in Changing Societies*. New Haven: Yale University Press, 1968.

Huntington-Wilson, Francis M. "The American Foreign Service." *The Outlook* 82 (January-April 1906): 499–504.

———. *Memoirs of an Ex-Diplomat*. Boston: Bruce Humphries, Inc., 1945.

Ireland, Robert E. "The Radical Community, Mexican and American Radicalism, 1900–1910." *Journal of Mexican-American History* 2 (December 1973): 22–32.

Jensen, Vernon H. *Heritage of Conflict: Labor Relations in the Nonferrous Metals Industry up to 1930*. New York: Greenwood Press, 1968.

Jessup, Philip C. *Elihu Root*. 2 vols. New York: Archon Books. 1964.

Johnson, William Weber. *Heroic Mexico: The Violent Emergence of a Modern Nation*. Garden City: Doubleday and Co., 1968.

Jones, Chester Lloyd. *The Consular Service of the United States: Its History and Activities*. Philadelphia: John C. Winston Co., 1906.

Jones, Edward T., ed. *Notable American Women, 1607–1950*. Cambridge, Mass.: The Beknap Press of Harvard University Press, 1971.

Jones, Mary (Mother). *The Autobiography of Mother Jones*. 2nd ed. Chicago: Charles H. Kerr and Co., 1972.

Kahler, Hugh MacNair. "Current Misconceptions of Trade with Latin-America." *Annals of the American Academy of Political and Social Science* (May 1911): 628–637.

Kaplan, Samuel. *Peleamos contra la injusticia. Enrique Flores Magón, precursor de la Revolución Mexicana, cuenta su historia a Samuel Kaplan*. 2 vols. Mexico City: Libro Mex Editores, 1960.

Katz, Friedrich. "Pancho Villa and the Attack on Columbus, New Mexico." *American Historical Review* 83 (February 1978): 101–130.

Kerig, Dorothy Pierson. "A United States Consul on the Border during the Mexican Revolution: The Case of Luther T. Ellsworth." Master's thesis, San Diego State University, 1974.

Konvitz, Milton R. *Civil Rights in Immigration*. Ithaca, N.Y.: Cornell University Press, 1953.

Landa y Piña, Andrés. *El servicio de migración en México*. Mexico City: Secretaría de Gobernación, 1930.

Langeluttig, Albert. *The Department of Justice of the United States*. Baltimore: Johns Hopkins Press, 1927.

Larralde, Carlos. *Mexican-American: Movements and Leaders*. Los Alamitos, Calif.: Hwong Publishing Co., 1976.

Levenstein, Harvey A. *Labor Organizations in the United States and Mexico: A History*. Westport, Conn.: Greenwood Press, 1971.

The Lincoln Star (Lincoln, Nebraska), 1950, 1956.

Lister, Florence C., and Lister, Robert H. *Chihuahua: Storehouse of Storms*. Albuquerque: University of New Mexico Press, 1966.

London, Jack. "The Mexican." In *The Bodley Head Jack London*, edited by Arthur Calder-Marshall. London: The Bodley Head, 1963.

Loomis, Francis B. "The Foreign Service of the United States." *North American Review* 169 (July–December 1899): 349–361.

Los Angeles Daily Times, 1907.

Lozano, Fortunato. *Antonio I. Villarreal. Vida de un Gran Mexicano*. Monterrey: Talleres de Impresora Monterrey, S.A., 1959.

Lubow, Sylvia. "The Espionage Act in Southern California." Master's thesis, University of California at Los Angeles, 1968.

Luna, Jesús. *La carrera pública de don Ramón Corral*. Mexico City: Secretaría de Educación Publica (SepSetentas), 1975.

Madero, Francisco Indalecio (Ignacio?). *Archivo de Francisco I. Madero.* 3 vols. Mexico City: Secretaría de Hacienda, 1960, 1963, 1966.

Mallen, Francisco. *Atentados contra la vida del cónsul mexicano en El Paso, Texas.* Mexico City: Tip. Mariano Lara, 1909.

Martínez, Pablo L. *A History of Lower California.* Translated by Ethel Duffy Turner. Mexico City: Editorial Baja California, 1960.

———. *El magonismo en Baja California (Documentos).* Mexico City: Editorial "Baja California," 1958.

Martínez Báez, Antonio. "Sarabia en San Juan de Ulúa." *Historia Mexicana* 10 (October–December 1960): 342–360.

Martínez Núñez, Eugenio. *La vida heroica de Práxedis G. Guerrero.* Mexico City: Impreso en los Talleres Gráficos de la Nación, 1960.

Medina Hoyos, Francisco. *Cananea: Cuna de la Revolución Mexicana.* Mexico City: [n.p.], 1956.

Mendieta Alatorre, María de los Angeles. "Galería de mujeres mexicanas en la revolución." *Revista de la Universidad de México* 28 (1973): 15–21.

———. *La mujer en la Revolución Mexicana.* Mexico City: Talleres Gráficos de la Nación, 1961.

Mendoza, Vicente T., comp. *El corrido mexicano.* Mexico City: Fondo de Cultura Económica, 1974.

The Mexican Herald (Mexico City), 1908.

Mexico. *Diario Oficial,* 1906.

———. Secretaría de Gobernación. "Informe del Señor Gobernador de Sonora relativo a los disturbios ocurridos en Cananea." *Memoria,* 1 December, 1904–30 June, 1906. Docs. no. 17 and 18, pp. 45–50. Mexico City: Imprenta del Gobierno Federal, 1909.

———. Secretaría de Guerra y Marina. *Memoria,* July 1906–July 1908. Mexico City: Talleres del Departmento de Estado Mayor, 1909.

———. Secretaría de Guerra y Marina. *Campaña de 1910 a 1911.* Mexico City: Talleres de Departamento de Estado Mayor, 1913.

———. Secretaría de Relaciones Exteriores. *Labor internacional de la Revolución Constitucionalista de México.* Mexico City: Imprenta de la Secretaría de Gobernación, 1918.

"Mexico." *The Engineering and Mining Journal* 81 (14 April, 1906): 731.

México y los Estados Unidos: Opiniones de intelectuales distinguidos y de los periódicos mas serios acerca de los ultimos acontecimientos. Mexico City: Talleres Linotipográficos de "Revista de Revistas," 1916.

Meyer, Michael C. *Huerta: A Political Portrait.* Lincoln: University of Nebraska Press, 1972.

———. *Mexican Rebel: Pascual Orozco and the Mexican Revolution, 1910–1915.* Lincoln: University of Nebraska Press, 1967.

Mignone, A. Frederick. "A Fief for Mexico. Colonel Greene's Empire Ends." *Southwest Review* 44 (Autumn 1959) 332–339.

Mijares, Aureliano J., comp. *Por la libertad de Ricardo Flores Magón y compañeros presos en los Estados Unidos del Norte.* Mexico City: newspapers of W.F.M., 1922.

The Miners Magazine (Denver, Col.), October 1906–December 1911.

Minger, Ralph Eldin. *William Howard Taft and United States Foreign Policy: The Apprenticeship Years, 1900–1918.* Chicago: University of Illinois Press, 1975.

"The Mining Riot in Mexico." *The American Monthly Review of Reviews* 34 (July 1906): 17.

Mock, James R., and Larson, Cedric. *Words That Won the War! The Story of The Committee on Public Information, 1917–1919.* Princeton: Princeton University Press, 1939.

Moore, John Bassett. *A Digest of International Law.* 8 vols. Washington, D.C.: Government Printing Office, 1906.

Morales, Vicente, and Caballero, Manuel. *El Señor Root en México.* Mexico City: Talleres de "Arte y Letras," 1908.

Morison, Elting E., ed. and comp. *The Letters of Theodore Roosevelt.* 8 vols. Cambridge, Mass.: Harvard University Press, 1948–1954.

Mounce, Virginia Ann Newton. "Mexican Women during the Porfiriato, 1877–1911: An Essay and Annotated Bibliography." Master's thesis, University of Texas at Austin, 1975.

Mowry, George E. *The Era of Theodore Roosevelt and the Birth of Modern America, 1900–1912.* New York: Harper and Row, 1958.

Murray, John. "Cases of Mexicans Persecuted by United States Officials." *Congressional Record* 45 (1910): 5137.

———. "San Juan de Ulua, the Private Prison of Diaz." *The Border* 1 (February 1909): 1–5.

Murray, Robert K. *Red Scare: A Study in National Hysteria, 1919–1920.* Minneapolis: University of Minnesota Press, 1955.

Myers, Ellen Howell. "The Mexican Liberal Party, 1903–1910." Ph.D. dissertation, University of Virginia, 1970.

Myers, John Myers. *The Border Wardens.* Englewood Cliffs, N.J.: Prentice-Hall, 1971.

El Nacional (Mexico City), 1933, 1945–1946, 1955.

Neal, Joe West. "The Policy of the United States toward Immigration from Mexico." Master's thesis, University of Texas at Austin, 1941.

Nebraska State Journal (Lincoln), 1901, 1942.

Nelson, C. Nelson. "The Sahuaripa District, Sonora, Mexico." *The Engineering and Mining Journal* 82 (6 October 1906): 629–631.

New York Daily Tribune, 1911.

New York Herald, 1906.

The New York Times, 1905–1906, 1908, 1922.

La Opinión (Los Angeles), 1939.

Overstreet, Harry, and Overstreet, Bonaro. *The FBI in Our Open Society.* New York: W. W. Norton and Co., 1969.

Pace, Anne. "Mexican Refugees in Arizona, 1910–1911." *Arizona and the West* 16 (1974): 5–18.

Park, Joseph F. "The History of Mexican Labor in Arizona during the Territorial Period." Master's thesis, University of Arizona, 1961.

Perkins, Clifford Alan. *Border Patrol: With the U.S. Immigration Service on the Mexican Boundary 1910–54*. El Paso: Texas Western Press, 1978.

Pletcher, David M. "The Development of Railroads in Sonora." *Inter-American Economic Affairs* 1 (1948): 3–45.

———. *Rails, Mines, and Progress: Seven American Promoters in Mexico, 1867–1911*. Ithaca, N.Y.: Cornell University Press, 1958.

Pollares, Enrique Lombera. "La huelga de Cananea." *Historia Mexicana* 9 (1958): 446–447.

El Popular (Mexico City), 1942.

Powe, Marc B. *The Emergence of the War Department Intelligence Agency: 1885–1918*. Manhattan, Kans.: Military Affairs, 1975.

La Prensa (Mexico City), 1932.

La Prensa (San Antonio), 1935–1936, 1938.

Preston, William, Jr. *Aliens and Dissenters: Federal Suppression of Radicals, 1903–1933*. New York: Harper and Row, 1963.

Putnam, Frank Bishop. "Teresa Urrea, 'The Saint of Cabora.'" *The Historical Society of Southern California* (September 1963): 245–264.

Quirk, Robert E. *An Affair of Honor: Woodrow Wilson and the Occupation of Veracruz*. Lexington: University of Kentucky Press, 1962.

Raat, William Dirk. "The Diplomacy of Suppression: Los Revoltosos, Mexico, and the United States, 1906–1911." *Hispanic American Historical Review* 56 (November 1976): 529–550.

———. "Ideas and Society in Don Porfirio's Mexico." *The Americas* 30 (July 1973): 32–53.

———. *El positivismo durante el Porfiriato*. Mexico City: Secretaría de Educación Pública (SepSetentas), 1975.

Ramos Pedrueza, Rafael. "Semblanzas Revolucionarios: Librado Rivera; Anselmo S. Figueroa; Práxedis Guerrero." *El Popular* (Mexico City), 4 and 18 May and 1 June 1942.

Rascón, María Antonieta. "La mujer mexicano como hecho político: La precursora, la militante." *La cultura en Mexico*, suplemento de *Siempre!* 569 (3 January 1973): ix–xii.

Rathbun, Carl M. "Keeping the Peace along the Mexican Border." *Harper's Weekly* 50 (17 November 1906): 1632–1634, 1649.

La Reforma Social (El Paso), 1907.

Regeneración (San Antonio; St. Louis), 1904–1906.

Report of Proceedings of the Twenty-Eighth Annual Convention of the American Federation of Labor. Held at Denver Colorado, 9–21 November 1908. Washington, D.C.: The National Tribune Co., 1908.

Revolución (Los Angeles), 1907.

Ríos, Plácido. "Testimonios." In *Huelga de Cananea, 1906*, by Manual Arellano Z.,pp. 19–35. Mexico City: PRI, 1976.

"The Riots at Cananea." *The Engineering and Mining Journal* 81 (9 June 1906): 1099–1100.

Rivera, Antonio G. *La revolución en Sonora.* Mexico City: Imprenta Arana 1969.

Roberts, Donald Frank. "Mining and Modernization: The Mexican Border States during the Porfiriato, 1876–1911." Ph.D. dissertation, University of Pittsburgh, 1974.

Romeo Flores, Jesús. "Maestros y amigos. Esteban B. Calderón: Precursor de la Revolución, maestro de escuela y constituyente." *El Nacional* (Mexico City), 11 October 1955, pp. 11, 19.

Roosevelt, Theodore. (See Morison, Elting E.)

Ruiz, Ramón Eduardo. *Labor and the Ambivalent Revolutionaries: Mexico, 1911–1923.* Baltimore, Md.: Johns Hopkins University Press, 1976.

Rynning, Thomas H. *Gun Notches: The Life Story of a Cowboy-Soldier. As Told to Al Cohn and Joe Chisholm.* New York: Frederick A. Stokes Co., 1931.

St. Louis Globe-Democrat, 1905–1906.

St. Louis Labor, 1906.

St. Louis Post Dispatch, 1905–1906.

St. Louis Republic, 1906.

San Antonio Daily Express, 1907, 1909.

San Antonio Daily Gazette, 1906–1907.

San Antonio Daily Light, 1907.

Sandels, Robert. "Antecedentes de la revolución en Chihuahua." *Historia Mexicana* 24 (January–March 1975): 390–402.

Sands, William Franklin, and Lalley, Joseph M. *Our Jungle Diplomacy.* Chapel Hill: University of North Carolina Press, 1944.

San Francisco Chronicle, 1906.

Scholes, Walter V. "Los Estados Unidos, México y América Central en 1909." *Historia Mexicana* 10 (1961): 613–627.

———, and Scholes, Marie V. *The Foreign Policies of the Taft Administration.* Columbia, Mo.: University of Missouri Press, 1970.

Secrest, Louis James. "The End of the Porfiriato: The Collapse of the Díaz Government, 1910–1911." Ph.D. dissertation, University of New Mexico, 1970.

Shanks, Rosalie. "The I.W.W. Free Speech Movement in San Diego, 1912." *Journal of San Diego History* 19 (1973): 25–33.

Silva, José D., ed. *Plan de Ayala. Fuente de información de Revolución Mexicana.* Mexico City: n.p., 1957.

Sinclair, Mary Craig, comp. *The Parlor Provocateur, or, From Salon to*

Soap-Box: The Letters of Kate Crane Gartz. Pasadena, Calif.: Mary C. Sinclair, 1923.

Sklar, Martin J. "Woodrow Wilson and the Political Economy of Modern United States Liberalism." *Studies on the Left* 1 (1960): 17–47.

Smith, Cornelius C., Jr. *Emilio Kosterlitzky: Eagle of Sonora and the Southwest Border.* Glendale, Calif.: Arthur H. Clark Co., 1970.

Smith, Robert Freeman. *The United States and Revolutionary Nationalism in Mexico, 1916–1932.* Chicago: University of Chicago Press, 1972.

Sonnichsen, C. L. *Colonel Greene and the Copper Skyrocket.* Tucson: University of Arizona Press, 1974.

Stevens, Horace J., comp. *Mines Register and Copper Handbook: A Manual of the Copper Industry of the World.* Vols. 6 and 8. Houghton, Mich.: Horace J. Stevens, 1906, 1908. (1908 issue simply titled *The Copper Handbook.*)

Stimson, Grace H. *Rise of the Labor Movement in Los Angeles.* Berkeley: University of California Press, 1955.

Stratton, David H., ed. *The Memoirs of Albert F. Fall.* Southwestern Studies, vol. 4, no. 3, monograph no. 15. El Paso: Texas Western College, 1966.

Stuart, Graham H. *The Department of State: A History of its Organization, Procedure, and Personnel.* New York: Macmillan Co., 1949.

Tucson Daily Citizen, 1906, 1909.

Turner, Ethel Duffy. *Ricardo Flores Magón y el Partido Liberal Mexicano.* Morelia, Michoacán: Editorial "Erandi," 1960.

Turner, John Kenneth. *Barbarous Mexico.* Introduction by Sinclair Snow. Austin: University cf Texas Press, 1969.

Turner, Timothy G. *Bullets, Bottles and Gardenias.* Dallas: Southwest Press, 1935.

Ulloa, Berta. "Diplomacy in the Borderlands: An Analysis of Some Research Material and Opportunities in the Archivo de la Secretaría de Relaciones Exteriores de México, 1910–1920." Paper read at the Conference on the Borderlands, 26 October 1973, at San Antonio, Texas.

———. "Las relaciones Mexicano-Norteamericanas 1910–1911." *Historia Mexicana* 14 (July–September 1965): 25–46.

———. *La Revolución intervenida: Relaciones diplomáticas entre México y Estados Unidos (1910–1914).* Mexico City: El Colegio de México, 1971.

———. "Taft y los antimaderistas." In *Historia y sociedad en el mundo de habla española,* edited by Bernardo García Martínez, et al., pp. 319–328. Mexico City: El Colegio de México, 1970.

United States. Congress, House. Committee on Rules. *Providing for a Joint Committee to Investigate Alleged Persecutions of Mexican*

Citizens by the Government of Mexico: Hearing on H. Joint Res. 201, 61st Cong., 2d Sess., 8–14 June 1910.

———. ———. Debate on H. Res. 542. *Congressional Record*, 61st Cong., 2 Sess., 21 April 1910, 45, 5135–5138.

———. ———. Subcommittee of the Committee on Immigration and Naturalization. *Communist and Anarchist Deportation Cases*, 66th Cong., 2 Sess., 1920.

———. ———. Report on Aliens Deported and Principal Causes, 1910–1920. *Congressional Record*, 66th Cong., 2 Sess., 1920, 59, Appendix, 9280.

———. ———. Debate on Espionage Acts, War Laws, Political Prisoners, and the Case of Ricardo Flores Magón. *Congressional Record*, 67th Cong., 4 Sess., 11, 14, and 19 December 1922, 64, 298–300; 485–490; and 682–697.

———. Congress, Senate. Message to the Congress from President Theodore Roosevelt. *Transmission Through the Mails of Anarchistic Publications*, 60th Cong., 1 Sess., 1908, S. Doc. 426, 11 pp.

———. ———. Committee on Immigration. *Immigration and Crime: Reports of the Immigration Commission*, 61st Cong., 3 Sess., 1911.

———. ———. Subcommittee of the Committee on Foreign Relations. *Revolutions in Mexico: Hearing on S. 335*, 62d Cong., 2 Sess., 1913.

———. ———. *Brewing and Liquor Interests and German and Bolshevik Propaganda*, 66th Cong., 1 Sess., 1919, S. Doc. 62, 2 vols.

———. ———. Committee on Foreign Relations. *Investigation of Mexican Affairs: Hearing on S. 106*, 66th Cong., 2 Sess., 1920, S. Doc. 285, 2 vols.

———. ———. Committee on the Judiciary. *The Immigration and Naturalization Systems of the United States: Report No. 1515 Pursuant to S. 137*, 81st Cong., 2 Sess., 20 April 1950.

———. Department of Commerce. *Annual Report of the Commissioner-General of Immigration to the Secretary of Commerce and Labor*, 1906, 1907.

———. Department of Justice. *Preliminary Report of the Domestic Council Committee on Illegal Aliens*, December 1976.

———. Department of State. *Papers Relating to the Foreign Relations of the United States, 1905–1911, 1916*. Washington, D.C.: 1906, 1909–1910, 1912, 1914–15, 1918, 1925.

———. ———. *Papers Relating to the Foreign Relations of the United States: General Index, 1900–1918*. Washington, D.C.: 1941.

———. ———. *Register of the Department of State: September 15, 1906*. Washington, D.C.: 1916.

———. *Statutes at Large*, Vol. 32. An Act to regulate the immigration of aliens into the United States, 1903. pp. 1213–1222.

El Universal (Mexico City), 1938, 1955.

Valadés, José C. "Apuntes sobre la expedición de Baja California." In *Memoria del Primer Congreso de Historia Regional*, pp. 655–663. Mexicali: Gobierno del estado de Baja California, Dirección General de Acción Cívica y Cultural, 1958.

———. "Más de cuatrocientos periódicos en español se han editado en los Estados Unidos." *La Prensa* (San Antonio), 13 February 1938.

———. "Memorias del General Antonio I. Villarreal." *La Prensa* (San Antonio), 17 November 1935–23 February 1936.

[———.] "Siguiendo la pista a políticos mexicanos." *La Opinión* (Los Angeles), 16 April–11 June 1939, 9 chaps.

Vanderwood, Paul J. "Genesis of the Rurales: Mexico's Early Struggle for Public Security." *Hispanic American Historical Review* 50 (May 1970): 323–344.

———. "Response to Revolt: The Counter Guerrilla Strategy of Porfirio Díaz." *Hispanic American Historical Review* 56 (November 1976): 551–579.

———. Review of "Emilio Kosterlitzky: Eagle of Sonora and the Southwest Border." *Hispanic American Historical Review* 52 (May 1972): 304–306.

Vera Estañol, Jorge. *Historia de la revolución mexicana*. Mexico City: Editorial Porrúa, 1967.

Wagoner, Jay J. *Arizona Territory, 1863–1912: A Political History*. Tucson: University of Arizona Press, 1970.

Weinberger, Harry. "Two Political Prisoners at Leavenworth." *The New Republic* 31 (5 July 1922): 162.

Wetter, Mardee Belding de. "Revolutionary El Paso: 1910–1917." *Password* 3 (April, July, October 1958): 46–59, 107–122, 145–159.

Weyl, Walter E. "The Labor Situation in Mexico." *Annals of the American Academy of Political and Social Science* 21 (January 1903): 77–93.

"What the New Mexican Ambassador Represents." *The American Monthly Review of Reviews* 35 (April 1907). 489.

Wilson, Henry Lane. *Diplomatic Episodes in Mexico, Belgium and Chile*. New York: Doubleday, Page and Co., 1927.

Womack, John, Jr. *Zapata and the Mexican Revolution*. New York: Alfred A. Knopf, 1969.

Woodbridge, Dwight E. "La Cananea Mining Camp." *The Engineering and Mining Journal* 82 (6 October 1906): 623–627.

Woodward, Earl F. "Hon. Albert B. Fall of New Mexico." *Montana* 23 (1973): 14–23.

Young, George. "Greene Cananea Copper Company and Subsidiaries: Historical Sketch." Mimeographed. Files of the Compañía Minera de Cananea, August 1920. Copy on file in Arizona Historical Society, Tucson.

Zayas Enríque, Rafael de. *The Case of Mexico and the Policy of President Wilson.* Translated by Andre Tridon. New York: Albert and Charles Boni, 1914.

————. *Porfirio Díaz, la evolución de su vida.* New York: D. Appleton and Co., 1908.

————. *Porfirio Díaz.* Translated by T. Quincy Browne, Jr. New York: D. Appleton and Co., 1908.

Index

Junta, 19, 91, 105; profile of, 25–27; in St. Louis, 21, 42; in San Francisco, 150; and socialists, 49–53, 56–57, 58–61; threatens Díaz's life, 37; in Toronto, 21, 79, 113, 117, 192; and Zapata, 259
floresmagonistas. See *Partido Liberal Mexicano*
Folk, Joseph W., 116
Fong Yue Ting v. *U.S.* (1893), 7, 168
Fort Huachuca (Ariz.), 83, 101, 136
Fort Leavenworth penitentiary. See Leavenworth penitentiary
Fort Rosecrans (Calif.), 57
Foster, Thomas, 184, 189
Fuentes, Joaquín. See Puente, Lázaro
Furlong, Thomas, 190n; and arrest of R. Flores Magón, 145–146; and arrest of López Manzano, 128; career of, 192–194; and Creel, 179; field report by, 196; and Madero, 213, 225–226; testifies against PLM, 155–156, 165. *See also* Furlong Secret Service Company
Furlong Secret Service Company, 46, 179, 183, 191–192; agents of, 40, 104, 185, 189, 193; assists *maderistas*, 225. *See also* Furlong, Thomas

Galbraith, W. J., 83, 88, 97
García, Luis, 137–142, 185
García, Trinidad, 184
Garibaldi, Giuseppe, 215, 217
Gartz, Kate Crane, 285
Gendarmería Fiscal, 83, 85, 101, 106
Germany, 254, 255; and Huerta, 253, 260; sends spies to Mexico, 256–257
Gillis, Walter, 130
Globe, Ariz., 191; W.F.M. in, 44
Gobernación. See Mexico, ministries and agencies of
Goldman, Emma, 4–5, 280; arrest of, 6, 8; in Baja revolt, 57, 61; deportation of, 276; in St. Louis, 42
Gompers, Samuel: supports Madero, 212; and Mother Jones, 47, 49; and Murray, 52, 54; supports PLM, 59,

147; racist practices of, 45; and W.F.M., 61
González, Abraham, 215–218, 224, 230–231
González, Jesús J., 157
González, Pedro N., 94
González, Cosío, Manuel, 180
Gottschalk, Alfred, 101–102
Gran Círculo de Obreros Libres (GCOL), 34, 35n
Gran Liga de Empleados de Ferrocarril, 98–99
Greene, Colonel William Cornell, 15, 122–123, 178–179; and Cananea strike, 81–83, 85–86, 91; career of, 67–72; copper stock of, 100; death of, 121; "empire" of, 69–70, 89, 177; espionage by, 121, 180; as founder of Cananea, 65; mansion of, 70, 84; opposes PLM, 105, 114–121; 142–143; opposed by PLM, 92, 138; and W.F.M., 119–121
Greene Cattle Company, 69
Greene Consolidated Copper Company, 13, 67, 74–75, 121
Greene Consolidated Gold Company, 69
Greene Gold-Silver Company, 69, 72
Griner, J. G., 29, 218; hired by Corral, 119, 129; as informant, 130–132, 179, 184, 197
Guadalupe-Hidalgo, Treaty of, 262
Guanajuato (state), 26, 255
Guerra, Calixto, 53, 131
Guerrero, Práxedis G., 21, 162, 230; in Chihuahua, 217; in El Paso, 192; as guerrilla fighter, 35; joins *magonistas* in field, 209; founds Morenci newspaper, 27; poetry of, 41; profile of, 19, 25–27; publishes *Punto Rojo*, 38, 117; in San Antonio, 193
guerrilla activity, 209n, 240, 257; organization of, 35–36
Guggenheim, Daniel, 100, 177–178, 246
Gutiérrez de Lara, Felipe (brother of Lázaro), 86